TWENTIETH CENTURY INTERNATIONAL HISTORY

A Reader

Edited by

STEPHEN CHAN AND
JARROD WIENER

I.B. Tauris Publishers
LONDON · NEW YORK

Published in 1999 by I.B.Tauris & Co Ltd,
Victoria House, Bloomsbury Square, London WC1B 4DZ
175 Fifth Avenue, New York NY 10010

In the United States of America and in Canada distributed by
St Martin's Press, 175 Fifth Avenue, New York NY 10010

A full CIP record for this book is available from the British Library
A full CIP record for this book is available from the Library of Congress

ISBN 1 86064 301 9 hardback
ISBN 1 86064 302 7 paperback

Library of Congress catalog card number: available

Set in Monotype Garamond by Ewan Smith, London
Printed and bound in Great Britain by WBC Ltd, Bridgend

Contents

Introduction:
Giving Thought

The twentieth century and the second millennium after Christ are drawing to a close. There will be enough events and vainglories to satisfy even the most ardent seekers after symbols and carnivals; enough books to declare that whatever epoch humanity has passed through has been tumultuous and meaningful. In a way, the calendar was almost an obstacle to the present book. We were afraid of publishing work that seemed portentous. Yet much has happened, and been thought, over one hundred years, to deserve comment. In the best of all possible worlds, we should have been pleased if we were heading towards, say, 1950 or 2050, and looking back to 1850 or 1950, without being sucked into the exaggerations the mere end of a century tend to bring.

Having said that, it is worth remembering that a thousand years ago the end of the first millennium was a time of very great tumult indeed. Millennial sects in Europe were seeking the portents of the last days prophesied by Jesus in St Matthew's gospel. There will be parallels drawn between the end of that millennium and this; so it is not merely a century ending but approaches towards comprehending the endgames of history.[1] Certainly, in 1989, when Francis Fukuyama first published a short article declaring an end to history, using phraseology borrowed from Hegel, it seemed as if we might shortly all compare the religious and secular thoughts of ending that were a thousand years apart.

But what was happening outside Europe a thousand years ago? Without Christ as the calendar's foundation, were there the same expectations of ending? Elsewhere there were continuations and beginnings. In the international relations of 1000 AD, Europe was a blip given to writing its histories well, but a blip all the same, on the great cultural and political maps of the world. Islam, India and China all had far grander civilisations at that moment in time.

The difference this time around is that, not so much Europe by itself, but a West with the thought of Enlightenment Europe as its core values (even if its greatest wealth, military power and technological knowledge are in the United States), behaves as a huge hegemonic influence, if not direct power, in the political maps of today's world. Fukuyama's talk of the end of history seemed to declare resistance over, and the Gulf War that followed seemed to demonstrate this. Enlightenment justice and late twentieth-century technology were set to end the century and this millennium with a euphoric bravado and a unity within international relations.

Meanwhile, the cultural maps of the world were less scrutable. The West defeated Saddam Hussein but, in a curious way, was reluctant to topple him. Who would engage the Iranians in this region? Who would occupy them regionally, to dissipate their energies globally, to prevent the values of their 1979 revolution and the era of their 'just men' from spreading further into the world, by conversions or violence, or both?

Thus, the endgame of history was not so simple. By the time Fukuyama released the book of the article, in 1992, he was speaking of the possibilities of destabilising agents at the end of history, ready to start history again; ready, in short, to challenge the triumph of the West. The language was curiously Greek and Hegelian: last men, 'men without chests', without gumption, might let the triumph slip away; first men, the first men of new history, bestial, having neither reason nor desire, might rise up to storm the fortresses of the West's completed historical triumph.

What is this 'without reason'? Others, more concretely but without nuance, declared the existence and competition of alternative reasons, what Samuel Huntington called 'civilisations'; opposing civilisations, he meant; Islam in particular.

Now, with all this, it seemed our project of a book at this time was good. Certain problems confronted the end of the twentieth century that perhaps would be passed over, or commented upon without nuance and subtlety, in the carnivals of ending. Moreover, we were mindful that our discipline, International Relations, was in need of two things. The first was a reminder that, whether it agreed with Fukuyama or not, it was becoming wedded to an Enlightenment method of thought and appreciation of values, and was consumed with the idea that there was a universal truth. The second was that, in becoming a more theoretical academic discipline, its reflexivity, its considering thought, was less directed on the world outside the library and more upon the books inside: reflecting on reflexivities past, and conceiving, just as in the German Enlightenment, ideal worlds of truth and justice. Not ideals of truth and justice, or views of ideal truth and justice, but an ideal world which they inhabited. Hegelian-derived thought on seamless constitution of citizens in communities of ideal civil society, so that the state might become purer, or be transcended in the development of a global civil society; Kantian-derived thought on a universe of moral values to which each citizen was inextricably linked. These were not the worlds that statesmen, diplomats, peace-keepers, aid workers, freedom fighters, and starving children found in their international relations.

Nor is their world as crude anymore as the simple state and power-based realisms of the Cold War. A child who starves is not a cipher who merely starves. He or she wonders why there is a necessity to starve. A teenager with a gun and fighting a guerrilla war is not necessarily an abused and abducted child terrorist or a piece of unreflective common fodder. He or she is aware of fighting for something. The aid worker who has just seen twenty people die that day, the peace-keeper who does not return fire while under sustained attack, but buries the bodies afterwards, seek justice under non-ideal circumstances. The failure of today's normative, reflective International Relations is that it does nothing for engaged people outside academies, sweating it out in the field. The test might be to lecture of Kantian ethics in a refugee camp.

There is an escape clause here. In 1997, as part of a lengthy debate with William Wallace, Steve Smith made a contribution to this debate in which he used the phrase, used before him by Vaclav Havel and Edward Said, of the need to 'speak truth to power'.[2] He related, in terms following Noam Chomsky's, the need to avoid speaking as policy-makers would wish, to avoid becoming mandarins who mediate whatever is decided to be truth in the exchanges between rulers and citizens, so that the rulers' decision about truth might be vindicated by academic authority. Academics needed, therefore, a critical distance between themselves and governments in order to reflect, unsullied, on true truth.

This is fine, as far as it goes. The fatal flaw here is that truth is not only spoken to power. It is spoken also to suffering, to forms of bad death, to dispossession and grief. A critical distance to these is an abjuration of the humanity of scholars. There is no such thing as 'Academia by Vocation', to turn a phrase of Max Weber's.

There is a second flaw. It is not the case that power will shirk from the truth. You can speak it, pure, nuanced, reflexively argued, in the full pomp of Enlightenment values, repetitively, and power will smile at you. In China today, you can talk about Hegel, Kant and Habermas all you like. Just don't make too many direct attacks on the government. The tragedy of this century is that power has mastered many truths. Nazi Germany spoke with what it called Nietzsche's tongue. It absorbed great thinkers like Heidigger. It appropriated Goethe and Wagner. So that truth, whether delivered philosophically or fantastically, was the Nazi servant. Who is to say any critical distance cannot easily be overcome?

There is a third flaw: why all the emphasis on truth? Why does International Relations not try to do good?[3] Good does not flow from truth, especially critically-distant truth. Feminism had to overcome certain 'truths' in the name of doing the good of equality to women. Liberation theology struggles against the 'truth' of the church. The anti-apartheid campaign had to struggle against the 'truths' of certain religious doctrines, selective histories, anthropologies and geographies. In South Africa, only after the good of majority rule had been accomplished has there been established a commission to look at the truth.

International Relations theory, of course, talks of a higher truth, abstract and above all these situations. But there are methods of abstract thought. These differ even within Enlightenment tradition, and certainly among different traditions. At a clear moment in time, there might be a simple statement that the truth that speaks to power must be capable of attacking and hurting power if need be. If, in the world of the end of the twentieth century, there are many powers, with very different animations and justifications, will they be hurt by the truth that does not understand their animations and justifications? And, if the power is not a state, but a militia, a clan, or a warlord, how then is truth transacted without the clean apparatus of government and citizenry that makes Enlightenment thought possible? Neither Kant nor Hegel were antagonists of what Napoleon left in his wake.

What is this book, therefore, in relation to this discussion? It is not abstract, but it does not try to do everything. It seeks chiefly to discuss the issues of the twentieth century, particularly as they lead on to the twenty-first, in terms of ideas that had some popular resonance, not merely in terms of International Relations theories. The latter are not shirked but, hopefully, there is a more balanced intellectual history implicit here than if it were only theoretically informed.

Secondly, it is mindful of the triumphalism the end of the Cold War and Fukuyama's accompanying gloss generated. Fukuyama, thus, features as a shadow actor throughout these pages. Never fully on stage until the last chapter, he is used to suggest that there are grave problems generated by this century which will ensure that the next does not have an easy time of it.

Thirdly, it looks at the complexities of, at first glance, easy formulations of what went before and what lies ahead. Globalisation is an easy term. Here, its difficulties are given thought.

And that, basically, summarises the book. It is a giving of thought to the century. It has certain shortcomings. Despite a commentary in the introductory passages, it does not give as much space as it should to what this giving of thought would have looked like if this book had been published in, say, Iran, China, or Sudan. So that there is a second shadow warrior dogging Fukuyama's footsteps: that of a silent Other. This one is not absent entirely. It is present enough to interrogate briefly what is more expansively here. This shadow warrior surfaces in our other books.

The reader should be mindful of four things. The first is that the introductory passages to the four sections should be read as continuations of this short essay. The second is that, in the deliberate choice of contributions, a blend between established and younger scholars was sought. This has meant some variation in reach but, we feel, not much. We are confident all the contributions give thought and stimulate. Thirdly, the section on 'Ideas and Economy' was the most difficult to represent as a giving of thought that was not overburdened by theory. Economics and International Political Economy are not easily given to immediately accessible renditions. We have tried our best here and, at least, have not made great excursions into econometrics.

The purity of econometrics, in the face of very real economic problems, is an exemplary warning for the pursuit, in International Relations, of an ideal world of truth and justice. Fourthly, all of the introductory passages, like the present essay, should be regarded as critical introductions. They do not merely introduce but seek, briefly, to engage with the contributions.

Having said all that, the completed book does not escape a certain feel of insipidness. Maybe this is the fault of all scholarly works. How many holocausts have there been this century? That is, how many premeditated, i.e. reasoned, even 'truthful' slaughters of huge numbers of people in cold blood? There is some scant comfort in the knowledge that other books will thunder in hotter blood on these terrors than we have. Finally, we have not escaped our discipline of International Relations. All this talk of shadow warriors might not be worth a bomb or two. But an exploded readership was not what we were looking for. We must finally all be alive and unalienated to be reflective and given thought.

Stephen Chan and Jarrod Wiener,
Takanini and London 1998

To Irene who said to write it with passion and
to Sarah for the inspiration to begin

PART I

Theory, Ideas and Ideology

CHAPTER I

The Optimism of the Century's End has a Fear of the First Men of the New Century's Beginning

Stephen Chan

At the dawn of the last decade, Francis Fukuyama wrote what briefly seemed to be the testament of the twentieth century. For one of those brief moments, which perhaps both fulfilled the technologically based idea of instant (if short, or shortened) fame, and was apt punishment for a borrowing of Hegel that, as Paul Bacon observes and comments upon in the last chapter to this book, was selective and had about it a certain sense of appropriation rather than fair usage, there seemed to be an historical pause in which a political Cold War was both won and recognised to have been won as part of the movement of history to its finest and highest point. A certain grandiosity seemed set to bathe the last years of the twentieth century in its glow.

By the time Fukayama had thought through his own suggestive comments of 1989, and had released his full-length book of 1992, the grandiosity came with, if not a health-warning, a caveat that there were, in the world of achieved history, potential dissidents or 'first men'. One of the suggestions of this present book is that the 'first men' are not merely those political Others that refuse the Western, apparently universally historical project, but may include those *within*, who, with the weapons of war in this late century, may celebrate the achievement of technology by both fetishing and propagating a deterministic use of a selective world order of weapons, rather than of ideas or ideologies, for their use on behalf of first, last, or any men or women. James Der Derian talks of this in the second section of this book. As ominously, and in a later section, Jarrod Wiener talks about the enemy within as liberalism's inability to sustain itself.

In this, the present section, three writers discuss some of the theories that even without Fukuyama's phraseologies, or neo-Hegelian phraseological view of the world, would concern men and women at the close, at least, of this century's history. Differently, they discuss what has been achieved as

3

global or as a world order, and what seeds, if not saplings of discontent are pushing through its smooth and flat tarmac. A.J.R. Groom presents, in his accustomed manner, a sweeping historical survey and speaks of the possibility of a global politics. Andrew Williams, using what Fred Halliday later calls a periodisation of history, discusses the recurring effort to achieve a larger, more stable world than that which small political communities can, by themselves, provide. For him, the movement towards larger community, and agreement on this movement, means movement towards a world order. Paul Rich conducts a brief inquisition on how a binding idea, or ideology, can traverse state boundaries and how, in the case of Iran, we have a revolution that has given way to certain state orthodoxies, but which might still wish to resist being globalised (within someone else's globalisation) or incorporation into (someone else's) world order. It should be said that, here, though briefly, Rich gives a far more sympathetic and intellectually based sense of why the Iranian revolution occurred than has often been the case.

Groom speaks of a post-Westphalian world where state frontiers are crossed and permeated. These are now crossed to such an extent that we may speak of the nature of order that itself must now traverse states. For Groom, global politics is where a totality of the world is engaged and an organic holistic sense may be said to pervade such a politics. By contrast, world politics *may* affect all the globe but not necessarily so. Certainly the efforts of Third World states to create, in Williams's terms, world orders – through the Non-Aligned Movement and the New International Economic Order – were said to have been of world importance but never achieved global subscription. This does, however, raise the question as to who does, indeed, create a global politics? Who can? If, as in the marriage between US triumphalism at the end of the Cold War and Fukuyama's view of the end of history, it is a global politics founded on a victorious politics with its achievement of hegemony, is that what Groom has in mind?

This is a problematic of which Groom is aware, but does not deeply address. Others, however, in this book do just that. It is not that Groom is himself caught up in the first naïve flushes of the *possibilities* that seem inherent in globalisation – and, leading off the last section of this book, Martin Shaw shows that what is under globalisation's smooth surface is an amazing messiness – but that he has hopes all the same for it. Nevertheless, Groom recognises a global apartheid at work, where the poor are not (in Wallerstein's almost clinical words) so much semi-peripheralised and peripheralised, as cast into cordons sanitaires and exclusion zones. Although Groom is fundamentally questioning the longevity of sovereignty, he is mindful of Hedley Bull's idea of a new medievalism, new and condensed separations, in which conflict becomes a greater possibility than seemed the case at the close of the Cold War and Gulf War and Fukuyama's 1989 article. Terrorist groups are among the 'first men' who, like other things loosely called global, are able to cross and permeate frontiers.

When Groom speaks of 'global riot control', therefore, what does he, in normative terms, mean? Who does the controlling? Here, his long fidelity to the United Nations is reasserted – notwithstanding his acknowledgement that the Permanent Members of the Security Council are not consistent and reliable in their own senses of moral behaviour and global normative vision. And, surely, if any states are sovereign, they are those of the Permanent Members? This book thus begins with a clear set of problems which the later contributors investigate.

For Williams, the notion of Woodrow Wilson that there might be a 'redemption of the weak nations' within a world order of (at least implied) equity, is an attractive one. Wilson and Lenin competed for the same audience with their opposing views of world orders. Both, in different ways, had in mind the project of integrating small states into, in Cobban's words, 'the fabric of a stable prosperous and peaceful world'. So that, for Williams also, the end of the twentieth century poses a choice between chaos or the continuing progress of the Enlightenment; between the last men of an accomplished history who gave way to the first men of chaos, or a global flourishing.

If there is much that here seems eschatological (the last days of chaos) and soteriological (a unified doctrine of salvation), this is where Rich's study of Iran is at least ironic. For, within Iran, once and perhaps still feared as the challenger against history and its flourishing, there were exactly these impulses of ending chaos and providing salvation; and, as noted above, Rich's tale is not the simple observation of theocracy that International Relations scholars have hitherto palmed off as reasonable explanation. Rich, first, however, discusses a problematic which underlies the in fact lesser problematic of globalisation raised by Groom and which worries Williams. That is, the nation-state, in the first instant, before the possibility of its transcendence into globalisation or integration into world order, cannot be described in rational and realist terms. The nation-state is a construct that both establishes an irony and the strait-jacket of realism: ironic because it is not real and strait-jacketing because it cannot then easily admit other realities. A cohesive nation-state is a romantic notion. In a hierarchy of historical progression, the tribal ethnic community, the nation-state, the society of states in world order, and the global community of humanity are all romances. The cohabitation, very naturally, of romance and realism provides not only a fundamental problematic, but one which is avoided in much International Relations scholarship. In this book, order and outlaws may be seen as living side by side – but very problematically so. The terrorists are part of globalisation, not its enemy.

For Rich, in Iran, the revolution in 1979 combined modernist and traditional thought. If traditionalism (briefly) won in the battle between the two, it has not yet achieved its own historical consummation. However, Rich is fascinated by the millennarian content of revolutionary discourse. In a way, to be general but bold, it was not unlike Fukuyama's. Only it did not, in a transition from article to book, sound doubts and warnings about last and first men. It was to be the era of *just men*. Whether it is the Fukuyamas and their brief beliefs in accomplished history, or the Samuel Huntingtons and their views of a certain history continuing to face challenges from Other civilisations, we must be aware not only of the contradictions and contingencies of these histories, but their romance and, above all, of their irony. What, at century's close, is just order? And who, exactly, are the just men? Who are the just women?

CHAPTER 2

The Construction of Ideologies in the Twentieth Century

Paul B. Rich

This chapter examines how ideologies are constructed in the course of twentieth-century international politics. It is divided into three sections. The first section discusses how scholars of International Relations (IR) have reacted to ideological issues in the post-war years. It shows how the main intellectual approaches within IR retarded for a considerable part of the post-war period serious analysis of ideological factors in international politics. This neglect is in some senses quite a surprise since the study of ideology frequently reinforces rather than undermines realism by showing how ideological conceptions interact with conceptions of national or state interest.

This argument is developed in the second section of the chapter when the focus shifts towards exemplifying the importance of ideology in understanding the operation of international power politics through a case study of Iran. The final section examines the importance of ideology in the post-Cold War era. It argues that the decline of superpower domination of the international system is likely to lead to a growing importance of ideological factors in international politics, though these will need to be seen alongside issues of national identity as well.

Ideology and the Study of International Relations

The study of political ideologies in global politics has been considerably neglected in academic International Relations. Ideologies usually have been seen by scholars in the Anglo-American tradition as part of the broad terrain of Political Theory. The discussion of ideological issues thus has occurred either within the confines of the nation-states and national traditions of political discourse or else in a universal intellectual framework that generally by-passed the constraints and pressures of international politics.

Moreover, within International Relations there has been considerable aversion to the study of ideology. Most of the mainstream theoretical

7

approaches within the discipline have tended to play down the significance of ideological questions and it is only comparatively recently that a serious re-evaluation of their impact on the course of international politics has begun to take place. These approaches or perspectives can be categorised broadly into the four distinct areas of (1) realism or power politics, (2) world systems theory, (3) economic interdependence, and (4) law and collective security.[1] None of these approaches paid much attention to ideology as such though it intruded at various points in their resulting analyses.

In the case of the first perspective, it would be broadly true to say that throughout most of the post-war years, the mainstream of academic IR on both sides of the Atlantic was dominated by a realist scepticism towards ideas and ideologies. Much of this scepticism derived from an intellectual reaction in both Britain and the United States to the supposed failures of idealists in the inter-war years to understand the nature of European power politics.[2] Realists saw ideological belief systems as largely peripheral to the operation of state-centred power politics where the central questions to ask concerned the military and economic capacity of states to project power beyond their borders. Hans Morgenthau, for instance, saw ideology as simply a 'flattering function' employed to conceal the imperialist pretensions of nation-states.[3] Within this paradigm ideologies had only a limited importance and were largely used by political leaders to legitimise their claims to political power.[4] Realists liked to point to the failure of efforts to promote ideological movements on international lines such as the ill-fated Socialist International before the First World War, the Soviet manipulation of the Communist International or the failure to develop a coherent fascist international in the inter-war years.

Such failures seemed to demonstrate all too starkly the shallow political roots of ideological beliefs. Realists such as E.H. Carr considered that it was a 'utopian' fallacy of the idealists to take ideology all that seriously since it had been precisely such a commitment in the form of pacifist and anti-war ideals which had driven the European powers into appeasing Hitler in the late 1930s. Carr's *The Twenty Years Crisis* (1939) was particularly influential in confirming a traditional view among foreign policy practitioners that ideologies were largely subordinate to state interests in international power politics.[5] As more recent research on 'idealist' thought in the inter-war years has shown, though, this assessment by Carr and the realist school was a gross over-estimation. Many of the prominent idealist thinkers in Britain in the 1920s and 1930s, such as Norman Angell, Gilbert Murray and Alfred Zimmern, were by no means unequivocally 'utopian' in their outlook and in many cases had a clear grasp of the realities of power and political decision-making.[6] Moreover, the realist conception itself stands subject to the charge that it too has idealist origins in the way that it has taken over and employed a romantic notion of the cohesive nation-state prominent in the writings of Hegel, Herder and Fichte in the early nineteenth century.[7]

Despite these limitations, the realist paradigm acquired a stranglehold on IR debate in the post-1945 years as the exigencies of the Cold War discouraged analysts from emphasising the ideological dimensions of international politics.[8] The very term 'Cold War' had been coined by the American journalist Walter Lippman to reflect the paralysis of international diplomatic dialogue and the tendency of the dominant superpowers of the United States and USSR to manipulate and hijack ideological and intellectual debate for their own great power concerns. Cold War liberalism in the West operated within relatively narrow confines and there appeared to be only a limited degree of autonomy for a free intelligentsia which could feel bold enough to speak truth to power.

One response from this beleaguered intelligentsia by the late 1950s in the United States was the thesis that the advent of modern industrialised societies had effectively rendered ideology obsolete and that politics had become essentially managerial and technocratic in orientation. The 'end of ideology' debate as it was espoused by Seymour Martin Lipset, Edward Shils and Daniel Bell appeared to provide, momentarily at least, a sociological confirmation of an essentially political view rooted in the idea of a triumphant managerialism in Western societies that no longer required any major ideological debate. This view did not prevail for very long since ideological politics made an abrupt return in US and Western politics in the following decade.[9]

By the middle to late 1960s the involvement of the United States in the Vietnam War led to a progressive unlocking of ideological debate over the nature of Western, and more specifically, US foreign policy. A number of radical critics, who began a sophisticated critique of the conduct of US foreign policy, emerged at this time. Noam Chomsky charged that the American policy-making apparatus was dominated by a class of 'new mandarins' operating in close alignment with academic research in universities. This class had undermined, Chomsky argued, the claims of liberal humanist scholarship which traditionally had rested upon the ideal of objectivity in social research. The imperialist pretensions of US foreign policy had now subordinated this ostensibly neutral scholarship to a 'counter-revolutionary' ideological purpose.[10]

The publication of the Pentagon Papers in the early 1970s, followed by the Watergate Crisis in 1973–74, revealed even more starkly the ideological nature of American foreign policy. There were signs that a major debate might ensue in International Relations on the ideological dimensions of state power. The China scholar Franz Schurmann pointed out in *The Logic of World Power* (1974) that these influences had been largely ignored by foreign policy scholars of US government and politics in favour of states elsewhere in the world.[11] Such influences were crucial to understand how the United States became embroiled in the Vietnam conflict and Schurmann suggested that it was the Roosevelt administration in the Second World War which secured the marriage of deep-rooted expansionist and imperialist forces in

American politics and its mobilisation behind a global policy of containment towards communism.[12]

By the mid-1970s it appeared that there might be the opening up in IR for a major debate on the nature and impact of ideologies in global politics. This was a period of mounting Third World pressure in international politics, symbolised by the North–South debate and the emergence of a number of radical Third World regimes such as Mozambique, Angola, Ethiopia and Nicaragua. Much of this debate, though, tended to flow by the 1970s into Development Studies and Area Studies and largely by-passed the concerns of International Relations, where the main terrain of radical criticism of conventional approaches took the form of World Systems Theory (WST) as it became espoused by Immanuel Wallerstein and his school.

World Systems Theory was largely structural in orientation and, like realism, tended to relegate ideological factors to a peripheral status. The theory was concerned mainly with explaining the marginalisation of developing states in what was seen as a dominant world capitalist economy. While Wallerstein was prepared to acknowledge that ideological 'commitment' acted as a major mechanism in the stabilisation of world systems, ideologies as such were of relatively little interest to world systems theorists.[13] The theory categorised states into those of the core (such as the United States, Japan and Western European states), semi-periphery (such as Iran under the Shah, South Africa, Brazil and Indonesia) and periphery (such as Bangladesh, most of Sub-Saharan Africa and Haiti). As with realism, WST largely explained ideological belief systems as *ex post facto* rationalisations of states in relation to their position within the structure of the world system. The theory drew heavily upon a structural Marxism that became intellectually fashionable in the late 1960s and 1970s. It emphasised the need for developing states to organise stronger economic alliances and cartels such as the OPEC cartel which had managed to increase the price of oil four-fold in 1973 in the wake of the Middle East War. Out of such alliances it looked to the southern rim of the globe, organising itself to transform the world capitalist system and reorganise it on socialist lines. The theory had little interest in the emerging debate about global human rights in the 1970s, following the Helsinki Final Act of 1975, and largely ignored issues about values and ethics in the conduct of foreign policy (perhaps because these were seen as largely the preserve of a guilt-stricken Western liberalism).

To this extent, then, World Systems Theory shared with mainstream realism a general disdain for ideologies in global politics. Interdependence theory, the third of the four main approaches to IR, largely shared the same viewpoint, despite its rather different view on the nature and operations of global capitalism. Like World Systems Theory, economic interdependence theory largely focused upon the structural imperatives within the global economy. Based upon the work of such scholars as Robert Keohane and Joseph Nye, this perspective emphasised how the expansion of global markets and international trade and investment rendered military conflict between nation-states increasingly irrational. The perspective up-dated in many ways older nineteenth-century Cobdenite ideas on international relations and saw nation-state decision-makers operating largely on the basis of a series of utilitarian economic calculations over their respective national interests. The global economic system was thus seen as containing an 'embedded liberalism' which would increasingly constrain the militaristic tendencies within nation-states and render unnecessary the domination of a hegemonic power within the international system in order for it to remain stable.[14]

The last of the four perspectives, law and collective security, is based on a considerably different focus. Here it is assumed that a state's preferences are based less on a simple calculation of economic utility than by the preferences of public opinion, which, if freely expressed in a democratic manner, will be inclined towards the pacific settlement of disputes with national rivals. This perspective is one of the oldest in IR, with its roots in the Wilsonian outlook that pervaded the founders of the discipline after the First World War. It was well exemplified in the inter-war years by many supposedly 'idealist' writers such as Alfred Zimmern, J.A. Hobson, Leonard Woolf and Philip Noel Baker, who hoped that the development of international law would help to underpin the slow evolution of structures of international authority to regulate and ultimately outlaw the pursuit of war between states.[15] Many of these writers broadly shared a liberal perspective on International Relations, though their understanding of ideology remained in many respects very limited. They frequently exhibited a Fabian disdain for popular and mass-based ideologies and their enthusiasm for building up structures of international governmental authority was aimed at curbing and controlling potentially explosive and revolutionary political ideologies which they feared would get out of control. Their proposals for international action tended therefore to be aimed at an enlightened elite which, it was hoped, would act to prevent more populist political movements influencing the conduct of foreign affairs. The failure of this group of rather well-intentioned liberals to understand the power of popular nationalism perhaps explains why they were so taken by surprise by the rise to power of Hitler in 1933 and their arguments increasingly lost credibility by the mid to late 1930s as war loomed over Europe.

The upsurge of nationalism in Eastern Europe and the Balkans since the end of the Cold War indicates that many of the issues that confronted the law and collective security approach in the 1920s and 1930s have re-emerged in IR. The study of ideology seems likely to increase in the post-Cold War era despite the appeal in some quarters of a Western triumphalist perspective rooted in an 'end of history' thesis. Some recent work in IR indicates that a careful re-evaluation has started to take place on the impact of ideas on foreign policy decision-making. In its most basic sense, the term 'ideology' denotes a strongly rational approach to the study of political ideas and values which fails to specify the various sorts of mythical and non-rational roots of modern belief systems. This highly rational approach is not especially surprising given that the discussion of ideology emerged among a class of secular and rationalist intellectuals in Europe following the French Revolution who saw themselves as free of religious belief. The word 'ideology' after all was originally coined by the French intellectual Destut de Tracy in his *Elements d'Ideolgie* (1801–5). This book propounded the idea that there could be a 'science of ideas' which would equip society to organise itself in an increasingly rational and harmonious fashion. It was on the basis of such rational forms that ideologies can be seen to be a product of the European Enlightenment. They became extended in the course of the nineteenth and twentieth centuries to the international level as the basis for programmes for the re-ordering of global society on to more rational lines, leading to the eventual end to war.

This rational interpretation of ideology can lead to a highly intellectualist approach, which, as John Hall has pointed out, tends to narrow our understanding of the nature and role of intellectuals. While it is intellectuals who give meaning and precision to ideas and ideologies, they do so in the context of particular communities. It is essential to have a grasp of the sort of identities that these communities have before we can understand fully the reason why intellectuals take up and propagate certain sorts of ideologies. International Relations can only ignore such identity issues at its peril since it is precisely these which frequently have led to the emergence of radical new ideologies with profound implications for international politics.[16] What sort of communities can be talked about in terms of the operation of politics at the global level? Since the emergence of the nation-state in the sixteenth and seventeenth centuries, there has been, in the West at least, three main visions of community at the international level in the form of nation-state, the society of states and the community of mankind.[17] In more recent years, there may be emerging a fourth distinct level of community in international relations in the form of the tribal or ethnic community which was formerly relegated to the terrain of sub-state politics but may now be emerging into prominence with the break-up of fragile 'quasi states' in many parts of the developing world and the emergence of various forms of ideological legitimation for the operations of warlords and local strong men.[18]

All these levels have contributed in varying degrees to ideological debate in international relations. It is at the level of the nation-state, though, that the operation of ideology traditionally has had the greatest impact. In varying degrees it has always been possible to identify political leaders and decision-makers who have exemplified either a greater or lesser attachment to political ideology ever since the emergence of the Westphalian states system in the seventeenth century. The issue acquired its peculiarly modern form in the wake of the failure of the 1848 revolutions in Europe when the pursuit of grand visions for European revolutionary reconstruction were replaced by the more amoral pursuit of naked national interest in the form of the doctrine of *Realpolitik*. This replaced the older eighteenth-century conception of *raison d'état*, which had been oriented towards the ultimate purpose of foreign policy. In its place, *Realpolitik* was rather more amoral in that it left open the ethical content of the final end to be pursued. The ultimate end could still logically be construed to be highly ethical and rooted in a clear ideological vision of mankind, but it did not have to be. Indeed, as the late R.J. Vincent has pointed out, it was morally flawed to the extent that it presumed at best only an accidental connection between state interests and something that could be demonstrated to be morally right and was thus very weak in its ability to control the activities of the unscrupulous.[19]

Conservative politicians such as Bismarck proved to be particularly adept at employing *Realpolitik* in the latter decades of the nineteenth century. The break-up of the European political order in 1918 provided the opportunity for revolutionary regimes to demonstrate that they too could learn its precepts. In the post-Second World War years the doctrine of *Realpolitik* spread to the rest of the globe and became employed by a variety of different states and regimes. Its amoralism of means has seduced many analysts into believing that it lacks any ethical ends, even though the careful scrutiny of the motives and beliefs of key decision-makers may reveal this not to be the case. In some senses, the issue ultimately becomes an historical one since the only way to arrive at a balanced assessment of an individual statesman and his or her motives will depend upon hindsight and access to the most intimate private papers. This is why the study of the impact of political ideology in international relations has tended to be highly uneven in its range and penetrative rigour since the omission of many leaders and regimes in the developing world or former Communist bloc is due not simply to a Euro-centric preoccupation with the West but also because access to documents and information frequently has been very difficult (this situation is now of course changing in many former Eastern bloc states).

The operation of *Realpolitik* in international relations can therefore provide considerable space for the operation of ideological factors. Much will depend upon the set of political and historical circumstances. The following section seeks to illuminate this issue by discussing the example of Iran in the twentieth century, centred upon the revolution of 1979 that overthrew the Shah.

Ideology and the Revolutionary Transfer of Power in Iran

The pivotal role that ideology can play in modern international politics is well exemplified by the case of Iran. The dynamics of domestic politics within Iran were influenced heavily during the course of the twentieth century by external actors, particularly those great powers with economic interests in the country and keen to exert a strategic and military presence in a geographically significant part of the Middle East.

Iran entered the twentieth century with a very weak and backward state that was under the informal imperial influence of Britain. A small Westernised middle class had tried to steer the country's political system in a more constitutional direction in revolution between 1905 and 1911 that had increased the powers of the country's Majlis, or parliament. This essentially constitutional revolution became undermined by the growth of the landlord-dominated central state that, with backing from external powers, increasingly took on the dimensions of a rentier state from oil revenues. After the First World War, the monarchy was restored in 1925 under the figure of a former cavalry officer, Colonel Reza Khan, who ruled as Reza Shah Pahlavi. In 1934 the Shah changed the name of the country from Persia to Iran to reflect its supposedly Aryan racial complexion and manifested strong leanings towards the Nazi regime in Germany, inviting in German advisers and establishing a Youth Corps modelled on the Hitler Youth. In 1941 he abdicated under Western and Soviet pressure due to his pro-Axis leanings. His son, Mohammed Reza, succeeded him and started modernising the state and economy on pro-Western lines.

Mohammed Reza Pahlavi began a rapid process of industrialisation in the post-war years, though he was forced to flee in 1953 with the emergence of a broadly backed nationalist regime led by Mohammed Mossadegh which had gained control of the Majlis in 1951 and demanded the nationalisation of the country's oil assets. A CIA-backed coup later the same year secured the overthrow of the Mossadegh government and the return of the Shah, who proceeded over the following two decades to build up an extremely strong and centralised pro-Western regime. The Shah's modernisation programme increasingly foundered in the course of the 1970s and his regime faced a militant alliance of Islamic clerics and bazaar owners which succeeded in mobilising a broad mass of the urban Iranian population. In February 1979 it was overthrown in one of the twentieth century's great revolutions, ushering in – to much Western surprise – a revolutionary government led by Shi'a clerics that declared an Islamic Republic ruling on behalf of the *mostaz'afin*, or oppressed.

The Shah can be seen as a classic example of a figure anxious to emulate the Western model of the nation-state, though his ultimate downfall owed much to the grandiose nature of his economic development schemes which led to an extremely rapid rate of urbanisation and social dislocation. After his return to power in 1953, the Shah cultivated his close ties with the United States and emphasised his strong support for Western interests during a period when superpower rivalries and Cold War ideological conflicts were extending to the Middle East. He projected Iran as a reliable Western ally that would resist the advance of radical Arab nationalism of the kind being propagated by Nasser in Egypt. Indeed, he played upon the fact that the

Iranian population were non-Arabic and stressed his opposition to Arabs 'who by ill-considered nature if not design would unlock the door for the Soviet Union'.[20] He urged the Eisenhower administration to build up his regime militarily since 'in this age of atomic warfare, the occurrence of regular armed conflict with conventional weapons is not to be ruled out as a thing of the past'.[21]

At this stage the United States was less interested in building up Iran into a regional hegemon than securing a reform of its domestic social and class relations. American containment policy in the 1950s became infused with counter-insurgency ideology following the Chinese revolution of 1949 and the development of communist-backed peasant guerrilla insurgency in such countries as Malaya, the Philippines and Vietnam. American counter-insurgency doctrine was not based, in the 1950s at least, on a widespread experience of guerrilla insurgencies. It was premised on the belief that all such guerrilla insurgencies were really partisan operations that depended upon outside support. Furthermore, it was assumed that these sorts of operations were the initial phase for later full-scale communist invasion.[22] Counter-insurgent doctrine therefore proved to be a powerful impetus behind US global strategy and represented what Fred Halliday has termed 'counter revolutionary internationalism' geared to prevent the spread of international communist-backed revolution.[23] It also reflected what can be termed a Cold War learning curve in US strategic thinking as American aid policy became re-oriented towards building up strong client states that were capable of engaging in programmes of economic and social modernisation.[24] As early as 1956 Iran had the largest American overseas aid mission in the world with some 300 employees. The Shah came under growing American pressure to introduce a land reform programme in order to deradicalise the rural peasantry, build up the indigenous middle class and release capital for the building up of a local capitalist economy. By these means it was assumed that Iranian society would be restructured in order to prevent the communist mobilisation of the peasantry, while in the towns an urban middle class would lead the society into an increasingly Western way of life.[25]

Iran therefore was a classic example of the way that liberal theories of modernisation, geared to a wider global strategy of containment, were prevalent in the 1950s in the social sciences in the United States and influential in political decision-making. Such theories drew upon a tradition of political science in the United States which in the decades since the 1920s increasingly had cut adrift from the democratic public as the root of political recon-struction and saw itself as a sort of surrogate citizenry engaged in a strategy of social control. Modernisation theory therefore had little to say as far as democratising Iranian society was concerned since it saw democracy as emerging not through political struggle between organised political groupings but emerging in a rather mechanistic manner as the end product of a process of social and economic modernisation.[26]

The application of modernisation theory to the Iranian example led to the idea that the rentier state of the Shah could build up its autonomy and restructure relations between the main competing groups in Iranian society as part of a programme of 'organic benevolent Statism'. The domination by the landowning class of the political system would be progressively phased out and a prosperous middle peasantry would emerge, capable of enhancing the growth of rural markets. It was envisaged that the whole process would be controlled by the state, reflecting in effect a domestication of US containment policy. For a period in the early 1960s the reform programme threatened to get out of hand when the radical figure of Hasan Arsanjani, the Minister of Agriculture in the government of Ali Amini, looked set to use it to take over control of the state. The policy was put into temporary reverse as the CIA became increasingly alarmed at the direction the policy was taking. Following Arsanjani's forced resignation in 1963, the Shah himself took over direct control of what became known as the 'White Revolution' in Iran. This led to the extensive commercialisation of Iranian agriculture and a sizeable increase in the number of small and middle-sized peasants owning their own plots. By the mid-1970s it was estimated that 930,000 plotholders of 2 to 10 hectares owned 28 per cent of arable land, forming in effect a new middle peasantry in Iran.[27] This still failed to stem the tide flowing into the cities as many of the rural plots still proved too small for the peasants to make a living and by the late 1970s an estimated 45 per cent of the total population had become urbanised.

Moreover, the development policies of the Shah built up the central state bureaucracy and by the 1970s a sizeable middle class had emerged in the urban areas without any significant access to political power. An estimated 500,000 of the million-strong middle class were bazaar owners and this group felt increasingly threatened by the impact of the Shah's industrialisation policies. These were developed in the wake of the four-fold increase in oil prices by OPEC in 1973 which increased the revenue to Iran from the sale of its oil from $482 million for 1.7 million barrels a day in 1964 to a staggering $4.4 billion for 5.9 million barrels a day in 1973.[28] The Shah's industrialisation strategy was oriented towards the development of large heavy industry and began to undermine small-scale trade and craft industries that traditionally had sustained the bazaar-based economy. Bound together by a network of guilds, the bazaaris began to act as a major political force when they became allied to sections of the Islamic clergy in the course of the 1970s.

It was thus in the towns and cities that the revolutionary upsurge in Iran was to come rather than the countryside, a dimension that the original modernisation theory tended to overlook. Some sections of the new urban middle class had become highly Westernised in orientation and looked to the Shah's regime being eventually superseded by a model of pluralist democracy. Likewise, some of the urban middle-class intellectuals drifted towards the Communist or Tudeh Party which also imagined that the Shah's regime would eventually be overthrown by a revolutionary alliance of peasants and workers leading to the installation of a socialist system. Both these groups employed Western concepts of progress and social evolution despite their differing end states. Neither took very seriously the clerical class of Shi'a *ulemas*, centred on seminaries such as Qom, who preached in the mosques for a return to an Islamic society in Iran governed by Sharia law.

To this extent, Western analysts outside Iran failed to grasp the drift of thinking among intellectuals from the 1960s onwards. A number of key intellectuals in Iran began to employ a form of orientalism in reverse as they saw the West as the quintessential 'other' to an authentic Iranian cultural identity that appeared to be under growing threat as a result of the Shah's rapid modernisation programme. One major figure in this regard was the radical writer Jalal Al-e Ahmad, who published a widely influential book, *Gharbzadegi*, in 1962. Al-e Ahmad came from a family with a strong Islamic faith, though he also belonged for a period to the Tudeh Party in the 1940s. He was important for moving between both religious and radical left-wing circles and never really lost his Islamic faith, unlike some more secular intellectuals on the left. *Gharbzadegi* was especially notable for launching an attack on the uncritical pursuit of Western values in Iran, a phenomenon that can be translated as 'Westoxification' or 'Euromania'. Al-e Ahmad lamented the dependency of Iran upon Western technology and its slavish subordination to a machine technology that destroyed its culture and ripped out the heart from its towns and cities. This was in some respects a variant of dependency theory that became popular among a number of Third World intellectuals at this time but went further by developing a theory of cultural autonomy that bore some resemblance to earlier intellectual movements such as that of the Slavophiles in nineteenth-century Russia.[29] Al-e Ahmad was critical of the impact of advanced capitalism on the values of Iranian society and urged a return to Shi'a Islam as an antidote to the 'tuberculosis' of *gharbzadegi*.[30]

Al-e Ahmad's writings helped to open up a space in Iranian intellectual debate for a variety of lines of critical thought, some liberal and some oriented towards trying to produce some form of synthesis between Shi'a Islam and a Marxist-oriented sociology. The key figure in the latter project was undoubtedly Ali Shariati, who began to fill the vacuum that was left by Ali-e Ahmad's premature death in 1969. Shariati sought to combine an intellectual commitment to Shi'ism with demands for economic justice and he was particularly notable for developing Al-e Ahmad's criticism of Euromania into a wider set of commitments to Third World liberation. Ali Shariati was wary of championing cultural autonomy for its own sake since this ran the risk of being hijacked by more conservative forces within Iranian society who could turn it into a more introverted fascist and racist ideology of cultural preservation. A variant of this was attempted by the Shah in 1971 in the form of the glittering celebration at Persepolis to celebrate 2,500 years of the Iranian monarchy. For Ali Shariati, the impact of Islam in Iran had been to cut its culture off from any pre-Islamic past and any return to the society's cultural roots meant a return to Shi'a Islam.[31]

This line of attack undoubtedly struck a popular chord in Iran, though the revolutionary coalition that emerged in the course of the 1970s was a broadly based one and it was by no means evident that the more conservative sections of the Shi'a clergy would eventually prevail over their rivals. However, the writings by Iranian intellectuals such as Al-e Ahmad and Ali Shariati helped to lay the foundations in Iran for a series of indigenous and nativist ideologies that rejected the Shah's close alignment with the West. These ideological movements acquired a popular base in the course of the 1970s as young militant clerics moved out of religious seminaries into political activism, forging in the process an alliance with the bazaar owners. The disparate groups involved became bound together by Shi'a revolutionary ideology which became the main weapon of mass political mobilisation. This seriously undermined structuralist concepts of revolution that were prevalent among 'third generation' theorists of revolution in the United States in the 1970s. It became clear that a state-centric theory of revolution centred on the inability of a 'Sultanistic' regime to devolve power down to the local level was not by itself adequate to explain the full complexities of the revolutionary movement.[32]

The Iranian revolution was a considerable surprise for a number of analysts since it appeared to contradict the basic conception of revolution since the late eighteenth century, that is revolution rooted in ideas of human progress and social evolution. The Ayatollah Khomeini wanted Iranian society to return to an earlier type of social model centred on theocratic notions of rule by a divinely inspired religious authority or *velayat i-faqih*. The revolution represented a denial of Western precepts of citizenship and pluralistic democracy. It led to widespread terror against its radical political opponents in the early 1980s, such as the *Mojahedin* and the Tudeh (Communist) Party, and the strict imposition of Sharia law as an Islamist state was created.

Some analysts have pointed out that the revolutionary regime's ideology was not simply geared towards returning Iran to the Middle Ages. Fred Halliday, for instance, has argued that, despite many obviously reactionary features, the revolution also engrained many modern features, including a huge array of popular forces which were brought together in a populist alliance against the Shah's regime. The revolution was also a generally urban revolution rather than a revolution by peasants and rural dwellers, and it occurred in a society with a far higher level of socio-economic development than Russia in 1917 or China in 1949. It did not occur as a result of external war or fiscal crisis – phenomena that the 'third generation' of analysts of revolution saw as the essential prerequisites for social revolution[33] – but through popular political mobilisation. These factors made February 1979 in Iran for Halliday not only the first contemporary religious revolution but also the first really 'modern' one as well.[34]

This effort to portray the Iranian in a basically modernist guise is not entirely convincing. As an analytical approach it can be criticised for seriously under-estimating the power of traditionalist Shi'ite social and political thought in Iran which has deep historical roots and which parallels some counter-revolutionary and anti-modernist thought in Europe. While a number of Shi'ite clerics did embrace various modernist ideas in a variety of different ideological mixes, the modernist impulse tended to lose its impetus following the death of Ali Shariati in 1977. By the time of the revolution in February 1979 the main modernist branch of the popular alliance that overthrew the Shah was the *Mojahedin* who became quickly marginalised in the months following the revolution. The traditionalist religious faction around Khomeini proved to be far better politically organised and were able to appeal to a strong power base not only in the mosques and bazaars but also in local religious associations (*hay'at mazhabi*) that met in the poorer parts of Iranian cities and reflected the views of the less well-educated urban petty bourgeoisie linked to the bazaar economy. These associations were generally far more receptive to traditionalist interpretations of Shi'ite Islam than more modernist versions that tended to be espoused by sections of the clerical intelligentsia educated in seminaries and universities.[35]

The Iranian revolution therefore ended up being led in 1979 by a group of petty bourgeois Islamic militants who succeeded in redefining 'twelver' Shi'a Islam into a utopian body of thought that rejected the basic precepts of the Shah's modernisation programme. The revolutionary clerics preferred to look backwards rather than forwards and championed the values of a previous golden age. Such a body of thought lacked Western notions of linear historical progress since it rested on belief in the occultation of the twelfth Imam, a direct descendant of the original prophet Mohammed. The projected return of the Imam was seen as heralding the end of the temporal history and the ushering in of a new millennium of social justice. Along with this there is a strong sense of martyrdom centred on the figures of Husayn, the son of Ali, and his companion Karbala who were murdered by an illegitimate tyrant. For Shi'ites revolution against what was perceived as an alien secular state did not represent the end of history as it did for Sunnis but the realisation of a promise or *Parousia* made by the hidden Imam.[36]

These religious precepts became gradually politicised by a political alliance of clerics and intellectuals in Iran who opened Shi'ism to a number of external ideological influences in a manner that was generally untypical in Sunni societies. The Iranian ayatollahs combined a legalism with a philosophical syncretism that has led to considerable ideological and theological debate over the exact nature of modern political authority.[37] Few senior clerical figures proved willing to support Khomeini's claims to being the *velayat i-faqih* which was only developed while he went into exile in Iraq after 1963. Khomeini's views largely prevailed as a result of the refusal of most of the senior *marjas*, or sources of imitation, to engage in politics. He was able to build up a huge network of political support at the local level with *hujjat al islam*, many of whom were his former students and who preferred political activism to religious studies.[38] This clerical-intellectual alliance was able to impose the 1979 constitution providing for the *velayat i-faqih* and succeeded in mobilising political support through the Islamic Republican Party (IRP) until it was disbanded in 1986. With such superior organisational resources the IRP majority in the Majlis was able to remove from the presidency in 1981 its most important ideological rival in the form of the modernist cleric Abolhasan Banisadr. It proceeded to engage in a wide-ranging religious purge of government ministries as well as introducing a draconian Penal Code. This did not stop continuing opposition from senior clerics such as Ayatollah Hasan Qomi though such figures failed to have strong organisational support.[39]

Much of the impetus behind the drive for a *velayat i-faqih* came from Khomeini himself and when he died in 1989 it proved impossible to maintain. Although the Assembly of Experts elected President Ali Khameinh'i as successor, it rapidly emerged that he could not inherit Khomeini's religious authority (even though he was made a Grand Ayatollah) and the *velayat* concept has more or less died a natural death. With this has come an implicit acceptance of the notion of a division of church and state and Ayatollah Qomi has declared that obedience is due to Khameinh'i only for his political and not religious rulings.[40] In the Spring 1992 elections to the Majlis barely a quarter of the candidates endorsed by the Islamic Clergy Association won, suggesting that there was growing public disaffection with Islamic radicalism at a time of falling living standards and riots in several Iranian cities. During the 1990s there has been a growing pragmatism in policy towards the West, though the *fatwa* issued by the Ayatollah Khomeini against the novelist Salman Rushdie has not as yet been lifted. Iran has resumed its membership of the International Monetary Fund (IMF) and borrowed from the World Bank. The regime in fact has begun to follow similar policies to the Shah in borrowing from the West to finance industrial projects, spending some $10 billion on steel and motor vehicle plants.

To this extent, there is some substance to the thesis that the Iranian revolution is unlikely to have the same sort of long-term impact on world history as the American, French or Russian revolutions. While the revolution initially sent considerable shock waves throughout the Middle East and provoked speculation in the West over the possibility of an 'Islamic funda-mentalist' offensive against Western interests, the impact of the revolution has tended to be generally local with the notable exception of the Hizbolah movement among the Shi'ite community in Lebanon and the Palestinian Hamas movement.[41] Some analysts have argued that a new coalition of forces may be emerging within the Iranian polity of islamic radicals and Persian nationalists which is bent on an ambitious expansionist policy towards its neighbours and eager to take advantage of the generally weak and chaotic state of the former Soviet Central Asian republics.[42] This view does not appear to have been born out by events, though it is hard at the best of times to assess the exact impact of political ideology on a state's foreign policy as ideological perceptions tend to be combined with more short-term goals. As with many other islamic states, Shi'ite revolutionary ideology in Islam has tended on occasions to give Iranian foreign policy a messianic edge and a sense of mission, though this may well be declining as more nationalist considerations come into prominence.[43] The full potential of Iran's revolutionary ideology in 1979 was never really realised since much of its force and energy became diverted into the long drawn out war with Iraq between 1980 and 1988, a war that was started by a pre-emptive strike by the Iraqi regime of Saddam Hussein against the Iranians through fear that the revolutionary ideological message of the new regime in Tehran would provoke a revolt by the Shi'ite minority in southern Iraq.

The protracted nature of the war led to Iran's revolutionary goals being subsumed by a more short-term goal of national survival. As the Irangate scandal revealed in the United States in 1986, the regime in Tehran was not even averse to pulling off an arms deal worth an estimated $27 million with the United States via Israel if it could secure its own national survival. Iran's foreign policy at this point reflected little or no sense of ideological consistency, though some revolutionary ideologues within Iran attached considerable importance to the distinction between dealing with the 'great Satan' of the United States via a (Zionist) proxy and dealing with it directly.[44] In the course of the 1990s even this ideological input seems to have declined markedly in Iranian foreign policy as the regime has shown itself to be wary of newer ideologically zealous regimes in the region, such as that of the Taliban in Afghanistan. The Taliban is Sunni-based and to many Iranian *mullahs* threatens to stir up dissent among the Sunni minority in Iran. The regime in Tehran opposes what it calls the 'reactionary' regime in Kabul and seeks a multi-ethnic governing coalition rather than the narrowly Pushtun-based Taliban. Such a strategy is part of a long-term goal of extending Iranian influence throughout the region and trying to counter US efforts to route oil from Central Asia out through Russia rather than through the most geographically obvious route of Iran.[45] At the end of the day, therefore, the exigencies of power politics and national self-interest can be seen to have largely taken over from the promulgation of Islamic revolutionary ideology. Iran's revolutionary regime has followed in the footsteps of other revolutionary regimes in the twentieth century of learning to postpone its immediate ideological goals in the interests of *Realpolitik*.

The Future of Ideologies in the Post-Cold War Era

The end of the Cold War can by no means be seen as ushering in an early 'end of history' and the termination of ideological conflict in global politics.

The era of superpower domination during the Cold War helped to simplify ideological divisions within international politics, reducing ideological debate at its crudest level to a battle between the 'free world' and 'international communism'. The era of decolonisation, stretching from the 1940s to the 1970s, was also marked by the dissemination from Europe of various ideological forms into the developing world. The emergence of nationalist intelligentsias provided fertile ground for the modification of various European ideologies such as nationalism, socialism, Marxism and liberalism into a variety of new ideological structures that provided legitimation to the new post-colonial elites that emerged to rule the large number of new states that sprung up in the wake of the retreat of the Western empires. In the continent of Africa, for instance, this led, by the 1970s, to various ideological forms, ranging from populist varieties of 'African socialism' in states such as Tanzania and Zambia, African capitalism as in Kenya, and a clutch of Afro-Marxist regimes such as Congo-Brazzaville, Guinea, Mozambique and Angola.[46]

The ideological debate on Third World economic development also acquired a relatively easily understood simplicity in terms of ideas of a 'New International Economic Order' and the re-ordering of 'North–South' relations. The highpoint of this debate was the 1970s when the prospect for growing Third World solidarity on such issues as debt repayment and the terms of trade with the West provoked fears that the global economy might be facing a major crisis. However, the inability of developing states to replicate the actions of the OPEC oil cartel in the sale of other commodities ultimately blunted the whole issue. By the 1980s it became largely by-passed by a new economic agenda pivoted around privatisation and the global extension of market economics.

The retreat of the superpowers in this decade also revealed an increasingly diverse and complex international system in which ideologies were developed rather more independently of superpower influence or control. The collapse of the Soviet Union in 1991 led to an increase in the number of states in the international system and this process may be continued by the break-up of some post-colonial states in Sub-Saharan Africa. This increase in the number of states raises the prospect of a growing diversity of national intelligentsias keen to assert distinct identities and intellectual autonomy from the conventions of global 'Westernisation'. As the Iranian example in the previous section has illustrated, such intellectual movements provide the essential basis for the construction of new or revitalised ideologies of national, ethnic or religious reassertion which can have important implications for the course of international politics. It is still possible, though, for such ideological movements to be contained by regional or superpower hegemons if they threaten major instability, as in the case of the Gulf War against Iraq in 1991.

Nevertheless, the decline of the superpowers to influence ideological debate indicates that contemporary ideological confrontation has moved beyond a geographical basis in the modern international system and taken on a global dimension.[47] This is clearly reflected in the way that ideas such as 'Thatcherite' strategies of privatisation and state withdrawal from the economy have become increasingly internationalised in the 1980s and 1990s. This perhaps bears out the argument of interdependence theorists that such an ideology reveals the 'embedded liberalism' within the global market economy that is ultimately beyond the capacity of any one hegemonic power to control.

It would be premature, though, to overlook the continuing capacity of states to control both people and ideas and utilise ideological belief systems for their own political purposes. Nation-states can still either foment or 'capture' ideological beliefs and resist pressures for their decision-making systems to be subordinated to supra-national imperatives. This issue is most dramatically illustrated in the fervent debate on further integration among the members of the European Union (EU) and the threat such integration poses to the national sovereignty of each member state. The defence of such sovereignties has begun to take on, in a number of West European states such as Britain and Denmark, populist features as it has become linked with emotive issues of national identity, a theme which cannot easily be replicated at the symbolic level by the EU itself.[48] Even if it is the case that many of the imperatives behind contemporary definitions of citizenship have moved beyond those of the sovereign nation-state, it can by no means be presumed that an automatic political realignment can easily take place. The notion of 'post-national' citizenship might be quite persuasive intellectually but contains a strong degree of utopianism to the extent that it continues to ignore the political capacities of nation-states to hinder and restrict its development.[49]

The nation-state still retains a considerable force in contemporary international relations through its ability to mobilise ideologies of nationalism in order to secure popular political legitimation. Nationalism can be seen as one of the three dominant ideologies in international politics in the twentieth century along with Marxism and liberal democracy. While Marxism in a variety of forms remained a major force from 1917 to 1989, its effective collapse as a major global ideology since the end of the Cold War has left just two major rivals in the form of nationalism and liberal democracy. In some sense this returns global society to a similar situation as at the end of the First World War when the Wilsonian vision for the reconstruction of the international order looked to the progressive extension of liberalism and democracy hand in hand with the liberal ideal of the right to national self-determination.

The doctrine of national self-determination, though, has been frequently mobilised during the twentieth century by nationalist groups in an anti-democratic manner, so cutting it off from doctrines of democratic political participation and citizenship.[50] As a doctrine, therefore, nationalism has an uneasy relationship with democratic and liberal ideologies and can often act to override them. At the close of the twentieth century this issue still does not appear to have been resolved in any way satisfactorily, though the successful prosecution of some of those guilty of 'ethnic cleansing' in Bosnia may go some way towards establishing in international law clear limits on the rights of ethnic groups to achieve national self-determination at the expense of the human rights of others.

CHAPTER 3

International Relations after the Cold War: from World Politics to Global Politics

A. J. R. Groom

The key institution in international relations, at least for the past four hundred years, has been the state. The state system has been rearranging itself structurally since the end of the Cold War, both politically and economically. However, the transformation from world politics to 'global' politics has been occurring since at least the 1960s. Perhaps the greatest transformation has been a social one, in the sense that individuals, ideas, images, and money have an unprecedented mobility across borders. The consequences of this may be such that we have entered a post-Westphalian world, a world characterised by global politics and 'globalisation'. The ending of the Cold War invites us to look back as well as forwards; to see where we are going implies a look at where we are coming from. Thus, this chapter begins with an assessment of the end of the Cold War and the emergence of global politics.

The latter part of this chapter investigates how we may be able conceptually to come to terms with the post-Cold War international system. The rate of change is increasing and therefore the period available for adjustment to changes is being shortened dramatically. Whereas Europe had one hundred years to adjust to the consequences of the military use of gunpowder from its first use to its generalised use, it took only half a century from the first powered flight of human beings, not merely to the generalisation of powered flight, but to putting a human being into space in *Sputnik*. Thus our technological ability is racing ahead, while the evolution of social, political, economic and cultural norms is proceeding relatively much slower. Therein could lie a recipe for disaster. All of our current nostra, or '-isms', were already in full flowering in the nineteenth century, save, perhaps, for globalisation. Yet our problems are those of the twenty-first century. Political theorists and practitioners have failed to imagine and develop the political, economic, social and cultural tools that fit the technological and scientific possibilities, not just of the approaching twenty-first century, but of the twentieth century. If we do not have adequate conceptual tools, the changing physical environment will impose itself upon us willy nilly.

The Cold War

An examination of the significance of the end of the Cold War implies, at the very least, a cursory analysis of the nature of the Cold War and of its effects so that we may determine that which has ended. The Cold War can stimulate many arguments. We may ask whether it was necessary, given the wartime agreements for the division of Europe, and with the willingness of both the Soviet Union and the Anglo-Americans to stay within the broad confines of those agreements. We may ask who started it, and quickly find ourselves embroiled in the arguments of revisionist historians. We may enquire whether the Cold War had cycles, perhaps to the extent of whether we can identify a first and second Cold War with periods of lesser tension and *détente*.[1] Moreover, if there were cycles, we may seek to clarify further what renewed the Cold War as each cycle came to an end. Again, why did the Cold War finally come to an end? Some of these questions are relevant for an analysis of the conceptual and theoretical implications of the ending of the Cold War. But first, what was the Cold War?

The Cold War was a perception of mortal threat by the predominant decision-makers of the major powers, beginning, at the latest, in 1947 and ending, likewise at the latest, in 1990 with the signing of the Charter of Paris. That this threat was perceived not only by decision-makers, both political and military, but also by the attentive public in general can be seen from any perusal of *Le Monde*, *Pravda*, the *New York Times* or, in earlier years, *The Times*. Their leaders and their reports illustrate graphically the sense of mortal fear that predominated at times to an extent that it almost numbed the minds of those who professed to be interested in global politics, or indeed, the fate of humanity. This perception of threat led to the creation of two blocs, each under the aegis of a hegemonic leader which engaged in a political competition not only with each other but also for the allegiance of the world at large, both in terms of elites and masses. It spawned an horizontal and vertical arms race in both nuclear and conventional weapons. It led to an economic rivalry in trade and in aid, and it formed the political underpinning of an ideological struggle on a global scale. No continent was spared from the exigencies of the Cold War. It was a global obsession that disenfranchised thought, and a prism through which life was conceived and lived. Although its heartland was in Europe and North America, its effects were global.

There were few factors at the global level that militated against this obsession. However, one such was the policy of non-alignment. Although a policy of non-alignment is not necessarily an adjunct of the Cold War, since it is almost a natural foreign policy for any newly independent state, as General Washington pointed out in his farewell speech as President of the United States, nevertheless the growth of the non-aligned movement was conceived in the context of the Cold War, and while the policy is still relevant, the movement has lost its way as the Cold War has receded into history.

A second phenomenon that, for a while, deflected global attention away from the Cold War was the demand for a New International Economic Order (NIEO). While the struggle for emancipation from colonialism had often been situated in a Cold War context, the demand for a NIEO was not so imbued with Cold War considerations. It was a demand addressed by developing countries to the West, that is Western Europe and North America, from which Japan was largely spared, and the Soviet Union, rather gleefully, stood aside. But a number of factors, notably the second major increase in oil prices at the end of the 1970s and the coming into office of President Reagan and Mrs Thatcher, led to a determined attitude on the part of the West and economic disarray in the developing countries. The way was thus clear for the second Cold War, symbolised by phrases such as 'the evil empire' and 'successive breakdowns of negotiations over nuclear arms'.

What has stopped with the ending of the Cold War is the all-pervasive fear of a mutual threat. There is now no global competition in any dimension between two blocs because one of those blocs has collapsed and the other is looking fitfully for a new role. The United States remains a superpower, if a superpower is defined according to superiority in four structures: military, economic, cultural, and knowledge. A superpower has a global military reach in the sense that it is able to project conventional military power effectively in any quarter of the globe, either using its own endogenous forces or in cooperation with allies that it can command, the possession of nuclear power, and the ability to develop and build its own capital military goods, implying the possession of a military-industrial complex. A superpower also has a domestic economy which is substantial in terms of its competitors, but of greater importance than size is the fact that its economy is at the cutting edge of scientific and technological innovations. A superpower must have a significant impact upon world trade and its currency must be a world currency, acceptable by others without fear. The definition of the cultural aspects of a superpower are more difficult to delineate. In short, a superpower must have a culture that is attractive to others. Culture in this context involves language, religion, political institutions, ideology and the like. A superpower is a country which others seek to emulate throughout the arts and sciences and to which they send their brightest and best for training. A superpower sets standards and it is found wanting in no major area of human endeavour. Finally, a superpower must have the will to act as such and the capacity to bear the sacrifices entailed, for being a superpower is not only a question of rights but also of duties. It must know how to set the global agenda, how to aggregate support for it, how to elicit decisions and how to ensure their implementation.

One reason for the end of the Cold War was that the Soviet Union was unable to maintain its position as such, and in particular in the economic sphere where it was able to accomplish to a substantial degree the first Industrial Revolution, as its performance in the Second World War indicated, but not the second Industrial Revolution. The United States, standing alone in the plenitude of this capacity, is not, however, and cannot be, a global hegemon. In each of the four dimensions of superpower status set out above the United States is not alone. In the military sphere Russia is a superpower. In the economic sphere likewise Japan and the European Union play an important role. In the cultural sphere there is no doubt that Europe has the cultural role, broadly defined, of a superpower, and perhaps in time so too might Japan. However, there is doubt whether any one of these actors has the will to play a superpower role, including the United States. There is therefore in each dimension a countervailing power which means that, should the United States so wish, it could not exert a global hegemonic role as the single superpower. Moreover, there are other major actors, such as India, China, Indonesia and Brazil, as well as important movements such as the Islamic movement, which crowd the global stage.

We have gone therefore from a world dominated by a bipolar East–West conflict to a much more complex interactive global system characterised by a marked diminution in the degree of polarity in all the important dimensions of military, economic, cultural and leadership functions. The end of the Cold War has therefore opened up the world to a wider variety of actors and a wider range of possibilities. We have also gone from a world dominated by an obsessive fear which paralysed thought to a new international order where new navigation points for political analysis are possible. What is not so evident is what shall constitute such navigation points. An all-pervasive enemy makes life, in one sense, simple, if dangerous. A complex and changing world is in itself a frightening phenomenon. The world had become more complex long before the watershed event of the ending of the Cold War, although that event perhaps has focused increased attention on the diversity and heterogeneity of international relations, and perhaps has also fuelled fears associated with the movement from international to 'global' politics.

From World Politics to Global Politics

It is a pointless task to attempt the identification of precisely the point at which an historic change occurred, since even signal events may be either a recognition of the culmination of past processes, or an intimation of future directions. Nevertheless, the designation of such benchmarks is useful, since they tend to indicate when a change of degree has become a change of kind. In this sense, the period around 1960 is such a benchmark for the movement from world politics to global politics. By 'world politics' is meant that events may affect all quarters of the globe, but do not necessarily do so.

In short, they are events which are not organic to the world as a single unit. 'Global politics', however, embraces the globe in such a manner that there can be no escape; global politics necessarily involve the globe as a totality and therefore global politics must be conceived in holistic terms.

This shift can be seen by comparing the Second World War with the prospect of nuclear war that became real in the 1960s. The Second World War was, as its name suggests, a world war. It involved every continent of the globe, albeit to degrees which varied substantially. However, that war did not necessarily involve the globe in an holistic manner. For example, indigenous inhabitants of the tropical rain forests of Brazil were, presumably, little affected by the Second World War. Around 1960 nuclear weapons and global delivery systems became available in significant numbers to the major powers. *Sputnik* in 1957 heralded intercontinental ballistic missiles (ICBMs) and Polaris. Accuracies were in sight which could distinguish between a warhead targeted on the House of Commons and one targeted on 10 Downing Street when fired either from California or Siberia. The nature of large-scale warfare had altered; henceforth the globe was potentially a nuclear battlefield, not only in terms of targeting but also in terms of effects, whether direct or indirect. A nuclear war, with the prospects of fall-out and nuclear winter would, of necessity, affect everyone; there could be no escape, even for those living in the furthest reaches of the Amazon Basin.

It is also at this time that the developed world could be considered to have recovered from the ravages of the Depression and the Second World War. This was signified by the establishment of the Organisation for Economic Cooperation and Development (OECD) in which more than twenty countries joined what was, in effect, the management committee for the global economy. It was evident at that point, with the Japanese and West European economies strengthening themselves apace, that there was now a global economic system for all but the Communist world. Since then the Communist world economic sub-system has collapsed and it has been integrated into the global system. But no single state can manage this system, and all are necessarily affected by what happens in any part of it. The 1960s also heralded the final stages of the de-colonisation process of the European colonial powers and in particular France, Britain, Portugal and the Tsarist-Soviet Empire. This process has given rise to an increasing number of formally independent states and the process has not yet exhausted itself. Yet, by 1964, with the creation of the United Nations Conference on Trade and Developement (UNCTAD), the centre–periphery aspects of the global economy were becoming ever more evident.

Similar globalising phenomena can be observed in questions of the environment. It was in the 1950s that such questions began to become a matter of public concern, and in the 1960s the movement grew apace until the United Nations Global Conference in Stockholm in 1972. Instrumental in this growing awareness was the work of the Club of Rome, and the discussions of its major contribution to the debate, *The Limits to Growth*,[2] which both crystallised and stimulated a growing concern with the environment in all its many aspects. It is now clear, whatever the weaknesses of a model underlying such exercises as *The Limits to Growth*, that the question of population growth, resource utilisation and environmental degradation are global problems, the effects of which will affect everybody willy nilly. No one, for example, can escape the consequences of the destruction of the Amazon rainforest. The historian Braudel reminds us of the consequences of the destruction of the wooded areas of the Mediterranean and all aspects of Mediterranean society – economic, social, cultural, political and military.[3] Our interaction with the biosphere can have similar consequences from which there is no escape.

We can look, too, to communications. The year 1960 marked the first time in which more people crossed the Atlantic Ocean by air than by boat. A new era of mass intercontinental travel was upon us, and by the 1960s the poor of the world could move in increasing numbers and distance. Tamils could arrive at Heathrow, Roissy, Schipol or Frankfurt along with others who are the poorest of the poor. The result of this has been a system of global *apartheid* where the Group Areas Act may have been abolished in South Africa, but its application is just as ruthless by immigration officers at these airports. But this movement of peoples has been more than matched by the movement of information. The development of powerful radio systems had a political effect even in the 1950s – consider the role of the Voice of the Arabs throughout the Near East, the Middle East and Africa. The global availability of radio, even to the world's illiterate, means that the reach of the privileged to send messages anywhere, even to the most deprived and oppressed, is virtually total. Television is now an important factor in foreign policy decision-making. Fax and email, and the information super-highway, have important implications for the time–space ratio. In no area is this better seen than in the global management, or lack thereof, of financial markets.

The list of changes in the last three decades or more is seemingly endless, but what is its significance for our theme? The end of the Cold War has meant that such factors which were crimped into the thought processes and transaction flows of the Cold War are now much freer. We can see more clearly because we are no longer mesmerised by a global adversarial system. Everything does not have to fit into one framework. Global systems are freer than hitherto to develop according to their own characteristic needs rather than be fired by the competitive interaction between the two antagonistic blocs. Perhaps this change can be seen in our evolving attitudes towards notions of sovereignty.

Sovereignty as an Anomaly

The European state system emerged in its full plenitude at the Peace of Westphalia of 1648. That system has now become a global one. It is predicated upon the idea of sovereignty, in which state authorities recognise no superior in the disposition of their internal affairs and recognise other states as a peer-group in the management of the inter-state system. Much political thought and much political action has been based on the notion of the sovereign state and indeed, the bifurcation of international relations and political science, as separate disciplines, has been based on the notion that intra-state politics are different fundamentally from inter-state politics. If that were ever true, it surely is no longer so and this has implications beyond academic boundaries for a key notion in political science and political action. Whatever the theoretical and juridical claims of absolute sovereignty, its exercise in practice is relative. In a situation of complex interdependence, the stage might have been reached whereby notions of sovereignty have been sufficiently attenuated that their utility as a starting point for analysis is so diminished that the need for a reconceptualisation is in order. Sovereignty in the sense of a competent and legitimised autonomy is now exercised by a variety of actors and not only by states. Moreover, the sources of social power are varied and changing.

The ending of the Cold War has enabled us to grasp more comprehensively the nature of the change from world politics to global politics, but it also takes us back to the basis of social power which Michael Mann has so ably demonstrated has four dimensions, namely the military, the economic, the ideological and the political.[4] Moreover, as he points out in a stunning historical overview, these four dimensions may overlap and interact, but they do not form an integrated whole. Indeed, never in human history have they integrated into a coherent whole, but rather they have formed an interacting, overlapping conglomerate. In such conglomerations at particular historic points, one dimension may take the lead and social organisation may be based more on ideological power than, say, economic power. Moreover, these dimensions do not necessarily push in the same direction. The ending of the Cold War enables us in our own time better to see this. Sovereignty is not something which either we have or we do not have. Sovereignty cannot be likened to virginity in that regard. Moreover, we must not forget, with 1648 in mind, that sovereignty is a Johnny-come-lately and it is bidding fair to be a Johnny-go-quickly.

Consider, for example, the experience in the European Union (EU), particularly the debate about sovereignty and federalism. Neither the substance of one nor the form of the other is at present a characteristic of the EU, nor are either likely to become so. Rather, what we see is a four-fold building process whereby we are 'building up', 'building down', 'building across' and 'building beyond'. In building up, to create an authority charged with the joint management of pooled competence in certain areas, the Commission itself has designated the process as being one of the joint management of pooled sovereignty. Thus the Union is not moving towards a federal goal, but rather towards a consociation of governmental elites in which national governments are not separate from a federal authority, but in fact constitute a major element of it.

This process of building up is balanced by an increasing thrust towards building down to regions and, by virtue of the principle of subsidiarity, there is no inherent reason that this process should stop at the boundaries of the member states of the Union. The emergence of regions in the EU, and not just in the traditionally strong Länder of Germany, but also in France, Spain, Italy and Belgium, is an innovative and necessary development. It is necessary because it responds to the growing need for a sense of identity, often regionally based in some parts of Europe; Catalonia is a prime example. It was perhaps symbolic in the closing ceremony of the Barcelona Olympic Games to see four flags leading the parade, that of the International Olympic Committee, and those of Spain, Catalonia and the European Union. Four different dimensions were therefore allowed full play, and the processes of building down are now beginning to be recognised in the institutions of the Union. It is interesting to note that in two countries where regionalism was not given full play, namely, Denmark and the United Kingdom, opposition to the Maastricht Treaty was relatively strong. The constitutional change effected by Tony Blair's government may well have significant consequences not only for the UK but for the EU as well. An independent Scotland in the EU is no longer a pipe dream.

Building across means the promotion and consolidation of transnational ties. In the field of education, for instance, ERASMUS, TEMPUS and the like are beginning to transform our educational systems. We can see it in other ways where transregional entities are beginning to develop, for example, in the forging of a myriad of links between Kent and Nord Pas-de-Calais in a Trans-Manche context. Finally, we are also 'building beyond' as we participate in partnerships and associations through formal links between the EU and other states and bodies. Building beyond entails reaching out, as in the Lomé Agreements in the European economic area, in the binding of links through the Commonwealth, *la Francophonie* and in the fostering of intercontinental Iberian ties. The context of these relations is complexity and diversity in economic, social, political and cultural dimensions, in such a manner as to create a degree of coherence without the establishment of a notion of Westphalian sovereignty, either within the Union, or beyond it.

We have just witnessed, before our very eyes, the break-up of states, peacefully as in the case of Czechoslovakia, in bloody war as in the case of Yugoslavia and with a mixture of both as in the case of the former Soviet Union. There is a movement towards devolution in countries such as Spain, Italy and Belgium, and it is hard to imagine that the Kingdom of Great Britain and Ireland will not evolve further towards the disuniting of the Kingdom, recalling, of course, the recent events in Scotland and Wales. In North America such phenomena are clear too, dramatically in the case of Canada, but there is no reason to expect that the United States will be immune from such tendencies whether it be through indigenous peoples, Hispanics or other groupings. What it behoves us therefore to do, as theoreticians, is to exert imagination in describing, and perhaps indeed prescribing, different forms of cooperation. We seem, however, to be, for the most part, enslaved by a rather old-fashioned typology and to be ignorant of our own past.

Surely experiences from the Ottoman Empire, from British India, or pre-British India, or from the Chinese experience can garner insights in our own need to develop a new typology both to reflect and to influence the phenomena that are changing around us. Such models are perhaps as relevant as that of 1648. A particular concatenation of events produced the European state system and its globalisation over the last 500 years. But Mann's argument would suggest that this is an anomaly. If that is the case, then we may gain insight from considering other models of historical societies, prior to the emergence of the European state system as exemplified by the Treaty of Westphalia.

In his treatise *The Anarchical Society*, Hedley Bull pointed to signs of the emergence of a 'new mediaevalism'.[5] He was referring to the complex mediaeval society with the independent towns, bishoprics, guilds, as well as feudal structures which were characteristic of Europe before the Westphalian system. Bull did not welcome such a system because he felt it was character-ised by conflict. Yet conflict, at least in its dysfunctional aspects, need not be the prevailing characteristic of such a society. Likewise, we can look for the diversity and complexity, but cohering qualities, of India both during and since the period of British predominance. The management of the Ottoman Empire, too, had elements which were not uncommon to our present experience, and perhaps there are some lessons for us to learn. Again, the management of the world centring upon China, like the other examples cited, was not based upon a notion of sovereignty in Westphalian terms. Clearly our future does not have to be like our past, but it is unlikely to be like our present.

It is not difficult to discern in contemporary global politics the emergence of three great groupings, that of North America, that of the Japanese co-prosperity scheme in East Asia, and that of the European Union. To be sure, there are other major actors such as Russia, China and India, not to mention Indonesia or Brazil, but nevertheless, the tri-lateral characteristic of the contemporary world is ever more striking. It is unlikely, however, that any of these groupings will be tightly integrated. Rather, they are likely to cohere, but by making a virtue of their diversity. But in none of these groupings will sovereignty in the Westphalian sense predominate. Moreover, there is no need to anticipate that the relationships between the groupings will necessarily be conflictual. To be sure, there are differing interests and differing values which give rise to controversies, but there are also com-monalities of such a nature that unless we hang together we shall surely hang separately. The global economy, the global environment and the need to avoid global war are strong reasons to ensure that the common interest is an integral and organic part of individual interest. Indeed, with the veil of the Cold War lifted, it is possible to perceive several long-term disturbing trends that mandate cooperation in global governance.

Long-term Disturbing Trends after the Cold War: Global Riot Control

Concurrent with the structural changes to the international system, and the organisational changes that are challenging notions of sovereignty is a growing list of long-term disturbing trends which require identification and conceptualisation. This list is by no means unknown to us, but it has been ignored to a dangerous extent because of the tunnel vision imposed on our thought processes by the Cold War. The phrase global riot control was probably coined by Robert Cox, but it is an apt characterisation of a number of concerns of the leading powers which constitute their global agenda and for the management of which they have evolved informal processes which push sovereignty aside. This agenda includes such issues as nuclear proliferation, the drugs trade, the full range of ecological and environmental questions, the problem of immigration, the promotion of human rights in a Western formulation, the suppression of terrorism, and the promotion of a market economy.

The agenda for global riot control has something in common with the agenda for the Cold War, such as the question of arms control, particularly over nuclear weapons, but its emphasis is different. Strategists, in an effort to stave off unemployment, are redefining quite correctly the notion of security. This includes traditional concerns, such as aggression, civil wars and wars of secession, but also the agenda is broadened to include a wide range of environmental questions and issues such as drugs, refugees, human rights and the like, which were given short shrift in the days of the Cold War. These questions are the immediate agenda of the United Nations system although they are but a reflection of a broader agenda which is circumscribed by a number of disturbing trends, both positive and negative, which are likely to throw items on to top decision-makers' desks in the thirty years to come.

The question of disarmament and arms control is still with us and likely to remain so. In particular, the issue of nuclear proliferation is one that will require new, more complex and far more sophisticated rules of the game. Not only shall we be dealing with the crude bipolar system of the past as it translates itself into a process of management of nuclear relations between four or five global nuclear powers, but also we shall have to give attention to regional rivalries, such as that between India and Pakistan. But besides the global and regional dimension, there is also a third dimension, that is the linkage between regional and global nuclear relationships. Little thought has been given to these. But the question of arms control and disarmament does not limit itself to nuclear proliferation; it is also concerned with other aspects of the arms race, such as the proliferation of high-quality conventional arms which means that determined countries with enough dollars in the bank can procure highly sophisticated conventional weaponry and that the producers of such weaponry would be willing to sell it, if for no other reason than to reduce their unit costs. Moreover, the procurement of weapons of mass destruction is no longer the preserve of state actors. Criminal organisations can exploit laxity in regulations to cater to the perceived needs of terrorist groups, and developments in chemistry can diffuse the instruments of mass destruction into the hands of individuals.

This implies that the traditional hierarchy of military capability will collapse and the superpowers will find that sending a gunboat will no longer do. There are already painful lessons to be learned from Suez, Cyprus, Indo-China, Vietnam, Afghanistan, Somalia, Yugoslavia and the like. There are, however, two temporary mitigating factors. The first is the resupply of weapons in case of combat, and the second is the inability of some recipients to service and operate sophisticated weapons systems. Thus, what is disturbing, above all, is the profusion of arms throughout the world. In a sense, the genie is out of the bottle. Conventional responses are mitigated further when the threat comes from within a state's borders, and very few states have been successful at securing themselves from terrorist attacks. We can no longer concern ourselves with limiting capabilities; though there is ample incentive to focus attention on safeguards, we have to concentrate our minds on intentions. The problem, therefore, has become a political one, purely and simply, rather than one of the politics of prevention.

Access to the means of violence is changing in another fashion. There has been a remarkable democratisation of access to effective means of coercion whereby small determined groups who think they have nothing to lose, and are therefore willing to risk everything, can have an impact, sometimes literally, out of all proportion to their numerical importance. Developed societies are open, liberal and therefore vulnerable. If they are to defend themselves against such groups they have to give up these very factors which have made them rich. In some ways, therefore, the tables are being turned. Rather than society being governed by a small, rich and immensely powerful elite, there is now an effective counter-elite. In the Lebanon in the early 1980s and in Somalia a decade later the United States was constrained to withdraw by determined local actors. In effect a superpower was defeated, in part because its threshold of pain on that particular issue was lower than that of a determined opposition which felt that it had nothing to lose, and therefore could risk all.

Such phenomena may have important consequences for global governance. It means that we cannot have great-power dominance because that is ineffective, and that we must work on the basis of consensus. If the poor and the dispirited finally lose hope in the existing system, what reason do they have for not disrupting it in a most devastating manner? After all, they have nothing to lose and those who benefit from the system are likely to lose their privileges if they resort to effective means of coercion. No one in his right mind in a warm room on a freezing winter's day will throw a brick through the window because it will create an icy blast. However, anyone outside freezing on the pavement will have no compunction in heaving a brick through the window. Western societies are rich and developed because they are open and complex. They are, therefore, extremely vulnerable. Anyone who lives in or near London knows of such vulnerability. If we continue on our present course, we shall not be liberal, open societies and will therefore be the poorer for it. Some form of global participatory democracy is being forced upon us. This factor is likely to increase in intensity as we become more aware of the structural violence which lies hidden in many aspects of global society, for such a growing awareness will give rise to greater demands for its abolition. If the changes cannot be brought about in an evolutionary manner, then the tools are at hand to destroy structures in a violent manner. This takes us back once again to the changing nature of authority, to the ubiquitous demands for participation and to the general problem of governance.

There is a clear need to enfranchise a wide range of disenfranchised actors in the global system. It is a nonsense to have Specialised Agencies of the UN system, including financial and trade organisations, which are made up largely of governments with little or no input from other major actors in the system. How can one discuss sensibly the questions of development or of the global financial regime without the participants of multinationals, whether they are viewed as benign or malign. It was only through a serendipitous anomaly that the Pope was able to make his influence felt at the World Population Conference in Cairo, yet the views of the hierarchy of the Roman Catholic Church are clearly of great moment for global population policy. Unfortunately, such anomalies do not exist in other functional dimensions. Our institutional structure therefore has to be ameliorated in such a way that it enfranchises key actors, that is, those without whom it is not possible to act whatever their status or standing. Thus the problem of governance involves an identification of systems boundaries and key actors, not merely of state boundaries. Moreover, the question of governance likewise causes us to give thought to the growing cleavage between human needs and institutional needs. While it is frequently the case that an institution grows out of a glaring human need, nevertheless, in ministering to this need, an institution may develop institutional values of its own which, over time, may take predominance over, or at least warp, the fulfilment of the human need for which the institution was established. Trying to get the benefits of the British welfare state, or what remains of it, without a fixed abode, is no easy task. Likewise, to get a loan from the World Bank of a few million dollars, forty pages of detailed statistical information are required, often from a government which hardly has a statistical service worthy of that name.

Countries the world over, and not only in the developing world, are in fear and trepidation of the International Monetary Fund (IMF). Unless the strictures of the IMF and the World Bank are met, then the international community is unlikely to afford help and assistance to those in economic need, and more generally, economic guidance is given by G8, which is closely linked to the work of OECD. Moreover, the Specialised Agencies of the United Nations system in Geneva are managed through the Geneva Group, which, in particular, takes a close interest in their budgets, and through the budget, their programmes. The Geneva Group is chaired jointly by Britain and the United States, but includes other Western countries, such as France and Germany, as well as having support from Russia. Thus we can see, with a melding of the permanent five members of the Security Council (P5) and G8, an informal institutional structure has been created for the purpose of global riot control.

There can be little doubt that not only those governments that have something to hide are fearful of these developments over the last decade. While many countries may share the aspirations of the P5/G8 group, nevertheless they feel that they do not participate in their decision-making processes in an adequate manner. Such sentiments are felt ever more strongly in the Third World where countries are more likely to be the object of the deliberations of P5/G8 rather than a participant in their processes.

During the Cold War, development too often was seen in terms of who could provide more material goods as part of the 'beauty contest' between Capitalism and Communism. Perhaps now we can give greater attention to other notions of development conceived as individual or group self-actual-isation, that is, situations in which individuals or groups are able to develop their capabilities to the best level possible within a given state of knowledge and technology. Perhaps then we will be able to avoid the hideous cocktail of the fusion of the poverty line and the race line, whereby the rich are predominantly the white global minority, with the Japanese as honorary whites as in *apartheid* South Africa, and the poor majority are non-whites. However, as we have seen, they have new effective means of coercion at their disposal and this raises the question about whether our future as a global minority will be analogous to that of South African whites under *apartheid*, or whether we shall have the good sense to see the way towards a more hopeful and prosperous future. To do this we must give proper consideration to questions of identity.

Given the onset of global politics since 1960, the notion of global riot control is not in itself an unhappy one. Where the difficulty lies is in the setting of the agenda for global riot control and decisions on the means for managing it. The institutions, such as the Security Council, OECD, the UN Specialised Agencies and the like, are amenable to democratic processes and participatory decision-making, but it is evident that the agenda for global riot control is, in essence, that of the leading Western powers. But if global riot control is to be effective globally, then the agenda has to be a global agenda. In particular, the questions of development and global structural inequities need to be included on that agenda. Whatever the manifold and manifest failures of Third World countries, the structural disparities of the global economic system have only been acknowledged by the West and they have not been addressed.

Towards a Global Governance

Some thirty years ago systems thinking was very much in vogue, but it fell out of favour equally quickly. Among the reasons for this were first of all, the normative aspirations of much of general systems theory (GST), and, secondly, the difficulty in getting a clear empirical picture (in under a lifetime's work) of any aspect of a particular system. Nevertheless, Mitrany, Burton, Deutsch and Rosenau pointed towards a conceptual framework that might now assume a greater relevance as the institutional structure of the Cold War has been stripped away.[6] But it will have to come to terms with a different global agenda, and particularly with the thorny problem of global governance.

The problem, of course, is not new. A half-century ago it exercised the minds of the founding fathers of the United Nations, who were careful to write Article 2.7, which safeguards the domestic jurisdiction of states, into the Charter. Domestic jurisdiction is now under some pressure from the intrusive activity of various international bodies and especially of UN bodies. An obvious example is that of the Security Council with the leading role played by the permanent five (P5), who have acted as a directing group since 1986 when Sir John Thomson, the then British Ambassador, brought his four fellow Ambassadors together in the context of the war between Iran and Iraq. The role of the P5 has been particularly important in the case of the Kuwait crisis, but it has also been concerned with Namibia, Cambodia, Afghanistan, Yugoslavia, Somalia, Rwanda and Haiti, as well as other conflicts.

The diplomacy of the P5, in seeking the authorisation of the Security Council for the application of military sanctions against Iraq in the Kuwait crisis, exemplifies particularly well the leadership function of the permanent members of the Security Council. In invading and annexing Kuwait, Iraq posed a threat to small countries the world over in so far as many of them are regarded with covetous eyes by their larger neighbours. Moreover, if Iraq had succeeded, it would have been a major independent action by a regional power against the wishes of the superpowers and other permanent members of the Security Council, thus debilitating their ability to manage the global system of international peace and security. Iraq had also violated the rule of law, the UN Charter and the very ethos of the international system based on the norm that international frontiers cannot be changed by coercive means. Notwithstanding its previous support from other Arab countries, the Soviet Union, some Western powers, especially France, and the arguability of its case in some aspects *vis-à-vis* Kuwait, Iraq's action had placed it in almost complete isolation. Moreover, it had done so in the context where the P5 had found a unity and, since the Cold War had ended but the peace dividend had not yet been implemented, there were ample military forces available for a coalition led and managed by the P5, and especially the United States, Britain and France.

In the Security Council, Britain, the United States and France were willing to apply military sanctions and advocated the use of Article 51 which permitted individual and collective self-defence, rather than the detailed provisions of the Charter itself. With France joining the Anglo-Americans, a degree of legitimacy was afforded to their leadership, and this made it easier for Russia and six non-permanent members to accede to the Western-led coalition, despite their preference for a strict interpretation of the Charter in the application of military sanctions. China, too, did not present any obstacle, since the crisis provided a useful opportunity for it to re-establish its diplomatic position after the catastrophe of Tiananmen Square. This left only four members of the Council, known as the Gang of Four, who were opposed to the application of military sanctions. They constituted neither a legal nor a political veto.

A striking example of P5 at work was Resolution 687 of 3 April 1991 which was accepted with only Cuba voting against and the Yemen and Ecuador abstaining. Known as the 'mother of all resolutions', this resolution embodied the terms for the ending of hostilities, which Iraq accepted, and which involved intrusive inspection of Iraq, on a continuing basis, for the purposes of ensuring that the provisions concerning the relinquishment of all nuclear materials, chemical and biological weapons, and ballistic missiles with a range of over 150 kilometres, were fully implemented. There is no time limit on such inspections, which represent a clear derogation of Iraqi sovereignty, and the system is likely to remain in place until after the demise of Saddam Hussein. Thus the P5 has asked for, and obtained, the approval of the international community, through the Security Council, for the suspension of Article 2.7 in regard to Iraq for the above measures of arms control. Humanitarian intervention is usually necessitated by a calamity of nature or one which has been brought about by a massive abuse of human rights. We can therefore see a link between the need for muscled humanitarian intervention and human rights, and that the solidarity of the P5 therefore has penetrated into the world of humanitarian organisations, whether UN bodies such as the High Commission for Refugees or non-governmental bodies.

The work of humanitarian bodies in Iraq, as well as in the former Yugoslavia is under the general aegis of the Security Council. It is, in fact, muscled humanitarian intervention and, in the case of Iraq, is in clear violation of Iraq's domestic jurisdiction. In short, the P5 have insisted that in this instance at least, the principle of humanitarian aid is superior to the principle of domestic jurisdiction. But since humanitarian intervention is often rendered necessary by a gross violation of human rights, and the Western powers, at least, have clear views on human rights, then the protection of human rights is beginning to take precedence over the question of sovereignty.

In January 1991 John Major presided over a meeting of the Security Council at which the Heads of Government of all member states attended. This was the first such occasion, and arising out of that meeting the Secretary-General was asked to write his *Agenda for Peace*. The Secretary-General's paper aroused a good deal of debate and it represented perhaps the high point of the P5 and the UN Secretary-General's confidence in their ability to institute a regime for global governance, at least in the area of peace and security. However, subsequent events have suggested that the previous conventional wisdom, which was challenged by Boutros-Ghali in his paper, had been founded on a hard reality and that the new, facile and fatal notion of peace enforcement is doomed to failure. It is now clear that there is a chasm between peace-keeping, which is based on the three principles of consent of the host countries, non-enforcement and impartiality, which is very different from enforcement, the like of which we saw in the Kuwait war. Between the two there are no real gradations. Rather, it is a slippery and treacherous skid zone from peace-keeping by consent to enforcement without consent. But this was not the only dent in the P5's notion of global governance.

Humanitarian intervention turned into disaster in Somalia. We have witnessed blatant examples of double standards by the P5 as the United States intervenes in Haiti, Russia in its neighbouring states and France in Rwanda, all with a degree of blessing from the Security Council. Yet violent abuses of human rights abound elsewhere and are ignored. This raises some interesting questions for the post-Cold War world. For example, how can P5 get its double standards right? What is more, have the superpowers or members of the P5 lost their taste for global governance? Again, still in power over seven years after his brutal invasion and annexation of Kuwait, Saddam Hussein is mocking the authority of the Security Council. At the same time the Iraqi people suffer from the sanctions imposed by the UN, and are cared for by the humanitarian organisations of that very same UN, but the brutality of Saddam Hussein's regime remains as do the abuses of human rights in that unhappy country. Perhaps the area of peace and security is one in which special circumstances are at play. Has there been any greater success in attempts at global governance elsewhere?

In another dimension, namely that of economic and financial affairs, the IMF and the World Bank, as UN Specialised Agencies, and the G8 have all undertaken a directing role which in many cases prejudices seriously the domestic jurisdiction of states. The controversies at the fiftieth anniversary of the IMF and the World Bank indicate public and political disquiet. Is it only the domestic jurisdiction of states that is being compromised or is their economic, social and cultural well-being being put in jeopardy likewise through the mindless and ferocious application of a rigid ideological doctrine? In short, the economic policies of clients are subject to the approval of the major powers through one or all of these institutions.

The activities of the P5, the IMF, the World Bank and the humanitarian bodies constitute a significant intrusion in the domestic jurisdiction of some states. It is not only Iraq that is fearful and it is not only Iraq that has much to hide. The activism of the leading members of the UN system in these matters is therefore inciting a reaction. It is, moreover, a moot point the extent to which the P5 may be able to carry China with them in the Security Council. There is a hostile reaction on the part of some states because they have things to hide. There is a growing anxiety on the part of other states because they fear that the major powers are acting in a very roughshod manner over the sensibilities of smaller powers and taking into account insufficiently their views and interests. There is a concern among others about the double standards of such interventions. In short, there is an urgent need to get our double standards right. Consider, for example, the different reactions to the occupation and annexation of Kuwait by Iraq, and that of Timor by Indonesia, not to mention ambivalence towards the Israeli occupation of the West Bank and annexation of East Jerusalem.

The anxiety of some states over such intrusion is partly a reflection of their concern over the nature of the agenda, of what is tantamount to global riot control. The agenda of the West includes arms control, particularly over nuclear weapons, terrorism, drugs, refugees, human rights, AIDS, the information super-highway, and a gamut of factors linked with the environment, not to mention traditional concerns about aggression, civil wars and wars of secession. This agenda is that of the developed Western countries who back, on the whole, the intrusive activism of the UN system. But such activities can be fully effective only if they represent a broad consensus. Otherwise, there is likely to be a strong reaction led by countries such as China and India, with the support of other major regional powers such as Nigeria, Brazil and Indonesia. Their objections may be somewhat mollified if the agenda of global riot control is broadened to include matters of their interest, such as the whole question of development on a global scale and the assymetries and inequities of the present world economy. An example of the growing irritation can be found in reaction to some of the environmental measures proposed by the developed countries and resisted by the developing countries. It is not that they are against global riot control, since they too have much to gain from it, but that they need to ensure that the agenda reflects the full gamut of everybody's interests, and not just that of the powerful few who have come, in effect, to control international organisations such as the UN.

In questions of global riot control the issues are global, the actors are many and varied, and the transaction patterns are transnational. The state system is incapable of responding adequately either on the basis of individual states or collectively through its formal institutions. This is not to argue that state administrative structures are irrelevant, but that they are not fully adequate. We need, therefore, in both setting the agenda for global riot control, and in implementing it, a wider range of possibilities than that afforded by the state or the inter-state system.

What of International Relations?

The end of the Cold War has perhaps given an incentive, or at least a stimulus, for thought. Where does International Relations theory stand in this? The decades of the seventies and eighties was dominated by the so-called 'interparadigm debate'.[7] What was that debate? Does it still exist, and can it carry us forward to meet the challenges that have been outlined above? What are the implications for these conceptual frameworks of the ending of the Cold War?

It has become customary over the last decade to identify three general approaches to the study of International Relations: the realist, world society approaches, and structural approaches, although the nomenclature may differ. However, our conceptual world is not a stable one, as Figure 1 suggests, and it is possible to detect a regrouping of approaches with concomitant implications for the appropriate units and levels of analysis.

Realism is concerned with power politics, which it takes to be axiomatic. It is actor-oriented in a state-centric world. The impact of structuralism has given rise to theories of structuration that might be best put under the heading of structural or neo-realism.[8] Such analyses scratch the surface of the relevant phenomena. Nevertheless, structural realism has incorporated some writers who first placed themselves in the transaction analysis stream, but who so interpreted ideas of complex interdependence and regimes as to move over into the tradition of realism.[9] However, the analysis of complex interdependence and regimes can also lend itself to non-state-centric, non-power approaches, as the work of Oran Young has exemplified.[10] In this sense, there is a bifurcation between structural realism and a variant of globalism in analysing complex interdependence.

While transactional approaches were initially in the category of world society analysis, other such approaches have developed in a different direction. For example, Burton's Cobweb model[11] and Mitrany's functionalism[12] have evolved through coalescence into an emphasis on human needs and thence to the individual as the unit of analysis, but this individual is seen in a universal context requiring a global response. However, there is a clear warning here that structures must bend to the needs of the individual for identity, participation, development and the like. We have, therefore, the individual in

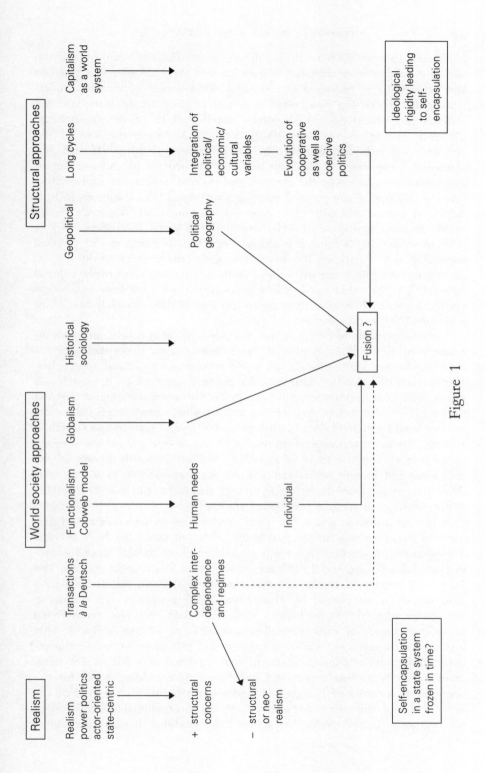

Figure 1

a universal context. We have already discussed globalism as a unit of analysis, and in particular its manifestation over the last three decades, but this can also be seen in an historical context as a world society approach of over-lapping and interacting dimensions of power, as the work of Mann attests.[13]

Such views meld easily with current manifestations of the geo-political tradition. The arguments of a Mackinder or a Mahan at the turn of the century were later distorted by the 'scientific' geography of Hitler's and Haushofer's theories, but the approach was rescued for the mainstream of International Relations by the Sprouts, and is developing a new and exciting lease of life among the political geographers.[14] Again, there appears to be a degree of consonance with more recent developments of long-cycle theory in the modern period of the last five hundred years. Modelski's work is particularly exciting because it is able to bring together elements of political leadership as a functional requirement in the contemporary world system, economic cycles and, tentatively, and as he admits, unsatisfactorily, cultural factors.[15] On the other hand, Wallerstein's notion of capitalism as a world system seems to have given rise to an ideological rigidity which has led to conceptual self-encapsulation.[16]

It seems possible to detect trends towards a possible fusion, although no estimate of probabilities is offered. Nevertheless, there is a potentiality for marching in step with some of the world society and structural approaches. In particular, the globalist approach, the political geographical approach and the revised long cycles approach seen in the historical sociological context have a capacity for fusion. As such, we will move beyond international society as conceived by the so-called English School,[17] beyond realism and structural realism, beyond traditional conceptions of world society, or the modern world-system, to a new form of globalism, but one in which notions of the individual and human needs can also be set comfortably. However, it is difficult to escape from the worrying thought that just as our world is complex and confusing, so are our conceptual approaches.

It is over a decade and a half since Michael Banks lamented that Inter-national Relations was 'an incoherent discipline', in which 'we have become a community of scholars who teach a muddled eclecticism'.[18] More recently, in 1994, John Burton and Tarja Värynen suggested in a chapter entitled 'The End of International Relations?' that International Relations, as a separate academic discipline, should be 'phased out'.[19] These authors were writing in very different periods in the history of the discipline, each one characterised by its own source of turbulence. The 'cutting edge' of the discipline, only just over a decade ago, was in contesting the still more or less dominant realist framework. Vasquez's reader in 1985 accepted as a fact of life state-ments about a nuclear winter and impending Armageddon, while for the contemporary reader of Burton and Värynen, the focus on the needs of the individual and the domestic sources of the international are no longer revolutionary. The discipline has always been muddied, because the waters that flow through the discipline are themselves unclear. Each successive lamentation of turbulence and a lack of discipline in the discipline derives largely from a lack of conceptual clarity in developing ordering principles for a world that is itself complex and lacks coherence. We require simplicity with substance, but we are far from acquiring it. It is clear what will not do, but it is difficult to feel satisfied with anything else. In short, confusion reigns.

There is a more fundamental criticism of the current state of International Relations theory which owes its current vigour to the opening of minds that the ending of the Cold War has brought about. International Relations theory normally takes on fashionable modes once they have passed their peak in other parts of the social sciences or beyond, and so it is with post-modernism. The attack on positivism cannot be gainsaid. We all know that we do not know what we know, but we know it all the same. In short, the post-modern argument is fun (if it is not wrapped up in incomprehensible jargon) and adolescent, but in the end we have to say 'so what' and get on with what we can, given the best inter-subjectivity on the market. We can act even if we do not know what we are doing. But that in no sense absolves us from trying to make sense of it.

The above suggests where some of the cutting edges of our discipline might now be found. Clearly the question of governance is paramount and, what is more, it is ubiquitous.[20] But governance requires an acknowledgement that the politics of identity are very much the politics of our time, particularly since the ending of the Cold War. Perhaps we need to conceptualise a notion of identity studies which involves not the traditional studies of nationalism or ethnicity and race but also gender and other factors as a source of identity. Identity is crucial because its denial is a denial of a person or group's moral worth and, indeed, its very existence. Since one of the great constraints on human behaviour is legitimised relationships, a denial of such legitimised relationships leaves the way open to anarchy. Why should those whose existence is besmirched or even denied have any compunction in pulling the house down around all our ears? How, therefore, can we conceive of identity and create institutions which allow it to flower? While we may need not a Leviathan, but global governance, to avoid life being 'nasty, poor, brutish, solitary and short', such a global governance can only be established on legitimised relationships, which in their turn will only be legitimised if they allow for a real sense of participation and do not deny the sense of identity of any individual actors or groups.

Yet the notion of identity is a very under-researched one. In the field of International Relations, studies of nationalism reach back into the nineteenth century, but other aspects of identity, such as gender, have only recently come on to the IR agenda. While nation, gender, race and ethnicity all have their idiosyncratic aspects, they do also have sufficient in common that they can be conceptualised together. This is a conceptualisation that has not yet adequately begun. Perhaps a little further down the road of conceptualisation is conflict studies. International conflict, and to a lesser extent inter-communal conflict, has been a feature of International Relations theorising for a long time. Indeed, the causes of war and conditions of peace was the starting agenda and remain a crucial element of the agenda of International Relations as an academic discipline. Yet conflict studies have now moved beyond the simple manipulation of threats to look at the causes, modalities and resolution of conflict in all its aspects at a variety of systems levels. Again, there is a need for holism. While partners in a marital conflict may not have nuclear weapons at their disposal, they do engage in escalations spirals, tunnel vision and many other phenomena that can be seen equally in industrial relations, inter-communal conflict, neighbourhood conflict or inter-state conflict. In many of these questions there is a spatial aspect. Recent and dramatic examples of ethnic cleansing are a case in point. What the ending of the Cold War has done in this context is to open our eyes to phenomena that were there for the seeing had we not been blind to them.

Conclusion

To change the world, we must first understand it. The study of International Relations has changed and must change further if it is to represent adequately the world in which we live. We cannot escape, and therefore we had better start thinking. Real power is brain power.

The nature of world society has changed in that its modalities and its agenda are becoming truly global. The nature of the agenda is such that not only states are primary actors, in either setting or implementing, the agenda. Both in Europe and elsewhere in the world, we are in the process of building up, building down and building across. In some of these activities, states play an essential role and may have a veto, but not in all. Is the nation-state in crisis or in change? It is, in fact, in both, for if it does not change it will be in crisis. The cry that 'The King is dead, long live the King' is inappropriate. It is not a matter either that the state should be dispensed with entirely, or that there is a ready alternative as a basic unit of analysis. To use the same analogy, perhaps there is to be no King but many barons. International Relations was, but is now no longer, as an academic study, state-centric, and our field has gone beyond the study of inter-state relations, while not neglecting them, to what might be defined broadly as the political sociology of world society with a concentration upon global politics.

The Cold War was an example of tunnel vision. Because politicians saw everything in Cold War terms, academicians felt obliged to do likewise. The end of the Cold War has enabled many of us to think differently, if not more clearly.

CHAPTER 4

Ideas and the Creation of Successive World Orders

Andrew J. Williams

It is now widely accepted that the warfare that has punctuated the twentieth century was fought not only about prestige and power but also about the intellectual agenda for the planet. A recent article on the Second World War states baldly that it 'was a war of ideas'. For that supreme student of the 'short twentieth century', Eric Hobsbawm, the period 1914–91 was a battle between competing ideologies, liberal, socialist and fascist (or ultra-nationalist and corporatist), 'an era of religious wars'.[1] The end of the Cold War has now given us a possibility to reflect on the whole of our 'short century' and to ask what were the key ideas that emerged, or at the very least now 'take ideas seriously' as John Gaddis has put it.[2] It is the contention of this chapter that the main cauldrons in which these competing ideas or 'ideologies' were brewed were the three great global conflicts of 1914–18, 1939–45 and the discussions since the end of the Cold War, and that the main resultant liquors can be described as the 'New World Order' (NWO) ideas. These have provided frameworks of 'meaning' for a large percentage of the planet's population that have proved more resilient than could ever have been expected in 1919 or 1945.

The NWO that we now tend to see as the axiomatic version is that proposed by a series of mainly, but by no means exclusively, American thinkers and policy-makers. It can be termed the 'Liberal Wilsonian–Rooseveltian' model, modified recently by the neo-liberal (or even 'hyperliberal' according to Robert Cox) influences of the 1980s. The alternatives, socialist and fascist, have largely failed, in spite of retaining some residual support. We have, to use the over-quoted Francis Fukuyama, reached the 'End of History' but we still have to beware of the 'Last Man' who might still surprise us out of our liberal dream.[3] Later in this chapter I will review some of the reactions that we have to this dilemma of 'triumphalism'.

Many tomes have been produced since 1991, and indeed before, purporting to explain the NWO phenomenon, and to a certain extent this chapter is an attempt to come to grips with this literature in a critical way. Some of them suffer from the strait-jacket of paradigmatic theorising on international relations, some of them attempt to paint the NWO projects, particularly those originating in Washington, as conspiracies against the suffering masses of the globe, and some of them suffer from an appalling a-historicism or at best a selective choice of facts.[4] I hope to avoid some of these pitfalls by what might be described as a 'de Tocquevillian' method, to see NWO ideas as part of the continuing debate between the main families of Western political thought and their reaction with the vagaries of history.

The central aim of this chapter is to look at the main architects of the NWOs and the ideas that they either laid down or developed after 1914. It will be suggested that there has been a certain continuity in these ideas. It is accepted that many of the ideas that have reached their current maturity in this century have echoes that go back many more. As Alexis de Tocqueville was able to see the 'droit fil de l'Ancien Régime' in the French Revolution so we must acknowledge the debt owed by NWO ideas to past periods.[5] We might even consider them as a central part of the Enlightenment project. However, it has been in the particular context of the twentieth century that these ideas have seen their apotheosis, a context defined by the 'age of the masses' and a previously undreamt of technological capacity for destruction and benevolent change.

A second leitmotif of this chapter is to come down somewhat heavily on the side of the 'great man' thesis in the elaboration of the historical process. There may lurk many an epistemological problem in associating particular ideas with particular statesmen (unfortunately we can search in vain for the great women until recently) but there is no gainsaying the perception that certain NWO ideas have been associated with particular people. Hence Alfred Cobban was able to write in 1944 that '[t]he leading part in the development of the general ideal of national liberation into an officially recognised Allied policy of self-determination was played by President Wilson, whose ideas on this subject were part of a long considered political philosophy'.[6] A much more recent commentator, Christopher Coker, wrote in 1994 that in 1914 '[i]t was almost an accepted fact that by mere force of will an inspired individual or people could change history or revise it, that history could be made most effectively by those who acted in conformity with the *Zeitgeist* of the age'.[7] NWO ideas were (largely) formulated in the particular circumstances of war or extreme national and international crisis and they are remembered for their particular human associations. Clearly it also has to be realised that Wilson did not 'invent' self-determination, nor Roosevelt the ideas of the Atlantic Charter, but the way in which they were presented by these men gives them a particular personalised character.

Nonetheless, the approach to world orders taken by, for example, Robert Cox, also has its great advantages. By putting the push of civil society (from 'below') and the structural forces that impose from 'above' he puts into important contrast the need to understand the 'forces of history'.[8] Social engineering à la Wilson or Roosevelt, or for that matter Lenin or Hitler, can ultimately only push the debate in a certain way, and the rest will be up to the currents of history. These names are therefore used here often as a shorthand, most usually as an historical 'flag' to a wider movement of ideas, but also because they can themselves be seen as key 'critical theorists' who looked at the international system of their day and saw the 'sources of contradiction and conflict in these entities and evaluate[d] their potential to change into different patterns'. They were in effect going beyond the usual 'problem solving' mode of the statesman, and acting as the revolutionary catalysts for potentially profound 'emancipatory' change.

None of the ideas espoused in 1919, 1945 or 1991 have had quite the destiny imagined for them by their patrons. Equally, there was no ineluctable reason for the 'End of History' seeing a triumph for an American (or 'Anglo-Saxon') version of liberal capitalism. Many other models of a NWO were posited, particularly those of Adolf Hitler and V.I. Lenin. However, there is a certain unity that we can discern in all these projects, in spite of their seeming and apparent differences of ideological emphasis. Most importantly, they all addressed the twin questions of allegiance and identity, whether it be to state, nation, people or some cosmopolitan ethic such as the 'dictatorship of the proletariat'. They all addressed the question of material welfare and its necessities, and they all addressed normative questions of rights and duties, most clearly with the emphasis on human rights after the defeat of Fascism in 1945.

The main definitional problem for a chapter like this therefore lies in what to select as the core of the 'NWO agenda'. Drawn widely this could include virtually all areas of political thought since 1914. It has therefore been necessary to make a somewhat arbitrary selection for this short piece by selecting those ideas that were identifiably at the heart of the NWO discussions of the Wilsonian and Rooseveltian projects and that seem to have been carried on by that of 1990. This core agenda must include the notion of 'self-determination' and the pursuit of functional alternatives to war, by which is meant the idea of the international organisation as the guarantor of peace and its twin ideal of the 'harmony of interests' through economics. Arguably we could also include the notion of human rights, but I have consciously left this aside as a subject both too big and too widely discussed elsewhere. The concentration in this chapter will be on what might be said to be the most problematic side of NWO thinking, that on self-determination, and the most successful, that on economics. It is hoped that this partial selection will be filled out in a subsequent book at present being written.[9]

Woodrow Wilson and Lenin

Woodrow Wilson's complex character and thought processes defy easy pigeon-holing. He can nevertheless still evoke awe in the manner in which he changed the way not only that the United States conducted its international relations but the way that international relations in the broad has been conducted ever since. Hence Henry Kissinger refers to him as one 'idealist' side of the 'hinge' of this century's diplomatic practice, with Theodore Roosevelt as the other 'realist' side. America, for Wilson, has to be 'unselfish' in sharing its benefits and attributes with the rest of the world. Whereas for Roosevelt ('the warrior-statesman') America should be internationalist in its national interest, for Wilson ('the prophet-priest') America should be internationalist in the global interest. For Wilson this meant an almost unbridled intervention-ism was necessary. For Kissinger the basis of this lay in his 'recognition that Americans cannot sustain major international engagements that are not justified by their moral faith' and that power must yield to morality.[10] It would, of course, be easy to see this internationalist urge as 'imperialist', as the 'revisionist' writers in the United States have done.[11]

As the First World War progressed Wilson came to define a new form of international society that was both a response to stirrings in the United States itself and in Europe, calling for a new way of organising inter-state relations and a recognition that the war had inevitably changed the nineteenth-century balance of power for ever. Wilson wanted initially to act as a 'mediator' in the European war, and when this failed to attempt to redefine the war aims of the participants so that such a war could hopefully not re-occur.[12] He had to decide whether the United States should enter the war in the full knowledge that this was not wanted by much of American public opinion, or by himself, by steering a middle path between 'preparedness' and not getting involved. America was at best an 'unwilling hegemon' at this stage. However, events militated against isolation as American shipping was increasingly becoming involved in the shipping war being fought in the Atlantic.

Wilson certainly wanted the war to at least result in a change of inter-national attitudes, as evidenced by a series of celebrated speeches during 1916 and 1917. American commentators always write of these in almost hushed tones, inevitably comparing each to the Gettysburg Address. Par-ticularly significant were the 'New Willard Hotel Speech' of 27 May 1916 and the 'Peace without Victory' address of 22 January 1917, the first ever by an American President to the Senate. The New Willard speech first laid down his commitment (he used the word 'creed') that 'every people has a right to choose the sovereignty under which they shall live' which was to apply to small as well as large states. It also made a plea for a right of the world to be 'free from every disturbance of its peace that has its origins in aggression and disregard of the rights of peoples and nations'. This 'creed' was given an institutional framework in the latter speech: 'There must be, not a balance of power, but a community of power; not organized rivalries, but an organized common peace.' This was to be guaranteed by the New Diplomacy, an equality of rights between nations, and government only by the consent of the governed. There was also to be 'freedom of the seas' and equality of armaments as part of this commonly enforced peace. The whole package has been termed 'progressive internationalism'.[13]

The final definition of Wilson's NWO proposals came in the 'Fourteen Points' of January 1918. They can briefly be summarised: Point I, 'Open Covenants of peace, openly arrived at, after which there shall be no private international understandings of any kind but diplomacy shall proceed always frankly and in the public view' – the definitive statement on the 'New Diplomacy'; Point II, guaranteeing '[a]bsolute freedom of navigation upon the seas'; Point III, 'The removal, so far as possible, of all economic barriers'; Point IV, urging the reduction of national armaments; Point V and (most of) Point XIV, referring to a settlement of colonial claims and the establishment of the League of Nations. Points VI to XIII were concerned mainly with territorial issues tied in with the principle of self-determination. In Wilson's supplementary speeches, referred to as the 'Four Principles' of 11 February 1918, which was mainly an elaboration of his views on self-determination, and that of 27 September 1918, commonly called the 'Five Particulars', the link was made between the notion of self-determination and the League of Nations.

This link can be seen as Wilson's major contribution to thinking about international relations, and a major modification of the principle of sovereignty. He firmly believed that the establishment of the principle would defuse most of the conflicts that had racked Europe in the nineteenth century and caused the First World War. He in particular believed that the United States had an almost God-given role to play in bringing this about. As he said on 11 February 1918: 'We believe that our [i.e., the United States] own desire for new international order, under which reason and justice and the common interests of mankind shall prevail, is the desire of enlightened men everywhere.'[14] However, as we shall see, his vision held within it a number of flaws when it was applied to practical politics.

Wilson's main rival for a vision of the future NWO came from Bolshevik Russia. Lenin's 'Zimmerwald Manifesto' of 1915 reflected his deep-seated cynicism about the 'enlightened men' who had started the war through their capitalist plotting. He accordingly used a language devoid of euphemism: 'Millions of corpses cover the battlefields. Millions of human beings have been crippled for the rest of their lives. Europe is like a gigantic slaughterhouse.' Lenin had a uni-causal explanation for this carnage, and a solution – 'the International Socialist Bureau has failed ... [so the] working class [must] ... take up this struggle ... for the sacred aims of socialism, for the emancipation of the oppressed nations as well as of the enslaved classes, by means of the irreconcilable class struggle ...'.[15] Wilson in particular recognised the strength of Lenin's claims. It has been demonstrated convincingly by Arno Mayer among others that his Fourteen Points speech was an attempt to outflank Soviet claims to be the advocates of self-determination (although only Poland is mentioned by name of the previous Czarist territories that must be freed)[16] and the defenders of a peace with justice.[17] In effect, both Lenin and Wilson felt that they could talk over the heads of governments directly to the 'people', not only among the Allies, but also in Germany.[18]

The Dilemma of Self-determination

The unforseen consequences of Wilson and Lenin's visions of self-determination have led many commentators since then to doubt the wisdom of encouraging it as an ideal for peoples and states. As Mortimer Sellers, among others, has pointed out, the debate about self-determination has also had to take into account the damage that it would do to the fundamental norm of sovereignty. It also has become clear that we need to link it to the concept of human rights, hardly addressed until the Nuremberg trials and the human rights discussions that took place within the United Nations in the 1940s and subsequently.[19] In recent times, many attempts at self-determination have seemed to disintegrate into arguments about minority rights, the collapse of state structures (the phenomenon of the 'quasi-state'), the mass and usually forced migration of populations and even worse forms of violence, such as the recent ethnic cleansing seen in the former Yugoslavia and elsewhere in Europe and Africa. Ethnicity has been the achilles heel of both Lenin and Wilson's vision ever since.[20]

   The dilemma is that of how to enable peoples to have their independence and dignity, while not denying that to others within the borders occupied by a dominant ethnic or cultural group and not allowing the granting of that 'right' to damage the cause of international or domestic order. One divide in such commentary can be observed in the position of one sceptical commentator on democracy. After seeing the mess that twenty years of self-determination had wrought in Central and Eastern Europe, George Kennan expressed the view that, '[g]ranted moderate and humane regimes in Berlin and Moscow ... I could see no objection to dividing all of eastern Europe (except Finland) up between them; and if only *one* of them, then it could be dominant'.[21] Kennan was not alone in believing that concepts such as self-determination were as pearls before swine for most of the planet's population. Democracy had to be learnt (as with the Germans), or earned.

   Andreas Osiander warns against historians like Webster[22] who assumed at the beginning of the 1920s that an idea that was by then on everyone's lips had always been so: 'At the time of the Vienna congress, national self-determination was present as an idea held by some, but it was not a consensus principle of the international system.'[23] By the time of Versailles the idea had taken firmer root with the conviction by Wilson and many others that the Empires of Europe and their linked notion of balance of power was the problem. So if the Empires were dissolved, there would be a reduced danger of war. However, as Alfred Cobban pointed out in 1945, '[i]t did not occur to the Allied Governments that the propaganda they employed against the Central empires would affect their own empires fundamentally, or that by proclaiming the principle of self-determination they had laid the axe at the roots of their own colonial domains'.[24]

Self-determination at Versailles

What was supposed to be the cornerstone of Wilson's plans for Europe and the rest of the world was in part a major casualty of the compromises made by the Allies in order to ensure a relatively easy passage of the Covenant through the various committees. Derek Heater points out that until 1914 Wilson had 'evinced little interest and little competence in this field'. He also points out that the expression 'national self-determination' does not actually figure in the Fourteen Points Speech, but that Wilson was nonetheless 'deeply committed' to it and that after the treaty was signed he singled the issue out as a reason for the United States to ratify it: it was 'unique in the history of mankind because the center of it is the redemption of the weak nations'.[25] Unsurprisingly, the main support for the Treaty came from the nascent nations of Central and Eastern Europe, and, until their hopes were thoroughly dashed, from the nationalist movements of what would later be called the Third World in China and elsewhere.

In the Middle East, in particular, Britain and France had effectively promised several different groups the same piece of land for their self-determination as in Palestine with the Sykes–Picot Agreement of 1917 giving Syria and Lebanon to France, and the Balfour Declaration of 1917 and T.E. Lawrence ('of Arabia') seemingly giving Palestine to both Arabs and Jews. The reasoning behind this had everything to do with *Realpolitik* and nothing to do with self-determination as a morally desirable allied war aim. Many in Britain realised that Palestine, in particular, might prove to be 'a thorn in the flesh of whoever is charged with its Mandate'.[26] The Ottoman Empire was perhaps the best example of how the principle of self-determination was sacrificed to the interests of the imperial powers. It was also one of the best examples of how difficult they found it to agree about the boundaries of these interests and stored up endless trouble for the future.

Within Europe any 'self-determination' that impinged on the perceived essential interests of the Allies was also rigorously excluded. The break-up of the Austro-Hungarian Empire left huge numbers of 'minorities' (as they were called from 1920 on). The attempts by Bolshevik Russia to capitalise on the discontent so caused made the Allies even harsher in their pursuit of strategic and economic goals at the expense of the interests of such 'minorities'. This was particularly true in the case of Hungary which lost three and a half million Magyars[27] and large areas of territory in the Treaty of Trianon in late 1919. This was to develop into one of the longest-lasting 'minority' problems in Eastern Europe, feeding Hungarian anger to the present day, while during the inter-war period was yet another example of British and French differences and their corrosive effect on peace.

Self-determination in the Inter-war Years

The 1920s and 1930s saw a host of attempted revisions of the issues raised by the question of self-determination at Versailles, although there is not room here to detail them.[28] Suffice it to say that Germany saw much of its resentment as being due to the inadequacies of such clauses of the Treaty that deprived it of the Saar (given back by plebiscite in the Rhineland and re-occupied in 1936) and, most significantly, the Polish Corridor and Danzig. It is not impossible that Alsace-Lorraine might have voted to remain German had it been given the choice in 1918, giving rise to Hardinge's comment that 'plebiscites taken in countries in our possession ... might be very inconvenient and certainly should not be encouraged'. It was also widely understood that the French wanted the Saar and the Rhineland in order to have a 'buffer' against Germany.[29] Equally, the victors of Versailles in Central and Eastern Europe were not too keen to let the population decide on its future state allegiance, thus creating, for example, a substantial Hungarian and German diaspora that was to cause many problems in later years.

Moreover, Heater is not wrong in his judgement that the 'several peace treaties [after 1918] were often drafted in conscious violation of the principle of national self-determination', or even that there was, as Cobban puts it, 'a hardly noticed substitution of an allied but different set of ideals for that of self-determination' at Versailles.[30] Its violation after the initial promise that it had held out was to prove in the long run the most corrosive factor in the medium-term collapse of the League of Nations and of the Treaty, and in the long run the stability of international order, an instability that was arguably not properly addressed until the Atlantic Charter of 1941 and the Charter of the United Nations in 1945. Cobban may well be right that the 'substitution' that took place was for a 'belief in small states' and in 'the equality of states', both enshrined in the UN Charter. Both in its promise and in its breach, it is hard to see that the introduction of the notion of self-determination did anything but increase the instability of the international system from 1919 on.

The 1960 Declaration of the Rights and Duties of States in the condition so post-colonialism defined self-determination within existing frontiers. However, in reality all these frontiers were imposed by imperial *fiat* and thus usually illogical in terms of the principles of self-determination. The resultant 'quasi-states' have suffered from a domestic lack of democratic legitimacy and an illusory 'unity' in their attempts to force the 'North' to implement a more just distributive order, which saw its culmination in demands for a 'New International Economic Order' in the 1970s.[31] In Europe the Hapsburg Empire has fragmented into ever more and smaller states since 1919. This process has been given a new impetus since the end of the Cold War, universally in the name of 'self-determination', sometimes peacefully (as with the break-up of most of the Soviet Union in 1991), sometimes with appalling violence, as in the former Yugoslavia. In Africa when this has happened it has always been by war and has been actively discouraged by local and global powers (as was the case with Biafra in the 1960s). Since 1990 self-determination has seen the creation of Eritrea and might well see the break-up of Zaïre. It is unclear where the process of fragmentation will end. Many certainly fear that it will prove destabilising for international order, the opposite of what Wilson intended.

One obvious response has to be that Wilson 'failed' with his emphasis on self-determination, as E.H. Carr and many others have indicated.[32] Writing in 1945, Alfred Cobban had attributed the collapse of the inter-war order, as did many of his contemporaries, to the 'balkanization' of Europe. As he pointed out, this had been translated by those on both ends of the political spectrum into a belief that 'the idea of nationality as a basis for statehood is obsolete' (the words of the British Socialist G.D.H. Cole) and by Hitler and the Nazis into a contempt for 'small nations' (*Kleinstaaterei*). But the Atlantic Charter had implicitly renewed Wilson's pledge of self-determination for all nations, so how could the dilemma be resolved? As Cobban put it, '[t]he real task is to integrate them [the small states] into the fabric of a stable, prosperous, and peaceful world'.[33] This is still the 'real task'.

Cobban's strikingly modern view of the problematique of the nation has been reinforced dramatically in its validity by the events since 1989 in Europe, which bear an uncanny resemblance to the problems of the inter-war period and before that, and in the problems encountered and still being faced up to by the emerging nations of the Third World. The emergent nations of Africa have refused to accept the existence of an interdependent world until recently, they have largely denied their peoples democracy, and they have cleaved to a spurious definition of cultural unity while neglecting the creation of a political state that also gives its citizens a large measure of liberty. The states that have succeeded the former multinational states of Yugoslavia and the USSR have similarly stressed ethnic identity over liberty of economic and political expression, thus guaranteeing that disintegrative forces have a field day.

Wilson, Roosevelt and Meaning through Economics

Carr also famously criticised the largely unstated, in 1939, but ultimately intimately linked, belief in the 'Harmony of Interests', the self-regulating

mechanism of the market. Wilson, in line with virtually all his liberal contemporaries, such as Norman Angell, thought that this would sort out the
economic future of the planet in 1919.[34] Wilson forgot that you have to pay
off the forces of economics, forces that were as damaged by the First World
War as had been the concept of the balance of power. The Treaty of
Versailles was bereft of any economic answers to the problems of the post-
war world. It indeed, as Keynes pointed out, exacerbated the economic
tensions that were recognised by 1939 as at the centre of Europe's problems.
Virtually all the NWO thinkers of 1939–45 came to see a better approach to
global economics as the key to the future of a stable and prosperous
international system, particularly in the United States. True, many of them,
in line with Karl Polanyi's *Great Transformation* and of course Keynes himself,[35]
saw an over-reliance on the market as the key problem. Hence planning and
regulation was to save the world, on a global level.

Wilson's Fourteen Points had among them some key economic demands,
including freedom of the seas for commerce (Point II), the removal of
economic barriers to trade (Point III), with the reduction of armaments and
decolonisation (Points IV and V) having a strong economic element. The
inputs to this thinking have been variously argued, but it is clear that for
Wilson economics was the key to peaceful cooperation among nations.
However, this was not operationalised in any way by either the Treaty of
Versailles as a whole or, until too late in the 1930s, by the League of Nations.
Wilson shared the beliefs of the pre-war thinkers like Norman Angell about
the 'irrationality' of war in the context of an interdependent economic global
system. His desire to include economic sanctions and measures short of
force to defuse international conflicts was stated very early on in his thinking,
and these are both ideas prominent in the Covenant of the League of
Nations, a clearly Wilsonian document, unlike the Treaty of Versailles itself,
which was as obviously a product of the balance of power thinking of Lloyd
George and Clemençeau. Wilson had the backing in this of a wide swathe
of conservative and progressive internationalism in the United States that
wanted to draw Europe away from its obsession with what Americans saw
as the causes of war – especially economic barriers, imperialism and secret
diplomacy.

But, of course, the Versailles Treaty was to be a grave deception to any
who believed that a new spirit of thinking about international relations might
be abroad in Europe. Even though he blamed the Germans for starting the
war, Keynes saw that 'the French and British peoples have run the risk of
completing the ruin ... by a peace, which if it is carried into effect, must
impair yet further, when it might have been restored, the delicate complicated
organisation, already shaken by war, through which the European peoples
can employ themselves and live'. To his disgust, '[i]nsofar as the main
economic lines of the Treaty represent an intellectual idea, it is the idea of
France and of Clemençeau'.[36]

But other Americans did try to implement an economic NWO even before 1939. Hoover's overall strategy as Secretary for Commerce (1921–28) and President (1928–32) was to enlist the forces of American (and indeed also of British) capitalism in forging a benevolent new world order fostered, in the words of Michael Hogan, one of the leading American historians of the period, by 'a limited and carefully delineated government action'.[37] Hoover recognised what we would now call a growing economic 'interdependence'. Hogan says that his aim was to 'avoid the pitfalls of pre-war imperialism and Bolshevik revolution',[38] steering what might be called a 'Wilsonian' path to global economic stability.

Hoover and other Republicans were thus adapting the Wilsonian agenda at Versailles to a new situation where a more lasting *economic* settlement of the war was to be imposed from outside the League of Nations and the Versailles *political* structure. Although it must be said that all the economic conferences organised under or outside League of Nations auspices in the early 1920s were also conspicuous for their lack of success and noteworthy for their high political drum-beating, it has been asserted by historians like Hogan that Hoover was in fact laying the groundwork for the later economic diplomacy of Cordell Hull and Roosevelt before and during the Second World War. This in turn created the economic NWO counterpart to the basic Wilsonian security NWO, also given a better institutional basis by Roosevelt through an observation of why Wilson had failed.

Roosevelt presided over a massive re-think of the 'errors' of Wilsonianism. He and his staff were nonetheless true believers, and like in all religions he had charismatic opponents and mutual charges of heresy to contend with. The holy texts – the Atlantic Charter in particular – were improvements and restatements of Wilsonian ideals but they were operationalised in a very different way than in 1919. Roosevelt took great pains not only to plan his NWO (which Wilson had not), and refrained from off-the-cuff philosophising, but also to make sure that his allies understood that the United States was firmly in charge (which it was not in 1919) and that his potential opponents in Congress were involved in the decision-making process throughout. His genius as a political animal gave life to Wilson's imaginings. His problem was that while he could cajole or overwhelm the British and the French, he was unsuccessful with the Russians.

During his period in office, and particularly during the war, there was nonetheless a development of many Wilsonian ideas to give them a more American and also 'realist' feel. The papers of the Post-War Planning (PWP) groups centred within the State Department are peppered with references to the need for such 'realism', but this did not exclude all sorts of forays into imaginative international social reconstruction. Economic reform was at the heart of the Rooseveltian NWO as it had been at the heart of the New Deal, and it was based on a notion of an economic 'harmony of interest'. Intimately linked to this was the setting up of some framework of international organisation that would ensure this economic development. His stated aim was wider: 'that ways be found for the creation of a system of international relations which would ensure the maintenance of great freedoms which lie at the foundations of modern civilisation.'[39] But this was again to be based on an *economic* agenda.

It would be very difficult to go into a lot of detail about this newly assertive American line in world politics, but there is ample evidence of what Dulles termed in June 1939 the 'almost mystic feeling that it was divinely ordered that we expand', first on the American continent, and now beyond it. The nature of this expansion would now be ideological rather than physical and the key to this for Dulles was the spreading of the American state model, and its corollary of federalism and the rule of law. The United States had shown how people could live in peace and that was by modifying the principle of 'sovereignty'. The European system of state sovereignty was pernicious because it made for 'barriers to opportunity [that had] to be broken down', it was a sovereignty of the powerful, of the 'status quo'. Inevitably this meant that peace 'tends to be identified with preserving the status quo', while war 'tends to be identified with adventure and change and the creation of opportunity'. It was therefore necessary to do what the United States had done, to create 'borders [which are] *structurally* porous and elastic'. Federalism would save the world from war by making peace more exciting and rewarding economically. Never had the world of the capitalist been more clearly identified with the pursuit of profit and peace.[40] Here was a redefinition of the 'harmony of interest' idea with a clear American backing. It was, in effect, the ideological justification for the process begun by Cordell Hull in 1934 that saw its fruit in the Bretton Woods Organisations and eventually in a united Europe and an emergent 'globalisation'.

Since 1990 it could be argued that this vision of the world has indeed triumphed, that we do not have an international economic system that demonstrates the applicability of the 'harmony of interests'. There is now a growing awareness of a globalised international economic system, free trade is more or less a reality, and the seas (and air) are more or less 'free'. The dangers of global anarchy are there for all to see, as many have pointed out, as are the patchy nature of the benefits of a global economy.[41] The 'harmony of interests', which seemed 'utopian' to Carr, is thus now bandied around as commonplace; capitalism is portrayed as the 'only game in town', and moreover the basis of civil society. It is clear that such over-optimistic hopes from 'globalization' run the risk of also being countered, and it is also true that there are many forms of capitalism. We are thus having to redefine what we mean by a lack of 'realism'. If this theory, essentially that of Angell, Brailsford, Wilson, Hoover and others (with minor internal variations such as how you exactly define liberal democracy), is correct, then what was utopian is now eminently 'realist'. In his recent study of the 'Twenty Years Crisis' Peter Wilson has suggested that rather than keeping the 'idealist–realist dichotomy', especially when looking at the inter-war period, we should substitute, as J.D.B. Miller suggests for Angell's thought, a 'short term ... long term' contrast or even reinsert 'the utopian disposition towards normative assertion and enquiry', as Ken Booth suggests in the same volume.[42]

Conclusions – Do NWOs Really Create Structures of Global Meaning?

It could be argued that the logic of the NWO derived from the active pursuit of a creative and progressive peace has now finally ousted the century's obsession with the search for meaning through war. 'Idealist' or 'utopian' thinkers, to use Carr's expression, all of whom seemed to be 'wrong' until 1989, are now being rapidly rehabilitated. Even federalist approaches, so long ridiculed, now look somewhat prophetic in the light of European Union. The most obvious return from the dead is that of Immanuel Kant, but other theorists of International Relations from the period 1916–45 (or so) will surely be resurrected. As David Long points out, the concepts of international organisation, what we would now call 'globalisation', or economic internationalism, and the emphasis on normative modes of thought were all common features of inter-war thinking on IR.[43] The early scholars of our profession saw IR as a functional alternative to war, it has again resumed this mantle of conveying meaning.

The purpose of the initial Wilsonian NWO project and its successors was to propose a vision of a unified approach to the future which would harmonise power and ideology (or what Zaki Laïdi calls 'power and purpose', of which more below). This simultaneous 'delivery of a universal message' and the generation of economic and military power[44] was the hallmark of both Wilsonian and Rooseveltian thinking and it was largely successful, at least partly in its second attempt and certainly in its third. The institutions (The United Nations, Bretton Woods institutions, NATO, EU, etc.) all operationalised the thinking of the two American presidents, a work that George Bush exhorted them to continue after 1990. It must be acknowledged that Bush's urgings have been more successful than many pessimists predicted even in 1994.[45] There are after all now a series of reasonably established and operational democracies in Central and Eastern Europe,[46] as well as in Africa, to add to the existing North Atlantic Triangle of liberal constitutional states. We do have a peace of sorts in Bosnia, Chechnya, etc. As John Hall puts it, 'skepticism should not become cynicism, and membership within an international liberal society is slowly widening'.[47]

In 1919, but most successfully in 1945, the harmonisation of power and purpose was attempted and brought together many of the essential diplomatic, economic and ideological elements of a NWO (if not for all peoples). In 1990 the situation was rather different, in that no war had been necessary for, ostensibly, the West's agenda to 'win'. The imagination had become reality (hence 'the End of History'), even if Laïdi and others have detected that this victory will prove hollow and that it heralds a new era of vicious American and European dominance of the poor and oppressed of the South.[48] Some of Laïdi's reasoning for this assertion is that there is now a dangerous '"non-fungibility" of vectors of power' between politics and economics, and a corresponding divergence between the two sectors, hidden by the Cold War, but now all too apparent. He asserts that there is no longer a hierarchy of power upon which stable regimes can be maintained.[49]

We therefore now have clear alternative visions of our collective future, one pessimistic, one optimistic. The pessimist sees the 'Enlightenment Project' of 'progress' and a linear development of mankind towards a better future being replaced by a rudderless descent into anonymity and chaos, the 'Heart of Darkness'. The optimists, like Fukuyama, see the future as the 'endpoint of mankind's ideological evolution', with the triumph of liberal democracy as the 'ideal [that] could not be improved upon'.[50] Others here might see social democracy as that 'ideal', but one could see that as a subset of the 'liberal' version, with the difference being essentially one of how much the individual should be helped to be free.

Which of these versions is right may depend on just *how far integrated* our 1990s world, as a result of the latest NWO, actually proves to be. Samuel Huntington provides a possible third path in our future 'imagining' which postulates that the 'fault lines between civilisations will be the battle lines of the future'. He clearly identifies 'civilisation' as being defined 'both by common objective elements, such as language, history, religion, customs, institutions, and by the subjective self-identification of peoples'.[51] The 'civilisation' that was consciously proposed as a universal model by Wilson, Roosevelt, Bush and their advisory teams was one which was firstly based on a particular interpretation of the nature of the nation-state and its problem as a category likely to lead to progress for mankind. It was also, secondly, a postulation of a set of values, often summed up as 'human rights', which derive their being from a narrowly Western cultural experience that were seen as universalisable.[52] Thirdly, it was underpinned by the notion of a mode of production, American capitalism, which was seen as a better form than that developed in Europe, one that underpins individual initiative in a global marketplace. Clearly there are paradoxes inherent in all of these ideas, but they nonetheless seem to encapsulate much of the main agenda of global politics in the late twentieth century.

Perhaps the greatest threat to this rosy picture has been suggested by Fukuyama himself, that liberal capitalist societies may implode as post-Fordist capitalism destroys our stock of 'social capital', which in turn he sees as the guarantor of a wider civil society, global or national. By 'social capital' he means that 'certain set of informal values and norms shared among members of a group that permit co-operation among them', a kind of capital that exists in and is created most naturally in traditional nuclear families, and stable communities that have widespread cooperative networks. Hence traditional societies like Japan might flourish more than those who allow globalisation to put work and productivity before family ties and religious belief, for example. Zaki Laïdi takes this view further in his warning that 'globalisation' cannot serve as a focus for global meaning given its vague locus, and its consequent inability to evoke trust or loyalty, the very basis of what Fukuyama says make up the formation of social capital. Perhaps this is Fukuyama's 'Last Man' to which we should pay urgent attention.[53]

New World Order ideas may thus well come to be seen by later generations as the last great attempt of global social engineering by statesmen before the lure of globalisation finally sucked us into ecological and cultural oblivion. They should rather be seen as the last attempt by powerful states to create a world safe for states to flourish globally. The ideal of self-determination gives the basis for a legitimated state existence, the ideal of the 'harmony of interests' gives the basis for global competition without warfare and a constantly increasing global prosperity. Both are essential for the NWO to result, for one without the other will lead to potential disaster, as the inter-war years may have been said to have demonstrated. Both together can potentially lead to a global civil society that recognises the right to difference and diversity. Critics of this utopia would assert that it assumes the benevolence of the initiating 'mind', that it assumes that the benefits will be distributed properly and that the results will not be catastrophic in terms of moral equity and environmental damage. These are possibilities that cannot be gainsaid.

It could also be argued that the latest of our NWOs demonstrates the failure of the human agency thesis that has informed this chapter. The leaders of the West were caught napping in 1989 by the fall of the Berlin Wall, indeed some tried Canute-like to make it topple in slower motion (like Mitterrand). Its main self-proclaimed architects (Genscher, Bush, Thatcher, etc.) have not seen their original plans fulfilled. The impersonal forces of 'globalisation' and its dualistic side-kicks liberal democracy or economic autocracy, as well as political or social disintegration, are widely touted as having won, not human hopes and aspirations. Thus, arguably the most coherent critique of the NWO would be 'post-modern' in style and approach, a rejection of the optimistic, progressive Enlightenment foundational thinking from which it ultimately springs. This would come especially from a denial of the universality of the appeal of the elements that make up the NWO project, and an assertion of the differences that exist between cultures (even 'civilisations'), ones that the American, or Western, project attempts to elide and obscure. Nietzsche could be wheeled out once more to demonstrate that all such ideal structures are doomed to fail, perhaps at their moments of greatest apparent success. Did not the great liberal dream of 1900 evaporate by 1914? Why should this one fare any better?

However, is this not a short-termist view of the agency–structure dichotomy? Should we not rather see the events since 1989 as part of a much longer interrelationship between structure (in which there are clear continuities over a *longue durée*) and human agency which has also manifested a long-term, progressive, even meliorist tendency? We now have a much more perfectly 'interdependent' world, a growing acceptance of the norm of civil society based on political, economic and social practices that are more or less universal than was the case in 1914. We could even admit to a parallel glorification of 'difference', although that would have to be the subject of another chapter. We could argue that this seemingly insane optimism is a statement of observed tendencies.

PART II

Ideas and Warfare

CHAPTER 5

Ideas and Warfare from the Nineteenth to the Twenty-first Century: War and the Self-consummation of War

Stephen Chan

Every day the technology that facilitates a moment of compression between the 'news' and the broadcast of that news, compression to a point of simultaneous action, brings to our screens the horrors of war or the prospects of horrific war. The same technological by-product of the late modernist age both makes war more destructive, but also allows war to be more restrictive – being more expensive than ever before, and because citizens can know and resist bellicose policy more immediately than before. Or might this not be so simple a case?

In this section, two authors, at first sight with very different views from each other, are brought together to discuss war and modernity. Fred Halliday argues that war has been, in the last two centuries, a product of modernity. Locating his argument within Europe, he provides an extensive historical survey which shows that war, though produced by modernity, is not its necessary feature. Nor, conversely, should war be seen as anachronistic or irrelevant to the modernist project. The complexity of it all was such, however, that when one considers war in the nineteenth century, that crucible of industrial mixes and political thought, no Battle of Waterloo, no matter who won or lost, could have stopped industrial and capitalist development. Yet it is almost impossible to imagine a Europe in the last century without its revolutions and wars.

Although there were lengthy periods when Europe was at war with itself, there were longer periods when war was a reserve power which could threaten or influence those outside Europe. In the twentieth century, however, because of what happened in two World Wars, Europe found itself looking at, for the first time, a major outside actor, a combatant power within Europe, that was not an invader. This was the United States. In the Cold War that followed, it may be said that there was a confrontation between two modernist projects – that of the West, with the significant addition of the United States to the idea of a modern Europe, and that of communism and the Soviet Union.

What, however, was this Europe to which the United States became affiliated and then became its leader? The United States, from the First World War, was an outside actor that became a combatant power within Europe itself, yet was not an invader. Previous outside actors were indeed invaders, such as the Mongols and the Ottomans. To a significant extent, invasion or the threat of invasion both delimited what was Europe from the threat of an outside world, but also provided the notion of a certain necessity for a united Europe. The sense of a common European identity became further consolidated with the universalistic ideas of the Enlightenment; though, of course, Europe remained politically and economically selective and hierarchical and, at times, grossly violent. So much so that, after the Second World War, Monet had almost to invent a certain idea of Europe and be hailed as a visionary for so doing.

Monet's was, however, a rational project involving economic benefits from the idea of cooperation and unity, and the absence, within Europe itself, of war. In the meantime, within the Cold War, different rationalities were being applied to war, including thermo-nuclear war. Herman Kahn's ladder of thermo-nuclear escalation was appallingly rational, to the point where its logic was unbearable to the people of Europe itself; so that modernity both helped unify and threaten Europe simultaneously. Within itself, however, the idea of nuclear war had its own contradiction. Established on technological possibility, it was also established on very costly technology, so that the capital investment into weapons of mass destruction also helped hold back that very destruction. It was now too costly to mount war, and even more costly to lose war.

From these contradictions the project of Europe slowly advanced and, within thwarted war, the ideas of the Enlightenment gained, if not sway or even full belief, sufficient credibility for them to help determine that reduction of political hierarchy and selectivity that had gone before. The ideas extrapolated from Kant, that constitutional republics in close cooperation with one another would not go to war with one another, made a non-warring Europe seem an artefact of the Enlightenment (even if Europe was still capable of committing appalling crimes elsewhere, or still capable of hosting, in the 1990s, war in Yugoslavia).

Halliday's point is that neither modernity, nor technology, nor ideology can be understood without an understanding of war; and nor might Europe itself be so understood. Where James Der Derian might be said to extend this sort of analysis is in the idea that modernism and its technology might have arrived at a certain moment where, even if war is not a necessary feature of modernity, the capacity for war becomes its own feature. Der

Derian talks, as his accustomed readers would expect, of voyeurisms and their satisfactions in the technological exhibitionisms of the high-technology simulations of war. The technology becomes so sophisticated and overwhelming that it outpaces by itself the rhetoric of military reasons. Thus, although Halliday draws on Clausewitz's dictum that war is a policy by other means, that is it is a rational extension of rational deliberation, Der Derian is saying that technology can acquire, then sustain, its own rationality and justification. Modernity, to use a neat shorthand, is resolved by itself into itself as its own product.

Now whether this is a rhetoric unto itself, a wordplay of, if not technological virtuosity, then inspired by it, this is an unusual chapter by Der Derian. It is an essay almost of reportage. It is not Der Derian who thinks like this, but strategists who think like this. This is, in short, a piece of fieldwork. It is, in the words of his interviewee, a revolution in ideas of war. Within Halliday's history, revolutions were part of the traumas of advancing modernisms in Europe. Modernism, who owned and used it, was contested. Now the revolution is not the instrument of political movement, but lies within the instrument itself. A revolution in war and modernity become one; just as war and its reportage on our screens become, if not one, then a seamless extension of a faraway reality into our reality. Where, in this condensation, this seamlessness, this revolution of modernity, are the ideals of the European project before the face of the universal technology that began in Europe? Although Halliday dismisses what might in fact be called post-modern arguments, Der Derian's question is not, simply at least, banal.

CHAPTER 6

Europe and the International System: War and Peace

Fred Halliday

The phenomenon of war is inextricably linked with the entire history of Europe, and never more so than with that of the nineteenth and twentieth centuries, the age of capitalist modernity.[1] War, like revolution, has been a formative influence on the very shape of Europe and on the character of its political systems: it has transformed the relations of European states with each other, and with the non-European world, and equally, has been a powerful constitutive factor in the evolution of European states and societies themselves. Yet this central historical and analytic place allows no easy understanding. On the one hand, it is not possible to talk of 'war' as a distinct, autonomously constituted factor in modern European history. In common with other formative factors – revolution, reform, state, nation, market, technology, ideology – war has been as much a factor shaped by the evolution of modern European societies and polities as an influence on it. The wars of nineteenth- and twentieth-century Europe have been wars produced by that Europe, and by the distinct phases of that European development, at least as much as they have been instances of an enduring, more trans-historical feature of inter-state relations.

On the one hand, war in the nineteenth and twentieth centuries has been shaped by the twin revolutions that were initiated at the beginning of the period, the political and industrial revolutions. If political change altered the impact and mobilisatory potential of war, the transformation of European societies through industrialisation changed the very character of war, leading to forms of destructiveness, and capacities for mobilising resources and people, inconceivable before the nineteenth century. We are not, therefore, looking at a simple recurrence, within increasingly politicised and newly industrialised societies, of a single, itself exogenous or autonomous, phenomenon: while some elements of war remained the same as they had been in, say, the eighteenth century or in earlier times, much of the character and function of war itself changed. War was as much a product of modernity,

68

conceived of in both its political and socio-economic forms, as a factor independently shaping the political systems of modern time.[2]

At the same time, while continuing in and stimulated by the economic and political transformations of the modern era, war was also mediately related to, in some periods an essential feature of, the reallocation of power with Europe. In others it was confined to relations with the extra-European world or maintained as a reserve power, used to threaten and influence, but not actually to engage with, strategic forces. This restriction is an important part of the story. From the beginning of the modern period there were those who argued that war was in significant respects alien to industrial society – the two centuries of modernity have seen both the most terrible wars and the most striking oppositions to it, be these in the form of overt political resistance to it, or in the development of transnational economic forces that have a decreasing interest in the prosecution of armed conflict. If at times it has appeared that modernity is intrinsically bellicose or, in a term coined to convey this character, 'militaristic', at other times it has seemed that war and modernity are contrasted, the former being an aberrant or residual feature in industrial society.[3]

A retrospective assessment of the past two centuries would suggest that neither of the two more absolute answers – war as a necessary feature of modernity, war as anachronistic or accidental irrelevance – can do justice to the record. Rather, the relation between war and industrial modernity historically was variant, necessary and central in some phases, irrelevant or restricted in others. A resolution of the mystery of this underlying historical question may only come through a periodised dissection of history itself. Analysis of the relation between the modern European age and war involves, therefore, a measured assessment both of the historical relation of war to European politics and of the evolution of these two underlying issues – the transformation of war itself by modernity, and the ambivalent relation of modern economies and political systems to war itself.[4]

Historical Patterns

Two Centuries of Conflict If war, either within Europe or conducted by European powers outside the continent, has been persistent over two centuries, the overall place as well as character of war has varied greatly as between different phases of this history. Taking the French Revolution as the starting point, we can distinguish at least four major phases of the relationship between Europe and war, each with distinctive implications for the European inter-state system, for the domestic character of European societies, and for the relationship of Europe to the external world. The French revolutionary wars (1789–1815) engulfed all the major states of Europe, as well as parts of the Middle East, and had a profound impact on the Americas, leading to the independence of most of South America. On the one hand, these wars introduced a period of mass popular mobilisation, for and against the policies of France, as well as setting in train a range of political movements that were to shape much of the world in the coming two centuries. The second of these phases, the long, ninety-nine-year European peace that lasted from 1815 to 1914, was not only marked by a general peace between the powers, but also by a growing intersection of the military apparatuses and technologies with the new industrialism, and by the use of force by European states to impose their control on Asia and Africa.[5] The third, from 1914 to 1945, was the height of conflict between European states, and of mobilisation in 'total' war, the latter so deemed because of the level of mobilisation of manpower and of domestic resources.[6] Equally, it saw the internationalisation of inter-state conflict beyond the European arena. Non-European powers, Japan and the United States, became involved in conflict with European powers, and the non-European arena became one in which, in addition to Europe itself, the European powers conducted their rivalry.[7] The fourth phase was that which began in 1945, one of Cold War, a division of Europe into two competing blocs which, while they did not go to war on European soil, or use in any region of the world their full nuclear potential, nevertheless contained the possibility of such an exchange and with it the destruction of modern industrial society itself. Equally, the Cold War, while not leading to the degree of 'total' mobilisation of resources seen in the two World Wars, involved a deployment of economic resources and manpower, and an intense ideological mobilisation, especially in the pro-Soviet states, that made of this an exceptional, semi-bellicose, confrontation. The collapse of the Soviet system in 1989–1991, and with it the end of the Cold War as a military and ideological conflict, brought this period to an end. The character of the epoch that succeeds it is as yet unclear. Assessment of how contemporary forms of modernity relate to war, of how and how far the relationship prevailing earlier in the century between inter-state relations and military conflict has changed, remain, however, central to any assessment of this post-1989 period.

This periodisation may, consequently, serve to highlight the changing, often contrasted, relation of war to the European political system and to European society as a whole. In the 1815–1914 period European states experienced war predominantly as conflict within societies, most significantly in wars of nationalist assertion and unification, or as conflict with non-European powers, especially after 1870, with the creation of new Asian and African empires. Wars between European states occurred, notably the Crimean (1853–54), Franco-Austrian (1859), Austro-Prussian (1866–67) and Franco-German (1870–71), but they were of a more limited duration and impact. In the twentieth century, by contrast, the history of European states was dominated by inter-state wars and associated forms of conflict. If in the period before 1914 there was the Russo-Japanese war (1904–5) and the wars between Balkan states (1912–13), this predominance of inter-state war was most dramatically evident in the two World Wars, and in the Cold War that, while never taking the form of a hot war, dominated the continent's international relations for the four decades after 1945. Levels of mobilisation and casualties in the two World Wars were on a scale not seen before in European history: 65 million men mobilised, and upwards of 14 million died in the First World War; 80 million mobilised, and an estimated 50 million died in the Second World War.[8] Nor were the major inter-state conflagrations the only instances: the twentieth-century history of several European countries was marked by intra-state, or civil, wars – Finland, Ireland, Spain in the inter-war period, Greece and Cyprus after the First World War and, later, former Yugoslavia and the Transcaucasian states in the post-Cold War period. Equally, throughout the latter nineteenth and twentieth centuries, and most evidently in the closing phases of the European empires after 1945, European states were involved in wars of colonial suppression. These, while not militarily costly, did disturb, to a greater or lesser extent, the political orders in the metropolitan countries. At some point or other over the century from 1870 the domestic politics of virtually every one of the major powers was disrupted by involvement in colonial conflicts. Such disruptions fell into two periods, the years up to 1914 and those after 1945. The British political system was wracked by conflict in Ireland from the 1870s onwards, and by the second Boer War of 1898–1902, that of Italy by the Ethiopian victory at Adowa in 1896, while that of Spain was convulsed by the loss of Cuba in 1898. In the period after 1945, France faced political crisis after the loss of Vietnam (1954), and from the war in Algeria (1954–62), the United States felt the shocks of its involvement in Vietnam (1965–73), while the Portuguese fascist regime fell as a result of its involvements in Africa (1974). Russia, for its part, encountered rebuff against Japan (1905) and in Afghanistan (after 1979): the result was, in both cases, an intensification of political crisis at home as a result of military setbacks.

An alternative, but equally dramatic, counterpoint of war and politics was seen in the Cold War, the dominant conflict of the latter part of the twentieth century. The Cold War deployed resources of men and of money almost comparable to any hot war. It also led, on occasion, to moments of dramatic military confrontation in Europe, most notably over Berlin in 1948–49, 1958 and 1961, which contained the possibility of an all out nuclear exchange. Yet, while it was fought out in the Third World in a series of sanguinary wars, some with little original relation to the Cold War itself, it was on the European continent a conflict between two social systems. The military conflict between the protagonists was at once dominated and restrained by the possession of nuclear weapons and the memory of the Second World War, but their social and political competition was conducted in unabated form. Each sought to insulate their own populations from the influence of the other, but, in the end, it was the coercive socialist system that collapsed. To the long-term erosion of its political and economic self-confidence, a trend of which the Soviet leadership after 1985 was acutely aware, was added in Eastern Europe the particular enabling condition of the withdrawal of the Soviet military guarantee in 1988. A system created, and legitimated, by military victory and protected by military means was, in the end, unable to protect itself against a series of peaceful challenges.

War and the European Map   The historical importance of war lies, as much as anything, in its formative role, between and within societies. At its most basic level, war was instrumental in creating the division of Europe into states, empires and spheres of influence that prevailed in the past two centuries. By the beginning of the nineteenth century the European political and economic system, propagated to a considerable degree by war, had already come to dominate much of the globe.[9] Four centuries of expansion, first by early modern imperial powers, then by mercantilist aggression in the seventeenth and eighteenth centuries, had subjugated and colonised the Americas, created the bases of a world market, and established the principles on which relations between states that were accepted as part of the system would be conducted – diplomacy, sovereign equality, and rudimentary forms of law.

The great explosion of the Napoleonic Wars, the first war that can be termed a 'world' war, in the sense that it encompassed significant parts of other continents, unleashed political processes that, in combination with the transformations of industrialisation, were to shape much of the subsequent two centuries – nationalism, democracy, revolution, and secularism. Yet the defeat of revolutionary France was to reveal one of the underlying secrets of war's role in shaping modern Europe: the verdicts of war, military and political, were in the longer-run to be eroded by the very processes of social and economic change. France's defeat appeared, for the moment, to re-establish the pre-existing inter-state system of dynastic entities ruling, in many cases, over disparate and multi-ethnic empires.[10] In many ways the greater challenge was that posed by the economic and social processes associated with the Industrial Revolution and the spread of capitalist modernity through Europe and North America. No Waterloo could stop these processes: the development of international markets, and the very pressure on states to compete, produced a set of parallel, if unevenly matched transformations in Europe, North America and, after the 1850s in Japan. It was only later in the nineteenth century that the delayed impact of the French Revolution became visible, in a fusion of ideological influences with the socio-economic transformations of the Industrial Revolution and the inter-state competition it generated, just as towards the end of the twentieth century the very supremacy of the European economic and social model, in its extended trans-Atlantic form, was to be challenged by the rise of a bloc of Asian states using the technological and economic lessons of their former masters to shift the centre of global economic gravity from the Atlantic to the Pacific.

War, linked both to political and to technological change, has played a central part in this creation and transformation of Europe in the three distinct, if interrelated, dimensions identified above: (1) in the internal, domestic, character of states and civil societies; (2) in the relation of European states to each other; and (3) in the relation of Europe as a whole to the non-European world. This experience of war had several general consequences for the European state system. In the first place, war served as the means by which the map of the continent itself was revised, both by the shifting of frontiers between established states, and by the changes, during or in the aftermath of war, in the number of states themselves. The wars of the nineteenth century produced some adjustment of frontiers – in favour of Germany, *vis-à-vis* Denmark and France, in favour of Russia or its protégés *vis-à-vis* the Ottoman Empire – as well as, in the 1860s, occasioning the reunification of the Italian peninsula. The wars of the twentieth century produced far more dramatic shifts, most noticeably in the successive truncations which Germany endured after both World Wars, losing land to France and Poland after 1918, and further territory to Poland and Russia after 1945. This redrawing of boundaries was matched by the emergence, and disappearance, of sovereign states. Thus, the French revolutionary wars were to see the disappearance of Poland, and, in the nineteenth century, in Italy and Germany, hitherto separate entities were absorbed into a single state. Elsewhere – in the Balkans, Belgium, Norway – new states came into existence. As a result of the First World War and the dissolution of European empires seven new states came into existence, most noticeably of all a Poland that had been eliminated by imperial partition in the 1790s.[11] The Second World War saw the reabsorption of three states into the Russian domain. But the decline of hegemonic systems precipitated a further increase: Malta and Cyprus gained independence from Britain in the 1960s, and the multi-ethnic Soviet, Czechoslovak and Yugoslav states disintegrated in the early 1990s.

A second major consequences of war is that it served dramatically to alter the distribution of power within the European continent. The term 'balance of power', for some the core concept of any theorisation of the international system, is open to many definitions, and qualification: too often it is used as an apparent grand explanation for all inter-state relations. It should be used with caution, for definite, but limited *ex post facto* explanation, rather than to denote some enduring, dynamic feature of the system.[12] In the case of the First World War the shift in the relative power of states came above all through the dissolution of the multi-ethnic hegemonic systems, imperial and other, that hitherto had dominated. The decline of the Ottoman Empire had begun long before 1914, going back to the first Russian advances in the 1770s. In the course of the nineteenth century the Ottoman hold on the Balkans was weakened steadily, leading to the independence of Greece, Serbia, Romania, Bulgaria, Montenegro and Albania. The First World War, while only slightly altering the frontiers of the Ottoman Empire in Europe, led to the abolition of the Empire itself and replaced it with the modern, aspirant nation-state of Turkey. The First World War also served to destroy the Austro-Hungarian Empire. At the same time it led to the withdrawal of Britain from its northern European colony, Ireland. The Czarist Empire also collapsed, and five new states emerged. Elsewhere, in the Ukraine and the Transcaucasus a multi-ethnic domain prevailed. Yet while the system produced by the First World War was inherently unstable, the Second World War produced a very different result: the elimination of Germany as a major power, the division of the continent into two rival military blocs, one under Russian domination and the other under the domination and of the newly involved United States.

Beyond these consequences, however, the First World War was significant in another respect: it broke the monopoly of European states upon European politics itself. It saw the introduction of the United States into European politics and conflict: by November 1918 there were two million US troops on the Western Front. Their belated entry, and rapid withdrawal thereafter, should not conceal the important, perhaps decisive, role they played in forcing Germany to concede defeat: the First World War, 'a close-run thing' in Churchill's phrase, might have had a very different outcome but for the US contribution. If for a millennium, from the fall of Rome to the Ottoman advances, Europe had been vulnerable to Asian attack, this was the first time a non-European power had played a significant military role in Europe since the pushing back of the Ottomans from Vienna in 1683. This draws attention to the third dimension of war's impact on Europe, namely in the relation of European states to the outside world. Beginning in the late fifteenth century, Europe had used war as a means of imposing its will, economic and strategic, upon the non-European world. This process of imposition had proceeded in waves, and had had its setbacks, most noticeably that of Britain in North America in 1783. By the late nineteenth century, however, the predominance of technical power guaranteed success to European states in their campaigns against others. Yet it was precisely at this point that the flow of history began to go the other way: the Japanese defeat of Russia in 1904–5 precipitated the first waves of unrest in the latter country. By the end of the First World War, and, even more dramatically after 1941, Britain had come to rely on the support of the United States to maintain its own military position. The result of the Second World War was not only that a non-European power had been introduced into the strategic map of the continent, but that it had come to dominate the Western bloc as a whole.

This internationalisation of the European strategic balance went together with another consequence of war, the reduction of the European hold on the non-European world. This was barely perceptible after the First World War: some colonies were reallocated from vanquished to victors, and the main areas of imperial dissolution were within Europe itself. After the Second

World War the process of colonial dissolution went much further, a result of three interrelated processes: (1) the rise of nationalist resistance in Asian and African colonies, itself in part a result of the Second World War; (2) the weakening of hegemonic power in the World Wars, for the winners as well as for the losers; and (3) the pressure, divergent in origin but convergent in effect, of Soviet and American hostility to colonialism. By the end of the 1960s the main colonial powers – Britain, France, Belgium, Holland – had withdrawn from their Third World positions. Only the most entrenched and conservative of colonialisms, the Portuguese, was to hold out, until a political revolution in Lisbon itself, in April 1974, the only such upheaval in Western Europe after 1945, led to a precipitate retreat. It was above all the desire of the Portuguese middle classes to break down their isolation from an increasingly prosperous and democratic 'Europe' that led them so expeditiously to break up what hitherto had been presented as a single, lusotropical, domain.

Defining 'Europe's Ideological Variations These shifts in the political map, and in geo-strategic alignment, were accompanied by changes in the conception of 'Europe' itself, in the very ideological presentation of this idea by the states of the continent.[13] The origins of the modern idea of 'Europe' lie in the simultaneous formation of a mediaeval Christian inter-state system, loosely united by common religion, and the confrontation with the major external threat to that system, the Islamic world. This conception of Europe was then transformed under the influence of two distinct processes: an ideological shift, whereby the unity of Christianity was displaced by a new unity born of revived cultural descent from the Greco-Roman origins; and simultaneously, a strategic shift whereby the Christian militancy hitherto directed at the Arabs in Spain and into the Crusades was now displaced on to the conquest of the Americas. However, contemporary with these shifts, the Islamic challenge in its original form, military expansion from the south, was revived, this time through the Ottoman conquest of Constantinople in 1453 and the advance through the Balkans towards Vienna. It was the response to this last challenge, which lasted until the end of the seventeenth century, that was to provide the strategic context for the modern idea of Europe. This modern concept was a two-sided one; on the one hand a supposedly objective geographic delimitation, on the other an ideological and normative one, pertaining both to what 'Europe' ought to be, and who should, and should not, be included within it.[14]

By the beginning of the nineteenth century, the ideological and strategic coordinates of 'Europe' had been defined further. On the one hand, the early secularised Christianity of the Renaissance had given way to the full ideology of the Enlightenment, with its universalist aspirations and cult of reason. From the mid-eighteenth century onwards, and even more so in the nineteenth, this ideology was linked to the idea of scientific advance and to progress. 'Europe' came to embody not just a distinct cultural domain, or a strategic interest *vis-à-vis* Arabs and Turks, but an idea of history, inevitably linked to the triumph of a particular concept of science and social organisation. If the concept of progress came to be central to this ideology, it received powerful confirmation from another, comparatively new, ideological element, namely that of race.[15] By the mid-nineteenth century European societies saw themselves as both distinct and superior, a superiority linked to the growth of modern industry and to the presumed inevitability of white domination thereof. The achievements of modern science, and the development of European society, thus came to fill the place of the supposedly more God-given superiority of the earlier Christian expansions, first to the south-east and then to the Americas. This ideological shift, building on, but markedly distinct from, the earlier versions, was to underpin and legitimise the establishment of the European empires from the mid-nineteenth century onwards. In the earlier part of the twentieth century this normative conception of 'Europe' was to be used to expel and massacre millions of inhabitants of European societies.

Within this ideology of 'Europe' there lay a distinctive conception of war.[16] War had long been accepted as a legitimate means of conducting inter-state relations, and of subjugating alien, 'non-European' peoples: in a fine example of cultural borrowing, Christianity fused elements of the Bible (Deuteronomy) with the Islamic concept of *jihad*, literally 'exertion' but in political terms a religiously sanctioned war, to promote 'Holy War', and 'Crusades'. In the nineteenth century, this served to allow for the conducting of military operations across the globe, to serve military, economic or even diplomatic interests. Yet even as Europe itself was largely at peace, the idea of war between major states came to be more thinkable again, so that by the latter decades of the century war had again come to occupy a central place in the conception which the major states had of their own destiny and options. War, far from being alien to Europe, or something only conducted between non-European powers, now came, under the influence of con-servative and Social Darwinist ideas, to be seen by many military men and not a few political thinkers as something which was central to the white man's conduct of international relations. While this reflected broader shifts within industrialising societies, and the parallel political and social tensions within them, it also served to legitimate preparation for war, the education of the young for participation and death in it, and, ultimately, war itself. If the First World War was neither inevitable, nor consciously prepared in advance, it was possible only on the basis of the combination of international rivalry and internal, social-economic, political and psychological foundations that had been laid since at least the 1880s.[17] The culmination of this fusion of war with the idea of European civilisation was the period 1914–45, when, in a frenzy of destruction legitimised by appeals to progress, race and destiny, the European states engaged in the two World Wars. External domination without, an extreme barbarism within – these were the fruits of this combina-tion of the European idea with the cult of war.

The period after 1945 saw the inversion of this ideological complex. On the one hand, the European states retreated from empire and from any presumed privileges, or burdens, associated therewith, and refocused their attentions on building a state system within the confines of the continent itself. On the other hand, the discrediting of war after 1945 served to bring to the fore another conception of Europe based on peaceful interaction between states and on closer economic and political integration. This, pacific, conception of international relations had been present both in a liberal, peace-oriented current of European political thought, and in the argument associated with many nineteenth-century sociologists as to the necessarily peaceful character of industrial society.[18] In the post-1945 period it was embodied in the Treaty of Rome and the growth of a European economic community: it was, therefore, a product of the discrediting of war over the previous half-century. Yet this abstention from war was, in other ways rather less acknowledged, still predicated upon the continued reality of war.

In the first place, if the states of Western Europe were increasingly united in their economic community, the urgency felt in initiating and continuing this had not a little to do with the confrontation with the Communist bloc to the East: economic stability and growth in the West, initiated by the Marshall Plan, served therefore both the insulation of Western Europe from communist influence and the erosion of the Eastern bloc's confidence through peaceful, economic competition. There was more strategy, and Cold War logic, in the early history of the European Community than was generally admitted. On the other hand, in their dealings with non-European powers, now part of a broader alliance led by the United States, the European states continued to be capable of conducting numerous wars in the non-European theatre: while the US now played the major role in 'Third World' interventions, France, Portugal, Britain and Belgium continued to be able to use war as an instrument for the defence of their national, and broader 'European' interests. Above all, of course, the major issues of military strategy and defence affecting member states of the European economic communities were settled elsewhere, in the military alliance linking them to the US – NATO. Like the Japanese, the European states could appear to be avoiding military responsibilities, because these were to a large extent assumed elsewhere.

Throughout this period, the shifting conception of 'Europe' was shaped by war in another, even more visible sense, namely that of the internal structuring of the continent itself. The extent and character of Europe was defined by those with power within it (the ruling monarchs, and later, ruling governments) or by those who aspired, through mobilisation of a continent-wide ideology, to justify their own campaigns for hegemony (most notably, and albeit with very different ideological characters, Napoleon and Hitler). Yet such definitions were, even as they proclaimed a common identity, selective and hierarchical. 'Europe' was never one, but rather several, that is a domain both fragmented and hierarchical. Here, of course, historical fractures were available: between Western and Eastern Christianity, between Catholic and Protestant, between the increasingly free markets west of the Elbe, and the re-enserved lands to the east. To these were added, with the rise of capitalist industrialisation, the inequalities of combined and uneven development, and, with the emergence of concepts of national identity and race, divisions between those considered pure Europeans and those, most commonly Jews and Slavs, who were not. If the extreme division was that created by fascism in the 1930s and early 1940s, a quite different but very effective division was constructed by the Cold War, which split the continent in two and created two competitive blocs each presided over by states that were in part at least extra-European. The Cold War also served as the context in which another division, between the prosperous West and the less wealthy East, could develop. With the collapse of that Cold War division the absolute fracture of the post-1945 period has been abolished, but other forms, based on the legacies of uneven economic development and the very real, institutionalised frontiers of the European Union, remain. As with any other ideological image, Europe has therefore been the subject of competing definitions, within a world of hierarchy and fragmentation. In that process of definition and redefinition war, and strategic competition in general, have played a formative part.

Theorisation and Myths

Structures of State   As this varied historical survey may help to indicate, the problem of locating war in the framework of modern European history and of social theory is not an easy one. If war invited generalisation, and invites assertions of how it has shaped, dominated, 'made' the modern European system, it is precisely because of these antinomies that an element of caution is needed. History and political theory alike abound with generalisations about war, and specifically about the relation of war to modern society, that simplify this complex relation. Such reflections are often of a reductionist, or even eschatological, character. Historians may be tempted to overstate the degree to which war had an autonomy, and an influence, irrespective of other political and social processes. Political and social theorists, not to mention theorists of war itself, may have been tempted to condense a multiple and changing phenomenon into one argument: yet in terms of political and social theory, there is no one 'question of war', no monadic totalisation of conflict, no single 'problem' for theory to solve.[19] Indeed, as indicated earlier, we can no more treat 'war' as a distinct, constant feature of European history than we can so treat 'family', 'market', 'nation', or 'state'. War is neither a wholly autonomous phenomenon, a product of a necessary plurality of states, nor is it simply the product of politics, or of contingency. Equally, while war destroys social orders and hegemonic systems, it often changes much less than might, initially, be thought. War has to be seen as interlocked with, but not necessarily predominant over, the other processes that have shaped modern Europe – economic change, democratisation, social revolution, technological development[20] – and as having a shifting relationship to these processes dependent upon the variant character of these broader contextual forces. A purely pacifist history, one that denied the efficacy of war, and, in some cases, the emancipatory outcomes of war, however horrendous the experience of war itself, is as much to be avoided as is one that sees all of European history through the lens of war, a 'bellocentric' reductionism that ignores the social and political context of conflict and the changing character of that conflict itself. A summary overview of the formative character of war in modern Europe, therefore, may have served as a prelude to an examination of the interrelationship of war with the broader evolution and internationalisation of the European system itself.

These issues were recognised by those who sought to comprehend war in the very first upheaval of the modern epoch, the wars of the French Revolution, the more dramatic, political side of the twin transformation accompanying the early nineteenth century.[21] If the fusion of modern, industrial technology with war was to wait another half-century or more, until the American Civil War, the fusion of modern politics with war was evident in the mobilisations of the French Republic against external invasion. On the one side, the *levée en masse*, a direct mobilisation of hundreds of thousands of citizens, marked a break from the limited recruitment of previous ages and signalled a decisive shift in the domestic character of wars, hitherto relatively insulated from the lives of subjects within the warring realms: a combination of aristocratic conceptions of war, and the seasonable requirements of agricultural society, had hitherto tended to ensure this result. On the other hand, the French revolutionary wars, despite the intention of those who waged them, politicised those they affected into a nationalist opposition to France itself. From the French revolutionary period onwards, we can, therefore, see the interaction of war both with socio-economic revolution, and with political change, the mobilisation that was to characterise so much of later European history.

One aspect of the new political character of war was recognised by the greatest strategic thinker of modern times, Carl von Clausewitz, who saw war not as the explosion of an irrational force, or the breakdown of a hitherto properly functioning system of states, but as the very continuation of that inter-state system and an extension of the wishes and strategies of its rulers.[22] Yet while von Clausewitz recognised the rationality, the intentionality, of war, he equally perceived that war escaped from the controls of those who conducted it. Herein lay a paradox that was to characterise European wars of the modern period – war promoted forms of technological advance and administrative control unparalleled in previous epochs, a modernisation and industrialisation of war that enhanced the power of states, yet it also stimulated processes that were to escape the control of states, or the intentions of leaders, not least in the technological field. The culmination of this process was to come in the period after 1945 when the invention of nuclear weapons provided states with a weapon that was both all-destructive and, simultaneously, unusable against other nuclear states.

Of parallel significance to the reflections of von Clausewitz, Immanuel Kant, writing in 1798 on the eve of the second round of French revolutionary wars, was to sketch out, in his thirteen-page *Zum ewigen Frieden*, an alternative, as yet immanent, political relationship, that, as European societies came more and more to acquire constitutional systems, what he termed a republican constitution, so the prospect of war between them would recede.[23] If Kant was perhaps as yet unaware of the economic transformations attendant upon the upheavals currently taking place in Europe, and of the potential im-plication thereof for war, he identified what came to be a recurrent theme in the history of modern Europe, and in political reflection upon it, namely the possibility that through the diffusion of constitutional government, war between European states would cease to occur. Some decades earlier, another political theorist, Rousseau, had come to the opposite conclusion: Rousseau, in many respects the originator of ideas of social and national emancipation expressed in the French Revolution, had an especially pessimistic view of international relations, believing that war was inevitable with a plurality of states. Kant, cautiously but perceptively, sought to develop an alternative argument. The implication was, however, that war between constitutional and unconstitutional European states, and equally between constitutional European and unconstitutional non-European states, could still occur. Kant was by no means unaware, and far less so than many later liberal optimists, of the destructiveness which war could inflict on Europe and on the more vulnerable, non-European world without.[24]

Beyond its impact on the map of states, war has equally served in a central way to affect the character of European state structures themselves, but the nature of this impact needs specification. It is easy to assert, with anthropological or archaeological reference, that it was ever thus: the state itself began as a war-making institution – protecting the interests of one group against depredation and promoting the pillage of others. This can be argued as much for the earliest states as for the emergence of the modern post-mediaeval state.[25] Such a reductionism is, however, disputable: if war has been a necessary activity of states, and peoples, it has never been the sole one, nor, in all cases, the object of major attention. Other activities – social conflict, religion, production, culture – have played their role. In the case of modern industrial Europe, a similar caution may be in order: the intersection of states with war is a central, but by no means determining, feature of the history of these institutions. If we try to specify how war has shaped the modern state, it can be said to have done so in three fundamental ways: (1) by fostering technological development; (2) by the promotion of state intervention in the society to prepare for, and wage, war; and (3) by fostering a sectional interest, within and without the state, in favour of military expenditures and war.

The history of economic development and of technical change, in particular from the early nineteenth century onward, is linked with that of warfare and preparation for war. Each of the main phases of war in modern European history was marked by technological and economic change, even if, as early as the 1850s, the development of military technology in the United States was also to play an influential role. Thus the Napoleonic Wars saw the development of industrial production of saltpetre for gunpowder, the first use of balloons for military technology, and the development of semaphore communications, linking Paris to the front.[26] The nineteenth century saw the application of industrialisation in two respects above all: the first was in the transportation of labour and material, most dramatically, in the first instance, the movement by rail of large numbers of men in the American Civil War, a phenomenon that was to become crucial for the outbreak and continuation of the First World War; the other application was in the field of fastest-moving technical change, naval competition, with the production of new forms of armour plating and, in reply, long-range artillery by the new navies of Europe. The naval arms race of the late nineteenth century was to produce an interaction of technology, political manoeuvre and public alarmism that was to be reproduced, in even more dramatic form, by the nuclear arms race a century later. Other inventions, and in particular the rifled handgun, first developed in the 1850s, and later the machine gun, first deployed to little effect by the French in 1870, were to be central to the waging of war in the twentieth century.

The First World War represented a new phase in both the mobilisation of people and in the application of modern technology to destruction, introduced on a mass scale, yet with a lack of any corresponding innovation of military strategy or moral concern: the result was the carnage on the Western Front, when the British could suffer 60,000 dead on a single day in 1916. During this World War several technical innovations were deployed: tanks, submarines, torpedoes, aircraft, poison gas. Yet while the last was banned by international agreement in 1925 and subsequent treaties, the former were developed and applied on a general scale only after 1918. If the First World War was fought with the innovations first seen in the Crimean War and American Civil War, it was the Second World War which was fought with the inventions, now generally applied, of 1918, combined with new strategies, that contrasted with those of 1914–18. Where the First World War had relied on protracted, static erosion of the other sides' military and psychological position, the Second World War involved above all rapidity and manoeuvre, evident first in the *Blitzkrieg* with which Hitler overwhelmed France in 1940 and then with the large-scale application of tank warfare on land, and of bombers and fighters in the air, that dominated the eastern and western fronts. The Second World War was characterised by the mobilisation of civilian economic resources, by war planning, on a scale unseen in the First World War.

The final chapter in this process of war-promoted innovation, and subsequent transformation of the character of war, was to be seen in the Cold War: this was dominated by the threat of nuclear weapons, an invention applied on two occasions at the end of the war, and by the application of new technologies of jet and rocket propulsion to the area of competition that was now the most technologically advanced – war in the air. The impact of these technologies was, mercifully, abstract, in so far as the states which developed them never resorted to war against each other. Yet the expenditures involved, the incessant process of arms race, and the evolution of new conceptions of military strategy, based on the use of nuclear weapons and a chimerical ability to control such wars, a grotesque misuse of von Clausewitz's instrumentalism, were to mark both relations between states and significant parts of their domestic economies and politics for the four decades after 1945. If nuclear weapons were not in this period used as weapons, they nonetheless served as instruments for the promotion of power and, through the arms race, as a means of wearing down the strategic rivals.

Modern war affected both the fiscal and economic roles of the state itself. Throughout history taxation for war had been the core of the state's raising of revenues; in this period, however, the demands of military competition, linked in many cases to the administration of empire, had led to an expansion and transformation of the states of Europe. This transformation was all the greater because, from the latter part of the nineteenth century onwards, it became evident that the state could not rely on the private sector for its military supplies, either for the production *en masse* and in sufficient speed of the material it needed for war, or for the promotion of that technological research that was essential to apply the findings of industrial society to war and, most importantly, maintain competition with rivals. The pace of change, in both civilian sectors and in the military technology of rival states, led states to become directly involved in military production, while promoting a civilian sector with major influence over the state and with an interest in prosecuting military competition with other states.[27] At the same time, the direction back into the economy of the fiscal resources so accumulated had a major impact on the growth of the societies concerned.[28] But this power of the state over society went much further than the extraction of resources or intervention of industrial and scientific processes. Education was reshaped to meet national and military needs. Conscription, mandatory in Germany from 1815, in France after 1870 and in virtually all European countries except Britain by the end of the century, served to educate, train and socialise male youth.[29]

War had, however, another potential, a relationship to politics which, latent in the nineteenth century, was to emerge with greater clarity in the twentieth. This was the fostering of a nexus of interest, some embodied in the state, some in society at large, which had an interest in international tension and war. Originally identifiable in the last decades of the nineteenth century, in the links between departments of state and private arms manufacturers, it was to become an enduring feature of developed societies thereafter, reaching its culmination in the post-1945 period, when it acquired the term 'military-industrial complex'. The emergence of this nexus of interests was linked to well-established calculations of political advantage: if established regimes had reason to fear the domestic consequences of war, and the heightening of tensions involved, they could also calculate that war served to preserve and consolidate their hold on society. For example, the outbreak of war, and the mobilisation of sentiment and resources involved, had been important means by which the British state had stifled sympathy for the French Revolution. The rise of nationalism both challenged established, multi-ethnic states and provided new means by which the established regimes could mobilise support. Equally, while the transformation of society in the nineteenth century provided the context for the emergence of new challenges, it also provided new means for the armed forces to obtain allocations of resources from the state and gave those traditionally associated with the armed forces, the officer corps and their families, an influential place within the new social order.

Combined with the growing emphasis on extra-European expansion, this process, broadly termed militarisation, was to pervade much of European life by the early twentieth century. The term militarisation itself connects several distinct strands within society – from the influence of the officer corps, to the distribution of state resources, the influence of the armed forces on the economy, and society to the tendency of such societies to go to war, or be more prone to doing so. In broad terms, however, it indicated the degree to which war, and those associated with its preparation, propagation and conduct, had come to find a central place in the state and economy of the modern Europe.

This intersection of war and political system, in a broad sense, the 'militarisation' of European society in the early part of the twentieth century, was to affect not only the major capitalist states of the continent, but also those which, taking advantage of the crises of the capitalist order, sought to establish a revolutionary alternative. From the middle of the nineteenth century onwards, and in contrast to the prevailing view that modern society was intrinsically peaceful, there had been those on the left who had stressed not only the possibility but also the inevitability of war between modern industrial states. Some sought to locate this in the continued influence within these modern, urban states of social groups linked to an earlier, agrarian and bellicose epoch. In this perspective the predominance of the officer corps, and the spread of ideologies of war and sacrifice, was a relic, an 'atavism', influential within, but fundamentally alien to, the modern industrial order.[30] For others, this linkage between war and modern society was not accidental, or a product of earlier epochs, but a necessary product of the new system itself: thus within the Marxist tradition, and in contrast to the earlier generally optimistic view of Marx himself, there developed the discussion of the necessarily imperialist character of the late nineteenth-century and early twentieth-century periods, 'imperialism' being here understood not just, or even primarily, as the search for colonies in Asia and Africa, but as the militarisation of the major industrial states both domestically and in their relations with each other.[31] Within this analysis, modern European society was inevitably militaristic and the ideologies of war and sacrifice an essential part of the maintenance of capitalist rule and mobilisation.

This perspective of inevitable inter-capitalist conflict, and the revolutionary opportunities resulting from it, was to receive apparent confirmation from the outbreak of the First World War and the ensuing period of political violence, first within and then between states. The First World War and the barbarism of the fascist movements that followed were, it was argued, proof of the inherently authoritarian and militaristic character of capitalism. By the end of the 1930s this process was to receive its apparent final confirmation in the outbreak of the Second World War and the victories of an authoritarian, genocidal capitalism in the first years of the war. Yet the Second World War, the ultimate conflict between developed countries, also contained the seeds of a different outcome. On the one hand, the alliance that defeated the fascist states comprised both the USSR, the revolutionary state whose destruction was a primary goal of German expansion, and also a coalition of liberal democratic states which, while committed to domination of countries in the colonial and semi-colonial world, had maintained a partially democratic political order within. The triumph of a militarised, brutalised capitalism was assured neither within states, nor, in the end, on the international scale. The outcome of the Second World War, far from confirming the triumph of such an authoritarian pattern of domestic and inter-state politics, contained within it other possibilities, temporarily united in the coalition against Nazi Germany and its allies.

The impact of war on liberal democracy was one in which the established orders were compelled, as a price for popular support for the wars, to make political concessions thereafter. In both the extension of the suffrage (the Second World War completing what the First World War had begun) and in the broader extension of welfare and other state provision, the two World Wars served to broaden the political space in these countries. If this was a gradual process in those countries that had avoided the experience of authoritarian capitalism (France, Britain, the US, the Scandinavian states) it was equally so, but in an abrupt manner, in the former fascist states which, through a combination of military defeat and subsequent occupation, came to adopt liberal democratic regimes in the post-war epoch. If the First World War had generated a set of contradictory options within capitalist Europe, the Second World War settled the argument within capitalism in favour of a liberal democratic order, albeit with many shades of interpretation. Once the defeat of authoritarian militarism had been assured, in 1945, the world, and in particular the European continent, was to be divided not by intra-capitalist conflict but by the four-decade-long confrontation between these two rival components of the wartime alliance, and, more broadly, two radically different variants of modernity, and their interpretation of the modern political project.

Social Revolution and Political Change Beyond these economic and long-term consequences, war also served, in shaping the social and political character of the continent's constituent countries, to constitute the forces of revolt and resistance within them. The two centuries since 1789 have been ones of continuous political change in Europe of revolution and counter-revolution, of democratic opening and authoritarian reassertion, of enlightenment and retrogression. The history of these processes, the inner life of the states of Europe, is inextricably linked to the outcomes of war itself. The course of war had its own logic and autonomy; but a continuous, reciprocal, interaction could also be observed between the incidence of war and the changing socio-political map of the continent.

The cataclysm of the French Revolution established a first variant of this relationship. The Revolution itself was caused by several factors, among which the weakening of the French state in the Seven Years' War was an important, if not in itself decisive, factor: wars weaken the capacity of states to rule, just as the costs incurred, by victor and defeated alike, can lead to the imposition of greater burdens, of taxation or mobilisation, upon the populations of the countries concerned.[32] In the 1770s, the British were forced to increase taxation in their North American colonies, the French, a decade later, to do so at home: the result was, in one case, the loss of colonies far away and the unleashing of political values, of impeccably European origin, that were to challenge dynastic states the world over; the result of the latter, in a configuration of conflicts within the hitherto dominant power in Europe, was twenty-five years of war and revolution.

In the period prior to 1815 the link between politics and war was evident to both sides: the Girondins, Jacobins and, in transmuted form, Napoleonic forces sought to use the occasion of war to promote social revolution across the continent, while at the same time believing that an increase in revolutionary allies, preferably ones able to take power, would help to consolidate the revolutionary regime in France itself.[33] Their opponents realised that the threat of the French Revolution was, beyond war itself, that of the ideas that it embodied: as Burke, a counter-revolutionary deploying a logic that any revolutionary could understand, was to argue, there could be no truce with such a regime, since its menace consisted not in its military challenge alone, which might or might not be contained, but in the defiance of the established principles of legitimacy. Pre-emptive counter-revolutionary war was, therefore, essential for the protection of the established states of Europe.[34] The outcome of the Napoleonic Wars was, however, to vindicate neither of these positions. The French revolutionary wars did not produce a revolutionary Europe after France's image: in some cases the French armies failed absolutely, that is in military terms. In others they succeeded on the battlefield only to face a political resistance, much of it inspired by their own ideals of nationalism and political freedom. As later revolutionaries were to learn, Lenin in Poland in 1920 and Khomeini in Iran in 1982 being examples, revolution could not be exported by military means. Yet the course of events after 1815 was, in other respects, to provide vindication of the longer-term perspective of the Revolution, as the intellectual heritage of that upheaval, unsuccessfully promoted by force of arms up to 1815, was, in the ensuing decades, to dominate political expression in Europe and later the world.[35] Burke was right to see that the ideas, and example, of the French Revolution posed a threat to established legitimacies: what he did not see was that mere military defeat could not, in the end, resolve this. The fate of the French Revolution was to illustrate what became a recurrent theme in modern European history, that wars may arrest or delay political and economic processes but they cannot in the end prevent them from developing.

The crises of the nineteenth century were ones in which such a conjunction of war and political change occurred, in which earlier military verdicts were challenged by political forces, but in which at the same time recurrent impositions of forces arrested further political change. If war was linked to revolution, it was also related, as both product and cause, to authoritarianism and counter-revolution. Thus the French upheavals of 1830 and 1848 sought to reverse, for France at least, the verdict of 1815. The most serious such crisis of all, the insurrection of 1871, was a direct result of the defeat of the French armies by Prussia. Yet the forces behind change, born of social and economic change rather than of military contingency, continued to grow: in the major states of Europe, social and political opposition continued, and the pressure on established states grew. A growing unification of economies was matched by an internationalisation of political ideas and organisation. The force of these conflicts was to find expression in the First World War and the upheavals which it generated, but in three contrasted manners. In the more developed Western states, world war and the accumulation of tensions within society led to a gradual cession of power, a broadening of the suffrage to encompass social classes, and women, hitherto excluded.[36] In the East, by contrast, where civil society was least developed, the regimes less confident, and the tensions of capitalist development greater, the First World War was to produce political revolution and civil war.

In the intermediate states, the defeated Central Powers of the First World War and the peripheral states of Western Europe, the ensuing years were to see the rise of right-wing extremists feeding on the bitterness and glorification of war to promote a new, bellicose, politics.[37] Here the crisis of the First World War both resulted from, and served to accentuate, this trend towards authoritarian rule. While, on the one hand, war led to the emergence of popular and democratic movements, it also provoked a crisis of the established states, and marked a radicalisation of many such regimes to the right. Where social revolution had failed, but where the established regimes were unable to make peaceful concessions to their own populations, a more assertive conservatism, backed by new ideologies of conflict and race, and drawing on the support of social groups either directly involved in the armed forces or broadly sympathetic to their authoritarian appeal, broke into the political realm. In Italy and Germany, later in Spain, Portugal and elsewhere, fascism emerged as a mass movement of the right, a product of both the impact and ideology of war, one determined to rectify the verdict of the First World War and to use war as a means of implementing its social programme. In this way the scene was set both for the onset of an even more destructive conflict, the Second World War, and for the mass suppression of opposition movements and the elimination of supposedly 'alien' ethnic groups. If the Second World War was the product of social and political tensions within Central European societies, and between the states of post-1918 Europe, the maturing of these tensions was itself a result of the First World War and of the anxiety at the social movements unleashed by it. The interaction of war and revolution was matched, at terrible cost, by the contrary enrichment which authoritarian and counter-revolutionary forces drew from the war and its consequences.

The fate of the revolutionary socialist component of the anti-fascist alliance was very different from that of its liberal capitalist counterpart. In its initial phases, the Marxist tradition had treated war in a neutral, scientific fashion, as a domain of political activity to be understood and mastered. While some had toyed with the possibility of there being a distinct, 'proletarian' approach to the conduct of combat itself, there was an equally strong argument, epitomised in the work of Trotsky, which stressed not the 'class character' of war as an activity but the dependence of war, in its course and outcome, on the broader social-economic context.[38] For his part, Lenin had seen in the First World War an opportunity to organise the first socialist revolution, and was to follow the seizure of power with a period of dire emergency, brought on by the civil war, invasion and famine, that was aptly titled War Communism. Later Marxists, most notably in China, were to wage wars of varying character over long periods before assuming power. The result was, to a considerable degree, a militarisation of the communist project, evident both in attitudes to war itself, seen in broadly positive terms as both inevitable and endowed with liberating potential, and in the mechanisms, many originating in wartime conditions and models, for administration and mobilisation. The very language of high Leninism – replete with references to 'combat', 'offensives', 'life-and-death struggle', 'militants', and the like – echoed the tones of war. Such indeed was this association of the communist project with war that, to many, it appeared that the two were inextricably linked. Some argued that the Soviet Union was an inherently aggressive, militaristic state, a left totalitarian regime comparable to that of Hitler's Germany on the right. Others, within the socialist tradition, believed that it was the wartime origins of the Bolshevik experiment, followed by the intervention and then, two decades later, by the Nazi attack of 1941, that had corrupted the whole socialist revolutionary project. War, which had given the opportunity to Bolshevism, had by the same token fatally destroyed its potential.

Neither of these arguments, claiming some close identification of communism with war, are sustainable. While committed to world revolution and locked into inter-state rivalry, the record of the USSR in international affairs, whatever the internal crimes of Stalin's regime, was in general one of caution and restraint, and in marked contrast to that of Nazi Germany. The USSR took advantage of 1944–45 to impose its will on Eastern Europe but this was a product of wartime itself. During the Cold War, more than in the inter-war period, the USSR took up a competitive posture in dealings with 'imperialist' states, whose potential it did not underestimate. But it always lagged in the arms race and exerted its main military influence through aid to other states and movements.

The argument on the military distortion of Bolshevism is also overstated. The assumption of power by the Bolsheviks in Russia in 1917 led, despite initial promises of democracy and mass participation, to the establishment of a coercive socialism: world war, civil war, external intervention all played their part, but these alone cannot explain the imposition of this authoritarian statist project, committed to the establishment of a radically different, in the event illusory, order. The argument that it was war and subsequent confrontations with the imperialist and fascist powers which account for the particular, bureaucratic and, to a significant degree, militarised socialism of the Soviet Union ignores the authoritarian, elite intent present at the very centre of the Bolshevik project. Moreover, while, in the initial period, war certainly served to accentuate this trend, and to render the tasks of the Bolsheviks more difficult, the subsequent conflict with fascism, in which the USSR played by far the greatest part, was to have, if anything, the opposite outcome: at terrible cost, and after many needless blunders of calculation, military and political, the Soviet Union defeated Nazi Germany. The result was a striking vindication of the system and of its legitimacy, domestic and international: the 'Great Patriotic War' served to provide the Soviet regime with a popular following that was to last well into the 1970s, while abroad it boosted the prestige of the Bolshevik system in a way that no achievements of an economic kind on their own could have managed. At the same time it provided the occasion for the consolidation of a new system of allied states, some imposed by military force in Eastern Europe, some created by mass revolutionary movements, themselves beneficiaries of the conflict with Japan, in the Far East. The result of the Second World War was, therefore, to provide an already coercive and authoritarian Soviet system with an apparent vindication.

Yet this 'triumph' of the Soviet model was in the longer run to prove illusory. In the first instance, the alliance system produced by the victory of the Second World War was to become subject to the strains of nationalist resistance and inter-state rivalry: the defection of Yugoslavia in 1948 was followed in 1960 by that of Russia's greatest ally, China. Within Eastern European states the regimes could only be maintained in power by military intervention – in the German Democratic Republic in 1953, in Hungary in 1956, in Czechoslovakia in 1968. Increasingly, too, the economic achievements of these states, immense in the initial phases of industrialisation and post-war reconstruction, were overshadowed by the successes of their capitalist rivals, in the European communities as much as in the United States and, later, Japan. In time the coercive socialist system was also to be undermined by one of its own greatest successes – the spread of urbanisation and education – and with it the growth of a middle class that aspired to the economic and political conditions of those in the capitalist West. For Europe, though not the Far East, 1989 ended, in peace, the experiment that had begun in 1917 in war.

War and Peace in the Late Twentieth Century

Cold War, European Peace: the Legacy of 1945 Such an outcome, unanticipated by almost all, can, in retrospect, be seen as a consequence of the particular outcome of the Second World War, a moment that, with hindsight, served as a point of arrested transition rather than as the end of an era. The liberation of non-Iberian Europe from fascism benefited all those, including the peoples of the fascist states themselves. It marked the end of a conflict, the most bloody in human history, that had been justified in the name of freedom. Yet, as the ensuing fifty years showed, that liberation concealed with it the contradictions of the modern concept of emancipation, and above all the contest between two, warped, competitors for emancipation: that contest was to end only in 1989–91. The Second World War had been a war fought by two rival inheritors of the Enlightenment against a third force, authoritarian and racist capitalism, that sought to deny that Enlightenment, even as it profited from the technologies and ideas of that Enlightenment, and rose to power on the very social and political conflicts that modernity itself had generated, above all in the inter-war period.

The history of the world after 1945 was, until 1991, dominated by the Cold War, the competition between these two modernistic projects. The original hopes of 1945, that a single emancipatory project continuing the project of the wartime alliance, and epitomised in the aspirations of the anti-fascist coalition, the United Nations, was soon confounded. Yet, for all the freezing of the Cold War, political and social change continued. The defeat of fascism in Germany, Italy and Japan led to the establishment of prosperous and, within strikingly eccentric limits, democratic regimes: whatever else, they ceased to be military threats to their neighbours. The impact of the Second World War on the European colonial states, combined with pressure from the USSR and the United States, led within the space of two decades to the ending of the European colonial empires. In the 1960s within Western Europe a series of emancipatory movements, many influenced, paradoxically, by the emergence of radical social and cultural trends within the United States, came increasingly to contest established systems of hierarchy and power, not least those of gender. In the 1970s, the authoritarian regimes of the right, entrenched in Spain and Portugal and more recently reconsolidated in Greece, crumbled in the face of democratic and social pressures. Finally, and most dramatically, at the end of the 1980s the contest between these two distorted forms of emancipation ended in the crumbling of the authoritarian regimes of the left: unable to prevail over its liberal democratic rival, and, even more importantly, unable to evolve into a democratic form capable of realising an alternative political path, the regimes of bureaucratic communism collapsed, with merciful speed and passivity.

Retrospective analysis of the outcome of 1945 can serve not only to identify the nature of the Cold War but to re-emphasise the contradictory character of Europe's place in modern history. Much of modernity and much of what is of universal, not restrictedly regional, value in terms of political liberties arose in Europe, a product not of some undifferentiated 'West' but of the social and political conflicts and movements for emancipation within the West. To reject this legacy as unacceptably 'eurocentric', 'ethnocentric', a product of some undifferentiated hegemonic narrative, is to lose an important element in the emancipatory legacy of humanity as a whole, and to concede, in the name of relativist uncertainty, to forms of oppression justified in nationalist, that is nineteenth-century European, terms. At the same time, the greatest crimes of the twentieth century, and the most inhuman ideas of our history, were generated in Europe. The authoritarianisms of right and left destroyed millions of people in the name of their historical vision. The liberal democracies, more benign at home, visited destruction on the Third World, through colonialism and post-colonial wars that added many more millions to the avoidable toll of the twentieth century. There is no place for piety about the defence of 'European' values, not least with regard to the wars of the Balkans of the early 1990s where such an invocation of the European past was frequently heard. Here it was irretrievably linked to sectarian and genocidal projects – Croatian neo-fascist hostility to the 'Byzantine', that is Orthodox, Serbs being matched by Serbian antagonism to the 'non-European' Muslims of Bosnia and Kossovo.

The outcome of the Second World War also reinforces our awareness of the contradictory character of modernity itself – evident in the rivalries of authoritarian left and right that dominated the middle of the century and in the many conflicts that dominate societies, and relations between societies, in the post-Cold War world. Such an awareness should warn us against many of the simplistic theories that are being generated to explain the post-Cold War world. The 'end of history' ignores the uneven, and itself contradictory, spread of economic integration and political change. The 'triumph of the West' ignores the destructiveness of the West, and the rise of economic centres that reject the mid-Atlantic hegemonies of the past half millennium. The most prominent pessimistic scenarios are also misplaced: talk of a 'new middle ages' or of an age of chaotic globalisation is inaccurate and sensational-ist – the state, as a unit of administrative and military power, had not disappeared, and is not about to do so. The strength of multitudinous ethnic and religious movements conceals their parasitic relation to modernistic ideas and preconditions, and should, if anything, reinforce the defence of values such as tolerance and reason. The condition avidly promoted as 'post-modernity' is but another factitious totality, a confusion of revived, but long-standing, philosophical conundra, with banal generalisations about yesterday's television news.

A Europe without Wars? The Contested Promises of Liberal Democracy

The evolution of Western Europe after 1945, and even more so the peaceful end of the Cold War in 1989–91, has brought back into view the possibility discussed by Kant in 1798: the prospect that, on the basis of constitutional political systems and reasonably prosperous economies, war will no longer be a feature of the European political system. If, throughout the two centuries since Kant, opinion has oscillated between those who regard war as inevitable and those who see it as avoidable, the pendulum would appear, in the aftermath of the end of the Cold War, to have shifted clearly towards those who envisage Europe as a zone of peace.

The arguments for such a prospect are substantial, and despite their contrast with the history of much of the past two hundred years, draw some support from that history itself. In the first place, democratic states, in the sense of those with full adult suffrage and developed economies, have not resorted to war with each other, but have found other means of resolving conflict. At the same time, militarism, in the sense of a military interest in war, or of widespread popular attitudes favouring war, appears to be in retreat, a result both of growing prosperity and of the very high cost involved in contemplating wars, whether or not nuclear weapons are needed. The growth of economic ties between states, whether transnational or organised, as in the case of the European Union, produces a network of linkages that makes contemplation of military force far less likely. This has led many to suggest that in some profound, possibly irreversible sense, we are now entering a 'post-military' epoch.[39]

Against this must be set arguments which, while avoiding the claim that war is inevitable, or a necessary product of capitalist society, would suggest that war will remain part of the European state system for the foreseeable future. As has been the case throughout the modern period, European states can still contemplate, and conduct, wars with those outside the continent: traditional colonialism may have passed, but a variety of occasions for war in the Third World have remained – from the defence of Kuwait against Iraqi occupation in 1990, to short-term interventions in civil war situations. No one could be sure that such occasions will not continue. Moreover, while throughout much of their history European states have intervened militarily in other areas of the world to pursue specific, national interest, the changed circumstances of the post-1945 world, and the creation of a new, international body, the United Nations, have produced situations in which European forces have acted on the basis of an international authority, be it for peace-keeping, that is non-combat, purposes, or, more rarely, for peace enforcement, involving combat itself. Within Europe itself, the prospects of peace within states have been by no means secure: the conflict that broke out in Yugoslavia in 1991, following the collapse of the multi-ethnic state, led to the deaths of over a quarter of a million people. At its root lay the inability of the Yugoslav state to make the transition from an authoritarian to a democratic politics and the manipulated explosion of ethnic issues which accompanied this, in which politicians desirous of protecting their now challenged interests resorted to chauvinism and violence to mobilise support: such eventualities could occur in other states. Much has been made of the importance of culture, of a national and popular disposition to go to war, in enabling European states to pursue the military policies they have over the past two centuries: the need for such a culture is an inevitable consequence of the political changes accompanying modernisation. Yet while there are obvious senses in which the political culture of European states has become less supportive of military activities, there is no reason to assume that such a reluctance is absolute or that, in situations where political leaders can point to a threat, there will not be support for armed actions, up to and including war. Most fundamental is the question of whether war, with or without nuclear weapons, remains a necessary part of any system of a plurality of states – a 'contingent' if not necessary part of a European system that will, for all its fusion in the European Union, remain one based on separate, legally 'sovereign', states.[40] This, exogenous, argument for the necessity of war, based on the Rousseauian plurality of states rather than any endogenous one, based on a 'militaristic' interest or on shifting popular attitudes to war, retains an ominous, if residual, plausibility.

Conclusion: the Transience of Outcomes

War has been a central part of the European experience, and a central factor shaping the politics and society of the continent, over the past two centuries. None of the other processes that have gone to make up the continent –

industrialisation, modernisation, nationalism, democratisation – can be understood without seeing how each has been influenced by war, and has, at the
same time, exerted its influence upon war. The map of Europe has, on
successive occasions, been drawn in war, as have, in conflicts with both
competing external powers and weaker non-European peoples, the relations
of the continent to the rest of the world.

In so far as European states are ceasing to conduct relations with each
other, or with other non-European states, through the medium of war, this
would mark a major break in the pattern of European history, not least in
the modern age. Such an eventuality can neither be precluded nor excluded:
what the previous analysis has suggested is that while war, in historical
perspective, has been a recurrent feature of modern European history, the
pattern not only of its waging, but of its relation to the politics and society
of Europe, has varied. If in the nineteenth century European states were
able to avoid war with each other, even as they conducted them against the
non-European world, and while in the first half of the twentieth century
they mobilised their industrial strength in a battle to the finish, this pattern
altered after 1945: with the establishment of a liberal democratic space, in
which economic relations were divorced from strategic confrontation, it was
possible for developed countries to avoid war with each other, even as the
prospect of war with the Soviet bloc, ever present, was contained. A spreading
and consolidation of such a bloc of liberal democratic states, a 'zone of
peace' based on shared economic and political principles, and assuming the
avoidance of major economic slump, would therefore enable the separation
of military power from capitalist state power to be maintained. Here, however,
as in earlier phases of European modernity, the relationship of war to
European society rested on the particular characteristics of the latter, on the
forms of power and rivalry it sustained, rather than on any necessary
militaristic or pacific relationship between industrial society in general and
the conduct of war.[41]

Precisely because it is not a discrete, autonomous, activity, war cannot be
understood in abstraction from the broader pattern of European history: its
causes, course and, above all, verdicts have to be seen in that, wider, context.
If from a moral and human point of view war has represented a succession
of disasters for the peoples of Europe, a folly of leaders who have failed to
use the diplomatic and legal mechanisms at their disposal, it has, in historical
terms, been subsumed into a broader pattern of European development that
could, in many respects, have been imagined without war at all. The rise of
nationalism and the spread of democracy were intimately, but contingently,
related to war, and in some parts of Europe at least bore only a secondary
relation to it. The processes of economic growth, industrialisation and
technological change were in some cases accelerated, in others delayed or
distorted, by war, but can again be seen as having had a dynamic and a
course separate from their military associations. This is also true, perhaps

most surprisingly, for the outcomes of war. France, defeated in 1815, was to see its power, and its ideologies, enhanced in the nineteenth and twentieth centuries. If the Russian defeats of the early First World War years paved the way for the emergence of a regime capable of victory in the Second, the victory of 1945, although protracted for four decades by the Red Army, was in the end to evaporate, leaving not only Russian power, but the very system created in 1917, in ruins. Germany was to experience a contrary fate: defeated in two World Wars, which its rivals fought in part to contain it, it was able to use the experience of humiliation and territorial loss to transform its economic and political system and to emerge, four and a half decades after the occupation of Berlin, as the dominant power of Europe. In the Far East a similar fate, of military catastrophe followed by economic and political rehabilitation, was to await Japan. In these perspectives the verdicts of war, a result of contingency as much as of necessity, appeared to be partial, temporary settlements, liable over time to erosion by political and economic changes that had longer, and apparently more irresistible, trajectories. In the context of the dual transformations that have characterised modern European history, 'war' as an autonomous, formative influence recedes in favour of the analysis of how military conflict itself, in both its conduct and consequences, has reflected the development of the twin revolutions of modern Europe.

CHAPTER 7

Virtual Security: Technical Oversight, Simulated Foresight and Political Blindspots in the Infosphere

James Der Derian

To be means to be for the other, and through him, for oneself. Man has no internal sovereign territory; he is all and always on the boundary; looking within himself, he looks in the eyes of the other or through the eyes of the other ... I cannot do without the other; I cannot become myself without the other; I must find myself in the other, finding the other in me. (Mikhail Bakhtin, *The Problems of Dostoevsky's Poetics*)

Alienation is no more: the Other as gaze, the Other as mirror, the Other as opacity – all are gone. Henceforward it is the transparency of others that represents absolute danger. Without the Other as mirror, as reflecting surface, consciousness of self is threatened with irradiation in the void. ... No longer the hell of other people, but the hell of the Same. (Jean Baudrillard, *The Transparency of Evil*)

In an escalating order of concern, four questions inform this chapter. How to approach a phenomenon so ubiquitous yet so elusive as surveillance? How to theorise – which from its Delphic origins (*thea* and *horao*) means 'to attentively look outward at something' – a technology that looks back at the theoriser with the reflected arrogance of science, a gaze that offers global knowledge dressed in the guise of objectivity and transparency? How to criticise something that has been deemed vital not only to national security but also to corporate, environmental, family and personal security? How to offer a plausible alternative to the collective belief that we live in a world at risk, and that our ability to foresee, perhaps even to forestall, danger requires a technology of surveillance which can oversee everything and everybody?

There are some extant theoretical responses, but each comes with shortcomings. Modernism, wedded to the idea of progress through technology, is deeply implicated by surveillance in the workplace, at home, on the battlefield, and indeed, by the mimesis of positivist modelling itself.[1] It is hardly conducive to the kind of intellectual distancing needed for a critical inquiry. Pre-modernist approaches offer historical depth and narrative breadth, but cannot explain, let alone anticipate the structural effects of rapid changes caused by innovations in surveillance techniques. Post-modernist approaches, like critical genealogies and intertextual analysis, offer a deeper sensitivity for the de-territorialised, chrono-political, and global effects of surveillance, but often fall short in the area of policy alternatives.

This array of practical and political difficulties prompts many academics to take the high road of meta-theory, to theorise about theory, or in my case, to put surveillance under surveillance. Aside from a few conceits offered as meta-theory, this will not be the strategy of this chapter: I've been there, done that.[2] Besides, I have come under other, more powerful influences. I have been compelled to throw caution, commensurability, and the cloak of meta-theory to the winds, and to morph pre-, post-, and modernist approaches for this investigation into surveillance. I could provide a host of intellectual justifications, but the reason why has become too difficult to conceal: too many viewings of *The X-Files*. The programme's (preposterous) slogans have become my epistemological mantra: 'The truth is out there' (often way out there), 'Trust no one' (especially the truth-sayers), and 'The Government denies knowledge' (an acknowledgement of guilt, ignorance, and epistemic drift). Radical measures, perhaps, but after a year in which a presidential candidate exalts *Independence Day* for its American values (a movie in which a replica of the White House is bombed by aliens),[3] the FBI's surveillance profiling turns a security guard at the Summer Olympics bombing 'from national hero to public zero',[4] and International Relations (IR) continues to confront increasingly irreal events, there is an even greater need for one's theoretical reach to exceed a discipline's grasp (or what's the extraterrestrial for?).

So I am a confessed *X-File*-phile. In fact, the origins of this chapter stem from an invitation for a conference on surveillance in Vancouver, the very city where *X-Files* is taped – an invitation that I could not refuse. Now that I have returned to Canada, those tireless purveyors of truth, FBI agents Scully and Mulder, have inspired new investigations. Flashing my ISA badge to gain entry into panels, plenaries, and publishers' booths, I have discovered that alien forms have infiltrated into nearly all ranks of IR theory. They have come as green-blooded, shape-shifters (a.k.a., the constructivist cabal), resistance-is-futile borgs (the critical security studies thuggees), gender-bending droids (the feminist coven), and, of course, those big-headed, bug-eyed mutants (the post-structuralist conspiracy). To recount a cheerier reaction to an earlier encounter of the third kind: 'They're HERE!'

This is not good news to the Syndicate: on *X-Files*, they are those old white guys who run the whole show from a smoky room somewhere on the east coast of the United States; in International Relations – well, just scrub the smoke from the picture. The job of the Syndicate, as one tells Scully, 'is to predict the future, and the best way to predict the future is to invent it'; not too far removed from the self-fulfilling prophecies of the 'neo(realist)-neo(liberal)' Synthesis in IR.[5] But the Syndicate has developed a peculiar relationship with the aliens. Unable to destroy what they fear, they now seek to control the aliens, first by suborning the shape-shifters – one of whom, the Bounty Hunter, becomes employed as a very scary terminator – and then by setting up a big research programme called 'Purity Control', whose goal is to extract DNA and other vital elements from the bug-eyed aliens for the production of hybrids (check your ISA programmes for details). This season opened with an episode in which Mulder was led to a Canadian farm tended by a cult-like community of clones. All of them were dead-ringers for his sister, Samantha, who at eight was abducted by aliens (or was it actually by the Syndicate?). When asked what the clones were seeking to achieve, she replies, 'Hegemony'. By the March sweeps, however, it is no longer clear whether the Syndicate controls the aliens, or the aliens have gained control of the Syndicate. Have the aliens come to save Earth from its own kind? Extraterrestrial eco-tourists on a mission of mercy? Or have they become pawns of the Syndicate, a kind of post-war solution for the fall of the evil empire? Worse, was there actually no one in control, and everyone afraid to admit it? Stay tuned for the next ISA meeting.

Aliens aside, let me get my own meta-theoretical conceits out of the way. Surveillance is Heaven (God). Surveillance is Hell (Sartre). Surveillance is fetishised desire (Freud). Surveillance is herd resentment (Nietzsche). Surveillance is patriarchal (Lacan). Surveillance is good (the V-chip). Surveillance is bad (the Clipper chip). Surveillance disciplines (Foucault), dissuades (Virilio), simulates (Baudrillard). Surveillance is everywhere (Agent Mulder). Surveillance is in your head (Agent Scully). My sole philosophical aim, to paraphrase Gilles Deleuze,[6] is to make theory worthy of the event, not by determining the cause of an event, but by interpreting the powerful and often ambiguous effects of surveillance.

This means that this chapter comes uncomfortably close to the kind of media spasm that reduces all phenomena and events – revolutionary or not – to superficial and ephemeral forms. Probably the greatest challenge in an age of information revolution is to slow down, to down-shift from media-hype and fast-and-easy stereotypes, to down-play crisis-mongering and crisis-management for more deliberative and experiential forms of analysis and decision-making. But this is not my immediate intention. This chapter moves from screen to screen, montage to holograms, sound-bites to buzz cuts, from substance to style – for nothing is so powerfully insubstantial, multiply mediated, and simulated as information – to alert us to the dangers rather than to pretend a solution for the most profound effects of the information revolution.

The bulk of my book *Antidiplomacy* is taken up with the theme that the current effects of surveillance cannot be isolated from the effects of simulation, and that they are more profoundly produced and sustained by an acceleration of pace rather than an occupation of space. My goal is to show how simulations through surveillance, from radar gun to spy satellite to computer screen, work as a technology and work on us as a technique of power through its ability to oversee and foresee, speed-up and slow down flows of information, capital, troops, refugees, drugs, viruses, and pollutants. In short, it is not the deep identities of geopolitics but the transparent differences of chronopolitics, where 'power is more "real" in time than space, it comes from an exchange of signs rather than goods, and it is transparent and diffuse rather than material and discrete'.[7]

Alloyed by the always renewable threat of terrorism, surveillance, simulation and speed form the undertheorised, overdetermined currency of the information revolution, and as such, it is inseparable from the issue of security. National security is endangered by too little (or too much) information; computer security is necessary to prevent the theft or invirillation of information; the Securities and Exchange Commission, draws a line between inside and outside information, and secures the borders of high capitalism; and at academic conferences we negotiate various meanings of security through our sharing (persuasion), withholding (manipulation), or distortion (propaganda) of information. We can freeze-frame factors of surveillance, simulation, and speed in all of these forms of security. But my brief is to focus on one particular aspect, the new surveillance effects of the so-called Information Revolution. Again, this is my attempt to get at the truth of the matter while trusting no single version.

Cut to CNN, General Shalikashvili, testifying before the Senate Foreign Relations Committee on the bombing in Saudi Arabia, 9 July 1996: 'Terrorism will always take the most indirect approach.'

Follow with Paul Verhoeven, director of *RoboCop*, *Total Recall*, and (regretfully) *Showgirls*: 'The US is desperately in search of an enemy. The communists were the enemy, and the Nazi's before them, but now that wonderful enemy everyone can fight has been lost. Alien sci-fi films give us a terrifying enemy that's politically correct. They're bad. They're evil, and they're not even human.'

Buzzcut back to Captain Kelvin Davis inside Kuwait City: 'I hate to say it, but once we got rolling it was like a training exercise with live people running around. Our training exercises are a lot harder.'[8]

Buzzcut forward to mid-March 1997, and the National Training Center in the high Mojave Desert, where Fort Hood's 1st Brigade of the 4th Infantry Division, kitted out with $250 million in computers, satellites and digital links, is about to face the Army's OPFOR ('Opposition force') for the fourth digitised rotation at the NTC. From *USA Today Online*, 'Cybersoldiers Test Weapons of High-Tech War' (6 March 1997):

The home team will try to find the Achilles' heel of the new system. On recent maneuvers, the high-tech suppliers swarming over the field headquarters, the

Tactical Operations Center (TOC), make it look like a movie set with the soldiers as actors. Five dozen new devices are being prepared for action. The soldiers are making progress. In less than six hours, the sweaty troops have transformed an empty clearing into a computerized control center. 'Barnum and Bailey has got nothing on us,' says Capt. Packard Mills, who oversees the TOC's operations. Outside, the tent and camouflage look typical old Army except for the satellite dish. Inside, video screens are coming to life amid the clutter. It's a long way from chalkboards and grease pencils. And a long way from battle-ready. 'When you first set it up, it looks like a scene in Star Trek when you just got hit by the Klingons,' Mills concedes. 'We've got people tripping over cables and plugging into the wrong thing. It's keeping me busy', says a harried Sgt. 1st Class Tyler Vandesteeg. He's one of an emerging class: a Webmaster of war.

Cut and paste: For the comfort of origins, I would say this investigation begins on a hilltop in the Mojave Desert, where I had been sent by *Wired* magazine to write about 'Operation Desert Hammer IVs', the first 'digitised' rotation of troops through the National Training Center at Fort Irwin. At the high end of the lethality spectrum there was the improved M1A2 Abrams main battle tank, carrying an IVIS (Inter-Vehicular Information System – 'Knowledge is Power' says the brochure) which could collect real-time battlefield data from overhead JSTAR aircraft (Joint Surveillance and Target Attack Radar System), Pioneer unmanned aerial vehicles equipped with video cameras, and global positioning satellite systems (GPS) to display icons of friendlies and foes on a computer-generated map overlay. At the low end, there was the '21st Century Land Warrior' (also called 'Warfighter', but never 'soldier' or 'infantryman'), who came equipped with augmented day and night vision scopes mounted on his M-16, a GPS, 8 millimetre video camera and 1-inch ocular LED screen connected by a flexible arm to his kevlar, and a 486 Lightweight Computer Unit in his backpack, all wired for voice or digital-burst communication to a BattleSpace Command Vehicle with an All Source Analysis System which could collate the information and coordinate the attack through a customised Windows program. 'Using the power of the computer microprocessor and digital electronics', digitisation was designed to be a 'force multiplier': the 'horizontal integration of information nodes' and the 'exchange of real-time information and data' was going 'to establish friendly force dominance of enemy forces'. In short, the Army was creating a C4I bundle (command, control, communication, computers and intelligence) of soft-, hard-, and wetware for the coming information war.

But up on that hilltop, as the simulated battle began at dawn with Black Hawks and Apaches flying so close to the deck they were below us, F-16s and A-10s roaring overhead, followed by the dust and smoke trails of M1 tanks, it was difficult to tell just what was going on. Our personable handler, Major Childress, former commander of an OPFORS unit and now head of public affairs at the NTC, did his best to explain, providing a running commentary for what we could see – and also what we could hear as we eavesdropped on the radio traffic among the combatants. Accounts of confusion and in more than one instance, fratricide or 'friendly fire', were overheard. But it was an aside from another member of the press that was to provide some much-needed historical perspective. For the most part my media cohort avoided me. I would like to think it was because of my intelligent questions and refusal to suck up to the brass, but it was more likely my failure to observe the press dress-code of Banana Republic safari vests, surplus fatigue pants, and desert jump boots. But at that moment, Austin Bay, ex-Army, military historian, and co-author of *A Quick and Dirty Guide to War*, turned to me, and said: 'It's just like Salisbury Plain.' I knowingly nodded, but before I could ask what this had to do with lunch, we were interrupted by 'Krasnovians' in simulated T-80 tanks, who were about to overrun our perch as they outflanked the 24th Mechanized. We got the order to move, and during a dash through the desert in an humvee, Bay filled me in. Salisbury Plain was the British forerunner of the NTC, and it was there in the 1920s that troops, tanks and airplanes, aided by wireless, came together for the first coordinated demonstration of mobile armoured warfare. It was, said Bay, a revolution.

Flashforward. A few years later, I had the opportunity to check out his story. Killing time at the Bodleian Library at Oxford, I began searching the microfiche rolls of *The Daily Telegraph*, not so much out of curiosity about the event as to how it was reported: was it recognized as a revolution at the time? I chose *The Daily Telegraph* because I knew that Liddell Hart had been its military correspondent – and much more.[9] Hart, a decorated officer during the First World War, had made a name for himself as an early proponent for mechanization, for a 'New Model' army based on 'tank marines' ready to use 'the indirect approach', to fight highly mobile battles on land as the navy fought at sea. At a time when Germany was disarming under the agreements of the Treaty of Versailles, and the French, under the direction of war minister André Maginot, were re-casting trench warfare and protecting falling birth rates by a defensive frontier of concrete, the British had the luxury (no real enemy threat), the temperament (no desire to repeat the slaughter of the previous war) and the technology (still the leader in industrial innovation) to experiment.[10] From August 1927 to 1931, Salisbury Plain became the premier laboratory of a new form of warfare. Armoured cars, light and medium tanks, motorized artillery, infantry in trucks and half-tracks, and even the odd horse were on the move, first during the day, later even at night. Hart's initial reports on the first exercises in 1927 were somewhat disdainful; aircraft were simulated, coloured flags stood in for anti-tank guns, and radios, where in evidence, rarely worked. But by the 'Armoured Force' exercise of 1928, the tone begins to change. One hundred and fifty wireless sets were used for a manoeuvre which left an assembled group of brass and members of parliament highly impressed. Hart considered the exercises a success in 1931, when the 1st Brigade Royal Tank Regiment, taking orders by radio, managed to manoeuvre through the fog in concert to arrive on time before a gathering of the Army Council.

Reopen USA Today Online, 'Cybersoldiers Test Weapons of High-Tech War':

> Assuming the digital force passes muster, the Army could soon be asking Congress for lots more money. The General Accounting Office estimates it would cost $4 billion to outfit all 10 active-duty divisions. But Maj. Gen. Robert Scales, author of the official Army history of the gulf war, warns it will be money ill-spent if all the Army does is perfect war as we know it today. That's what France did after World War I with its Maginot line, a defense easily overrun because it failed to anticipate Adolf Hitler's high-speed mechanized attack.

What follows is a brief sampling of his fluent – and influential – accounts in *The Daily Telegraph* of the first exercises on Salisbury Plain in 1927. On the front pages were stories about the Naval Conference in Geneva (most notably, friction between the US and Great Britain – with Japanese support – on cruiser tonnage and gun size), death sentences for Nicola Sacco and Bartolomeo Vanzetti, Italian anarchists, 'Trotsky's Victory – Stalin's Move Checked – Surprise for Moscow', 'a world not ripe for disarmament'. Hart's early articles were on page five or later, mixed in with military bands and tanks bogged down in the mud; gradually the articles moved up to page one. Entertainment is liberally mixed with education. They read like the bread and circus of late empires – much like our own evening news.

The Daily Telegraph, Monday 1 August 1927, 'Tidworth Tattoo – Modern War Staged' (p. 6).

> Tidworth is the home of the mechanized force which is expected to play a great part in the future development of the Army. Therefore it is fitting that the star attraction of the Southern Command Tattoo, which commenced before many thousands of people in the arena in Tidworth on Saturday night, should be a 'battle' in which the latest mechanized units take part. When an interesting programme was nearing its end, the searchlights flashed on to an Eastern fort, where picturesque Eastern marauders were taking rest. Almost immediately the battle began. A signal for assistance sent by the British commander brought a reconnaissance car to the spot, and, following quickly in its wake, came the mechanized machine guns, the latest swift-moving tankettes spitting fire, with a self-propelled gun giving protection to the British force, and in doing so adding to the din. The mobility of the new armoured units enhanced the realism of the episode, and undoubtedly this battle will prove one of the most attractive features of the performances.
>
> There is plenty of variety in the programme, for following community singing and the fanfare of trumpets, massed bands of the 2nd Cavalry and 7th Infantry Brigades enter the arena in peace-time uniform, the cavalry bandsmen mounted, and all playing delightful music ... Lancer trick riders carry through amazing

feats and some remarkable jumping, the obstacles including a donkey and cart, bed, fire hoop, and fire bar. … The concluding item before the reassembling of the soldier actors is a display by the Royal Air Force in illuminated aeroplanes. …

The tattoo was a huge success on its first night and will be continued during the week … the railway companies are running excursions from all over the South of England and buses are expected to bring many hundreds of spectators.

Flash sidewise. To 'Hearing a Face – Television Broadcast', *The Daily Telegraph* article next to Hart's first account of the 'Tidworth Tattoo', 1 August 1927:

> Giving a broadcast lecture at the British Empire Exhibition at Edinburgh on Saturday night, Mr. J.L. Baird, the inventor of television, said he had asked three chance acquaintances the meaning of the word 'television'. One said that it was an island off the Coast of Africa, the second that it was a form of telepathy, and the third that it was a kidney disease. Television meant actually seeing by wireless. The scene was first turned into a sound, which was then broadcast, and turned back into an image at the receiver. Every face had its own particular sound.
>
> A phonograph record was then played on which the television sound of Mr. Baird's face had been recorded. It sounded something like the rasp of a file with a peculiar rhythmic whistle underlying it. This was broadcast by the B.B.C., so that listeners for the first time in history had the opportunity of hearing what a face sounded like. The lecturer went on to describe his discovery of television, and said that the first person ever seen by television was an office boy, who had to be bribed with 2s 6d to submit to the experiment. The latest development of television had rendered it possible to see in total darkness, invisible rays being used. Steady progress was being made in developing the invention to a commercial stage, and he hoped that television would very shortly be available to the general public.

Historical note. One year later, the same year that motorised and wireless transmissions were linked in simulated warfare, similar breakthroughs in television were made by engineers at General Electric. From experimental station 'W2AXAD' they broadcast the second-ever television image, about the size of an index card. What did they choose to broadcast? A simulation of a missile attack on New York City. The point of view was from the missile, a flight ending in an explosion, then nothing.[11]

Hammering the point of the missile home. Paul Virilio, in his preface to the English edition of *War and Cinema*, writes: 'A war of pictures and sounds is replacing the war of objects (projectiles and missiles). In a technicians' version of an all-seeing Divinity, ever ruling out accident and surprise, the drive is on for a general system of illumination that will allow everything to be seen and known, at every moment and in every place.'[12]

The Daily Telegraph, 'Tanks "In Action" on Salisbury Plain' – Bombing Attack Thrills – Triumph for Mechanised Army, by Captain B.H. Liddell Hart, Tidworth, Friday Night, 20 August 1927:

To-day the training proper of Mechanized Force was inaugurated on Salisbury Plain. More definite localization is impossible because the exercise covered too wide an area, and that is a point to the good, for an immense broadening not only of space but of mental horizons is the only way in which full value can be obtained from these tentative experiments in mechanized warfare ...

Further, one discovers that common-sense again has overcome another of the apparent drawbacks of the Mechanical Force as originally constituted – by distributing this mechanical potpourri into groups according to the qualities of the mechanized units which compose it. Thus for marches it is divided into a fast group, comprising only the Armoured Car companies, whose normal rate of march is reckoned at 25 m.p.h; a medium group, comprising light batteries, field companies R.E., machine-gun battalions, and mechanized transport, all conveyed in semi-track or six-wheeled vehicles, whose normal rate of march is reckoned at 10 m.p.h.; a slow group, composed of tanks, tankettes, and mechanized artillery, whose normal rate is reckoned at 7 m.p.h. These normal rates are, of course, on the conservative side, with the sound object of allowing for hindrances and reducing wear and tear.

'Attacks from the Air'

To-day's test was a 'peace march by day', a phrase which implies not that it was under peace conditions, but that it was conceived as taking place in rear of the advanced forces and so not likely to encounter the enemy. But the serpentine column which wound its length in coils over a distance of some thirty-two miles, suffered bombing and machine-gun attacks from the air, when checked by road blocks, and had also to pass through an imaginary gassed area – presumably by enemy aircraft.

'The First Test'

... [T]he umpire created an impassable block by the declaration that a vehicle had broken down – or been blown up. It was about as severe a test as could have been imposed on a new-born force, and it was not surprising that twelve minutes elapsed before the first vehicle moved off the road to lead the way along an alternative route hurriedly reconnoitred on the flank of the sunken road – a route which, incidentally, enabled the whole column to display their cross-country ability and to get on to another and wider road altogether. ... At this juncture flights of single-seater Gamecocks came diving over the trees and swooped down on the vehicles in the road, dropping 'flour' bombs and firing their machine guns. So low did they come, so spectacular was their handling of these bullet-like machines that the spectators had a series of thrills. That they would have caused heavy casualties there is little doubt, but even in a stage-managed affair they were late enough behind time to lose several minutes of their opportunity, and in war, given greater practice by the mechanized troops, it is not often that such an ideal obstacle, such a heaven-sent breakdown, and the appearance of the enemy aircraft would all three combine ...

'"Mechanical Gods" of Modern Warfare – Tanks in Night Move – Driving Feat in the Dark', Hart, 23 August 1927 (p. 11):

Between 10 p.m. last night and daybreak this morning, the Mechanised Force, under Colonel R.J. Collins, carried out the second of its trial schemes – a night march along some fourteen miles of rain-steeped roads to a rendezvous near the Bustard, north-east of Shrewton, and a return in two columns across country. … If the test was severe for a newly-assembled and still inchoate force, the condition increases its severity to such a pitch that even an ardent believer in mechanisation was astonished at the practically hundred percent fulfilment which was achieved.

'Primeval Monsters'

I watched the column for a point close to Stonehenge, and in the apt and eerie setting of that dreary monolith-surmounted down, at midnight, little imagination was needed to picture it as the passage of a herd of primeval monsters or legendary dragons, with glassy eyes shining in the darkness, fiery breath, and scale-coated body. So irresistible was the impression that I pity any belated motorist who met them, unprepared on his homeward road. And the passage by Stonehenge had also a symbolical effect, for there the gods of the prehistoric past could be conceived as watching from their long-abandoned altars the procession of the mechanical gods of modern man – both equally the creation of man, but the one expressing the static mentality of the past, and the other the ever-changing, restless motion of the mind of to-day.

Historical sidebar. The next day, Sacco and Vanzetti were electrocuted.

Impressed, but not convinced, the British general staff failed to learn the lessons of armoured warfare wargames on Salisbury Plain. Defeated, and some might even say rendered desperate by disarmament and the fiscal restraints imposed by reparations, the German staff did not. They carefully studied Hart's writings as well as Brigadier Charles Broad's 1929 booklet *Mechanized and Armoured Formations*, which conceived of the tank not as a support for infantry but as a fast-moving independent force that could create shock, chaos, and demoralisation in enemy forces. In 1939, they applied those lessons with spectacular results.

Exterior. Bodleian. Film-noirish voice-over. Why, when Austin Bay looked down from the desert hillside, did he see Salisbury Plain from his desert perch, rather than Poland or France, collapsing under the speed and fury of the Panzer *Blitzkrieg*? And if we were the British, who then, or rather, who now, are the Germans?

Travelling shot. It would take a few more manoeuvers in the field before I would find an answer. Two tours at Fort Irwin; two trips to the annual Interservice/Industry Training Systems Conference in Orlando, where simulation industries like Boeing, Lockheed, Loral, Silicon Graphics, Evans and Sutherland paraded their wares to their military; Central Command in Tampa, on the heels of Schwarzkopf and the wargame that took us to Iraq, Internal Look 90; Fort Knox, home to our dwindling gold supply and to the ultra-modern tank SIMNET; Hohenfels, Germany, to observe the 1st Armoured

Division as they 'peacegamed' their intervention into Bosnia; Advanced Research Projects Agency (ARPA) in Virginia, to learn how the Synthetic Theater of War (STOW) was created to integrate virtual, live and constructive simulations of war in real time; and finally, the Office of Net Assessment at the Pentagon, where I found the Yoda of the 'Revolution in Military Affairs'.

Outtakes. In many ways, the itinerary for the journey was determined by an air-express package that I received from the Office of the Secretary of the Army the day before I was to leave for Fort Irwin. Although it did not come with an acronym de-coder ring, I was able to make some sense of it. Officially it was identified as the press kit for the Advanced Warfighting Experiment, or 'AWE' for short. But this did not do it justice. Collected in a large three-ring binder with the triangle logo for 'The Digital Battlefield' on the cover (satellite, helicopter and tank in each corner, connected by lightning bolts to a Warfighter in the middle) were over thirty press releases, brochures and articles on the Army of the future. In style and content they replicated the corporate publications that I had picked up three years earlier in Orlando. Computer-generated images were mixed in with all kinds of fonts and graphics. Indeed, it all looked a bit like *Wired*.

Leading the paper charge of the simulation brigade was a prolegomenon from the office of the Chief of Staff. It bears quotation, not just for its Toffleresque rhetoric, but for its encapsulation of the rationale behind the 21st Century Army, Force XXI:

> Today, we are at a threshold of a new era, and we must proceed into it decisively. Today the Industrial Age is being superseded by the Information Age, the Third Wave, hard on the heels of the agrarian industrial eras. Our present Army is well-configured to fight and win in the late Industrial Age, and we can handle Agrarian-Age foes as well. We have begun to move into Third Wave Warfare, to evolve a new force for a new century – Force XXI.

A series of categorical imperatives for the Force XXI follow. They call for nothing short of a paradigm-shift:

> Force XXI will represent a new way of thinking for a new wave of warfare. We must be strategically flexible and more lethal. We must leverage the power of the best soldiers in our history through the use of state-of-the-art simulations and realistic, simulator-enhanced training. We must accommodate the wide-range of operations being demanded of US. Intellectual change leads physical change – the mental shift goes before the software and hardware.

One brochure, slicker than all the rest, maps out how the Army was making the future present. It bears the short yet pretentious title: 'The Vision'. It leads with the now common litany of the national security mandarins, that with the fall of the Berlin Wall, the dissolution of the Soviet Union, the rise of regional powers, and the advent of MTV (reading between the lines here) no one can safely predict what is to come, nor who is to be the next enemy.

The Chief of Staff, General Gordon Sullivan, asks 'What's next?' and answers 'No one knows'. Therefore, 'We are relatively safe in predicting, however, that the strategic environment in the next decade will be dynamic, uncertain, and unstable.' Military jargon married to technospeak usually calls for high waders, so I was surprised to find a few pages later a box in the section on 'Exploit Modelling and Simulation' that read, well, like a good cyberpunk novel:

> The Distributed Simulation Internet, projected for the turn of the century is to a creature of another order entirely from SIMNET. Ten thousand linked simulators! Entire literal armies online, Global real-time, broadband, fiber-optic, satellite-assisted, military simulation networking. And not just connected, not just simulated. Seamless.

It gets better, and for good reason: it was written by Bruce Sterling for *Wired*. What does it mean when *Wired* is appropriated for the Army's 'Vision'? Perhaps in the idea-void of post-Cold War strategy, shortly after 'enlargement' (of democracy and free markets) is offered by the Clinton administration as a plausible foreign policy replacement for 'containment' (of the Soviet Threat), it is wholly understandable that the Army's visionary reach should exceed its rhetorical grasp. Indeed, I had come across much stranger intertexts in the course of the visit to Fort Irwin. One briefer had described the intensity of Desert Hammer as somewhere between the Gulf War and Red Storm Rising. Not such a surprise, considering that former Vice-President Quayle had once defended Star Wars (the anti-missile system, not the movie) by citing the same Clancy novel.

Or perhaps something else was going on, something I sensed at the NTC when I was in the MIA2 tank, and again when I was granted video-taping access not once but twice to the Star Wars building, command central of the NTC from which the battles are run and to which the signals from hilltop remote video cameras and overhead reconnaissance are beamed for the after-action videotape reviews. Was my presence at Fort Irwin – no less so than Bruce Sterling's in 'The Vision' – just one more tactical exercise in the Army's much-vaunted Information War? Was journalistic simulation one more front for the successor to Salisbury Plain?

As early as 1964, after reading a breathless promotional account of the 'Cyborg' under development by General Electric and the military (from the photographs it looked like a robotic elephant), Lewis Mumford warned of the coming of a new 'technological exhibitionism'. Thirty years on, was I bearing witness to an even more powerful, possibly perverse hybrid? What happens when you combine media voyeurism, technological exhibitionism and strategic simulations? News flash: In the Twenty-first century Army, you get the cyber-deterrent.

If this sounds farfetched, remember the worst-case scenario that currently underlies strategic thinking. As CIA director James Woolsey put it at his confirmation hearings, a 'bewildering variety of poisonous snakes' has sprung forth from the slain dragon. With the dragon went the mighty if mainly illusory deterrence value of nuclear weapons. On a quest since Vietnam (to fight only quick, popular, winnable wars), and imbued by the spirit of Sun Tzu ('Those skilled in war subdue the enemy's army without battle'), the Twenty-first century Army has perhaps now found in the cyber-deterrent its Holy Grail. It is fast, digitised, and as spectacular in simulation as it is global in surveillance. The digitised option also has the advantage of being out of reach of all but the richest rogues. And it makes a hell of a photo-op.

Moreover, the digitised deterrence machine bears an important similarity to its nuclear counterpart: it does not necessarily have to work in order to be effective. Its power lies in a symbolic exchange of metaphysical signs – give or take the odd reality-check in the desert to bring religion to the doubters. Hence spectacles like Desert Hammer IV, to render visible and plausible the cyber-deterrent for all those potential snakes that might not have sufficiently learned the over-hyped lessons of the first (if prototypical) cyberwar, Desert Storm. Once again the desert functions as a backdrop for the melodrama of national security. With assistance from Disneyland, Hollywood and Silicon Valley, the National Training Center, full of video cameras, computerised special effects, not to mention thrilling rides, has superseded Los Alamos and the Nevada Test Site to become the premier production set for the next generation of US strategic superiority. Can the Army go on to win the information war without firing another (real) shot? Of slightly lesser concern, can one conduct a critical enquiry of the information war without becoming, well, just another informant for it, a box in the Army's sequel issue, '(Re)Visions'?

Cut and run (and paste). Combat and Maneuver Training Center (CMTC), Hofenfels, Germany. The US Army owns, or more precisely, has 'manoeuvre rights' over a significant piece of real estate in southern Germany, 178 square kilometres' worth in Hohenfels alone. Spread out over the State of Bavaria like an isosceles triangle are the three major sites of the US Seventh Army Training Command, through which the European-based US troops, as well as some units from the British, Spanish, Canadian, and German armies and the Dutch marines, rotate through for some laser-simulated warfare as well as for live-fire exercises. The centres have an interesting heritage. Grafenwoehr, the oldest, was set up by the Royal Bavarian Army in 1907 to 'play' some of the earliest *Kriegsspiele*, or wargames. It served as the southern tactical arm of the northern Prussian head, most infamously represented by Count von Schleiffen, Chief of the General Staff, who in 1905 designed the famous Schleiffen Plan that was supposed to anticipate the next German conflict. Instead, its iron-clad 'war by timetable' helped to precipitate the First World War as one mobilisation triggered a cascade of others throughout Europe. The two other training centres owe their origins to Hitler's rejection of the Treaty of Versailles, the peace of the victors of the First World War which

included the humiliating 100,000 troop limitation for Germany. Rapidly filling
up the ranks with new conscripts, the *Wehrmacht* found itself short on training
space. Grafenwoehr was expanded, and two new sites were created: Wild-
flecken in 1937 for the IX German Corps, and Hohenfels in 1938 for the
VII German Corps. It was here that the lessons of Salisbury Plain were
applied.

The morning I drove past the front gate and into the Hohenfels Combat
Maneuver Training Center, I learned a less-known part of its history. The
tank-crossing sign, resembling more First World War lead toys than the M1
behemoths that skidded up the hill ahead of me, momentarily caught my
attention. But it was the more conventional warning sign for 'Cobblestones:
slippery when wet' that seemed out of place. I later asked my handler, the
very smart, very affable Colonel Wallace, why the short strip of quaint
cobblestone interrupted the finely graded, modern asphalt road into the base.
He thought it had been left intact as a tribute to the Polish construction
workers. Later I filled in the blanks: Hohenfels, begun in 1938 and finished
in 1940, had evidently been built by Polish *sklavenarbeiter*, slave labour. Wars,
when gamed, tend to lose their history of blood and deception: 'Slippery
when wet' joined 'Trust no one' as my coda during my visit to Hohenfels.

The reason I was there had taken on a special urgency. Two weeks before
my arrival at Hohenfels, NATO air strikes on Bosnian Serb ammunition
dumps triggered the hostage-taking of over 300 UN peace-keepers. The cold
peace flared hot when French soldiers in Sarejevo fought back after Bosnian
Serbs disguised in French uniforms and UN blue helmets tried to take the
Vrbanja Bridge. Britain and France announced plans to send a rapid reaction
force: debate ensued whether it would be under UN-command – and whether
the new artillery, armoured vehicles and helicopters would be painted UN-
white or sovereign-camouflage. President Clinton, breaking with the stated
policy of only providing US troops in the event of best- and worst-case
scenarios – to monitor a peace accord or to cover a UN withdrawal –
suddenly announced that he was ready 'temporarily' to send troops in support
of the British and French forces. But morning-after polls and the shootdown
of an F-16 US pilot by the Serbs quickly reversed that readiness. In fact, as
I drove through Hohenfels for my morning briefing I spied in the *Stars and
Stripes* newspaper box in front of the PX Burger King a tall headline and a
big photo: 'A Hero's Welcome' ... 'Air Force Pilot Capt. Scott F. O'Grady
looks mighty glad to be back – alive – at Aviano AB'.

It seemed like the right time to come to Hohenfels to observe an 'Operation other than War'. Just what that meant was supposed to be the subject
of the morning brief. But there was some initial confusion, not least because
somewhere between the time of my fax-barrage requesting a visit to the
base and my arrival, a name-change had taken place. 'Operations other than
War' had been replaced by the more anodyne 'Stability Operations'. Word
had not quite got through the ranks, and people kept shifting back and forth

between the two. The confusion mounted as I sat in a darkened theatre with my two handlers, Captain Fisher and Colonel Wallace on either side, and listened to the opening to Major Demike's multi-media, name-negating 'brief'. The Major was clearly in a take-no-prisoners attitude towards the English language: 'Army units from USAREUR [troops in Europe] rotate through the CMTC [I got that one] at least once a year for 21 days of Force-on-Opfor training' (good guys versus bad guys), 'situational training with MILES in the Box' (dial-a-scenario field exercises using lasers rather than bullets), 'BBS training' (not bulletin-board systems, but networked computer battle simulations with units based elsewhere), and 'after-action reviews' (video presentations of what went wrong on the battlefield).

It was all very impressive, but after five years of research on wargames and probably one too many jarring rides in a humvee, I had just about reached my tolerance for military-speak. I had gone one brief too far, and I was ready to go in search of that faceless desk-jockey sitting somewhere in an inner-ring, window-less office of the Pentagon, whose sole mission was regularly to abbreviate and if necessary change the name of anything in the military that becomes decipherable to the layman before its half-life of usefulness is over.

But it would have to wait until after the mother of all techno-briefs. Major Demike got into it with vigour: 'We have at CMTC the most realistic battlefield. The instrumentation system is state of the art. No other training centre in the world has an instrumentation system like ours. It is the best in the world.' He skipped through technology like the MILES (Multiple Integrated Laser Engagement System) for firing and recording laser hits, the microwave relays which allowed for near real-time production of the video after-action reviews, and the simulated mortar and artillery fire. To punctuate the point, Colonel Wallace stepped in: 'Once a unit goes into the Box, with the exception that they're shooting laser bullets, and that a guy, instead of falling down with a gunshot wound, will read from a card he's carrying in his pocket how badly hurt he is, virtually everything we do is real. There's nothing simulated in the Box.'

The Major became more animated when he moved into the details of the technological capability of the CMTC. Instrumentation systems gather and process battlefield data that observer/controllers use to provide instant feedback for both sides of the operation. There is a seamless web of command and control between Building 100 (the 'Star Wars') centre from which the battles are run, and the troops in the Box. For instance, simulated artillery attacks are launched via Sun Microsystem work stations, and hits are assessed according to probability software which calculates trajectories, terrain, and the grid locations of vehicles and troops which are constantly updated by Global Positioning Systems. Hits are then transmitted to each vehicle, as a 'commo kill' (communications knocked out), near miss, or 'catastrophically destroyed'. News of a simulated death comes in a female voice: the female voice gets the attention of the adrenalised or battle-fatigued soldier. My query about what happens when women eventually get to join in on the combat simulations was met with a blank stare by the Major, but the Colonel picked up on it: the female voice will always stand out from the background of male ones. My stock question about the realism of the simulated battlefield received the stock answer, but with a raising of the technological ante: the National Training Center, CMTC's better known state-side rival in the Mojave Desert (see *Wired*, 2 September) was still using the first generation of MILES to simulate weapon's effects, while they had the interactive MILES 2 with data communication interface ($9,000 a unit). 'Everything is wired' said the Major, who clearly had an ear for a soundbite.

After a long slog through computer graphics on the organisation and function of the CMTC, we finally got to the geopolitical gist of tomorrow's 'Stability Operation'. Up came a map of 'Danubia', trisected into 'Sowenia', 'Vilslakia', 'Juraland', and, looking very much like a small fiefdom among them, the CMTC. The Major's pointer started to fly: 'Three separate countries have split off from Danubia – Sowenia and Vilslakia are at odds with each other. When we want to transition into high-intensity conflict, we have Juraland, which has heavy forces, come in on the side of one or other of the parties.' Prodded to just once utter the word 'Bosnia', he would go no further, except to say that the scenario was based on intelligence sources, CNN reports, and the 'threat books'. But for my benefit he did add, 'You don't have to be a rocket scientist to figure out what this is modelled on'.

No rocket scientist, I resorted to a kind of semiotics to sort out the countries. The new countries of the disintegrating Danubia bore some obvious similarities to the region of Yugoslavia: to the former republic, now independent state of Slovenia, or perhaps the western enclave of Slavonia contested by the Croats and Serbs; and, of course, to the Jural mountain range. 'Vilslakia' remained a mystery. The countries surrounding Danubia were familiar enough that I sought out my own intelligence source, Microsoft's CD-ROM version of Cinemania '95. It was not needed for the country to the northwest: 'Teutonia' referred back to the early Germanic tribes. However, 'Freedonia' to the northeast of Danubia was clearly taken from the 1933 war satire *Duck Soup*, in which Groucho Marx so effectively played the power-hungry dictator of said-country that the real dictator Mussolini banned the film from Italy. And below Danubia was 'Ruritania', the country in the clouds which provided the surreal setting for W.C. Field's 1941 classic, *Never Give a Sucker an Even Break*. What should one make of the Army's strange choice of simulated countries? Probably nothing much, except that some wargamer had a sense of humour as well as history – and, perhaps, also something for Margaret Dumont, who plays in both comedies the great dame (or great dane, as Fields might have said). But I was left wondering: play by the intertext, die by the intertext?

The briefing ended with a short video of a 'Stability Operation'. By way of introduction, Colonel Wallace informs me that 'none of this stuff is staged, it's all from live footage taken by the Viper video teams in the Box'. Before I can enjoy fully the Colonel's knack for paradox, the lights dim, the screen flickers, and Graham Nash is singing something about 'soldiers of peace just playing the game'. The first clip is of a confrontation between partisans and soldiers that escalates into heated words; the last is in the same tent, with hand-shakes and professions of friendship being exchanged. In between, UN convoys are stopped by civilians, soldiers go down, wounded or dead, a body-bagged corpse is spat upon by a partisan, food supplies are hi-jacked by townspeople, a female member of the media gets shoved around, an explosion and panic in the town streets, a sniper fires on a humvee, dogs sniff for explosives, infiltrators are caught in a nightscope, a UN flag waves defiantly, and an old man drops to his knees in the mud in front of a humvee, begging for food. More in the sentimental aesthetic of an AT&T advertisement than an hyperreal MTV clip, it is strangely moving. I am disarmed by it.

But the mood shifts quickly when the Major concludes the briefing by handing me a three-inch-thick pile of documents. The rest of the day was a whirlwind of briefs-to-go. First stop was the 'Warlord Simulation Center', full of desktops and more Sun Microsystems for planning, preparing and running simulations in the Box, out of the Box, or through the cyber-Box, that is, simulation networking (SIMNET), 'remoting via satellite in and out of the Box to anywhere in the world'. Next stop was a cavernous warehouse, full of MILES gear under the watchful eye of Sergeant Kraus, who probably gave the best brief of the day. A man who clearly loves his job – or just eager for some human company – he was as articulate as his lasers ('instead of a bullet it sends out 120 words on a laser beam, in the centre are eight kill words, anything else is a wound or near miss'), as he made his way through the various shapes, types and generations of laser and sensors, all set up on a variety of weapons and menacing mannequins. He was stumped only once, when I asked what would happen if a Danubian snuck up and hit one of his dummies on the head. Would any bells and lights go off? 'Excuse me?', he said. 'ROE?' Colonel Wallace intervened to explain: 'Against the Rules of Engagement. One-metre rule. No physical contact in the Box'. It seems that one conveys body-to-body harm with real words, not laser words, for example, 'I am butt-stroking you now, so fall down'. I would later find out that in Operations other than War, the Rules of Engagement were there to be broken.

The day ended with an interview with the pugnacious commander of the base, Colonel Lenz, who made a persuasive case for Stability Operations as essential training for the increasing number of missions in that 'grey area between war and peace'. He would not, however, be drawn out on the relationship between Stability Operations and Bosnia, especially when I queried him about the possibility that some might find the notion of stability based on the *status quo* to be offensive, in both senses of the word, when stabilisation is perceived to be an enemy of justice, or simply just desserts. 'That's above my pay-grade.' At the end of the interview he kindly suggested a de-brief after my visit to Box: 'I've got people upstairs who can suck a guy's brain dry.'

That was sufficient incentive to stay up that night and wade through the stack of papers that I had been given. The bulk of it was a four-hundred-page document called the 'Coordinating Draft of the 7th Army Training Command White Paper of Mission Training Plan for Military Operations other than War'. A substantial part of it breaks down the 'Critical Tasks of the Task Force', like the establishment of a quick reaction force, checkpoints, lodgments; conduct liaison with local authorities and convoy escort operations; provide command and control and protect the force; and of no lesser importance, plan for media. Specific scenarios for battalions, company and platoons are spelled out. The philosophy of operations other than war is conveyed in the introduction, and after wading through all the acronymic muck and bureaucratese ('Traditional MTP crosswalk matrixes for references and collective tasks are also included in this MTP') – the final paragraph emerges as a reasonably clear summary of the purpose of the plan:

> As we continue to maintain our proficiency in traditional wartime operations, our forces must also be ready to operate effectively in non-traditional roles. Units involved in conflicts anywhere within the full spectrum of operations will always face some elements of a complex battlefield. These elements include civilians in the area of operations, the press, local authorities, and private organizations. This White Paper is designed to assist leaders at all levels to more fully understand and prepare for these new challenges.

In other words, this 'White Paper' was this year's model for the hi-tech, post-Cold War simulations and training exercises which would prepare US armed forces for pre-peace-keeping non-interventions into those post-imperial spaces where once- and wannabe-states were engaged in post-war warring. In terms of past experiences rather than future threats, Somalia, Haiti, Rwanda, and – judging from the many references to the British Wider Peace-keeping Manual – Northern Ireland lurked between the lines. But in this simulated shadowland between military combat, police action and relief aid, other ghosts could be discerned; Bosnia, yes, but why not as the next operation other than war a counter-narcotics operation in Mexico? Or a quarantine of a para-military survivalist camp in Idaho? Or checkpoints and convoy escort through a persistently riotous Los Angeles? This week, however, the enemy at Hohenfels reflected the headlines.

Very early the next day I was heading for the Box, where the warring ethnic groups of a disintegrating 'Danubia' were about to make life very hard for the visiting 1st Armoured Division. The next morning began with a low fog – confirmed by the weather report provided at the 'Battle Update for Rotation 95–10'. The mission: 'to provide humanitarian assistance and separate belligerent factions'. Computer graphics were projected in meticulous detail, breaking the mission from the highest level of 'UNDANFOR' (United Nations Danubian Force) commander down to equipment lists, tactical rules of engagement, task force organisation, and maps with vehicle and troop positions. A schedule of major events was put up, some of which required translation, like '1100 – Scud Ambush of Convoy' (not the missile, but the 'Sowenian Communist Urban Defenders'), or '2230 – Jerk Raid vs. Care Facility in Raversdorf' (again, not Steve Martin, but the 'Jurische Ethnic Rights Korps', guerrilla forces operating in the south sector). I was in bad need of a scorecard.

Finally we were on our way to the Box. There was a bit of delay as I struggled with the camouflaged ensemble of gortex jacket, pants and boots (for the mud), and as my faith in our humvee was tested when the door handle came off in my hand. But Colonel Wallace proved to be as good a handle-fixer as he was a handler, and we were soon off. During the short ride through a gently sloping open terrain with trees on most of the hilltops, Colonel Wallace did the eco-army routine – 'there are more trees and grass growing now than when we got here' – and as if on cue, a substantial herd of deer dashed across the road in front of us. The valleys and hillsides looked pretty chewed up by all the manoeuvres, portaloos dotted the land-scape, but the fauna seemed to appreciate the fact that the US Army – unlike the Bavarian hunters outside the Box – were shooting blanks.

The first stop was a UN checkpoint, one of many where civilians were stopped and forced to do kind of 'self-search' for weapons or explosives. Most of M1 tanks and Bradleys had their turrets reversed, the universal symbol of non-aggression (or surrender). We arrived with a UN food convoy which was supposed to pass through the mock-town of Ubingsdorf. The town came complete with the steep-roofed houses of Bavaria, a church with a steeple (no sniper in sight), a cemetery (no names on the gravestones), a mix of Vilslakian and Sowenian townspeople (dressed by a retired psy-ops sergeant in what he described as 'the eastern-European, grunge-look', ac-cessorised with the requisite MILES vest), and a mayor in a green-felt fedora, who was insisting that the food be off-loaded for his hungry people.

Language differences, a belligerent crowd, an aggressive reporter with an intrusive cameraman, all jacked up the tension level. 'Lt. Colonel Vladimir', commander of the local Vilslakian garrison, was refusing to bring the rabble to order. Chants for food in a kind of pidgin German – 'Essen, Essen' – made voice communication difficult. Suddenly the crowd began to move towards the trucks, and a few rocks were thrown. The US troops began to retreat back to the trucks, but already some of the townspeople were clamber-ing up on to them. It was then that the first rule of engagement, right up there with the 'Prime Directive' of no-no's, was broken by one of the soldiers when he grabbed a civilian to toss him off. 'One-metre rule, one-metre rule!'

was shouted by the observer/controllers on the scene. Some tanks and Bradleys, probably called up by the besieged sergeant in charge of negotiating with the mayor, came roaring up to join the convoy. The situation died down when the townspeople were rounded up and put under guard. Negotiations resumed, resulting in something of a compromise: the food would be unloaded at the local UN headquarters. But after the troops pulled out, I watched as some of the townspeople pulled off the most realistic manoeuvre of the day: they scampered off with some of the large crates of food, evidently for their own purposes. Colonel Wallace later told me this was not in the script. I had witnessed some Box Improv.

The script-writers clearly had it in for this convoy. At just about every checkpoint, food had to be traded for safe passage. And now, as we roared ahead in the Colonel's humvee for high ground, I noticed an observer/controller crouched in the ruins of a building probably dating back to the *Wehrmacht* days. A bad sign. As the convoy descended down the hill all hell broke loose – machine-gun fire from the hills, smoke bombs marking hits, and the light-and-sound show of MILES sensors going off. The M1 tanks and Bradleys reacted sluggishly to the ambush, not moving, and worse, keeping their turrets reversed in the defensive posture which made it impossible to identify the enemy with infra-red or thermal sights. Instead, someone called in for a Cobra helicopter gunship, breaking another rule of engagement: only 'minimum' or proportional force should be used in a counter-attack, to prevent a needless escalation of violence. From the last two engagements, it seemed apparent that the shift from war/sim to peace/sim was not going to be an easy one.

Salisbury Plains Forever. During my interview with Andrew Marshall, Director of the Office of Net Assessment, the intertext went into monalisa overdrive. For five years I had managed to avoid the Pentagon. It was not just the reports of the rats in the basement that kept me away. I had learned the hard way that when it came to the Revolution in Military Affairs, the hype-to-reality ratio skewed as one went up the ranks. But at every pit-stop I got the same name, regardless of stripe on the sleeve or political colourings: go talk to Andy Marshall.

Several faxes later, I was sitting across from him in his spacious, paper-filled, very unmilitary Pentagon office, with what looked to be a small primitive rocket on the ground between us. Seventy-four years old, Andrew W. Marshall has been around. Brought in by President Nixon, he helped set up the innocuous sounding 'Office of Net Assessment', 'to weigh the military balance in specific areas, what the important long-term trends are, and to highlight existing or emergent problem areas, or important opportunities that deserve top-level management's attention to improve the future US position in the continuing military–economic–political competition'. His memoranda are legendary, and for the most part classified. They have ranged from broad politico-strategic issues like the decline of the Soviet Union, to no less important tactical debates about the advantages of sending Stingers to Afghanistan. The one that I kept hearing about bore a simple title – 'Some Thoughts on Military Revolutions' – and was only seven pages long. When it was circulated on 23 August 1993, it was an idea in the wind; a year later, there were five task forces at the Pentagon alone, exploring the ramifications of the 'RMA' – the Revolution in Military Affairs. He agreed to talk to me about it, on the record.[13] Here are some excerpts:

JD: Could you tell me who you are and what do you do?

AM: Well I'll start with the history. I went to Rand at the beginning of '49 and I was there until the beginning of '72. Then I went and worked for Henry Kissinger at the National Security Council, and a couple of years later came here to set up this office.

I've been here ever since. This is the Office of Net Assessment and fundamentally what it tries to do is assess military situations with the intent of surfacing for the very top managers issues that they should pay attention to. I mean, based on emerging problems or opportunities. Of course, when I was first here we focused very much on the Soviet Union, and the more intense military, political, economic competition. Now we really are working fundamentally on two things. One is exploring this idea of, you know, that the next twenty, thirty years may be another one of these periods where warfare changes in some very significant ways. We've done some earlier analyses of that before but, about four years ago, began a much more intensive effort. I suppose we really began in '89 or so, and put out a preliminary assessment in July of '92 and have been pursuing a variety of activities to try to understand the potential character of the change, to better understand the actual nature of what the change might be.

So that is one thing we are doing and the other is trying to take a very long-term view of Asia and where it may go, again, over the next twenty or thirty years.

JD: Would you call it a revolution or not?

AM: Well, I mean, we have picked up this terminology of revolution and, I think, at one level, or in one way, that's appropriate. It turns out that tactically it gets you into a lot of arguments you don't really need to be in about whether it is a revolution, or what things can be called a revolution. Anything that can happens over a couple of decades can't be called a revolution, for some people ...

JD: Would you call it a revolution?

AM: Yeah, I would ...

JD: Why?

AM: Well I think, again if you look back, there is all this historical work that people have done on, way back to the fifteenth century, looking at periods where over the course of, you know, couple of decades or so many new forms of warfare emerge that just dominate whatever was dominant before and that seems, you know, reasonable to call it a revolution. It was the Russians that first brought it to my attention, the writings that they began to put out in the late seventies and early eighties.

JD: You mean your counterparts in Russia were speaking about a military revolution?

AM: Well, yes, beginning in the seventies and on into the early eighties they began talking about the fact that we were entering, or that the world was entering another period of what they initially called a 'military technical revolution'. And they cited two previous periods as exemplars. One was the twenties and thirties where you get the big change in many areas of warfare, because of, well, in some ways, the technologies of the internal combustion engine, radios and so on. Then the second period, right after World war Two, where it's a combination of nuclear weapons, ballistic missiles and the beginnings of computers lead to big changes. Their function, as military intellectuals, was to diagnose when there were these periods of big change. And, so they began to say one of these periods of big change was coming, because of the micro-processor and other related technologies. It was triggered, I think, by a programme to develop a system that they called the 'assault-breaker', that conceptually was a reasonably long-ranged rocket with a smart front-end coupled to long-range sensors.

JD: I was out for the first digitised rotation at Fort Irwin when the Fort Knox brigade was out there, and did some interviews. I've been looking at this from the bottom-up, from the field, and it seems there's a lot more scepticism about a revolution going on.

AM: Yeah, I would think so. I wouldn't particularly expect to see it down there. It's also spotty on the top, although growing, I would say. What I tend to argue with people is that we ought to see ourselves as in something like in early twenties where we don't fully see what the outcome would be. But there is just enough, on the one hand, to see that the technologies are moving rapidly and it's plausible that there would be a big impact. We are about in a position, where people say, at the Naval War College, we were about in '22 or '23, where we now have a bunch of wargames that are being played, that are beginning to explore, in some sense, the logic of the situation that would exist if you had, let's say, twenty years from now, a number of new kinds of systems.

JD: Are you familiar with the exercises on the Salisbury Plain in the twenties –

AM: Yes, '27 and so on, oh yes ...

JD: Last fall I checked out the back-issues of *The Daily Telegraph*, where Liddell Hart wrote about them, and what struck me is that he didn't really call it a revolution, or understand it as such. When you are really in the middle of it, you are least aware of it.

AM: Yes, well I suppose to an extent there were people in the military in the twenties that thought of things as revolutions that were primarily associated with air. Even the Germans, who really boast of being a hell of a lot better than the British, were not consciously thinking in terms of a revolution. So, what would be unique this time, in a certain sense, I think, or more so, is that because of things that have happened since the twenties and thirties – both the historical literature that has been built up that looked at these kinds of periods and the Russians who began intellectualising about it and raising it as a kind of intellectual issue – that one of the unique things about the next twenty or thirty years, if in fact we will go through such a thing, it will be almost the first time in which it is, in a wide-spread sort of way, self-consciously – you know – pursued or experienced as a revolution.

JD: Who do you see as our next enemy?

AM: Well, I'm interested in Asia mainly because of some general reasons. You look at long-range projections, that's the place where the most rapid economic growth is going to take place. Also, Asia has been dominated by the West for over 150 to 200 years and that's over. And so, exactly what Asia would be like, what kind of internal rivalry will be there is something that really needs to be looked at.

JD: Can you really compare our times to any other? When suddenly everything is wide open, do you think a global threat is going to emerge?

AM: No, I think not in my time. But if you look back into history I think you can see ... I think the twenties was like that. The twenties turned out to be a period of illusion about what the world was going to be like. I think we are in the twenties. Both in terms of the beginning of technical change which is working out its implications, and in terms of, well, in the twenties the United States didn't really have any big immediate threat, and the forces were very small. Whether something like the thirties is before us, I don't know.

JD: But to what extent do we create our enemies? Do you think it is completely a unilateral action, or do you think it's more like the whole idea of the security dilemma?

AM: Well I don't see that right now. You have a little of that in Asia with the growth of China and how we react against it, and to the extent that we get to be seen as, you know, the people who are intervening in this place and that place ... to the extent that we have gotten ourselves in the position of being the leader of the interventions for the UN.

JD: In the way that the nuclear deterrence maintained a relative peace for some, do you think there is such a thing as a high-tech deterrent, in the way that people would see what happened in the Desert Storm and then would not want to take on the US?

AM: I think so, I mean it's a deterrent in a sense, but it also has these other effects. I mean it deters people from taking us on in this way. But it may substantially increase incentives to go after nuclear weapons, or look for other clever ways of using the technology.

JD: It's clearly part of your job here, but do you really think war is persistent, we will always have it?

AM: I tend to be pessimistic about it and not just because of my job. If you just look at history and human behaviour you can't be very optimistic about it ...

JD: You don't want to think of war as obsolescent?

AM: I would tend towards that view, yes.

Closing shot, a shadow looming over the White House. Ronald Reagan, at a final press conference before the National Strategy Forum in May 1988:

But I've often wondered what if all of us in the world discovered that we were threatened by a power from outer space – from another planet. Wouldn't we all of a sudden find that we didn't have any differences between us at all – we were all human beings, citizens of the world – wouldn't we come together to fight that particular threat?

Paul Virilio, from his *Popular Defense and Ecological Struggles*:

> Meanwhile, damage and disaster occur just like the emergence of war popula-
> tions, nihilistic spectre of the speed of those with no name, who cannot be
> named and who nonetheless arrive, those whom Chaucer in the fourteenth
> century already called 'builders of smoke jails ... greenish men, couriers of the
> Great Fear ...'. The modern myth of UFOs is mixed with that of the terrifying
> immanence of assassination attempts, cataclysms, crime, epidemics, enemy
> threats.

And finally, Walter Benjamin, from Charles Baudelaire, *A Lyric Poet in the Era
of High Capitalism*:

> In times of terror, when everyone is something of a conspirator, everybody
> will be in a situation where he has to play detective.

Agent Mulder probably would agree.

PART III

Ideas and Economy

CHAPTER 8

Ideas and Economy in the Twentieth Century: Liberalism ... Forever?

Jarrod Wiener

Provided that no structural crisis occurs on the day that our reader glances at these words, a universe of activity will occur in the international economy. On that single day, ships will set sail carrying goods to be sold in other states that will contribute to the $5 trillion worth of annual world trade; decisions will be taken to make foreign investments that will make 'foreign' products available in a given market without them having to be loaded on to ships, thereby contributing to the growth of annual foreign direct investment four times greater than that of trade; about $1 trillion worth of money will change hands in international currency markets; and about $5 trillion will traverse through the computerised inter-bank payments networks. Driving this activity in the universe of the international economy on that single day are capital investments, technology, labour, and knowledge. Guiding all of this are ideas.

At the micro-level, the guiding idea is, basically, that profit should be made; the international economy is, of course, a capitalist one. The underlying reason why goods are being produced, ships are sailing, investments are being made, and money is changing hands is to make profit. At the macro-level, ideas about the economy are concerned with providing stability; the capitalist economy, driven by private individuals, coexists with an international system of states whose interests are primarily in stability. These two interests in profit and stability can be complementary; economic growth – the accumulation of wealth – can provide stability and power, and can make politics less divisive. However, these goals can conflict; growth can be destabilising to order if it produces vast inequities, or if centres of power shift in ways that are unforeseen or undesirable. The turbulence affecting South East Asian economies at the end of the 1990s quite possibly may show the dangers of organising any political association on the basis primarily of economic growth without it being supported by other mechanisms of legitimation.

The art of synthesising ideas that can be conflictory is governance. It has been said that the history of human civilisation is the history of ideas. Basic ideas give rise to a mode of governance, or 'governmentality' to borrow the word from Foucault; the rationality of governance gives expression to mechanisms that execute those ideas. However imperfect the form that the expression of ideas finally takes – because of compromises, bureaucratic necessity and mistakes – all such expressions, or modes of governance, are based on some ideal – theory, model, or ideology. All ideas about the economy are subjective, because they are based on a particular conception of 'the economy', a normative belief about how it should operate, and what the relationship between the state and market should be.[1] Aware of the subjectivity of ideas, the astute reader would ask the questions: why are ships sailing from particular ports carrying specific goods? Why are investments being made by particular individuals in specific places? And, why is money passing through – and stopping in – the hands of particular individuals? The astute reader on this day will be aware that 80 per cent of global GDP is in the hands of twenty-four high-income countries representing 14.5 per cent of the world population, and that only 5 per cent of global GDP is shared by forty-five low-income countries, representing about 55 per cent of the world population.[2] The reader may appreciate that this is because certain ideas about how to govern the international economy have triumphed over other ideas, whether by force, the forging of beneficial alliances, the appropriation of knowledge, 'scientific' rationale, and the moral high-ground.

There has been a succession of ideas about how to organise an international capitalist economy, and if history informs us of anything, it may be that ideas do not retain currency for very long. The history of the international political economy has been punctuated by periods of stability in which dominant mechanisms of governance were favoured, and by periods of instability in which order was challenged by another idea, or worse perhaps, by instability that resulted from floundering without guiding principles.

One such incidence of floundering occurred from the mid-1920s to the mid-1930s. Although the crash of 1929 was due to a range of factors, not least of which were misguided macro-economic policies, particularly in the United States, and, of course, malevolent economic policies in Europe, the discipline of International Political Economy seems to have been most concerned with its consequences on the multilateral trade system, rather than with its causes. The enactment by the United States Congress of the Smoot–Hawley Act in 1930, and the retaliation by its trading partners, particularly Britain and the Commonwealth, which implemented a strict system of trade preferences in 1932, has been taken by many as the paradigm result of a breakdown in cooperation.

The 'solidification' of 'trading blocs' often is taken as synonymous with a breakdown of liberalism, the memory of which still haunts policy-makers at the end of the 1990s, as Rorden Wilkinson illustrates. Wilkinson shows that while much of the 'institutional memory' of the 1930s may be exaggerated, and at least misunderstood, it nevertheless continues to operate as the lifeworld that guides policy rhetoric: if the 'bicycle' of multilateral liberalisation loses momentum, the edifice will fall down and we will see a reversion to 1930s style beggar-thy-neighbourism. Much of this is due to a Realist 'afterglow' – that competition leading to rivalry among the core powers is the proper focus of attention. However, the regional integration areas of the 1990s are not threatening to the prevailing order for a host of reasons that Wilkinson explores; an important one is that they have been created to be complementary of liberalisation. The early 1930s were a time of vacuous ideology; the 1990s are a time of unprecedented dominance of a mode of governance – and it is one that reinforces itself in a range of ways, including by faulty analogies warning of impending disaster if alternatives are contemplated.

The international political economy has traversed the past four centuries like a serpent, undulating between forms of cosmopolitan and collectivist ideas, usually expressed in grand terms as the contest between Liberal and Mercantilist systems of capitalism on one spectrum, and between capitalism and socialism on another, but which certainly is more complex given the permutations of these grand labels. A predominant characteristic of the present international political economy is a lack of such a contest about how to organise an international economic system – liberalism has become dominant – and there is a consequent paucity of other ideas. In the past, those excluded from the privileges bestowed by a dominant idea formulated counter-hegemonic pedagogies: Mercantilism and Marxism – and 'neo'-Mercantilism and 'neo'-Marxism arose as critiques of Liberalism by those excluded from its sphere of privileges, just as various styles of socialism arose among those who could not perceive, in their experience, the benefits of prevailing ideas. After the end of the Cold War, however, those not benefiting from the prevailing system are attempting with vigour to integrate more fully into it, to become more liberal. As Jarrod Wiener and John Kennair argue, this change in attitude is illustrated in the sea-change in the attitude of many former 'radicals' of the international economy towards foreign direct investment (FDI). Once seen by many as the vector of exploitation of the rich countries, multinational corporations are now seen as the best means to attract the capital and knowledge necessary to sustain development. Corollaries to the welcoming attitude to FDI are changes in the municipal national laws of most states to conform to an emerging international 'regime' to protect foreign investors, and participation in free trade agreements.

To some, this acceptance of liberalism indicates the 'end of history'; that the great contest of ideas played out along the linear progression of history has burned itself out. To others, less committed to liberalism, it may well signal the triumph of a sophisticated structure of power. E.H. Carr observed that ideas, particularly those espousing universal principles, often serve as an 'ingenious moral device invoked, in perfect sincerity, by privileged groups in order to justify and maintain their dominant position'.[3] But perhaps this paucity of perceived alternatives – although some, like Marxism, have yet to be burnt out completely – presents the greatest ever challenge to the International Political Economy. It is poignant to recall Francis Fukuyama's last words: 'liberal principles had a corrosive effect on the values predating liberalism necessary to sustain strong communities, and thereby on a liberal society's ability to be self-sustaining'.[4]

Perhaps, with the decline of radically different alternatives in the Western system – to be sure, there are varieties of liberalism – an ideology can become unbridled, lose its frame of reference, and become self-consuming. We have always known that unbridled liberalism can be predatory, but silent are the dissident voices. Perhaps it is for fear of labels. Standing indignant in the institutions of Western economic organisation and labelling another's policy as 'Mercantilist' – even if it is not – is to claim moral high-ground. To label a policy as socialist is a convenient off-the-cuff rebuke. But perhaps all of this is just romanticising the recent past of second-last men.

Perhaps the real danger to the international economy today is not an ideological challenge from the outside at all, but the fact that the present ideology is in the process of burning itself out. Perhaps too much liberalisation is a rather bad thing indeed, and in its programme to extend to new areas – trade in services, intellectual property, agriculture – the system may undermine itself. Liberalisation in the post-war era was not true liberalism – it had inbuilt mechanisms to protect itself. As we witnessed in the agriculture and cinematographic films negotiations of the Uruguay Round of the GATT, international trade seemed, at least to the communities concerned, to be impinging upon valued norms and raising concerns for 'societal security'. This is to say nothing of the threat to human life thundered quietly by developing countries at the prospect of 'liberalising' – an interesting use of the term – their patent systems for pharmaceutical products. The 'compromise of embedded liberalism' need compromise no longer.

Similarly, we no longer have to worry about a drying up of credit as we witnessed in the 1920s. The collapse of the financial 'regime' feared in the early 1970s has not come to pass, primarily because the assumptions of hegemonic stability that guided such fears have proved to be false. Perhaps we do have to worry that credit is too freely available and money can change hands almost instantaneously and in such large volumes that governments are forced to rescue their currencies from speculators. No longer do we worry about there not being a counter-cyclical flow of liquidity provided by a hegemonic state, but do we have to worry that too much power over currencies has been vested in the hands of private individuals? Perhaps the danger is not that we do not have enough money in the system, maybe we have too much. Maybe the system that can hide gigantic fraud on the scale of BCCI is a dangerous system. Perhaps that is one danger of too much liberalisation.

Perhaps the enemy is us; perhaps the next great challenge to order may be not a challenge from the outside by those excluded, but by the inability of the dominant idea of liberalism to sustain itself. Liberalism involves individualism – some of the perils of which have been pointed out by many conservatives – and on the international level it also implies a loss of control over the actions of individuals. As Wiener points out, the liberalisation of international finance, while welcome from an economic perspective, has empowered the criminals, from dealers in drugs and body parts to white-collar fraudsters, to launder their proceeds under the cloak of the activity in the international financial system. With liberalism has come a loss of state control, and a decreasing ability to enforce the standards of conduct on which the stability of the system ultimately is founded.

CHAPTER 9

Reconciling Regionalism and Multilateralism in the International Trading System

Rorden Wilkinson

The collapse of the Cold War, more than any other event in world politics, has left scholars and social commentators with a common dilemma: what shape will the new world order take? Many have discussed the possibility of the fragmentation of the international system into three dominant economic blocs. Others have suggested that this tripartite world order has already taken root, and is currently consolidating its form. The possibility of world order evolving into three highly regionalised blocs directly challenges the multilateralist projects of the latter half of the twentieth century. Multilateralism seeks as its primary goal the standardisation of certain political and economic practices across the wider international system, whereas regionalism operates on a much more geographically exclusive basis. The conflict between regionalism and multilateralism is not, however, a new feature of international discourse.

E.H. Carr, in discussing the ill-fated League of Nations, wrote that the globalist project of multilateralism was hindered from the very start by the complications that naturally arose when 'sixty known states differing widely in size, in power, and in political, economic and cultural development ... attempt [to] standardise international political' practices.[1] George Orwell, prompted by the jealous isolationism of the 1930s, wrote a fictitious account of the world divided into three macro-regions poised in a conflict perpetuated by institutionalised social control.[2] More recently, Samuel Huntington has predicted that with the end of the Cold War, and its accompanying ordering mechanisms, the international system will degenerate into 'seven or eight' competing, and ultimately conflicting, civilisations.[3]

In a parallel of Huntington's account, Lester Thurow has argued that the post-Cold War climate has facilitated the emergence of economics as the primary issue of international concern. Accompanying this elevation of 'low politics', he argues, is a consolidation of global commercial activities, based around three competing regions centred on the industrial powers of the US, Japan, and Europe. He characterises this tripartite world view as the 'head to head' conflict of the twenty-first century.[4]

What is interesting about these accounts, apart from the common assumption that conflict is an omni-present feature of international relations, is that there is little room for reconciliation between regionalism and multilateralism. Simply, the tendency to regionalise is perceived as greater than global collectivisation. Therefore, the former will necessarily triumph over the latter. There can be no middle ground, no accommodation.

Apocalysing aside, the recent proliferation of regional trading agreements has led to much debate. Some suggest that the multilateral framework of international trade regulation is threatened by regionalism. The consolidation of the European integration process, the apparent abandonment of multi-lateralism by the US in favour of a more regional role, and the 'Asianisation' of Asia are understood to illustrate this emerging threat. However, others strongly criticise this position, suggesting that the process of regionalisation acts in compliment to the wider multilateralist agenda. Nonetheless, what is clear is that regionalism is an important feature of the International Political Economy.[5]

The increase in contemporary regionalism has its roots in previous waves of regionalist activity. Immediately following the Second World War, Europe embarked on a number of regionalist projects in the belief that the welfare functions of its individual states were better served through such means. The first of these was the Organisation for European Economic Cooperation (OEEC). This, in turn, spawned the beginnings of the European integration process under the auspices of, first, the European Coal and Steel Community (ECSC), and then through the establishment of the European Atomic Energy Community (Euratom) and the European Economic Community (EEC). Europe also regionalised its security relations under the North Atlantic Treaty Organisation (NATO), and later through the Western European Union (WEU).

At the global level, the structure of international relations became highly regionalised by the ordering tendencies of the Cold War. The US and the Soviet Union embarked on an ideological conflict, and set about ordering global relations into two diametrically opposed series of alliances. The world divided, somewhat untidily, into East and West.

Regionalism re-emerged in the 1960s, in part, as a consequence of the consolidation of the European integration process. Other European countries attempted to aggregate their resources under the European Free Trade Agreement (EFTA). The developing world embarked on several, largely unsuccessful, attempts at collectivisation, primarily as a means of meeting the challenges of the post-colonial era. The most notable organisations here were the Latin American Integration Association (LAIA), the Andean Pact

(AP), the Central American Common Market (CACM), the Association of South East Asian Nations (ASEAN), the West African Economic Community (CEAO), and the Organisation for African Unity (OAU).

During the late 1960s and early 1970s another form of hemispheric regionalisation emerged. The general easing of Cold War tensions under *détente* uncovered a global divide that previously had been obscured by the severity of East–West tensions. This new hemispheric regionalisation differed from the macro-regionalism of the Cold War in one particular aspect: it was distinctly economic in nature. The world witnessed the partition of North and South; the separation of the industrial countries from their largely underdeveloped counterparts. This hemisphere regionalisation was reinforced by the construction of the Non-Aligned Movement (NAM), and the Group of 77 – a broad coalition of Southern states seeking delinkage from the dominance of Northern economic policies and military bipolarity. A key element in this delinkage was the development of micro-regionalist bodies. This led to the establishment of various organisations throughout the 1970s and 1980s. Organisations such as the Organisation of Petroleum Exporting Countries (OPEC), the Economic Community of West African States (ECOWAS), the Southern African Development Coordination Conference (SADCC), the Gulf Cooperation Council (GCC), and the South Asian Association for Regional Cooperation (SAARC) were formed in the hope of enjoying the benefits of unhindered geographic collectivisation. However, during the early years of the Reagan administration, the macro-structuralist tendencies of the Cold War again reasserted themselves. International relations once more became preoccupied with bipolarity.

Contemporary regionalism in the international trading system can largely be attributed to the existence of Article XXIV of the General Agreement on Tariffs and Trade (GATT). Under this article, contracting parties are permitted to establish customs unions and free-trade areas (FTAs) in the pursuit of accelerated welfare maximisation. It is the apparent effects of this clause that have prompted debate over the future shape of the world economic order. Some suggest that by enabling states to act in such a way a breakdown in the multilateral trading system will occur, while others argue that such regionalisation acts as a compliment to the globalist agenda. This is the dichotomy between pessimistic and optimistic regionalism.[6] This prompts the question: does regionalism undermine multilateralism, or does it enhance the achievement of globalist goals? It is because of this lack of consensus that this chapter attempts to assess the impact of economic regionalism on the multilateral trading system. It will be shown, hereafter, that although there is evidence to suggest that regionalism does threaten the international trading system, upon more careful examination this threat is without foundation.

Multilateralism, Regionalism, and the International Trading System

What is multilateralism? John Ruggie defines multilateralism as a particular type of institution which, through the set of rules it embodies, requires that inter-state relations are organised in accordance with certain generalised principles of conduct. These principles, he posits, are indivisibility and its corollary diffuse reciprocity.[7] The consequence of organising inter-state relations in accordance with these generalised principles is that multilateralism seeks to standardise certain political and economic practices across a group in the pursuit of a desired goal. As multilateralism is most commonly associated with the organisation of a large number of states throughout numerous geographic locations, this project can be described as globalism, though strictly speaking it is not truly global.[8]

The GATT, and its recent manifestation the World Trade Organisation (WTO), can be understood in these terms. The rules embodied by the WTO require that institutional activities are organised in accordance with the principle of most-favoured nation (MFN) in its unconditional form.[9] This is the economic interpretation of Ruggie's principle of indivisibility. As an institutional rule, the principle of MFN requires that 'any advantage, favour, privilege or immunity granted by any contracting party to any product originating in or destined for any other country shall be accorded immediately and unconditionally to the like product originating in or destined for the territories of all other contracting parties', except in those instances agreed otherwise.[10] Also embodied in this rule is the requirement that all trading concessions are made reciprocal.

Throughout the evolution of the GATT several other Agreements have been negotiated in an effort to expand the standardisation of liberal trading practices to areas other than conventional trade in goods. These are most prominently the General Agreement on Trade in Services (GATS), the Agreement on Trade-Related Aspects of Intellectual Property Rights (TRIPs), the Agreement on Trade-Related Investment Measures (TRIMs), and the four Plurilateral Agreements relating to Trade in Civil Aircraft, Government Procurement, Trade in International Dairy Products, and Bovine Meat.[11] More recently the WTO has successfully concluded the Agreement on Telecommunications.

Unlike multilateralism, regionalism is less easily defined. It refers to a diffuse group of arrangements, operating at a number of behavioural levels. Generally, regionalism is taken as the organisation of political and socio-economic relations on a geographically proximate basis. Such organisation commonly occurs at three levels: the micro-, sub-, and macro-level.[12] Regionalism, therefore, is a domestic, transnational, and international phenomenon.

This does not, however, provide us with a satisfactory definition of regionalism. Even in its statist form regionalism has many manifestations both political and economic.[13] Each exude different qualitative characteristics, though all, as Paul Taylor observes, enable the constituent parts to fulfil a particular function.[14] Hence regionalism is only homogeneous in that it enables a group of states to fulfil a specific function, otherwise it is qualitatively heterogeneous. By extension, then, and in the context of this chapter, regionalism is broadly interpreted as the spatial organisation of inter-state activities for the purpose of fulfilling a pre-determined function. By defining regionalism in this manner we can encompass a wide variety of statist arrangements. Yet, in the context of the multilateral trading system, we are specifically referring to economic collectives constructed for the purpose of liberalising internal trading environments in an attempt to maximise national welfare.

The Threat Posed by Regionalism

The threats posed by regionalism to the multilateral trading system can be placed into two broad categories reflecting (1) the contemporary nature of multilateralism, and (2) the specifics of regionalism. Let us deal first with the multilateral system itself. There are two issues at hand here. The first is to do with the existence of Article XXIV of the GATT; and the second concerns the relative stagnation of the globalist project. Article XXIV permits states seeking to aggregate their commercial activities to qualify their pro-curement of MFN. This is done by conveying preferential treatment to regional associates at a level over and above that provided to the wider membership (though the wider membership must still enjoy at least the same level of preferential treatment previously procured). To undertake such activity states must meet certain criteria. The Agreement requires that states: (1) acknowledge that the purpose of such arrangements is to facilitate trade liberalisation among the constituent parts of the group, rather than to increase trade restrictions in relations with other states or similar arrangements; (2) eliminate duties and other restrictions for 'substantially all trade' between the constituent countries; (3) ensure that the general incidence of tariffs and other barriers encountered by third parties does not exceed previous levels; and (4) set out a schedule for the construction and formalisation of the proposed FTA or customs union, and the application of the requirements of Article XXIV.[15]

Although Article XXIV requires that FTAs and customs unions operate in accordance with the wider agenda of trade liberalisation, it is commonly held that the ability to qualify MFN procurement in such a manner unjustifi-ably discriminates against third parties. Under MFN, each Member is required to provide all others with the same level of preferential treatment, unless otherwise collectively agreed.[16] This acts as a brake on the adoption of trade discrimination policies where one receives more preferential treatment than a third party. However, by aggregating commercial activities under the auspices of Article XXIV, states are able to act more favourably towards those members of the sub-group than they are obliged to do in relations with third parties. And, as extra-preferential treatment is enjoyed within the sub-group, the incentive to seek further liberalisation in the wider system is removed. Hence, it is argued, the encouragement of regional organisations serves only to facilitate, rather than militate, the adoption of discriminatory trading practices.

Secondly, the increase in regional activity can, in part, be attributed to the relative sloth of the globalist project. During the early years of the GATT trade liberalisation appeared to thrive. Up to the mid-1970s, progressive rounds of trade negotiations ensured a certain degree of economic success. Between 1950 and 1975 the merchandise trade of the industrial countries grew at an average rate of 8 per cent per annum, 4 per cent above gross national product (GNP).[17] During the Dillon Round over four thousand tariff concessions were exchanged. And, at the Kennedy Round, barriers to trade fell at an unprecedented rate, falling 35 per cent over a total of sixty thousand products, and 30 per cent over a range of industrial goods.[18]

However, by the mid-1970s the process of trade liberalisation had stagnated, and, to some extent, had been partially reversed by the imposition of non-tariff barriers. The growing scepticism that accompanied this stagnation was compounded by the GATT's apparent inadequacy in dealing with issues of agriculture and development.[19] Much of this inadequacy was put down to the hopelessness of coordinating policies among such a large number of con-tracting parties; the preoccupation, particularly by the US, with issues of sovereignty; and the relative decline in the bargaining power of less developed countries (LDCs). In response, states increasingly sought other means of satisfying their national welfare functions. For many, regionalism provided the answer.

The notion that national economic interests might be better served within the confines of a regional environment fed on a growing body of literature which asserted that, in international organisation, small is beautiful. This literature drew heavily on rationalist research programmes. Mancur Olson, for example, argued that effective large-scale cooperation was unrealistic in the absence of a 'special device'. Instead, he argued, the smaller the group the more beneficial the gains.[20] Other scholars increasingly advocated that states embark on strategic trading policies outside the multilateral environment designed to maximise national gain[21] – policies that were notoriously bilateral in nature. Simply, confidence in the multilateral system's ability to deliver the fruits of liberalisation had fallen.

Economic, historical, psychological, and socio-political factors reinforced the perception that state interests might be better served through regional-isation. States sharing common geographic spaces often encountered similar, though not always comparable, economic problems. Spatial co-habitation facilitated the historical development of commercial links. Furthermore, this co-habitation had, in some instances, nurtured a sense of familiarity which, in turn, fostered a sense of regional cooperation. Moreover, the transaction costs associated with conducting commercial activities on a regional basis were relatively less than those encountered globally. And common socio-political experiences linked geographically proximate countries.

Evidence, as well as reason, appears to support the threat posed by regionalism to the multilateralist agenda. Between 1947 and 1994, 108 regional agreements were acknowledged by the GATT. During the latter stages of the Uruguay Round, thirty-three notifications were made to the GATT Secretariat by states intending to establish new regional groupings under the provisions of Article XXIV.[22] Moreover, the regional programmes already under way in Europe, the Americas, and Asia appeared to be gathering steam. The European Union ratified the Maastricht Treaty. The progress made by the North American Free Trade Agreement (NAFTA) evolved into talks about a wider American Free Trade Agreement (AFTA); and East Asian regionalism gathered steam under ASEAN, the East Asia Economic Caucus (EAEC), and the Asia–Pacific Economic Cooperation forum (APEC).

The consolidation of regionalism appears to be borne out in the incidence of trade patterns within these geographic areas. According to WTO figures, the share of world merchandise trade conducted intra-regionally rose from 40.6 per cent in 1958 to 50.4 per cent in 1993.[23] Between 1990 and 1994 intra-regional trade increased in both Asia and North America.[24] Taken over a longer time-frame, between 1983 and 1993 intraregional trade grew in Europe by approximately five percentage points, in North America by two points, and in Asia by seven.[25] In 1994 Western Europe conducted a staggering 68.1 per cent of its trade intra-regionally, with Asia and North America registering figures of 48.5 and 36.9, respectively.[26]

This trend of proliferation and consolidation brought with it the fear that, like a contagious disease, regionalism would prove infectious. As Siegfried Schultz posits, regionalisation in one area can 'spill-over' into others. Those not included in the regional programmes of others may seek to establish competing economic collectives in an effort to increase bargaining power, or to offset the relative loss of markets due to trade diversion.[27]

In general, the main concern of regional pessimists is that as each region becomes increasingly preoccupied with events in its own back-yard, less emphasis will be placed on trading with other areas. Hence regionalism will take on a trade diverting, rather than a trade creating, characteristic. This will result in a *de facto* increase in international protectionism which will, in turn, undermine the multilateral system. It would, therefore, appear that the process of regionalisation challenges the very foundations of multilateralism. Or does it?

The Myth of Regionalism

Historically, regionalism, in its three-bloc manifestation, has not posed anything other than a *threat* to the multilateral trading system. Although much inter-state economic activity has been concentrated around the commercial activities of a few predominantly Northern states, the apocalyptic accounts of systemic fragmentation have yet to be realised by the structure of world order. Indeed, the process of multilateralism appears to be more robust than ever. The completion of the Uruguay Round and the establishment of the WTO has given the system new vigour. Moreover, the necessity of continuing such multilateralist projects is acknowledged by many.[28] This is the case with both the WTO and the United Nations.

The reasoning behind Article XXIV of the GATT is that, by enabling states to conduct accelerated regional liberalisation processes through collectivisation, spill-over will occur into the wider system. Hence the process of regionalisation is envisaged as facilitating, rather than deconstructing, multilateralism.[29] A bi-level process is at work here. Slower movements towards liberalisation take place at the multilateral level wherein states negotiate tariff and other barrier reductions and take on fewer binding disciplines, while at the regional level, the relatively greater intensity of shared interests among the sub-group, in conjunction with the logistical manageability of negotiating tariff and other reductions within a relatively smaller environment, ensures that at the micro-level liberalisation gains are achieved faster than would otherwise have been possible. Taken to its logical extreme, this process envisages an international system composed of several regional groupings, which are then better able, logistically and otherwise, to liberalise trade within the multilateral environment.

Ultimately, regionalism, it is argued, can act as a model for multilateralism. Achievements made at the regional level can, in time, be applied to the system as a whole. Therefore, the proliferation of regional groupings is perceived as a welcome feature of the International Political Economy, that is, if one accepts that the universalisation of liberal economic doctrines is a desirable one in the first place. Regionalisation does, however, pose some pertinent questions as to the affect that such a process may have on the state as the political unit of organisation.

The logic of collectivisation can be carried over into the negotiating patterns of states within the wider multilateral framework. During the Uruguay Round negotiations, the formation of regional, as well as other, linkages between states enabled many to propose, and extract, concessions that otherwise would have been unattainable. The negotiating power of the Cairns Group, and the construction of NAFTA as a political lever by the US *vis-à-vis* the EU, are two cases in point. Negotiations were conducted in, what Michael Hart characterises as, a 'multilateralised' manner.[30] Parties, or groups of parties, negotiated bilaterally, and then, in accordance with the principle of most-favoured nation, conveyed the results to the membership at large. This manner of negotiations was designed to reduce what Bruce Bueno de Mesquita characterises as the 'unfairness and unpredictability' of multilateral negotiations.[31] Logistically speaking, small numbers of participants are better able to conduct satisfactory negotiations than large numbers of competing parties.[32] By extension, then, the formation of regional and other alliances serves to contract artificially the number of negotiating participants. It logically follows that by engaging in such activity, smaller, less able, countries are better placed to negotiate relevant concessions by aggregating their negotiating power, especially in dealing with relatively more powerful counterparts.

The emergence of fragmentary tendencies can also be called into question by examining the particular *kind* of regionalism under way in the areas in question. Most certainly the consolidation of existing regional organisations has occurred, as has the proliferation of such groupings. However, there has also been a proliferation of regionalist projects which overlap the traditional areas of regionalisation. For example, the development of the APEC seeks to establish an economically beneficial collective centred around the Pacific Ocean that includes the countries of North and South America, the Newly Industrialised Countries (NICs) of South East Asia, Japan, New Zealand and Australia. Mention has also been made of the possibilities of establishing a Transatlantic Free Trade Area (TAFTA) linking the industrial powers of North America with Europe, with, perhaps, Latin American and Africa.[33] Under the auspices of Lomé IV, Europe has committed itself to the continuation of its relationship with the African, Caribbean and Pacific (ACP) states, and a number of proposals have emerged seeking to establish a pan-American arrangement.

What is more, regional groupings also demonstrate various levels of cohesiveness, and, therefore, degrees of collective activity. While it may be the case that the economic collectivisation of Europe paved the way for further social and political standardisation within the sub-group, it does not necessarily follow that similar consolidation will occur in other regional organisations. Furthermore, the integration processes under way in Europe have been relatively successful. There is no evidence to suggest that similar success will occur if, say, the Americas were to undertake a comparable project.

This can be illustrated by examining the regionalist projects in these areas. The Member states of the European Union, for example, have applied a common external tariff in commercial activities with non-Members. Moreover, 'Project 1992', the date agreed as the target for the consolidation of the Single European Act (SEA), has involved the liberalising of service markets, eradicating discrimination in government procurement, freeing up capital markets, and derestricting labour movements within Europe.[34] This regionalism is qualitatively different from the collectivisation of other areas. NAFTA and the Asian Free Trade Association (AFTA) merely entailed that the

Member countries have lower tariff barriers on particular goods and services and undertake some liberalisation of capital movements. Neither arrangement required the removal of national tariff structures in commercial dealings with third parties.[35] Furthermore, NAFTA was constructed as an agreement between three states wherein the sovereignty of each was zealously preserved, whereas the framework of the EU lends itself much more favourably towards supra-nationality.[36]

The reasons behind the regionalisation of particular geographic areas, when examined in further detail, suggests that regionalism is rather a means for dealing with specific and/or common problems, than a method of introversion. Europe's concentration on its integration process, rather than a feature of a general desire to establish regional autarky, is a function of the need to address the problems posed by integration. Much of Europe's energy during the early years was directed inwardly as a means of rebuilding after the Second World War, and more recently attention, particularly by Germany, has been directed at the problems posed by reunification and the collapse of the communist system in Eastern Europe. Indeed, by concentrating on the problems of the East, European actions can be interpreted as building bridges between two formally opposed regions. Similarly, the Organisation for African Unity (OAU) has sought to foster a pan-Africanism aimed at tackling specifically African problems. It has not sought introversion, or systemic delinkage.

Paul Bowles and Brian Maclean suggest that further error can be found in the three-bloc thesis by examining the manner in which statistical data is employed. Bowles and Maclean take particular issue with the use of intra-regional trade flows as evidence of economic regionalisation in East Asia.[37] They demonstrate that while increases in intra-regional trade flows may be indicative of the increasing importance of an economic area, in East Asia at least, much of this increase in trade can be attributed to national economic growth, rather than bloc consolidation. Intra-regional trade figures naturally increase as the units involved themselves grow and expand. Hence the growth of intra-regional trade, in this case, is more relative than absolute.

Bowles and Maclean suggest that the accurate predication of an emerging tripartite global system is impossible when simply observing aggregate trade flows.[38] This, in East Asia, is for three main reasons. First, aggregate trade data for the 1980s was artificially high as a result of the high importation function of 'Reaganomics'. Hence the subsequent decline in inter-regional trade between North America and East Asia must be viewed with this in mind. Secondly, capital flows, particularly foreign direct investment (FDI), are important indicators of movements towards bloc formation. These have clearly had little place in the calculations of the regional pessimists. And thirdly, bloc formation itself is undertaken as a response to a number of internal and external factors. These factors cannot be accounted for by trade flow data alone.

It is worth taking up Bowles and Maclean's second point as it is useful for our purposes. They observe that in recent years much of Japan's FDI has been directed towards the establishment of productive units in Europe and North America. This has, by extension, obscured the level of Japanese activity within these areas. While it may be that the incidence of Japanese trade with both Europe and the United States has fallen over the last decade, the level of Japanese production within these areas has actually increased. Therefore, the relatively high levels of FDI flowing to these areas, and the economic strategy of constructing settler production units, has had a *trade replacing affect*, as opposed to the *trade diverting* function that regionalism, in its pessimistic form, is supposed to generate. In other words, the increase in interregional FDI has offset the fall in trade between these areas. It does not necessarily indicate a consolidation of regionalist activity.

The incidence of FDI occurring between the developed regions centred around North America, Europe and East Asia has increased markedly of late. According to a 1995 *World Investment Report* nearly two-thirds of all FDI occurred between the developed world. In general Western Europe exported $106.5 billion worth of FDI in 1994, US FDI totalled $46 billion, and Japanese overseas investment amounted to $18 billion in the same period.[39]

The notion that FDI plays an important role in militating the pessimistic effects of regionalism leads naturally into discussions about the role of globalisation in the global political economy. Arguments about the nature of the effects of regionalism aside, we have noted that it is a tendency at work in international economic relations. In addition, it is commonly accepted that social behaviour is currently subjected to a process of globalisation. Simply defined, globalisation is the 'social process in which the constraints of geography on social [economic, political] and cultural arrangements recede and in which people become increasingly aware that they are receding'.[40] Globalisation should not, however, be confused with globalism as employed herein. Globalism is the statist project of multilateralism, which seeks the standardisation of certain practices across a group. Globalisation is, on the other hand, a multi-level process.

Schultz argues that globalisation actually reinforces multilateralism by increasing calls for multilateral solutions to common problems.[41] Globalisation, though more dense in particular regions, operates transnationally. Goods are exported to markets to satisfy demand, the geography of production is increasingly diffuse, capital is exported on a global scale, and the phenomenal development of communications networks has reduced drastically the transaction costs normally associated with operating 'internationally'. In order to assist this process wider-ranging solutions than those offered by regionalism are required. For example, the failure to de-restrict investment flows on a global basis will, it is commonly assumed, discriminate against those markets that remain relatively more protected. It is Schultz's contention, then, that the underlying process of globalisation acts as a natural counter to the fragmentation tendencies of regionalism.

The WTO recently conducted a study into the effects of regionalism on the post-war international system. The Organisation's general conclusion was that there was no evidence to substantiate the fragmentation thesis. First, the report noted that, with the exception of the European Union, few regional arrangements have attempted to regulate trade in agriculture and services, or to specify disciplines pertaining to intellectual property or investment. Rather, regional arrangements have tended to seek the liberalisation of trade in goods, and usually only certain goods. This is in direct contrast to the achievements of the Uruguay Round which has ensured that these areas are now subjected to multilateral standardisation.[42] Hence the regionalisation of commercial relations has been only partial. Because of this, the report argues, the multilateral system has gone further than the majority of regional organisations in standardising certain practices, and has thus secured its future.

Secondly, the report concluded that the coexistence of regional integration agreements and the wider multilateral framework had been satisfactory, if not 'broadly positive'. However, there were a number of concerns raised. In particular the report highlighted that many contemporary interpretations of paragraph 8 of Article XXIV of the GATT, requiring that FTAs and customs unions affect 'substantially all' the trade between the constituent parties, were unsatisfactory.[43] Furthermore, some discrepancies were noted in the level of trade barriers operated with regard to third parties after the establishment of regional arrangements.[44]

Reconciling Regionalism and Multilateralism: Some Concluding Comments

This chapter has attempted to reconcile two apparently contradictory tendencies affecting the international trading system: the fragmentation affects of regionalism and the globalist project of multilateralism. At their root both regionalism and multilateralism share the same objective, the liberalisation of a particular trading environment through the standardisation of certain practices. Where they differ is in the relative size of their operational space. Regionalism takes as its spatial boundaries a particular geographic area, more often that not based on continental lines, while multilateralism perceives global space in its entirety as the arena within which its project can be undertaken. These two practices have, however, been perceived in markedly different ways in the international trading system.

We have seen that a number of factors cast doubt on the notion that the multilateral trading system is evolving into a tripartite order. We noted that historically regionalism has failed to re-order the international trading system to any significant degree. Furthermore, Article XXIV of the GATT can act in complement to the multilateral system. Regionalism can also be a positive means of conducting trade negotiations. States, by the action of collectivising, can gain micro-political advantages within the macro-political environment.

Indeed, much of this regionalist proliferation can be attributed to increased political activity within the broader multilateral framework. This regionalisation has the additional benefit of making negotiations logistically more manageable, as it artificially reduces the number of participants.

Doubts are also raised about the three-bloc thesis when examining the nature of contemporary regionalism. We have observed that regionalism is not an homogeneous process. Each form differs by degree and, as a consequence, the threat posed by this type of international organisation is relatively less than pessimists like Thurow suppose. And, as Bowles and Maclean demonstrate, there are sufficient problems with the value of the data employed by the pessimists. By extension, then, regionalism does not threaten the multilateral trading system. Indeed, in certain instances it acts in compliment.

Although it has been shown here that regionalism does not necessarily pose a threat to the multilateral trading system, it does create some problems for certain states. While the ability of states to aggregate their negotiating strengths by collectivising is of value, it does not ensure that all states will benefit from engaging in such activity. The logic of collectivisation, when applied to trade negotiations, presupposes that each state has something desirable to offer for exchange. This does not ensure that each state will be able to negotiate concessions that are of particular benefit. Under the auspices of 'multilateralised' negotiations, the preoccupation with collectivisation runs the risk of marginalising the negotiation agendas of less developed countries. This is because, although collectivisation makes smaller actors relatively more able at the multilateral level, it does not stop middle-ranking powers from exercising disproportionate influence within these collectives, at the expense of LDCs. Indeed, the marginalisation of less able states is a very real danger within regional arrangements. What is more, policies adopted to stop this happening suggest that a degree of relative homogeneity must exist within an arrangement to ensure the relative benefit of all, unless some kind of redistributive mechanism, other than those already embodied by such arrangements, is employed.

Secondly, much of the concern raised by regionalism has been caused by increases in activity among members of the developed world. Largely it has not affected the developing world. Although it is possible to demonstrate that Latin America and the less developed areas of South East Asia are increasingly being brought into the arena of international economic activity on the backs of their more powerful neighbours (and even these countries are struggling), the majority of the developing world is still marginalised in the international trading system. While there may not be sufficient evidence to substantiate the fragmentation of the international system into three predominant blocs, there is sufficient evidence to suggest that a wider, more familiar hemispheric regionalism is taking place. For example, in 1994 developing countries as a whole attracted only 37 per cent of all FDI, of which just two per cent went to the least developed.[45] The value of goods imported into Europe, Japan, and the United States from the least developed countries fell between 1990 and 1994, with only Japan increasing the value of goods exported to these countries over the same period. And trade within and between Asia, Europe and North America accounted for over 80 per cent of all trade in merchandise in 1994.[46] Indeed, the worsening situation of many Southern countries facilitated the adoption of a Plan of Action for Least-Developed Countries at the WTO's 1996 Singapore Ministerial Meeting.[47]

It would appear, then, that inter-regional activity between these three areas of the North is at the expense of inter-regional activity with the South. Ironically, this hemispheric regionalisation does not figure in the arguments of the regional pessimists. They appear preoccupied with the threat posed to the multilateral trading system as defined by its most significant constituent members, and not the hemispheric re-emergence of North and South.

CHAPTER 10

Foreign Direct Investment: the Globalisation of Ideology and Law and the Regionalisation of Politics

Jarrod Wiener and John Kennair

A New World Order for foreign direct investment (FDI) emerged after the collapse of communism as a viable alternative for development. According to the United Nations Centre for Trade and Development (UNCTAD), economic and political liberalisation 'is the most important policy trend of the 1990s as part of broad-based efforts to attract foreign investors'.[1] During the Cold War, there were options: developing countries could choose to open their markets and permit foreign companies to operate on their territories, or they could choose the path of autonomous development by operating national industries. In the 1960s and 1970s in particular, many developing countries chose the latter option. In fact, many developing states were hostile to multinational corporations (MNCs) to the extent that many of them expropriated foreign-owned assets and expelled MNCs from their territories. The New World Order for FDI is characterised by an overwhelming acceptance of neo-liberal ideas of development, which involve liberalisation, privatisation, and integration into the international economy. Indeed, some might suggest that there are no longer alternatives: all states are attuned to the benefits of FDI, and are in competition with each other to attract it.

But at the end of the millennium, the new order for FDI is also characterised by a polarisation of economic activity in regional zones: most FDI remains in the 'triad' of Europe, North America, and East Asia. A strategy of developing states is to court politically these economic zones, and to establish bilateral investment treaties (BITs) and bilateral free trade agreements (FTAs) with them as a way to 'get in on the act'. This is illustrated here in the context of Chile's economic relations with the states of the North

American Free Trade Agreement (NAFTA), and with Canada in particular. It is most likely that what this millennium will hand to the next as regards the politics of foreign direct investment is a platform for the creation of ever larger investment zones through gradual expansion.

Of Political Ironies

The strategy for autonomous development was most attractive in the 1970s. In that decade, the most less developed countries (LDCs) embarked on projects for national ownership of production, evidenced by the high number of expropriations of foreign assets: 423 cases in total, with 85 cases in 1975 alone.[2] The practice of nationalisation, and the strategy for autonomous development that it served, were informed by a particular view of the international economy, and of the nature of multinational corporations within it. Generally speaking, that view was that MNCs were agents of exploitation of the northern capitalist states. They were thought to exploit workers in developing countries through low wages and poor working conditions, to exploit the environment through irresponsible mining and waste disposal techniques, and to exploit the natural resources of developing countries by extracting profits that were funnelled to their First World headquarters. In the words of Stephen Hymer, MNCs assisted the capitalist class to 'centralise control by imposing an hierarchical system'.[3]

The idea that the structure of the liberal international economy was inherently inequitable had sufficient currency in the 1960s and 1970s to inform the creation of a Third World bloc to rally against global liberalism. By the time of the Fifteenth General Assembly in 1960, 60 per cent of UN members were developing states. In 1961, the General Assembly declared the 1960s as the first United Nations Development Decade,[4] and by 1964, the General Assembly convened the United Nations Conference on Trade and Development (UNCTAD), at which the Group of 77 (G77) was formed. The G77 sought to legitimate the programme of developing countries to gain legal authority over economic development as a right, which, in the words of Lawrence S. Finkelstein, constituted nothing less than an attempt at 'value allocation' through international law.[5] The idea that Third World states should own the factors of production located on their territories gave expression to two important declarations that they were able to pass in the General Assembly by virtue of their numerical majority. The first was the principle of permanent sovereignty over natural resources (1962) which stated that states enjoy 'the inalienable right freely to dispose of their natural wealth and resources in accordance with their national interests'.[6] E. Jiménez de Aréchaga observed that, 'the description of this sovereignty as permanent signifies that the territorial state can never lose its legal capacity to change the destination or the method of exploitation of those resources, whatever arrangements have been made for their exploitation and administration'.[7]

The second Resolution was passed in 1974 in the context of the Declaration and Program of Action on the Establishment of a New International Economic Order (NIEO). The Charter of Economic Rights and Duties of States extended this principle of sovereignty such that, 'every state shall freely exercise permanent sovereignty ... to regulate and exercise authority over foreign investments within its national jurisdiction'.[8] The concept of sovereignty over economic activity was thus taken to relate to the whole of the economy, including production facilities and other factors of production and administration, and not simply limited to natural resources. The expropriations of foreign assets were justified, according to many Third World states, by virtue of the fact that their sovereignty was permanent; beneficial ownership of economic resources could be revoked by the state.

In practice, strategies for autonomous development rarely succeeded to generate growth, and a number of factors showed them to be misguided. Less developed countries that had pursued such strategies very soon found that nationalised industries suffered from a lack of managerial expertise, a lack of research, development and innovation, and a lack of markets since most upstream marketing continued to be controlled by the First World corporations. A number of other factors pressured LDCs to accept liberalisation, privatisation, and a greater interaction with the world economy. Among these was the debt crisis of the 1980s, which forced most LDCs to seek rescheduling of their debts, and in the process to accept liberalisation as part of the conditionality and structural adjustment programmes of the international financial institutions. Another factor was the demonstration effect of the rapid industrialisation of the newly industrialising countries (NICs), such as Malaysia, Singapore and South Korea, as a function of market-driven development which highlighted the benefits of greater interaction with MNCs. The NICs had attracted 90 per cent of FDI to developing countries,[9] and as a result, they benefited from transfers of technology, training, management and international marketing skills, increased levels of employment, and higher wages relative to those offered by national industries.[10] Finally, an important force for market opening was the end of the Soviet Union as the bastion of the socialist model of development and an alternative 'way forward'.[11] These factors, among others, contributed to an 'all change' in LDCs' musings about alternatives to the liberal capitalist model of development, and in their attitudes towards foreign direct investment.

The failure of alternatives, coupled with the pressures for marketisation, contributed to a change in both practice and ideas. There were only fourteen cases of expropriation between 1980 and 1987, and none at all between 1987 and 1992.[12] The practice of expropriation vanished along with the demise of the radical critiques of the world economy. In the 1970s, the Dependistas had lamented the 'political irony' that the exploitative capitalist system perpetuated an inequitable distribution of wealth whereby the majority of the world's population lived in poverty, while the minority controlled most of the world's resources.[13] This, sadly, is still the case, as 80 per cent of global GDP continues to be appropriated by twenty-four high-income countries, while 55 per cent of the world's population share 5 per cent.[14] But the greatest political irony of the 1990s is the realisation that the ideas about how to remedy this were fundamentally wrong. The fashionable cure for underdevelopment at the end of the millennium is 'more of the disease' – greater interaction with the capitalist system and more FDI. The irony is that most LDCs are privatising state-owned industries, and are actively attempting to encourage FDI. As Michael Minor noted, 'not only has expropriation activity largely ended, but in some countries it is being reversed, in very literal terms by reversion to the former owners'.[15] Along with this change in practice, the ideas that informed programmes for autonomous development[16] were, by the early 1990s, 'due for the junkyard', in the words of Susan Strange and John Stopford.[17]

By the early 1990s, MNCs were very much 'back in fashion'.[18] Nowhere was this more conspicuous than in Eastern Europe when the former communist states began to liberalise and to call for the participation of foreign firms in privatised industries, particularly in Russia,[19] Ukraine,[20] and more spectacularly in Hungary, the Czech Republic, and Poland.[21] Perhaps nowhere was the political irony more apparent than in the attempts of the former radicals of the international economy, such as Vietnam,[22] North Korea,[23] Cuba,[24] and Iran,[25] to attract FDI. On the whole, there were no less than 206 liberalising policy changes in twenty-six developing countries between 1977 and 1987.[26] UNCTAD, the forum which had given rise to the demands for an NIEO and which had 'spent decades tut-tutting about these firms and drawing up codes of conduct to control them, now spends much of its time advising countries how best to seduce them'.[27]

States seeking to import foreign capital increasingly are promising greater incentives to attract foreign investors. Among these are tax shelters for defined periods; reduced restrictions on the repatriation of capital and profits; the lessening of limitations on the share of ownership of enterprises, including the ownership of privatised state industries; the streamlining of bureaucratic procedures, such as easing the requirement for licences and permits; and the lessening of restrictions on foreign firms' access to credit. Many states with a history of hostility towards FDI are providing particular assurances as to the continued integrity of foreign investment.

Until the 1980s, among the most important incentives to an MNC to make an investment were access to natural resources, access to a large market, and relatively cheap labour. However, these factors are now insufficient, particularly since much production is technologically advanced. An educated and skilled workforce and reliable communications networks are equally important. However, political factors are at least as important as economic incentives. Political stability and favourable regulatory regimes are crucial determinants to an MNC's decision about an investment location.[28] As Strange and Stopford observed, it is crucial for states to provide a rule of law that not only 'appears reasonably stable', but one that is not plagued by frequent, arbitrary alteration.[29] Indeed, as Minor reported, in contrast to the high level of expropriations that took place in the 1970s, 'many developing countries now protect foreign direct investors from expropriation'.[30] At present, many states are according MNCs some form of guarantee against the unilateral change in the terms of their investment, including assurances that they will not be divested of their equity. States have enacted municipal legislation to 'outlaw' expropriations; have agreed to specific contractual provisions with MNCs, known as 'stabilisation clauses'; and have committed, at the inter-state level, to bilateral investment treaties (BITs), also known as investment promotion and protection agreements (IPPAs). As the following section will show, BITs are a superior tool for attracting MNCs in terms of the legal assurance that they provide.

The Relative Superiority of BITs as a Legal Assurance

It should be noted at the outset that the right of a state to expropriate foreign-owned assets on its territory is a settled norm in international law. It is a prerogative of a sovereign state to exercise its power of eminent domain to expropriate property within its jurisdiction so long as this act is for a public purpose, is not discriminatory, and is accompanied by compensation.[31] The main issue raised by state promises not to expropriate is whether a state can be bound by its own commitment to restrict this sovereign right.

Policy statements, either oral or in the form of Proclamations, often seek to assure the foreign investor of a stable political and legislative climate. These can range from outlining the state's intent to privatise certain industries, to more specific statements that the state promises to refrain from ex-propriation. An example of the latter can be found in the Proclamation of the State of Eritrea. As one of the most recent states to have attained formally its independence (on 24 May 1993), Eritrea adopted in August 1994 an 'Investment Proclamation' that provides that foreign investments 'shall not be nationalised or confiscated'.[32] This would appear to represent a promise on the part of the State of Eritrea to refrain from exercising its sovereign powers of eminent domain.

However, such general promises relate to an unspecified contract, at an undetermined time in the future. It is recognised in positive law that such a promise cannot have legal effect upon any eventual contract. However, it would hardly be reasonable to presume that a state is justified in confiscating the equity of an investor who had committed a substantial amount of capital on the territory of that state if the investment had been made due solely to the fact that the investor had accepted this promise in good faith. The principle of estoppel − defined as 'a rule preventing states from denying assertions which they have made and which are relied on by others'[33] −

requires the performance of a promise, which is accepted in international law. However, there is the question of whether there is an estoppel when the representation relates to an intention rather than a fact, as in the application of the concept to the law of evidence, for example. Yet, as Schwarzenberger observed, good faith in commerce has a 'long pedigree' as 'the word and honour of princes were the pledges on which foreign merchants had to rely'.[34] The *Eastern Greenland Case* demonstrated that a promise can have legal effect, although, importantly, only if the promise is made by a competent authority, and is specific to a particular circumstance.[35] The International Court of Justice held that good faith constitutes 'one of the basic principles governing the creation and performance of legal obligations *whatever their source*'.[36] And, paragraph I of the UN Resolution on Permanent Sovereignty over Natural Resources reaffirmed that agreements shall be respected in 'good faith'.[37] Therefore, general policy statements which provide a promise against future nationalisation measures do not have legal effect, by virtue of their general nature. However, a specific promise could be a mitigating factor in determining the amount of compensation awarded in the event of a nationalisation.

Of greater formality than general statements of policy are municipal foreign investment laws (FIL). A number of states have adopted FILs to appear more attractive to foreign investors. Such laws provide special dispensations from the payment of tax; guarantee freer repatriation of profits; reduce or eliminate the need for permits, such as for the handling of foreign exchange; liberalise domestic-ownership requirements; reduce or eliminate the minimum capital investment requirement; and guarantee indemnification for expropriation.

It is interesting that 'almost all of the developing countries that have enacted foreign investment laws since 1979 have recognised a state responsibility ... not to expropriate foreign-owned assets except with adequate compensation'.[38] This is significant in light of the contention that had existed between developing and developed countries over the issue of compensation. The developed states have long argued for a formula elaborated by US Secretary of State Cordell Hull in a Memorandum to the Mexican government in 1938 for compensation to be 'prompt, adequate and effective', where 'prompt' means without delay, 'adequate' means of fair market value before the act of expropriation became known, and where 'effective' relates to payment in a freely convertible currency. The LDCs had maintained that compensation must be based on their ability to pay, taking into account the profits already made by the investor.[39] As an example of the acceptance of the Hull formula, the 'Law on Foreign Investments in Russia' is interesting.[40] Chapter 2, Article 7 stipulates that 'foreign investments ... are not subject to nationalisation and may not be requisitioned or confiscated except by the legislative acts in the extraordinary events when such measures are taken in the public interest'. In the event of a nationalisation, the foreign investor is entitled to 'the payment of swift, adequate, and efficient compensation ... including lost profits' in a convertible currency. Clearly, this is a reaffirmation of customary state practice regarding expropriation, and the guarantee of compensation not only restates in spirit the Hull formula, but also provides for the added protection against lost profits.

The FIL of Vietnam goes further, as it guarantees outright that 'enterprises with foreign investment capital shall not be nationalised'.[41] Such guarantees can be appealing to the foreign investor, but what is the extent of their legal force? The predominant view of scholars appears to be that the protection accorded is minimal. In the particular cases of Russia and Vietnam, the promises would not be iron-clad due, prima facie, to the fact that the FILs of both states provide for national treatment, as per Article 6 and Article 101, respectively.[42] Article 6 of the Russian investment law states that '[T]he legal regime applicable to foreign investments ... may not be less beneficial than the regime applicable to the property, property rights and investment activity or juridical entities and citizens of the RSFSR'.[43] The national standard of treatment has long been the preferred standard of capital-importing states, which holds that investments are purely an internal matter, and that foreign investors should be treated in a manner not less favourable than that accorded to nationals. As such, the investor is subject to national laws, as well as any changes thereof, and to the settlement of disputes within national courts.[44]

Indeed, it is a settled norm that a state can amend or annul any of its laws simply by passing another. For Minor, this means that 'municipal legislation will not necessarily prevent expropriation'.[45] De Lupis agreed that, a 'nation is always free to amend [its laws] even if foreign investors would suffer'.[46] Therefore, by an act of eminent domain, the promises made to foreign investors can be negated. There *could* be exceptions to this, namely if the investment agreement is internationalised, that is not governed by the municipal law of the state, and if it is held to be a contract in private, rather than public law.

This issue arises most clearly in the context of the 'stabilisation clause'. Due to the ability of a state to change its legislation, there have been included in a number of investment agreements clauses to guard against changes in tax laws and other elements of fiscal policy, which can amount to 'creeping expropriation'. Stabilisation clauses can be classified conceptually in terms of 'freezing clauses',[47] which are intended to provide a guarantee that certain national laws will remain the same as at the date of the entry into force of the agreement for a defined period; 'enclave clauses', which provide for the laws to be grandfathered notwithstanding any subsequent changes to them; and 'intangibility clauses', which prevent the exercise by a state of its sovereign powers to alter unilaterally an investment agreement, including expropriation, by providing that any change must be subject to mutual consent.[48] Such stabilisation clauses raise mainly the issue of whether such promises take precedence over sovereign powers. This, in turn, raises the question of (1) the nature of the investment agreement; and (2) the force of United Nations General Assembly resolutions asserting the permanence of such sovereignty.

These stabilisation clauses are by no means new; they featured in the investment contracts of Middle Eastern states with oil companies in the 1950s. The arbitral awards of the ensuing nationalisations, famously known as the 'hot oil cases', were the first to consider in depth the legal status of the stabilisation clause. The Texaco Concession Agreement with the Lybian Arab Republic contained numerous stabilisation clauses. One enclave clause read: 'The concession shall be interpreted during the period of its effectiveness in accordance with the provisions of the Petroleum Law and the Regulations issue thereunder at the time of the grant of the concession, and any amendments or cancellation of these Regulations shall not apply to the contractual rights of the Company except with its consent'.[49] In other words, the laws that prevailed at the time that the contract was consummated were 'grandfathered'; they would prevail notwithstanding any subsequent alteration in the law of Libya. Another, intangibility clause, in the Texaco Concession provided that: 'The contractual rights expressly created by this concession shall not be altered except by mutual consent of the parties'.[50]

However, it is important to recognise that such stabilisation clauses will *only* have legal effect *if* the nature of the contract between the state and the foreign investor is deemed to be private in nature, rather than public. There is a view that an investment agreement is a private law contract. In the *Liamco* case, Arbitrator Mahmassani stated that although a concession has both a public and private law character, 'it retains a predominant contractual nature ... and [is] governed by the principles of the private law of contracts'.[51] He continued that the stabilisation clause renders the two parties equal in status with respect to the contract, as it serves to 'strengthen this contractual character in Liamco's and similar other concessions agreements as a precaution against the fact that one of the parties is a state'.[52] Professor Dupuy, Arbitrator in the case of *Texaco*, also held that the stabilisation clause rendered the investment agreement the character of a private law contract. He stated that, 'the state intended to contract on a footing of strict equality with its partner ... if the clause were not in the contract, one would have to presume that the state had intended to conserve intact, in respect of its contracting partner, the full and free exercise of its privileges and usual powers'.[53] This was also the position taken by Arbitrators Dupuy and Rouhani in *AGIP Spa*. They argued that it is 'recognised by positive international law that by entering into an international agreement with a private person the state exercises a sovereign power, seeing that its consent is freely given'.[54]

This view holds that the act of a state binding itself in an agreement is an expression of sovereignty; that is, it is the state's sovereign will to be bound and to abnegate its other rights as a sovereign. This view is contentious. It cannot be denied that states can subrogate mutually their sovereignty in an international treaty, and that this must be respected under the maxim of *pacta sunt servanda.* The *Aramco* and *Liamco* arbitrations argued that the principle *pacta sunt servanda* applies, in the words of Mahmassani, to 'ordinary contracts and concession agreements'.[55] Mahmassani went so far as to state that 'the sovereign right to nationalisation is limited by the respect due for contractual rights', and cited Professor Lapradelle's statement that 'nationalisation, as a unilateral act of sovereignty, shall respect validly concluded agreements, whether by treaty or contract'.

However, the principle *pacta sunt servanda* is not without qualification, as Mahmassani seemed to imply, as it can be limited by the principle of *conventio omnis intellegitur rebus sic stantibus,* which provides that a treaty is binding so long as the circumstances surrounding it do not alter fundamentally.[56] If the principle were as sacrosanct as Mahmassani suggests, the International Monetary Fund (IMF) would still be operating on a gold standard. More pertinent, perhaps, is that the principle *pacta sunt servanda* cannot take precedence over the public interest. Maniruzzaman concluded after an analysis of major representative legal systems that the principle 'is limited ... especially in the domain of public or state contracts ... the state party to a public contract has exceptional prerogative powers to vary or even terminate the contract for the public interest, subject only to the duty to pay compensation'.[57]

More importantly, to assert that a state is so bound is tantamount to elevating a juridical person, namely the MNC, to the level of statehood, and the investment agreement to the status of a treaty. And, there is convincing support for the argument that a state and a private investor cannot be held to be equal. For, notwithstanding the contractual elements of the relationship – that there is a negotiated agreement and a meeting of wills – the important element of motive must be taken into account. The state acts in the public interest, whereas the investor acts only to serve a profit-motivated interest. This, according to Maniruzzaman, is sufficient to render the contract a public law character. He stated: 'In the blend of public and private law concepts and rules applicable to economic development agreements, the public law rules will prevail over the private law ones, in case any conflict arises between them, because of the predominance of the public interest aspects of those agreements.'[58]

Thus, where there is an investment agreement between a state and a foreign investor, the contract will be of a public law nature, rather than of private law. And, notwithstanding the principle to respect contracts in good faith, the state will retain prerogatives to alter the contract in the public interest, notwithstanding any number of stabilisation clauses that provide for the contrary.[59] These prerogatives have been reinforced by the UN General Assembly resolutions noted above, particularly that of Permanent Sovereignty over Natural Resources. The opinion of jurists seems to be mixed as to the legal force of this particular principle. In the *Aminoil* case, the arbitral tribunal found that a state could bind itself to refrain from expropriation regardless of the principle of permanent sovereignty.[60] However, in the *Texaco* case, the

arbitrator held, 'in respect of the international law of contracts, a nationalisation cannot prevail over an internationalised contract, containing stabilisation
clauses'.[61] And, interestingly, in the *Liamco* case, where the stabilisation clause
under consideration was expressed in precisely the same terms as in that of
Texaco, Mahmassani held that it was well within the right of Libya to terminate
the investment agreement, subject to compensation, notwithstanding the
stabilisation clause.[62]

The reason for this discrepancy in view lies in the legal force that is
accorded to the General Assembly resolutions in general. Some contend that
these do not represent the force of law.[63] Dupuy, in the *Texaco* arbitration,
held that the General Assembly resolutions are of 'no binding force',[64] and
Mahmassani in *Liamco* argued that they 'cannot be invoked as a source of
international law'.[65] The argument put forward is that, at best, the General
Assembly can create 'soft law', which has only *de lege ferenda* effect, and that
only states that have accepted them can be bound by them. This argument
seems to be confirmed by Article 38 of the Statute of the International
Court of Justice, in that treaties and customs are the main sources of
international law.

However, there are many views to the contrary. First, even accepting the
objection that General Assembly resolutions are binding only on those who
assent to them, it is debateable whether a private investor can be held to be
a 'persistent objector' of the resolutions of an inter-*state* organisation. Second,
as argued by Maurice Mendelsen, some General Assembly resolutions are, in
fact, binding.[66] Moreover, as stated by the UN Secretary-General in 1971:
'the principle of national sovereignty over natural resources has been
proclaimed so frequently and so solemnly that it has by now acquired the
weight of a Charter principle'.[67] This view holds that it has the status of *jus
cogens*, 'a preemptory norm from which no derogation is permitted',[68] which
would take precedence over an agreement that constrains this state power.
Therefore, since sovereignty is permanent, stabilisation clauses are negated,
and have no effect. This view is most persuasive, as it is debatable as to
whether the General Assembly actually had stated any novel principles that
had not already been part of conventional state practice relating to expropriation. The principle of eminent domain is well established. From
Friedman's overview of the history of state practice regarding expropriation,
it is apparent that the General Assembly did not articulate any principles that
were new, but merely affirmed customary state practice.[69] Indeed, as Brigitte
Bollecker-Stern observed, the UN resolutions were 'not based on a new
principle of international law, but on a more sophisticated expression of an
old and uncontested principle of the sovereignty of states'.[70]

A final point which arises as a development of this is whether the
stabilisation clause can somehow survive the termination of the contract,
and have an independent life of its own, or 'float'.[71] Indeed, for the stabilisation clause to mean anything, the law on which it is based must provide for

the clause to have legal effect. And, if the law that governs the entire contract is changed by the state so as to render it null and void, so too must the stabilisation clauses within the contract become null and void. Many foreign investors, particularly in the 'hot oil' cases, argued that the stabilisation clauses can survive the termination of the contract. However, as Philip Wood has explained, the proper law applying to an investment agreement 'is the law as it exists from time to time', and that 'if the law changes, the entire contract will be affected'. As held by the House of Lords in *Kahler v. Midland Bank*, 'the proper law, because it sustains, may also modify or dissolve the contractual bond'.[72] The freezing clause is therefore regarded as an incorporation of law into the contract, and not as the proper choice of law. This particular clause will therefore be modified by a change to the proper law, which, as shown, the state has the power to do.

Therefore, notwithstanding any promises the state makes to the foreign investor, even in the investment agreement itself, the foreign investor is still subject to the power of eminent domain of the state. The most protection that can be afforded by properly formulated stabilisation clauses is to increase the amount of compensation. As observed in *Aminoil*, the stabilisation clause had a legal effect with regard to the 'necessity for a proper indemnification'.[73] For both E. Jiménez de Aréchaga and O. Schachter, the violation of a stabilisation clause is a circumstance which must be taken into account in determining compensation, to the extent of compensating for prospective profits.[74]

And, like the promise of good faith, the stabilisation clause, to have any legal effect, must be specific. This was observed in the *Aminoil* arbitration. The stabilisation clause in the agreement between the American Independent Oil Company and Kuwait provided, vaguely, that the agreement was protected from any legislative acts, and for mutual consent in order to make alterations to the agreement.[75] The Tribunal stated that 'a straightforward and direct reading … can lead to the conclusion that [the stabilisation clauses] prohibit any nationalisation'.[76] However, it added the qualification that, 'the case of nationalisation is certainly not expressly provided against by the stabilisation clauses', and that the restraint on the exercise of the power to expropriate 'would be a particular serious undertaking which would have to be expressly stipulated for'.[77] Moreover, the Tribunal argued that the stabilisation clause would have to be limited in duration as well.[78] Rosalyn Higgins concluded from this that stabilisation clauses are 'not to be read literally'.[79] At the very least, the fact that the permanence of sovereignty has been reaffirmed in the UN resolutions can reduce the quantum of compensation liable in the event of a nationalisation. It is affirmed that nationalisation does not involve a delict, thus there is no duty to pay damages.[80]

It is for these reasons that bilateral investment treaties (BITs) concluded between capital-exporting and capital-importing states offer by far the most trustworthy promise for the protection of foreign investments. There is at present a network of over 600 BITs involving 133 states which protect foreign investments by mandating indemnification by the nationalising state. Bilateral investment treaties offer legal protection to private investors, who are not subjects of international law, by providing them with recourse to remedies for a breach of an agreement at the international level. In other words, if a state that is party to a BIT with the home state of the foreign investor does not honour the terms of an investment agreement, the investor may seek the protection of his home state in the form of diplomatic representation and arbitration at the inter-state level. The failure to honour a BIT, which, like any international treaty, is legally binding on the states, *is* an international delict. The breach of the BIT would therefore be a breach of a treaty, and a breach of international law. An investor could therefore seek the assistance of his home state to enforce the treaty on the international plane on his behalf.

A common provision of BITs is that disputes between a host state and a foreign investor shall be settled through compulsory international arbitration, rather than governed by national laws which can be changed arbitrarily. A survey of 335 BITs conducted in 1991 found that all but one provide for international arbitration, and most provide for arbitration under the standard provisions of such institutions as the International Centre for the Settlement of Investment Disputes (ICSID).[81] To return to the example of Russia, notwithstanding the fact that Article 6 of the Russian FIL provides for national treatment, an American investor with a grievance against Russia can seek international arbitration by virtue of the BIT between Russia and the United States.[82] Another important common clause in BITs is that investors shall be indemnified in cases of nationalisation. All of the 335 BITs surveyed were found to contain the 'prompt' and 'effective' elements of the Hull formula, while 195 adopted the Hull formula in its entirety.[83] It is another of the ironies of foreign investment that the BIT between Argentina and the United States contains a reference to the Hull formula.[84] Argentina is, of course, the home country of Carlos Calvo, the leading advocate of the developing country alternative to the Hull formula.

The existence of such a network of BITs containing common clauses raises the issue of whether these construct a 'regime' which endorses a particular norm to govern international investment, just as the developing states were attempting to forge through 'value allocation' activities in the General Assembly. Some believe that they do not, such as Friedman who expressed in 1953 the view that such treaties 'do not go so far as to express a general principle of law'.[85] This opinion was repeated in 1986 by Sornarajah.[86] But, irrespective of whether these treaties comprise a general norm of international law – and there are those who argue that they do[87] – the fact remains that their common provision is illustrative of a massive sea-change in attitude towards FDI. Moreover, the fact that BITs include liberal principles and have legal force at the international level means that investors whose states have concluded a BIT are guaranteed recourse to their own state to seek remedies. For these reasons, the United Nations Centre on Transnational Corporations (UNCTC) has stated that BITs are the most reliable instrument available to ensure the continued integrity of a foreign investment since these are 'legally binding on the parties'.[88]

The Political Dynamics: Chile and NAFTA

For a developing state to create a welcoming aura for FDI is not sufficient to guarantee that investors will establish on their territory. Less developed countries find themselves in competition with other developing states, and with developed states, to attract FDI. Multinational corporations have preferred to invest in the relatively more stable atmosphere of the OECD countries, particularly in the 1980s. For instance, in 1988, 96 per cent of FDI remained in the OECD,[89] with the US attracting 60 per cent of the flow of FDI in the 1980s.[90] By contrast, the stock of FDI in Central and Eastern Europe reached only $13 billion in 1994, equal to that of Thailand.[91] Between 1989 and 1996, only $31 billion was invested in the states of Eastern Europe.[92] This has been attributed by the IMF to, among other things, 'a lack of an effective administrative and legal infrastructure with respect mainly to uncertainties over property rights'.[93]

The distribution of FDI owes also to the fact that MNCs require access to a relatively large national market, or access to a large regional market that is not hindered by tariff and non-tariff barriers. This factor, among others, explains the fact that most FDI remains within the 'triad' of regional economic areas, the European Union (EU), the Asia–Pacific area, and the North American Free Trade Area (NAFTA). In fact, 75 per cent of stock of FDI and 60 per cent of the annual flow of FDI is among the members of this triad.[94] Thus, perhaps the best strategy for a developing country which is attempting to attract FDI is to conclude a BIT and a free-trade agreement with a member (or, preferably, all members) of one of the large economic zones. This would not only assure foreign investors a relatively stable legal footing for their investment, but it would also assure them access to large markets.

The North American Free Trade Area is the largest regional economic area currently in force, incorporating Canada, the United States and Mexico. Signed in 1993 and coming into force the following year, NAFTA built upon the 1988 Canada–United States Free Trade Agreement (CUSFTA). In December 1994, a plan was put forth to expand NAFTA into a 'hemispheric zone of free trade' by the year 2005 to encompass Latin American and Central American states. Such an expansion is certainly desirable for those states currently outside NAFTA, for there are clauses within the agreement that give trade favouritism to products manufactured within the regional area. For instance, NAFTA contains domestic content requirements whereby the tariff classification for certain goods changes according to the 'regional value content' of the good.[95] For instance, textiles are subject to a 'triple transformation test', which is a measurement of the content of NAFTA-added value which is required for textiles to achieve tariff preferences in the region.[96] There is also a requirement that assembled automobiles must contain at least 62.5 per cent North American content to qualify for duty-free treatment within NAFTA.[97] Because of such clauses, there have been fears that NAFTA, and other regional economic zones like it, could evolve into 'investment blocs' that discriminate against products manufactured outside.

Therefore, in order truly to take advantage of liberalisation and privatisation, it is not sufficient that Latin American and Central American states attract FDI. It is imperative that they also establish a political rapport with NAFTA. The twin pillars of this are bilateral investment treaties to guarantee the fair treatment of MNCs, and bilateral tree trade treaties to provide these MNCs access to the large regional market of NAFTA.

Canada's recent bilateral agreements with Chile, signed in May 1997, illustrate this dynamic. Traditionally, Canada has had very limited relations with Latin America, since the majority of its interests have been focused on the United States and Europe, and to a lesser extent with its Commonwealth partners. Within Latin America, Canada had most of its ties with Common-wealth states, and these ties were mainly related to bilateral aid relations. The nature of Canada's relations with Latin America and the Caribbean began to change in 1969, when Canada tried to encourage more private investment into this region. Tourism was one aspect of business which attracted financial support, but this was given mainly to Caribbean countries. Support was given to a few Latin American countries, mainly in the mining industry, and this still pertains today. However, in 1993 the new Liberal government in Canada, under the leadership of Jean Chrétien, indicated that it was looking at Latin America and Asia as part of its new foreign policy. Ottawa finally acknowledged that Canada was both an Atlantic and a Pacific state.

Prior to this, Canada maintained an almost distant relationship with Latin America on the whole, although there is a history of Canadian investment and trade with Chile.[98] Though opportunities availed themselves since the 1930s for Canada to play a more active political role in Latin America through the Pan-American Union and the Organization of American States (OAS), various political issues, mainly dissuasion by the United States, discouraged Canada from joining these organisations. It was not until Canada took a more proactive continental approach in its foreign policy in 1988 that it joined the OAS the following year.[99] In 1993 Canada actively engaged in a new foreign policy direction which sought to improve both its foreign and trade relations with South East Asia and Latin America.[100]

Notwithstanding the fact that Canada had distanced itself from the region politically, Canada had economic relations with Chile for some time. And, interestingly, Chile is a state which historically has been hostile to MNCs. In the early 1970s, the Allende regime, a socialist government, nationalised a number of industries in an attempt to assert control over its economic destiny and to repatriate the funds which were leaving the country through profit-taking by multinational corporations.[101] Most famous among these, perhaps, was the 'intervention' in the ITT telephone company.[102] However, due to Canada's good relations with Chile, very few Canadian investments were affected. In fact, Allende had invited Prime Minister Trudeau to visit in 1971. Canada, according to the Department of External Affairs' documentation, saw this as an opportunity to encourage better trade relations with Chile in the hope of allaying the fears of Canadian businesses that their companies may be nationalised. Canada's confidence in such an approach rested in the fact that it possessed much technology and skills needed by Chile and that it did not have the same 'reputation' as the United States.[103]

On 11 September 1973, General Augusto Pinochet led a successful *coup d'état*, overthrowing Salvador Allende, and establishing a military dictatorship which lasted for seventeen years. The immediate policy of the Pinochet government was to reverse the trend set forth by Allende, and to turn Chile into a market-led economy[104] (although it continued the expropriation of ITT 'in the national interest' and 'for public utility', but committed itself to arbitration to determine the quantum of compensation[105]). On 29 September 1973, eighteen days after the coup that deposed Salvador Allende, Canada recognised the government of Augusto Pinochet and continued business as usual.[106] Early in 1974, a study by the Canadian Imperial Bank of Commerce assessed Chile's new economic policies favourably, although it included a caveat that the economic damage afflicted upon Chile's economy by Allende's mismanagement would take years to recover.[107] At the same time, while Canada was concerned with its trade relations with Chile, it was taking in the 7,000 political refugees displaced by the Pinochet dictatorship.[108] In other words, Canada did not allow its political convictions to interfere with its economic interests. Canada's relations with Chile continued to be relatively stable until 1990 when the Chilean economy began to improve dramatically. From the early 1970s until 1982, Canada gave Chile approximately $7,416,000 in overseas development assistance (ODA) (see Table 10.1). After 1982, when the Latin American debt crisis affected Chile, Canada's ODA increased dramatically until the end of the 1980s.[109]

Canada's trade with Chile continued to expand, and to blossom, in the 1990s as the Chilean economy began to perform much better. From 1974 to 1990 Pinochet set in process the revitalisation of Chile's economy through the re-privatisation of those industries nationalised under Allende and through seeking foreign investments into its economy mainly from foreign banks.[110] It took at least five years for confidence to be restored in Chile. In 1978, Chile's balance of capital recorded a significant increase from $737 million the previous year to $1,855 million. The following year, portfolio investments stood at $50 million. Though these are not great sums, what is significant is

Table 10.1 Canadian official developmental assistance to Chile, 1970–90*

1970–71	2,357
1971–72	819
1972–73	2,174
1973–74	371
1974–75	371
1975–76	123
1976–77	144
1977–78	131
1978–79	69
1979–80	18
1980–81	247
1981–82	574
1982–83	2,782
1983–84	3,347
1984–85	4,717
1985–86	4,332
1986–87	6,703
1987–88	5,745
1988–89	5,966
1989–90	5,752

* These figures exclude multilateral assistance and are represented in thousands of Canadian dollars.

Source: James Rochlin, *Discovering the Americas: The Evolution of Canadian Foreign Policy Towards Latin America*, UBC Press, Vancouver, 1994, pp. 243–6.

that in 1976 and 1977 these figures show negative balances, indicating that more funds were being taken out of Chile than were being invested into Chilean markets. There was also a remarkable shift in direct investment in 1978, when it increased from negative growth to $1 million in 1976, and then jumped to $17 million in 1977, and finally to $177 million in 1978. Interestingly, Chile's new foreign investment laws, of 18 March 1977 and 30 November 1985, both provided for national treatment of foreign investors, and contained no state promises or provisions for international arbitration.[111]

Yet, by 1990, there was proven stability in the economic policies of the Chilean government.[112] As Chile's economy stabilised and strengthened, more foreign investment was forthcoming. From 1985, portfolio investments increased remarkably to $50 million.[113] This increased to $262 million in 1986, $826 million in 1987, and $1,309 million in 1988. In 1992, a report by Standard & Poor, a large American credit-rating agency, announced that 'Chile became a safer bet for foreign investors', and was 'the first Latin American country to meet international standards of creditworthiness since the debt shocks of the 1980s'.[114] By 1992, a World Bank publication on the privatisation of state-owned firms showed that Chile's actions were very profitable to Chile's economy and to its people as a whole.[115] The result of the privatisation and liberalisation policies was that Chile was able to become a dominant economy in Latin America in the 1990s. It is for this reason that Chile was suggested as being the link tying NAFTA and Mercosur together at a conference to discuss Pan-American trade held in Santiago in 1997.[116]

A middle class is growing in Chile, which is stabilising both the political and the economic situation,[117] and the disparity of wealth between the 'have' and 'have nots' is becoming less obvious with a large middle-class buffer. A middle class is an important indicator in assessing a state's economic transition, as such disparities of wealth have encouraged the growth of Marxist politics in Latin American countries – Chile included.[118] The development of the middle class in Chile has taken place since 1974. According to Gary Macoein, Chile did not have a middle class in the 1970s.[119] Yet, in the run-up to the 1993 elections, Senator Eduardo Frei ran his campaign for president on a platform based on middle-class principles and policies,[120] which demonstrates the change in attitudes that had come about in Chile since its increased democratisation in 1987.[121] Though President Patricio Aylwin forbade 'ministers to talk of Chile as a Latin American Tiger' and he continued to insist that 'Chile is a poor country', these statements fail to negate the fact that the number of poor in Chile has decreased, as has unemployment, indicating the increase of a middle class.[122] In 1995, Pepsi-Cola invested $100 million into Chile, introducing Pizza Hut and Kentucky Fried Chicken, two 'fast food' franchises.[123]

Chile's economy has shown signs of growth, and the economic indicators have already shown the propensity of Chileans to spend their money on luxury services and to invest in both Chilean and outside markets.[124] Thus, confidence in their own economy is growing. What is more interesting is the number of foreign investors speculating on the Chilean economy's potential since 1990. In agriculture, Chile has been a recognised producer of grapes and wines. In recent years, however, the quality of these products have increased, and these products are rated quite highly internationally. What makes this market even more interesting to investors from the United States is that it does not compete with their domestic agricultural industries, but rather complements them as Chile's and the United States's growing seasons occur at different times of the year.

The fishing industry has also attracted foreign investors, most notably within the luxury sector, namely salmon. As natural fish stocks of salmon – in this case Pacific salmon – are fought over by Canadian and American fishermen, and as these natural stocks diminish while demand increases, the need for 'farmed' salmon has increased. With fewer environmental restrictions on such industries, as compared to Canada for instance, Chile was well suited to take advantage of this market, and has prospered, making it one of the world's largest producers of salmon. So successful is this industry that Chile recently has been accused of 'dumping' salmon in the United States market.[125]

In the mining sector, fresh capital is now opening up Chilean ores for development. Such industries existed before but were poorly subsidised, and lacked much-needed modern technology. The new investments from Canada and the United States have injected the needed capital and technology to develop the copper fields, bringing the mining industry up to its full potential. The next logical step would be the development of secondary industry in Chile, with the refinement of ores locally, so that a high-quality finished product could be produced.[126]

The banking sector also has taken advantage of the changes in Chile, and in Latin America as a whole, as banks have been more willing to lend money. A recent flux in banking regulations in Latin America as a whole has led a number of foreign banks to buy Latin American banks, and Chile has not gone untouched by this trend. Banco Bilbao Vizcaya, a Spanish bank fronting European interests, has already invested heavily in Latin America with over 1,200 branches, becoming Chile's second largest bank. Such investments have introduced better credit-risk analysis, which for Latin American banks traditionally has been poor.[127] It has also introduced new banks in competition to the traditional state-sanctioned ones, as banks from Europe, Asia, and North America build alliances with local banks and open up their own branches in Chile. Furthermore, as speculators themselves, North American banks have realised the market potentials in Chile and have invested there in a bid to increase their own profits.

All of this indicates a growing confidence in the Chilean market. The production of finished products with lower labour costs than those found in Europe or North America allows for cheaper products of similar quality to be produced and exported. The problem with this, however, is that without a reasonable export market – and one that is not faced with import duties – these opportunities could be stymied. It is here that bilateral treaties with members of NAFTA becomes most important. Because of this rapid economic growth, the membership of NAFTA expressed an interest in Chile as part of its expansion, and on 11 December 1994 they invited Chile to apply for membership. The reason that Canada has spear-headed economic treaties with Chile is due to the historical relations between Canada and Chile, and also to the fact that the United States Congress has been reluctant to pursue such programmes with Latin American countries following the crash of the Mexican peso in 1994.

On 24 March 1997, Canada and Chile signed a bilateral trade and investment treaty which was designed to improve their bilateral investment relationship, trade relations, and market opportunities.[128] This document sets out a comprehensive structure for trade between these two countries, listing the various sectors which are involved, the matter of import and export

Table 10.2 Canadian exports to and imports from Chile, 1945–96*

	Exports	Imports
1945	2.6	0.6
1950	6.9	1.4
1955	3.8	0.3
1960	6.6	6.6
1965	10.5	1.7
1970	22.9	2.8
1972	10.8	6.5
1975	30.8	50.0
1978	56.9	51.4
1980	112.4	97.1
1982	68.0	119.0
1985	82.0	130.0
1988	141.0	160.0
1990	200.0	180.0
1991	150.0	184.0
1992	145.0	202.0
1993	–	–
1994	–	–
1995	386.0	–
1996	330.0	342.0

* All figures are measured in millions of Canadian dollars.

Sources: James Rochlin, *Discovering the Americas: The Evolution of Canadian Foreign Policy Towards Latin America*, UBC Press, Vancouver, 1994, pp. 238–43; and *Chile's Business Update*, Vol. 4, Spring 1997, http://www.chiletrade.cl.

tariffs,[129] a mechanism for dealing with trade disputes[130] that might arise along with an agreement regarding anti-dumping practices.[131] As part of this agreement there are no import duties on products travelling between Canada and Chile. Article (A–02) of this agreement states:

1. The objectives of this Agreement, as elaborated more specifically through its principles and rules, including national treatment, most-favoured nation treatment and transparency, are to:

a) eliminate barriers to trade in, and facilitate the cross-border movement of, goods and services between the territories of the Parties;

b) promote conditions of fair competition in the free trade area;

c) increase substantially investment opportunities in the territories of the Parties;

d) create effective procedures for the implementation and application of this

Agreement, for its joint administration and for the resolution of disputes; and

e) establish a framework for further bilateral, regional and multilateral co-operation to expand and enhance the benefits of this Agreement.[132]

Table 10.2 indicates that trade between Canada and Chile has increased dramatically in the last decade, and it is likely that trade will increase further with the negation of import tariffs. Sub-section (e) of this Article gives the promise that such increased trade and investment will be extended in a wider regional context than simply bilaterally between Canada and Chile. Indeed, it would appear that such bilateral trade and investment treaties are a stepping-stone to Chile's eventual integration into a more complexly integrated regional economic zone, if not to the expansion of NAFTA itself. Of course, this also offers Canada the opportunity to expand into other areas of South America using the Canada–Chile Free Trade Agreement as a model.

Conclusion

There is a indeed a New World Order for foreign investment. It is one characterised by an overwhelming desire by most states to attract FDI. It was shown that this desire has been given expression in all manner of state promises in foreign investment laws, as for instance, in those of the former 'radicals' of the international economy, Vietnam and Russia. Legal and political stability are undoubtedly important, which could explain in large part why Eastern European countries, on the whole, have not experienced very rapid growth in FDI. However, it was shown that while most legal assurances seem golden on the surface, they have very little substance in terms of the protection accorded to investors. Sound economic policies and confidence retain an important place in investors decisions, as illustrated in the case of Chile.

Moreover, due to the polarised nature of global investment patterns, which remain mainly confined within the 'triad', sound trade relationships and access to a market, such as the Canada–Chile Free Trade Agreement, provide investors with an even greater incentive to invest in a given state. At the end of this millennium, the race to attract FDI involves not only providing legal and economic assurances, but politics plays a crucial part. States on the fringes of the large economic zones are courting politically the larger markets to 'get in on the action'. The bilateral agreement between Chile and Canada could be a first step in Chile's eventual incorporation into NAFTA, if such expansion takes place at all. If it does, the dynamics of foreign investment in the next decades will be determined as much by politics as by economics. This is not to suggest that the current politics of FDI is free of ideology; however, unlike the 1960s and 1970s, economic considerations are *prior* to goals mandated by any particular political ideology.

Technology, Business and Crime: the Globalisation of Finance and Electronic Payments Systems

Jarrod Wiener

The size of a market economy has always been a function, in large part, of technology. Prior to the consolidation of nation-states, economies were limited to geographic nodes of no more than about twenty miles in radius. This was due to the fact that traders and merchants had to transport to marketplaces not only their wares, but also their fuel (in the form of food for their horses, etc.) for the journey there and back which limited the size of markets.[1] The international economy developed more rapidly, due to superior sea transportation. As Immanuel Wallerstein observed, 'the size of the world-economy is a function of the state of technology, and in particular the possibilities of transport and communication within its bounds'.[2] Equally important has been the way in which technology has promoted the evolution of stored value. Paper negotiable instruments are more easily transportable than specie, and electronic impulses can transfer a greater volume of wealth with ever greater speed.

The speed at which money flows through the global financial system has increased dramatically in the wake of the technological revolution, most important of which are twenty-four-hour electronic trading in money markets, electronic fund transfers (EFTs), and electronic data interchange (EDI) in the inter-bank clearing systems. In the UK, the Clearing House Automated Payments System (CHAPS) handled an average of 32,000 transfers a day in 1991, with an average daily value of £75 billion.[3] In the United States, the Clearing House Interbank Payments System (CHIPS) handled an average of 148,801 transfers a day in 1990 with an average daily value of $885 billion, while FedWire processed 67 million transfers with an aggregate value of $199 trillion.[4] In 1995, the number of FedWire transactions increased to 76 million, involving $223 trillion.[5] It has been estimated that the payments systems in the United States, Germany, and Japan turn over the equivalent of their annual GDP every few days.[6]

Money is, after all, a signifier of wealth. When the transfer of that wealth is purveyed through electronic impulses – disembodied from its physical representation – the size of the economy depends more on the bounds of *communication* than of transport. More correctly, it depends on the bounds of communication of information about wealth. The revolution in communication technologies in the latter part of this century has provided a very great impetus to the speed at which the global economy has developed, defined for present purposes by the parameters of those in possession of the technology rather than by geographical demarcations. While the definition of globalisation of Ian Robert Douglas as, 'the eradication of space through the domestication of time'[7] is perhaps strong for general usage, it is nevertheless an appropriate working definition here to denote the empowerment of individuals by innovations in communication technologies to defy, or at least to compress, territorial space – the borders of sovereign states in many cases notwithstanding – for the purposes of moving wealth. Indeed, an estimated $1.2 trillion passes daily through the international foreign exchange market, and $6 trillion of money passes daily through international inter-bank payment and settlement networks.[8]

In addition, it is important to recognise that the functioning and size of a market economy is also a function of a supportive legal framework.[9] Governments must support a monetised economy either through a commitment to underwrite a gold standard, or to formulate internationally agreed rules and act as lender of last resort in diffuse market-led systems.[10] Systems of law must also guarantee and enforce at least such essentials as the sanctity of contract and private property rights. National systems of law differ in many respects, including mandatory contract terms, usages and practices, such that there are likely always to be legal risks in international commercial transactions. Nevertheless, the development of a highly integrated system of international commerce would have been impossible without the legal frameworks of commercial states sharing sufficient commonality to provide at least the necessary confidence for the business community to undertake contracts and some guarantee against crime.

Economic crime is arguably just as old as the market, or at least as old as the concept of value. It is defined here as the coercive transfer of the ownership of wealth (i.e., theft, fraud, extortion) and the concealment of the beneficial ownership of wealth for the purposes evading or avoiding taxation and government regulations, or to disguise the illicit source of funds (money laundering). The potential for such economic crime has evolved in tandem with the evolution of the market economy, and more precisely with the manner in which money has evolved into new and different forms.

Until the time that banks implemented central accounting and clearing procedures among themselves, the movement of material wealth (in the form of gold or notes) was almost always accompanied by mercenary soldiers to guard against theft.[11] Apart from robberies of armoured cars, electronic clearing and payments systems have effectively eliminated pirates and bandits 'cutting-off at the pass' money on the move. That is, until the summer of 1994. From June to July 1994, individuals in St Petersburg succeeded in breaching the security of Citibank's private network, the Citibank Cash Management System, and conducted several unauthorised transfers of funds totalling approximately US$3 million from the Philippine National Bank to a bank in Finland, and from Djakarta and Buenos Aires to San Francisco and Israel.[12] It seems the more easily transportable money becomes, and the more ways in which it travels through complex communication networks, the greater the geographical area in which such crime can take place.

Similarly, money laundering on an international scale is arguably easier and preferable (for criminals) to the laundering of funds within a single legal jurisdiction. Those who seek to hide their money can use electronic communications to move money in and out of different financial instruments and in and out of national jurisdictions without leaving an easily observable paper trail. As Bruce Zagaris and Scott B. MacDonald commented, 'open economies, growing interdependence and the sheer instantaneity of financial transactions can be, and is being, abused by those who intentionally seek to conceal the source of their earnings. ... As new technology allows information to move faster around the globe in new forms, so money can also move faster and in more mysterious ways.'[13]

To the extent that the economy is transnational, so crime also has become transnational, in the sense that criminals can utilise transnational electronic networks to their advantage, and even reach into the legal jurisdiction of a state to commit a crime without having to breach physically the borders of that state. An important current of the twentieth century is that which carries criminals through transnational electronic networks while keeping the sovereign state land-locked. At the dawning of the new millennium, a major project for International Relations – defined in an interdisciplinary sense to include International Political Economy, International Law, and Law generally – will have to address the problem of economic crime in a global sense. The input from International Relations could be many, but two important areas come immediately to mind.

The first is to assist debates to conceptualise the role of states in the face of increasingly empowered civil society actors with a greater transnational reach than the states. An important question that concerns policy-makers and law enforcement officials centres on the increased potential for economic crime as communications technologies are diffused to individuals. Prior to the 1980s, technological breakthroughs were confined mainly to large corporate users, banks, and governments. For instance, approximately 14,000 large corporations are connected to electronic payments systems, such as BACS, through the gateways of their clearing banks, so that they can input directly their high-volume payment instructions, such as automated payrolls.[14] However, the proliferation of the personal computer and the growth of computer networks has diffused the technology into the hands of individuals, including criminals. Electronic payments systems now used routinely – including credit cards, debit cards, wire transfers, automatic-teller machines (ATMs) and other proprietary payments networks – present businesses and individuals alike with security risks from computer-literate criminals.

Many unfortunate individuals who have been victims of 'electronic mugging' know all to well that the fraudulent use of ATMs and counterfeit credit and debit cards is a disturbing problem. As Chuck Owens, a Section Chief in the criminal investigative division of the financial crimes section of the FBI stated before a hearing of the House Banking and Financial Services Committee, 'credit card fraud and the financial abuses that arise therefrom' are a 'problem of growing and, indeed, alarming proportions'.[15] The newest innovations in electronic money ('e-cash', 'digital cash') that can be traded transnationally in exchange for goods and services already have raised serious concerns about security and the appropriate ways in which to adapt existing legal and law enforcement systems.

Related closely to this, the second concern for International Relations is to assist in breaking conceptually and practically the mould of compartmentalised sovereignties, either through cooperation by treaty, or more problematically but more interestingly, by the functional harmonisation of states' municipal laws. Criminals operate transnationally, whereas the jurisdiction of states is bound to a particular territory (apart from notable exceptions for extraterritorial application and bilateral cooperation treaties). Indeed, criminals utilise state sovereignty to their advantage; for instance, money launderers count on the fact that different legal systems have different bank secrecy laws and different reporting and disclosure requirements.[16] Transnational challenges could be met effectively, for instance, if states were to harmonise their laws so that certain activities are recognised everywhere as 'criminal' (problems of relativism noted) and that the laws are enforceable separately in the courts of each state.[17]

Whatever path ultimately is chosen for the regulations of transnational challenges, including those presented by 'cyberspace', the fact remains that one of the main challenges of International Relations in the coming decade will be to devise ways to reconcile the compartmentalised Westphalian system of legal jurisdictions with increasingly internationally mobile civil society actors – some of whom are thieves, or dealers in drugs, body-parts, people, and hot money – who exploit communications technologies and sovereignty to their own ends. As Barry Rider commented insightfully, 'there is really no international capability at present to deal with serious organised crime at its own level of operations'. He continued, 'much of our criminal law is tied to notions of physical property that were no doubt meaningful in the seventeenth century but which hardly accommodate developments in communications technology'.[18] Elsewhere, Rider stated: 'To attempt to deal with these problems with tools fashioned by the criminal courts several hundred years ago to deal with essentially property-related crimes taking place within a very limited environment, both socially and geographically, is like trying to fight a nuclear war with King Henry II's bow and arrow.'[19]

The purpose of this chapter is to investigate one aspect of the 'darker side' of globalisation, namely the challenge of transnationally mobile criminals that raise difficulties for the effective application of political authority, defined as municipal law. It does so guided by the belief that International Relations should contribute a wider perspective to policy debates currently raging. However, to do so effectively, International Relations scholars must first adopt an interdisciplinary understanding of the issues, for instance by delving into the minutiae of legal intricacies. To that end, this chapter explores the ways in which electronic banking and digital cash are challenging our notions of money and commercial transactions, and the new opportunities that this could create for fraud, theft and money laundering.

On Governing a Permeable Society

There seems to be an emerging consensus among international political economists and international commercial lawyers that the 1990s has been 'the decade of telecoms and other forms of electronic communication'.[20] According to at least one visionary businessman, Bill Gates, communications technologies promise to revolutionise nearly every aspect of our lives, from the way we learn, the way we work, the way we relax, to the way we go shopping.[21] Futurists imagine a world in which individuals can obtain vast amounts of information from on-line 'virtual libraries', can 'tele-commute' to work, and can dial up interactive 'video-on-demand' entertainment systems and 'virtual shopping malls'.

The basic outline of such a vision emerged early in this decade when, on 15 September 1993, the Clinton–Gore administration launched the National Information Infrastructure (NII) in the United States.[22] In December of that year, former European Commission President Jacques Delors outlined similar measures for a European Information Society (EIS).[23] Both plans envisioned national (in the case of the United States) or regional (in the European Union) computer networks promising precisely these benefits. A year later, media reports abounded of Fortune 500 companies reducing fixed overhead costs by equipping their workers with laptop computers and mobile telephones. In 1994, Ernst & Young was reported to have reduced its total US office space by 50 per cent, and IBM in Denver was reported to have reduced its office space from nine to four floors, at an estimated savings of $6 million over five years.[24] The innovation in interactive entertainment services was also unveiled in 1994 in the form of the 'Full Service Network' of Time-Warner, Silicon Graphics, AT&T and Scientific Atlanta.[25] Computer-shopping is increasing rapidly. In 1994, there were estimated to be over 14,000 businesses with a presence on the Internet which hoped to take advantage of the transnational reach of on-line advertising to service a seemingly infinitely expandable market.[26] That number has grown almost daily, with many businesses accepting electronic orders from on-line computers. VISA, MasterCard and others have already unveiled electronic payment systems,[27] known variously as 'digital cash', 'e-cash' or 'cybercash'.[28] Finally, the amount of full-text information available on the World Wide Web is increasing daily as libraries, research organisations, and other information providers up-load documents to the Internet. The 'virtual library' envisioned by the US Congress as a massive storage system for 'hundreds of trillions of bits of data … giving thousands of users simultaneous and nearly instantaneous access to that data'[29] is an emerging reality.

What all of these technological innovations have in common is the empowerment of the individual to defy, or at least to compress, territorial space. No longer do workers in innovative firms have to move physically to a fixed workplace, and no longer must researchers travel to documents that more effortlessly and efficiently can be pulled to them by their computers. A corollary to this compression of space is an increase in speed. Businesses and individuals alike can enjoy cheap and nearly instantaneous communication across vast distances with a minimum of paper – a revolution that the money and commodities trading markets have enjoyed since the 1970s.

At first glance, the implications of this for International Relations appear fairly straightforward. Once physical boundaries are conquered by electronic networks, territorial space and time lose practical meaning. That is, it makes little difference whether a person is tele-commuting to an office in the same city, or to an office on another continent. Many services industries have already realised this. As early as 1994, the administration of the global British Airways booking system took place at its Message Editing Unit in New Delhi in order to capitalise on low-wage computer terminal operators and fast, cheap communications.[30]

One must pause to reflect on the novelty of this, however, lest the author be accused of reifying an imaginary revolution. All of this can be seen simply as an extension of the practice of using the now common telephone, or the practice long established in commerce of utilising electronic data transfer (EDT). In fact, most components of international trade transactions are conducted through the electronic transmission of data 'from negotiation through contract formation, performance, insurance, and payment'.[31] And in international capital markets, 'banks contract among themselves for the placing and taking of millions of dollars with little more documentation than an ordinary sales slip'.[32] There is very little new in essence in the use of electronic communication in commerce; the novelty lies in the application of the media to new aspects of it; the entirely new commercial potential of entertainment and information service provision; and, importantly, in the fact that some of the technologies previously available only to banks and currency traders can be found in the living-rooms of wealthy computer-literate individuals.

Many in the discipline of International Relations have rushed to state the extent to which this transnationalisation of communications challenges state sovereignty. The 'traditional' arenas in which telecommunications technologies have been used – most notably in international capital markets – have raised concerns about state sovereignty, and it did not take long for such concerns to be transposed to the new areas.

Perhaps nowhere has the erosion of state sovereignty been feared more than in the international financial system, where individual currency traders have been empowered by the market and twenty-four-hour electronic trading to determine the value of a state's currency and to discipline governments' economic policies. To be sure, there are examples of traders pressurising the central banks of states, ranging from the selling short of the money supply of New Zealand by Andy Krieger to the collapse of the European Monetary System in 1992 by the trading activities of George Soros and others.[33]

From this, many have over-stated the extent to which there exists a 'stateless' transnational financial system, 'delinked' in some fundamental way from the control, and perhaps even the oversight, of states.[34] For instance, Malcolm Waters has referred to a 'postmodernising effect' in the international economy, which is that 'the entire system has become more difficult to control. States are placed at the mercy of financial markets.'[35] Phil Cerny has referred to 'the crystallisation and consolidation of a genuinely transnational and increasingly autonomous financial market'.[36] In the words of Eric Helleiner, 'all states have been losing power to the international markets in the financial arena, making their management of such markets more difficult in recent years'.[37] And Gregory Millman, in journalistic style, commented that 'the new markets in risk baffle old-school bankers, humiliate presidents, and elevate twenty-something traders to a rankless power from which they determine the fate of nations. They are a sign of capital's triumph over all social constraints.'[38]

As digital communications technologies spread from the capital markets into new areas of commerce – and indeed into many aspects of individuals' daily lives – similar concerns have been transposed to them. There have been commensurate concerns about the ways in which the communications technologies challenge the whole structure of authority relationships, and particularly the way in which the traditional mechanisms of state control are challenged. These have ranged from the impact of communication on cultural identity; the debate over the control of socially sensitive or unacceptable material, such as pornography on the Internet; and indeed to the maintenance of national security.

A White House paper assessing the NII warned, 'if access controls and security concerns are not addressed ... vulnerabilities to US national security may be inadvertently affected by making information readily available to foreign governments, competitors, or criminals'.[39] Reports have abounded of computer hackers gaining access to sensitive information, such as that which occurred from the central computer of British Telecommunications in November 1994 in which, allegedly, the telephone numbers of MI5, MI6, Ministry of Defence installations, as well as the locations of NATO fuel depots and nuclear weapons storage sites were made available over the Internet.[40]

The new technologies have raised societal and cultural insecurities. It has been said that 'information technology ... is beginning to cause a deeper social transformation, by affecting the flow of information and ideas by which people define their culture'.[41] Arguing that the power of images constructs social reality, France has attempted to resist the 'coca-cola–McDonalds–Mickey-Mouse' culture that is transmitted through films and television and undermining what the French government believes to be traditional social values of France.[42] Similarly, Saudi Arabia also has attempted to ban videos that were morally reprehensible (though largely in vain because such efforts were undermined by satellite and on-line technologies). Singapore has instituted a programme to become an 'intelligent island' to take advantage of information processing opportunities, but has also attempted to force users of Teleview, its network, not to use it 'for sending to any person any message which is offensive on moral, religious, communal, or political grounds'.[43] More recently, the United States has attempted to control transmissions of obscene and lewd information through the Computer Decency Act that failed in the Supreme Court.[44]

All of this, and more, can be gleaned from even the most cursory glance at reports about the 'dark side' of the Internet. It is difficult to dispute that due to growing global electronic communication networks, states are permeated by transnational forces even without these physically breaching their borders. And, the flow of information over the Internet is exceedingly difficult to control. In fact, the Internet was created in such a way as to route information around damage in the system. Conceived during the Cold War to ensure continued communication in the event that a part of the system would become damaged, the Internet perceives censorship to be damage and routes around it. Thus, the attempt to deal with perceived socially unacceptable challenges as profanity and pornography on the Internet on their own terms, namely through technological 'fixes', is difficult.

Yet, the basis of the concerns outlined above fundamentally are not new. Indeed, with every opportunity there are risks, and with every freedom there are costs. As we, an advanced society, become aware of the ways in which communication technologies promise to shape more aspects of our lives, so too do we become aware of the dangers. As early as the 1980s, the Organisation for Economic Cooperation and Development (OECD) was embroiled in a debate about transborder data flows (TDF) precisely because these challenged government control. William J. Drake and Kalypso Nicolaidis reported that 'the rapidly expanding corporate use of TDF raised concerns about the implications for national sovereignty, economic welfare, legal autonomy, and cultural integrity'.[45]

The same sorts of concerns that have been raised about foreign currency traders and individual Internet users have been raised at one point or another about transnational corporations and international travellers carrying infectious diseases.[46] At the heart of all such concerns is that state authority – defined as the ability to exercise control over a well-defined territorial space – is being challenged because the security threats are not easily defined within territorial terms of reference. The strong thesis has been put forth by Paul Virilio, that 'space is no longer in geography – it's in electronics. ... There is a movement from geo- to chrono-politics: the distribution of territory becomes the distribution of time.'[47] Since this statement was made in the context of a discussion of war, it cannot easily be excused for overlooking the numerous ethnic, national, and territorial wars spilling real blood daily. But the sociological circumstances that prompt such statements to be made are themselves interesting. With every innovation in civilisation there are concerns about the applicability and adaptability of the traditional methods by which societies protect themselves. Leaving aside the range of possible responses by authoritarian regimes and any technological 'fixes', the first response of a free society to challenges to its 'societal security' is to assess the extent of incongruity between the newly perceived risk and its principal mechanisms of control, which are, namely, its systems of law and their attendant mechanisms of enforcement. This is then followed by an attempt to adapt them to the new realities. The frames of reference for the debate about how to so adapt the laws and coercive apparati of the state concern the balance between individual freedom and social costs. An ideal-type of political debate in a free society involves the extent to which the state, as the guarantor of rights and the arbiter of social and political conflicts, should intervene to limit freedoms for the wider good of the society.

However, the ground-work upon which this debate takes place shifts fundamentally once an individual's *will* (to move money, to obtain information, to enter into a commercial transaction) translates into *actions* that are able to traverse space irrespective of sovereign borders without this also entailing the physical movement of the corporeal individual. The difficult question arises – as indeed it has arisen in public debates about regulating the Internet – whether one state's criminal law, which by definition is bound territorially (with certain qualifications), should apply to the disembodied will or actions of individuals corporeally situated in another jurisdiction but breaching the laws of that state. To take a civil case as an example, electronic mail over the Internet gives a person in Australia an avenue through which to defame another person in Canada with whom that person otherwise would not have had contact. Moreover, that defamation potentially can occur in hundreds of different legal jurisdictions simultaneously if the comments are posted to a bulletin board and read or downloaded all over the world.[48]

As the recognised boundaries drawn by public officials on a physical map of the world become challenged, difficult questions arise in the search for consonance between threats to 'societal security' and the law. As the borders of a political community become permeable to the will and actions of individuals outside them, the risks to the values of that political community become transnationalised. Commensurately, the ability of the state, defined as public authority, to act as arbiter between the rights and freedoms of its constituent members and the social costs that emanate from outside its jurisdiction is called into question. The ground upon which political authority is able to be exerted is shifting, and many fear that it is shifting in favour of transnationalised forces. At issue is nothing less than the ability of the state to exercise sovereign control.

Perhaps it is the problem of regulating the activities of individuals who can be in many states at once, of responding to challenges that cannot be seen, and of stabbing with inadequate laws at shadows in cyberspace that has led some post-modernists to throw in the towel on behalf of the sovereign state. Lawyers and regulators are more proactive.[49] The fear of lost sovereignty could be well-founded, though it must be emphasised heavily that it is so only *unless* public officials comprehend properly the challenges and adapt appropriately to them. As the following will show, systems of law have always adapted (with greater or lesser comfort) to advances in technology, and the regulation of economic crime on the Internet is not a hopeless enterprise.

On the Nature of Banks and Money

To respond appropriately to something, one must know what that thing is. For some commentators, the ground-work has shifted to such an extent that what constitutes a bank is no longer certain, nor even what constitutes money. This debate is not new, though recent developments have added fuel to it.

In the early 1980s, the American bank that has advertised widely its commitment to the use of innovative communications technologies, Citibank, ironically was the first to initiate a searing debate over what actually constitutes a bank. Citibank had supplied customers software for use on their personal computers to review a bank balance, to see if a cheque had cleared, or to view the stock-market closing rates. This was at the time when ATMs were posing problems for US banking regulators. A peculiar feature of the US banking system is the prohibition under the MacFadden Act of national banks (which belong to the Federal Reserve System) from branching across state lines. Whether an ATM represented a 'branch' or merely an over-glorified telephone was debated hotly in the Supreme Court.[50] Citibank's actions extended the debate to whether a person's home, effectively, could be considered to be a 'branch'. That debate opened perhaps the most fundamental philosophical question raised by modern banking. That is, 'what is a bank?'

In the Citibank case, reason prevailed and it was held that a customer's living-room does not constitute a branch of a bank. Of course, there is much more to banking than the transmission of information concerning negotiable value, such as making loans and taking deposits. But the debate which this case fuelled concerning the nature of a 'bank' and what constitutes 'money' remains an interesting question, particularly in light of the development of digital cash.

The term 'digital cash' as used here subsumes the various forms of electronic payments currently marketed under various brand names. Though the precise mechanisms of each system differ slightly, the essential mechanics are as follows. An individual maintains on his or her personal computer a 'digital wallet' to which he or she can transfer funds by accessing directly his or her bank account. That individual can then use the digital cash to make on-line purchases by transferring the required amount of digital cash from his or her wallet to the 'cybershop', to pay bills, or to transfer the digital cash to a wallet of another individual.[51]

Returning to the question of what constitutes a bank, is a bank defined by structural features, such as a vault, with layers of (one hopes) impenetrable security measures? No, these features are mandated by the fact that a bank is a place to conduct transactions, such as depositing and withdrawing currency. But if electronic commerce does not depend on the movement of physical currency, but rather *information about currency*, the vaults become redundant for these transactions. As Chris Reed stated, 'all banking transactions, except for those involving cash, are at bottom only transfers of information from one bank to another'.[52] As Carl Felsenfeld put it:

> The receipt and disbursement of money as an intermediary becomes less and less important as money continually and inevitably evolves from specie, through paper, to electronic impulses. The developing role of banks is not so much moving money as supplying information so that money can be moved. Less and less do banks even think of themselves as depositories on one side and lenders on the other, but as generalised suppliers of services to the financial marketplace.[53]

Thus, in Internet commerce, deposits, withdrawals and transfers of funds can be handled by individuals themselves. Therefore, where is the 'location' of the bank in Internet commerce? The answer is that these functions, traditionally performed by banks, will be performed by individuals using the various commercial products collectively known as digital cash. Indeed, among the different commercial providers are 'Ecash', 'Digicash', 'BankNet', 'Checkfree', 'Clickshare', 'Commercenet', 'Cybank', 'CyberCash', and 'Cyber-Source', among at least fifty others.[54] Of course, the banks will have a role in keeping money, as any virtual economy, whatever its level of abstraction, depends on a real economy with real wealth creation and storage. Thus, banks will continue to hold the money, but they will not be the only ones moving it.

It is true that telephone banking, credit-card companies, and others have been challenging the hegemony of banks in the payment system for some time. However, with digital cash, the payments segment of banks' activities are increasingly open to competition. Banks, fearful of this competition, commissioned in 1995 a report by the Bank Administration Institute and Boston Consulting Group entitled *The Information Highway and Retail Banking*. This report urged the industry to develop electronic delivery systems under pain of 'losing ground to technology companies [forcing] them off the road'. As stated by David Van L. Taylor, the Institute's Executive Vice-President: 'The payment system just keeps moving out further and further, and banks could be left sitting with a little piece of it if they're not careful.'[55] Many banks have done so. A fact-finding mission of the Financial Issues Working Group of the European Commission reported that:

> a great number of banks are aggressively embracing the Internet. The number of Web sites offered by US banks is forecast to increase from 285 in the early 1995 [*sic*] to 900 in 1991, and 2000 in the year 2000. ... Banks offering Internet banking in the year 2000 will represent some 40 per cent of the deposit base, over 16 million households. ... Close to 50 per cent of Internet banks plan to offer full-fledged services, including real-time access to accounts and on-line payments.[56]

What concerns us here is not that banks are losing market share. Of importance is the fact that the regulatory regimes that have developed to guard against fraud, to safeguard the individual from electronic crime, and to arrest money laundering traditionally have applied to 'conventional' banks. Indeed, the Bank for International Settlements considered these issues in a report entitled 'Implications for Central Banks of the Development of Electronic Money', though it did not make any firm recommendations.[57] Perhaps the most important issue is that regulations must also now be applied to the non-bank enterprises that provide digital cash. As the following section will show, it is relatively easy to apply the current banking practices and regulations to digital cash regardless of whether banks or other providers are involved, at least in so far as the individual can be protected from 'electronic mugging'. However, as will be shown, the regulation of money laundering could be exacerbated.

Electronic Mugging

A poll conducted in 1995 by VeriFone, Visa and MasterCard found that 32 per cent of World Wide Web users already had purchased products and services on the Internet, and that 91 per cent planned to do so in the future. Credit cards were found to be the preferred method of payment, followed by digital cash, ATM cards and prepaid cards.[58] Those polled stated that the prevention of fraud was the most important concern impeding the development of commerce on the Internet. Indeed, as late as February 1996, Joel

Lisker, Senior Vice-President for Security of MasterCard International stated: 'MasterCard doesn't recommend the use of the Internet now ... We would advise against using the Internet for credit cards transactions.'[59]

Policy-makers and law enforcement officials are also fearful of fraud over publicly accessible networks using digital cash. 'Electronic mugging' through the unauthorised use of the conventional credit card is already indicative of the growing problem of policing electronic transactions. VISA is the largest credit-card organisation, with 442 million cardholders and 19,000 member financial institutions world-wide. MasterCard is second largest, with 300 million cardholders and 22,000 member institutions. Losses in the United States alone from transactions involving counterfeit credit cards in 1984 amounted to $40 million,[60] which rose to $147.5 million in 1991,[61] and to $700 million in 1995.[62] (And this despite redesigned cards which incorporated additional security features such as watermark magnetics.) According to the House Banking and Financial Services Committee, counterfeit credit-card schemes are estimated to be worth $1.5 billion annually in underground business.[63]

It has been estimated that electronic commerce on the Internet is expected to grow from $730 million in 1996 to $2.74 billion in 1997.[64] Longer-range forecasts are less certain; projections range anywhere from $22 billion to $10 trillion in on-line sales by the year 2000.[65] The potential for 'electronic mugging' may increase commensurate with the volume of transactions and the variety of ways in which digital cash can be used. However, the current legislative framework, to the extent that it guarantees individual's rights for existing electronic payments (such as in automatic teller machines (ATMs) or electronic fund transfers at the point-of-sale (EFTPOS)), along with new security measures in the form of cryptography, potentially can eliminate individuals' concerns about electronic fraud.

The Regulatory Framework

Banking has always had to react to changes in technology. One need only consider the challenges presented by the increased use of electronic fund transfers (EFTs) which enabled vast amounts of money to be transferred among banks with great speed, ease, and reduced cost as compared with the traditional paper-based clearing of funds. Electronic fund transfers raised questions relating to security, liability, and risk. However, many issues were settled with reference to existing law and practice of banking. Where the new technology simply did not 'fit', the issues were settled by the terms of the contract of the individual EFT systems. Indeed, there was some debate as to whether the issues raised by EFT could be settled within the context of the rules developed with reference to cheques. Some argued that EFTs are fundamentally different. An EFT is not only much faster than a cheque, but is essentially a credit transfer which is a 'push' of funds, whereas a cheque is a 'pull'. Thus, the EFT is an instruction from a customer to his or her own bank; that instruction does not confer rights upon a third party as does a cheque, which by its nature embodies the rights of the payee to demand payment.[66]

One issue that arose in this debate concerned the point at which an EFT instruction becomes revocable. A cheque can be countermanded at any time up to payment. Similarly, although an EFT is not a negotiable instrument, it is 'an authority and instruction, from the customer to the bank'.[67] The bank must act upon the mandate of its customer. So, if the customer revokes the instruction before payment, the bank is obliged to honour the cancellation of that instruction, otherwise it exceeds the mandate given by its customer.

Thus, the question of when payment is actually made became the central issue. Is it made when the funds are transferred to the recipient's bank, or when the recipient's bank places the funds at the disposal of its customer? As Chris Reed explained, 'the problem of identifying when a payment is irrevocable is particularly intractable', not because of the peculiar nature of EFTs, but because of a lack of any generally agreed rule.[68] In an execution of an EFT, 'payment' is deemed by English banks to be the point at which the funds are transferred by the recipient bank into the account of the payee. The practice of continental banks, on the other hand, is that the funds cannot be recalled after reaching the recipient bank.[69]

However, the rules of CHAPS (Clearing House Automated Payments System) is that an instruction becomes irrevocable once the payee bank sends an acknowledgement to the payer's bank. The payee bank is then under an obligation to give same-day value to its customer.[70] In sum, according to Roy Goode: '[T]here seems to be no reason why automated EFT should in any way affect the rules as to the time when payment is completed through a transfer of funds ... the sole effect of EFT is to accelerate the process.'[71]

Another issue surrounding EFT concerned liability relating to errors and fraud. It is established that banks are liable for things within their control, such as their equipment and the conduct of their employees. If an EFT instruction is received by a bank, but is not acted upon, or is acted upon improperly, then the bank would be liable to its customer for those errors. An incorrect transfer – one that is either paid to the wrong payee, or to the correct payee in the wrong amount – would be effected without the customer's mandate and the bank would thus not be able to debit the customer's account. When the customer's instructions are ambiguous, 'the bank is protected if it carries out the instructions in good faith and upon a reasonable interpretation of the customer's intentions'.[72] Of course, if the customer provides the bank with the wrong instructions, the customer is liable for his or her own loss. Thus, this issue, too, is settled with reference to the fundamental rules and practice governing the banker–customer relationship. Electronic fund transfers therefore did not raise particularly novel issues.

If the bank makes a payment without a proper mandate, the customer is not liable for the loss. Most EFTs are transmitted to the bank in paper form which bears a signature, or by magnetic tape in the case of large corporate customers. If the bank proceeds with an unauthorised, fraudulent EFT, the situation is the same as if the bank paid a cheque with a forged signature; it acts outside its mandate.[73]

In the United States, the Uniform Commercial Code (UCC) Article 4A provides that the bank and the customer must establish commercially reasonable security procedures between them (such as passwords, or a call-back to confirm the transaction). Where no security measures have been agreed, the bank is liable for loss, which provides the bank with a strong incentive to formulate general security and contract terms with its customers.[74] And, where the code is silent on the question of liability, it has been argued that common law negligence should provide a basis for recovery 'where a bank reasonably should have known of a fraud but still pays out a wire transfer to an unauthorised recipient'.[75]

The Electronic Data Interchange (EDI) system administrator, that is, the 'value-added' network which operates the EFT system – such as BACS-tel (the Bankers' Automated Clearing Services Limited) – is liable for damage to or loss of a transmission.[76] Such systems use encryption and other data security measures, such as passwords and other protocols, to ensure safety in transmissions. Many EFT systems provide their own rules for settling the issue of fraud. For instance, the US CHIPS (Clearing House Interbank Payments System) places the onus to detect fraud on the beneficiary's bank, because this is the place where face-to-face contact is most likely to occur, and damages are not incurred until the funds are released.[77]

Other EFT transactions, such as EFTPOS, are more complex than wholesale EFTs between clearing banks. Electronic fund transfers at the point-of-sale comprise a series of arrangements between the customer who uses a credit or debit card, the merchant who accepts the cards, and the clearing bank or financial institution. Certain peculiarities accompany EFTPOS, or cheques that have been supported by a cheque guarantee card, such as the fact that a customer generally cannot countermand these transactions. Such provisions are generally included in the contract between the customer and the bank. In fact, the entire EFTPOS relationship is a 'web of contractual relationships' which sets out at the outset the rights and obligations of the parties.[78] As Eric Woods put it, 'Contract, all the way!'[79]

Thus, it is likely that issues concerning a customers' liability for a fraudulent transfer will be settled with reference to current practice applied to the new media. Just as EFTPOS transactions and the liability for fraud of value-added networks in EFTs has been settled by contractual agreements, it is likely that a significant dose of contract terms between the individual and the digital cash provider will provide sufficient assurance. For instance, the liability of the value-added service provider would apply for issues arising from bi-directional digital cash transfers. If one 'customer's' transmission of funds to another 'customer' goes awry, the issue will be settled with reference to the contract terms of the digital cash provider.

However, it is likely that the majority of issues concerning fraud and theft that will arise from the use of digital cash will resemble more the current issues relating to plastic cards, such as credit and debit cards, used in automatic teller machines. In other words, the issues arising from a case where a criminal manages to gain access to an individual's code for his 'electronic wallet' will not differ substantially from those which arise when a criminal manages to obtain the personal identification number (PIN) for an individual's ATM or credit card. And again, the regulatory framework governing ATMs and plastic cards could be applied to digital cash.

Indeed, one of the central issues raised by ATMs involved the authentication of an instruction to the bank. That is, while a cheque or other written instruction carries a signature which authenticates the customer's mandate to the bank, when ATMs first came into use it became difficult to prove the genuineness of an ATM transaction initiated by a debit card and PIN. Without a signature, it became difficult for a bank to prove that a PIN was put into the ATM by the genuine card-holder, and equally difficult for a customer to prove that he or she did not authorise a particular transaction and that it was performed fraudulently.

This issue was addressed through statutes. In the United Kingdom, the Consumer Credit Act 1974, s.84(1) stipulates that a customer is liable for any unauthorised use of a credit card or lost PIN up to the first £30. In the United States, Section 909 of the US Electronic Fund Transfer Act 1978 provides that a customer is liable for the first $50 where the customer reports the loss or theft of the card or PIN to the bank within two days, or $500 if the loss is reported up to sixty days after the theft or loss.[80]

Such formulae are not, in essence, novel. Such statutory provisions merely update and apply to the electronic media earlier maxims that governed questions of liability between bankers and their customers. Indeed, it can be seen to be a compromise between the principle that a customer must act in a way that minimises fraud and the principle that the bank must be vigilant to ensure that it acts only upon a genuine mandate of its customer. The customer's responsibility was expressed by Lord Finlay in *London Joint Stock Bank Ltd v. Macmillan & Arthur*: 'If a [customer] draws a cheque in a manner which facilitates fraud, he is guilty of a breach of duty as between himself and the banker and he will be responsible to the banker for any loss sustained by the banker as a natural and direct consequence of this breach of duty.'[81] Thus, it follows that the customer has a duty to keep his or her PIN secret, and should be liable for some loss if he or she does not report the likelihood of a fraudulent use of his or her card.

The bank's responsibility stems from the essence of the banker–customer relationship as that of a contract between creditor and debtor.[82] The bank can act only upon the mandate of the customer; if it acts otherwise, it cannot debit the customer's account. This was expressed in the Bills of Exchange Act 1882, s.24, which provided that a forged or unauthorised signature to a bill was wholly inoperative.[83] If the bank does not recognise that the bill is a forgery and pays the holder of the bill, it acts contrary to the mandate of its customer, which it is bound by contract to carry out with reasonable skill and care. Thus, the bank would be liable for the loss.

It should be noted, however, there is nothing in the US Electronic Funds Transfer Act which gives any clear guidance of how to resolve the 'yes you did, no I didn't issue' when it comes to proving the authenticity of an electronic transaction.[84] Yet, as Chris Reed found, in the 'vast majority of disputed ATM and EFTPOS transactions which have come before the Banking and Building Societies Ombudsmen, the presumption has been that the bank's records are correct … the customer has no way of proving otherwise as all the relevant information is in the bank's possession'.[85]

This disadvantages individuals since the ATMs do not record the series of key-strokes that precede a transaction; they record only that the transaction has taken place. The machines do not record the unsuccessful attempts by a fraudster to use a stolen card in various locations unsuccessfully until finally hitting upon the correct PIN. More disturbing is the sophistication of many fraudsters. At a recent hearing of the House Banking and Financial Services Committee it was reported that credit cards are being counterfeited on a very large scale by organised, transnational groups and that fraudsters have devised sophisticated means to obtain and use the PINs and account numbers of unwary customers.[86] Thus, the original debit or credit card may still be in the possession of the customer while fraudsters are using counterfeit duplicates. Customers are therefore not likely to be aware that fraud is taking place until it is too late, and thus would have no reason to alert the bank to fulfil statutory requirements. The statutory solutions that limit customers' liability *if* they notify their bank perhaps unfairly place inordinate risk upon the individual customers.[87] This form of electronic crime is disadvantaging the individual.

However, digital cash promises to be more secure than ATMs, because of sophisticated cryptography, known as 'Secure Electronic Transactions' (SET). VISA and MasterCard have cooperated on secure payment systems to develop protocols for a secure Internet payments system based upon RSA Data Security. The result is a public-key encryption system.[88] Simply, the system operates by encrypting transmissions that can be decrypted only if the 'keys' (electronic codes, known as 'digital signatures' or 'digital certificates') of the sender and receiver are compatible and recognise each other.[89]

The main challenges to stopping electronic crime are therefore not that daunting. National legal systems must be adapted to the technology, but as the foregoing has illustrated, this has been the practice with each successive innovation in banking technology. The challenge here is to apply to digital cash the statutes and practices developed for plastic cards. Electronic 'fixes' must also be put into practice, such as secure payment systems, which recently have been developed. However, the very thing that makes digital cash payments safe for individuals makes it easier for money launderers to hide their activities. For if encrypted systems are completely anonymous, the transactions are opaque to all observers except for the sender and receiver, which could frustrate governments' efforts to observe dirty and hot money in flight.

Money Laundering

It has been estimated that the turnover from organised crime in the United States amounted to between $170 and $250 billion in 1989, and that the world-wide figure approaches $1 trillion.[90] Large-scale money laundering threatens the integrity of global financial institutions and particularly the confidence that the international financial system must maintain. This is apart from the fact that money laundering enables criminals to reap the profits from other illegal activities, including economic crime, such as firm fraud, commodity futures trading abuses, and drug trafficking.

Sophisticated attempts to conceal the source of money can involve hundreds, perhaps thousands, of bank accounts in numerous jurisdictions in an attempt to create as complex a web of transactions as possible – a process known as 'layering'. As the case of the Bank of Credit and Commerce International (BCCI) indicated, it was relatively easy to structure the corporate matrix of the bank such that its headquarters was a holding company incorporated in Luxembourg, with its principal operations in Luxembourg and the Cayman Islands, two states which had relatively strong bank secrecy requirements. The bank also engaged in complex layering. As reported by Daniel Laiffer:

> Drug money was first deposited in a non-BCCI bank in any city in the US. The money was then wired to an account at BCCI in Tampa that was set up for the laundering operation. From Tampa the money was transferred by wire through a non-BCCI New York bank to BCCI headquarters in Luxembourg. From there the money was wired to BCCI in London, where it was placed in a certificate of deposit. This certificate of deposit was used as a basis to generate a loan in the Bahamas to a phony corporation set up by the drug dealers. From the Bahamas the money was wired back to the undercover account in Tampa, where it was transferred by wire to the BCCI branch in Uruguay. From Uruguay, the money was transferred as cash into Colombia.[91]

Such layering makes it difficult to trace transactions by presenting law enforcement authorities with administrative barriers against obtaining financial details, and by making it difficult to obtain other evidence and to freeze assets.

Criminals also take advantage of the speed and complexity in an EFT to conceal the source of the funds. The simplest EFT takes place between two clearing banks. However, many EFTs involve numerous intermediary banks and many payment orders. Intermediaries sometimes use different protocols to complete the transfer, which can leave bits of information out along the way, and sometimes the intermediaries will not even know the name of the originator or the payee, only the name of the two banks on either side of the chain. This can make the construction of a paper trail especially difficult for law enforcement officials, and hence also makes EFTs a preferred medium for money laundering.[92]

Thus, money laundering operations are more noticeable, and thus easier to stop, when the money is first introduced into the system – the 'placement' stage – since deposits without an apparently bona fide commercial reason more easily arouse suspicion. Even the most complex schemes start in some bank account in some state's territory.[93] It is this philosophy which has guided the approach of the United States and the United Kingdom, two states with stringent anti-money laundering legislation. Both states place the onus of vigilance on banks.

The United States has a barrage of anti-money laundering legislation, including the Money Laundering Act of 1986, the Anti-Drug Abuse Act of 1990, the Annunzio–Wiley Anti-Money Laundering Act of 1992, and the Money Laundering Suppression Act of 1994. The obligation of the bank to report suspicious activity under these laws is emphatic. There is a blanket threshold above which all transactions must be reported.[94] Under the Currency and Foreign Transaction Reporting Act (CFTA) provisions of the Bank Secrecy Act of 1970 (BSA), all financial institutions are required to file a Currency Transaction Report (CTR) for any transactions of any financial instruments totalling more than US$10,000, including a payment, receipt, transfer inside the United States or to foreign bank accounts.[95] It is an offence to wilfully violate any record-keeping requirements under the CFTA, to wilfully or negligently to fail to file a CRT, or to wilfully make false statements in a report filed under the CFTA.

In the United Kingdom, the laundering of money derived from drug-related crimes was criminalised by the Drug Trafficking Offences Act 1986, which was re-enacted in 1994 as the Drug Trafficking Act 1994.[96] The Northern Ireland (Emergency Provisions) Act of 1991 criminalised the laundering of money connected with terrorist activities. This made it an offence for anyone to assist another to retain (Section 53), conceal, convert, transfer or to move from the jurisdiction of the courts (Section 54) the proceeds of terrorist activities if that person had knowledge of, or suspected, the source of the funds as having derived from terrorist activities. The Criminal Justice Act 1993 (CJA) implemented the European Community's Council Directive on Prevention of the Use of the Financial System for the Purposes of Money Laundering, which itself was drafted in conformity with Article 3(1)b of the 1988 United Nations (Vienna) Convention Against Illicit Traffic in Narcotic Drugs and Psychotropic Substances, which called upon all states to establish criminal offences for money laundering.[97] The CJA made the laundering of proceeds of all serious offences a crime. Section 93A outlines several related offences of direct relevance to banks and other financial services institutions: first, to facilitate the retention or control of monies derived from criminal activities; secondly, to conceal such proceeds by its removal or transfer from the jurisdiction of the courts; and thirdly, to fail to disclose knowledge or suspicion of money laundering. Finally, Section 93D made it an offence to 'tip off' a person about an actual or impending investigation.

Thus, in both the United States and the United Kingdom, the onus has been placed on financial institutions to police the financial system. It is an offence to fail to report any unusual activity, and this relates both to the directors of a financial institution as a whole and to individual employees of the institution for failing to report internally. Banks and other financial institutions are required to maintain identification and verification procedures, record-keeping, internal reporting procedures and to train employees in the procedures and in the laws relating to money laundering and to take other procedures 'as may be reasonably necessary' for the purposes of preventing money laundering. Banks must now be wary of such things as persons acting through intermediaries, and to assure that they know the true identity of a new customer. In the case of a one-off transaction, if money laundering is suspected banks must report if a single transaction exceeds Ecu 15,000, or if it appears that a transaction for over Ecu 15,000 is being structured. Institutions which do not implement internal procedures can face a criminal charge under Regulation 5(3), irrespective of whether money laundering has occurred.

Digital cash introduces two fundamental problems in enforcing anti-money laundering regulations. The first is that the anti-money laundering legislation has placed the onus on banks to report suspicious transactions. However, the transmission of digital cash could be performed without using the bank at all for the transfer; rather, it could be done by using one – or, more complexly, all – of the commercial service providers offering digital cash services. Indeed, money launderers conceivably could set up rows of personal computers programmed to make intricate and complex transmissions of digital cash through thousands of digital wallets in and out of all of the systems offering digital cash. The anti-money laundering legislations therefore will have to be extended to all financial institutions that offer these services. Moreover, it conceivably also could have to apply to all the shops offering goods and services on the Internet, otherwise payments could be made for fictitious goods and services in order to render the money 'clean'. However, extending the legislation thus could be problematic, as the legislation already has been the subject of substantial criticism for failing to apply to, for instance, commodity trading institutions, where money laundering can occur just as easily as through bank accounts.

The second problem raised by digital cash is that it could provide greater secrecy to money launderers. Anonymity is necessary to protect individuals as they go about their business of using the new technology. That same anonymity could present a barrier to governments' efforts to monitor transactions. Indeed, a recent Financial Action Task Force (FATF) report warned that the 'speed, security and anonymity' of Internet transactions could frustrate government monitoring.[98] As expressed by a European Commission fact-finding report:

> The idea of anonymous and untraceable software tokens, which could be used by anybody, raises the spectre of ... marginalisation of both commercial and central banks, not to mention the risk of fraud and forgery. Small wonder that ... the central banks expressed concern about the potential use of e-cash for money laundering.[99]

However, having said this, it is important to point out that some states, such as France, already have adopted a system of encryption whereby 'trusted third parties' must be supplied with the two security keys to digital transmissions, and to disclose to enforcement officials a user's private key if required to do so under compulsion of law.[100] It is therefore likely that, even if current anti-money laundering legislation lags behind technological developments, governments will retain the ability to rip peek-holes through the shadow of cyberspace.

Conclusion

It has been argued that the main challenges to individuals' security raised by the use of successive technologies has been resolved by adapting existing legislation. Issues of liability, risk and security have been fundamental questions ever since banking moved from the physical transfer of specie to paper-based transactions where the paper instruments embodied rights and obligations, and to the transmission of information about wealth disembodied from physical tender. These issues have been more or less settled through statutes (such as the UCC and the Electronic Funds Transfer Act in the United States, and the Consumer Credit Act in the United Kingdom), by common practice based on the principles of the banker–customer relationship which have been adapted to deal with the new ways in which the old problem can manifest in electronic banking, and by contract terms of the EFT systems themselves. Electronic methods for banking up to now have not challenged fundamentally the regulation of market economies, but have enabled market economies to do what they always have done, only much cheaper and faster. Other issues, such as the ability of governments to eavesdrop into otherwise secure Internet communications, doubtless will rage for some time, but in a free society such debates, quite properly, should rage as new opportunities are balanced against social risks and costs.

So, what of the task for International Relations? Quite simply, the global system which assists the spread of transnational crime raises interesting questions about the way in which states can deal with the problem. In a word, they cannot do it alone; such global problems mandate global solutions. So long as law is tied to territory – and so long as those laws are different – while crime increasingly is not, such threats to all states will continue. Internet commerce and payments of digital cash can be made as effortlessly across borders as they can be made within them, and as has been shown, economic crime using communication technologies does not stop at the water's edge. By definition, the task for International Relations is to study the ways in which states can cooperate to meet these challenges, for the Westphalian system of compartmentalised legal jurisdictions is simply not up to the task of disciplining civil society actors that are more mobile than the representatives of the state.

Bilateral and multilateral treaties can be one effective method – among a range of alternative methods – to tackle problems of common concern. A government can commit itself in a treaty concerning any number of issues, so long as the state is in a position to comply with the treaty. For instance, governments can agree upon security protocols to ensure interoperability across borders upon which the Internet, almost by definition, depends. Governments can also agree to settle issues of their municipal law relating to the risk and liability to individuals and commercial services providers arising from the fraudulent use of technology.

Another effective method could be the functional harmonisation of national laws in these areas. The foregoing analysis of legal regimes was confined to comparative developments in two states only, the United States and the United Kingdom, due to spatial constraints. However, it is interesting that the mechanisms that these states have evolved have been remarkably similar. No doubt this owes in some measure to their shared common law traditions. However, it surely must owe as well to the fact that the integrated global economy presents states with the same risks. It is therefore not surprising that the approach of different sovereign states to deal with common problems have been similar. Perhaps an agenda for International Relations could be to investigate the ways in which globalisation is promoting the functional harmonisation of the laws of distinct sovereign entities.[101]

It could be that as states attempt to rein-in certain negative aspects of globalisation, such as money laundering, they are more or less forced to do so in similar ways. Elsewhere in this volume, Martin Shaw writes about the development of a 'global state'. His level of analysis is that of global riot control, which orients his analysis to the military responses of governments, and to the locus of decision-making and political power within the global state. It could very well be the case that a global state is also emerging at 'lower' levels of analysis, in regulating the behaviour of civil society actors through harmonised systems of municipal law.

Harmonisation may be an effective way in which to govern a global society while maintaining the parameters of the state system. Such harmonisation is problematic. Not only are there differing national priorities, but to expect all states to enact the same laws raises problems of relativism. For instance, the criminalisation of money laundering extends deeper into what states define as a 'crime'. To criminalise the movement of money derived from 'illegal' activities requires that all states 'criminalise' the same things, otherwise definitions of what constitutes 'dirty' and 'hot' money will also vary. Even in the area of drug trafficking, which has received the most attention in discussions about money laundering – perhaps unduly, to the exclusion of economic crime – one need only look to the Netherlands to see the very different views that are taken towards this issue.

And, for harmonisation to be effective, it must be not only global, but it must involve the harmonisation of a host of related areas. This 'harmonisation creep', for lack of a better word, is not unprecedented. International trade negotiators have long recognised that once border measures, such as tariffs and quotas, had been addressed, the next phase was to harmonise rules regarding non-tariff barriers, which involved examining complex government policies ranging from health and safety regulations to workers' rights. Advanced stages of integration, such as in the European Union, have shown that complex markets require the harmonisation of a host of areas ranging from competition laws to taxation. It may be that a global Leviathan could be bred by such incrementalism, but that is a topic best not pursued here. The fact remains that the only way to address global economic crime is to reassess the territorial approach to dealing with it.

PART IV

The Agenda for the Twenty-first Century

CHAPTER 12

What is Obvious and What is Beyond the Obvious

Stephen Chan

The question of time, or at least the construct of time, has us all questioning the wherewithals of a crossover from one point in time to another: in this case, from the twentieth century to the twenty-first. Even the technology of high modernity – computers – approach 2000 as a year zero, which may throw the orders and receipts of an instrumentalist world into what some might regard as an appropriate anarchy. Thus might the liberal capitalist project be (at least temporarily) thrown into its own consummation of itself; or be, rather expensively, spared such consummation. Who would have thought, in a world of global technology, each computer, one by one, might have to have its date reset?

The conceit, for technophobes, is that something is messy under the surface. Yet this is more than a mere conceit. In this section, Martin Shaw speaks of messiness within the system or arrangement (or whatever) of globalisation. Like A.J.R. Groom in this book's first section, he sees a movement to a global politics, but, more precisely than Groom, sees the contingencies and conditionalities of it all. The time, at least, of simple dyads, of neat oppositional sets that may or may not interrogate each other, may certainly be passing. Indeed, if one is to talk of conceits, it was always one of the most precious of conceits within International Relations that the world order, the globe, or intellectual reflectiveness on the universal nature and moral order of the world could be seen or explained as a series of oppositional sets. As if it were all tennis. So that, in its most fundamentalist and realist manifestation, it was the rivalry between the two great superpowers. At its most sophisticated, it was the crude if erudite parading of a cosmopolitan thought against a communitarian thought – close enough, in the context of a careful reading of Enlightenment intellectual history, to be twins; but separated at the birth of International Relations' concern to have its own, philosophically anchored, normative project. And the separations and oppositions continue in debates on structure and agency; on what is purposive in international behaviour and what is merely practical.

Martin Shaw argues that the world is indeed, to borrow the sort of communitarian terms used by pioneering International Relations writers like Mervyn Frost, constitutive. We are all constituted by what we appear within. However, says Shaw, this is not simultaneously determining. No neat dyad of structure and agency here. Global politics, in its messiness, affords scope for a *mélange* of disciplines to be assembled, in order to do what single disciplines have not. Michael Mann has spoken of 'overlapping networks of interaction' and, though problematic, overlapping discourses may be the way forward, even if not immediately successful. The globalised world is not easily amenable to any instant or single culturally bounded explanation.

Some of this has obvious echoes of, if not inspiration from, Anthony Giddens. However, the sociology of it all, of a globalised world and its politics, is (to use the term again) messier than in a society within modernity, never mind high modernity. Just as Gunnar Myrdal once talked of 'soft' states which could not deliver the promise embedded in a citizen's relationship with his or her government, so also we may now be heralding a 'soft' global politics. In what way does a starving, limping and uneducated child soldier in Rwanda partake in a global civil society? This child is not concerned to transcend his or her local and parochial civil society. He or she would like a local civil society *in the first instant*. This is the same response to the self-stimulated rhetoric of post-modernism: what about those who must live in the pre-modern?

However, discussion of the local within the global must be aware of a number of non-constituting factors. Not just that local states might not have formal constitutions, but that, below the state, whether it be 'soft', ruthless or incompetent, the local leaderships of village communities might not be as Body Shop advertisements deem them to be: paradigms of cooperative self-help, hard work, and deliberative leadership enshrining values that are both resplendently moral and ancient – traditional. Rajni Kothari has spoken of a pluralism within International Relations which begins with the village. If there are units of analysis, here is the first. However, as David Humphreys acknowledges, in this section, the community control that ecologists and environmentalists might talk about is not necessarily in keeping with assumptions of pastoral-romantic local leadership and community.

This is where Keith Webb's chapter presents itself as a point for taking stock. Of course the millennium time-bug in computers will be overcome – no matter what rhetorical benefit it might bring to an introductory essay which will say a few things about the end of time, the end of history, and what lies beyond the point history has now reached. The electronic facility of IT resources will greatly abet International Relations scholars, and Webb is quite right to give a low-key but slightly didactic opinion of the worth, for instance, of the Internet. However, there are those not only without computers, but without electricity. And a great many of those with electricity suffer blackouts; or live in conditions of such feeble security that owning a computer is not only the investment of years' salary, but an invitation to be burgled and to have all your other possessions, even if meagre, vandalised or appropriated. Having said that, the outreach of globalisation is felt. The days are gone when, once, a decade ago, I observed Webb taking a new group of graduate students to their first data-processing session in the University of Kent's computing laboratory, and heard a Tanzanian student say in wonder, looking at a computer terminal, 'ah so *that's* what they look like!' But global outreach is itself messy, uneven, and contingent. Webb understands the irony explicit in the Internet and other electronic resources being at the increasing disposal of International Relations scholars, both as a research and a teaching tool. In a post-realist intellectual world, such possession merely adds to those already empowered. There is the added irony that the Internet is, in a sense, and a reasonably if contingently global sense as well, anarchic. What price complete abjuration of realism now, when its more subtle problematics might only be beginning to be discerned?

International Relations, in the midst of discourses, modernities, pre- and post-modernities, oppositional dyads, and even within global messiness, can be said to have been concerned with the discovery of, if not truth, then statements about the world that are true; at least not false. Beverley Neufeld, however, remarks that feminist theory, whether within or without International Relations, has been less concerned with truth as with goals. It is not given to be a case of problematising what is true but to insist that, in the future, International Relations should have something to do with what is *right* and *good*.

Like Martin Shaw, she argues that community and individuals are mutually constitutive. The state is not the sole community, however, nor is citizenship the sole identity. For instance, womanhood is an identity. The danger of mainstream International Relations ascribing community to states, or of a newer International Relations, represented, say, by Andrew Linklater, talking of 'a search for an imagined international community, by conceptualising it as some sort of mystical entity to be conjured up', is deficient in the face of a feminist call. What may have been gone beyond is a concern to theorise the state; but what has not fully been recognised is a need to theorise community, and, within it, what might be the good life (as satisfied need and desire) and what might be the good life (as moral conduct).

Where, then, does this lead us? It is the end of the twentieth century. The conceptualisation of the global is messy. The not-yet-undertaken theorisation of community seems, if not messy, tricky. Panaceas, conjured by our imaginations, can be pastoral or romantic. Technologies embed us further in the undertaking of modernism: that we cannot live without the products of modernity even in the face of the bulk of the world barely living at all, or having no product of its own by which to live.

Fukuyama certainly recognised that technology confers advantages on those who had the advantage in the first place to possess it. So, to end this section and, indeed, this book, Paul Bacon looks more deeply and, to a significant extent, more sympathetically at Fukuyama than, for instance, Derrida (see Bacon's note 3), or the present editor. Fukuyama does go beyond the Enlightenment project, of which Hegel was a part, and from which project the idea of a spirit of history, working towards its consummation, arose. Looking at Greek thought, he calls upon Plato's idea that a soul has a desiring part, a reasoning part, and a *thymos*, a part of spiritedness. It is this last part that seeks recognition. From here, Fukuyama tends to leap back to Hegel, and to relate what is well enough known of his work – that the beginning of history was a battle to the death for recognition, for prestige. This is where Hegel's work on the master and the slave arose. With the revolutions in eighteenth-century France and America, however, history was brought to an end by way of the clash between master and slave being replaced by the reciprocal recognitions of state and citizen.

In this (rather politically concrete) sense (and not in any real metaphysical sense at all), the end of the twentieth century, with its triumph of the West, with exactly those values of the Western revolutions in France and America (and with French tanks and American warplanes doing most damage in Iraq), the end of history merely had a coda; and it was not unlikely there should have been a restatement of Hegel to commemorate concrete political acts and their forms of rhetoric. If this were all there was to Fukuyama, well then, a footnote in intellectual history is at least a parallel to a coda to the end of history itself.

However, the idea of the desiring and spirited soul is an intriguing one. Fukuyama uses the part, the *thymos*, as that strategic ingredient that does not allow a soul merely to bask in the products of modernity. It seeks recognition. It is ever a citizen. This overcomes Jarrod Wiener's earlier pessimism, in this book, on the inabilities of liberalism.

Here, however, two further arguments present themselves. The first, Fukuyama himself recognises. What if there has not been a reconciliation of master and slave within democracy? What if it has been merely the triumph of slaves and a slave's morality; and history has bred only a class merely comfortable in the freedom it finds itself within, will seek to preserve itself, perhaps within continuing freedom, but will not die for it, has no spiritedness, no *thymos*? The second argument Fukuyama skirts. The end of history has not seen the end of the slaves left *outside* history itself. The masters may have been supplanted within the West, but the West is not the world, and not the globe. Catching up with history perhaps, or achieving their own history, those Other states and communities are exercising forms of *thymos*. Fukuyama recognises this by conceding nationalisms may be just such an exercise. However, nations are new, at least recent, and certainly contingent. History can and probably will move beyond any individual nationalism. Perhaps all nationalisms. But, what about our present moment, now, at the end of the twentieth century? At least the triumphalism has gone. But the question has not gone. What about the first men? Those dissatisfied by the premature time and limited space of the so-called end, resolution, consummation of history? Who live within present nationalisms or indeed, against them? Or against *inter*nationalisms?

Fukuyama misidentifies these people. They are not just the last men of history, slaves who have triumphed over a master and now brutally squander their inheritance. They are authentically 'first' men, or the first people of that large omission of our history. More to the point, in terms of the early part of this book, in Paul Rich's chapter, are they the 'just men' of the vision behind the Iranian revolution? Was this the aborted paradigm of a true historical *thymos*, combining new desires and new reasons?

In the space of this question, never mind the ideas of history and time, is it enough to say we are mutually constitutive? *What* is being constituted here? And in what *struggle* is the constitution taking place? The politeness of normative International Relations is that it *must* excise struggle from its discourse, since struggle, with its death and ransack, cannot exist in a normative vision. Normative International Relations, therefore, exists not at a time within history, or before history's progress, but *beyond* the struggles of history.

What is being constituted? I wrote that we are beyond simple dyads. We are beyond simple realism and pluralism. Within pluralism we have rogue states (they behave outside the *system* of states), tribes, clans, religions, criminal gangs, warlords, outlaw community leaders, and the protectors of trees. How will these people face or, more to the point, seek to create history? Or overthrow our history?

What if Fukuyama is wrong, not only perhaps about Hegel, but in his use of Plato? He suggests that a slave victory over the masters, but with a slavish mentality intact, might constitute a society of desire and reason, but without *thymos*. Arising from the inadequacies of such a society of 'last men', he suggests 'new men' of *thymos* alone, without desire or reason, so bestial, might storm society. There is an obvious other use of this perhaps too neat typology of the soul. What if the 'first men' are those of *desire*? Perhaps without our reason?

In this book, both A.J.R. Groom and Fred Halliday talked of the banality and posturing of post-modernism. They take a vocabulary at its face value. There were forerunners in the absurdity stakes, and the writers of their own youth, Sartre and Camus, sought a vocabulary of *actions* in the face of the empty and hostile, senseless, universe. Men and women have gone to firing squads clutching copies of Byron's poem of freedom's banner fluttering against the wind, certainly; but have also stood on scaffolds with copies of Camus *The Rebel*. Is this one of John Burton's basic needs? One of John Vincent's human rights? Or, is there a desire to rebel, both as a desire in itself and as a desire in the face of omission? Some readings of Nietzsche might here be as well as readings of Hegel. Or simply, perhaps overdue at the end of the century, a re-reading of Sartre's introduction to Fanon's *Wretched of the Earth*; an end to the polite discourse of International Relations, before the first men force an end.

I do not want to misuse Martin Shaw beyond his usage by me to date. He speaks of the critical importance of 'Western values like human rights and democracy becom[ing] globalised, and a genuine global politics develop[ing] around them'. They do not, however, have to be *Western* values. Fukuyama makes an unconvincing foray into Eastern values; but this does not mean a convincing foray is impossible. Why should Shaw foreclose this effort? More convincing is his use of Michael Mann, who spoke of 'polymorphous crystallisation'. Although he spoke of this within states, it may also be spoken of within global politics. It is not the end of history. It is merely the end of the twentieth century. In no culture is 20 a magic or symbolic number. However, in certain systems of numerology, 21 is a number where the first, 2, is halved in its second, 1, to become 1 again; and this is necessary before there can be a 22, in which the number is composed of two equal figures. It would be a Freudian jest to say that what is polymorphous might satisfy that which is desirous. But it is not a jest in idleness. History has not ended, but perhaps needs to be rewound a century or two so that it might become, through the admixture of other histories, and overlapping discourses, more polymorphously crystalline. At the end of the twentieth century, this might be the messy but ultimately beautiful task of an International Relations of the twenty-first. It will be harder to say what is true. But it might speak *of itself* as good.

CHAPTER 13

The Global Revolution and the Twenty-first Century: from International Relations to Global Politics

Martin Shaw

In this chapter I discuss globalisation as a profound transformation, the roots of which can be traced through modern world history. In contrast to much literature which sees its contemporary form as a product of market liberalisation, I argue that global change entered its critical phase as a result of the political-military changes of 1945–47, and that the end of the Cold War completed this. The twenty-first century, which in historical terms began therefore in 1989–91, is a period in which global relations are recognised as defining and the global revolution is beginning to be seen in its full significance.

The meaning of this for the social sciences is not limited to understanding the characteristics of globalisation as a discrete process or set of processes. Rather, we are on the threshold of a conceptual revolution, in which the methodological nationalism of the domesticated traditional social sciences is being challenged in non-core disciplines and interdisciplinary fields. In order to accomplish the theoretical changes which are entailed, we need to re-configure the meaning of key concepts such as society and culture in global terms.

The global revolution has particular implications for the field of International Relations. My discussion argues that the need to rethink the concept of state, in terms similar to those in which I discuss society and culture, is central to reconstituting the subject as a constitutive discourse of a wider global social science.

The Global Revolution and the Twenty-first Century

In the ubiquitous debates about globalisation, the phenomenon has often been identified with late twentieth-century forms of political economy –

notably market liberalisation – and the associated changes in political thought. Important as these forms have been, however, they are hardly the essence of global transformation. Globalisation is not simply or mainly either an economic or a recent historical phenomenon, indeed not a single process at all, and requires a much deeper and broader understanding. Only when this is grasped can the significance of the global for the social sciences be understood.

Globalisation can be defined as a complex set of distinct but related processes – economic, cultural, social but also political and military – through which social relations have come to be understood in a common world framework. In this sense globalisation includes the development of trans-national relations of many kinds as well as specifically global forms. It can be linked, as Anthony Giddens among others has argued, to profound changes in the relations of time and space in the development of modernity.[1] The preconditions for globalisation have been developing for something like six centuries, in the processes through which the 'multi-power actor civilization of the West', as Michael Mann calls it,[2] originating in Europe, has come to dominate more or less the entire world.

Each century – or more precisely each historical period (obviously these do not coincide precisely with the chronology of centuries) – has made its own contribution to world transformation. From the European exploration of the 'Indies' and discovery of 'America', in the fifteenth century, through the heyday of the Spanish and Portuguese empires to the eighteenth- and nineteenth-century dominance of Britain and France, a Western-dominated world order came into existence. At the heart of this process of change was the extraordinary dynamism of Western economic and cultural life, which by the end of the nineteenth century had produced the core of a modern industrial economy and society on a world scale.

Although some like Immanuel Wallerstein[3] have seen in this development the progress of a capitalist world-system, global market relations have always developed within political frameworks. State forms have not merely expressed but have also shaped global markets. For centuries, the world order has been marked by great political divisions. First it was segmented by the evolving system of European empires. In this sense there was not one world order but several, each centred on a different European metropolis. Twice in the twentieth century, the rivalries of these European orders embroiled large parts of the world in total war. The outcome of the Second World War was the common decline – in some cases ruin – of the traditional empires, and their replacement by a new form of world political division. In the second half of the twentieth century, ideologically polarised blocs replaced nationally-centred empires as the basis of two rival orders.

The Cold War system was the final form of a politically divided world order. Despite its formally reciprocal bipolar character, this system was substantively unbalanced in a way which was quite critical to the emergence of the contemporary form of globalisation. The Soviet bloc centred on historically backward regions of the world economy; it failed to develop legitimate state or inter-state institutions; and it fragmented through both insurrections and inter-state rivalries. The Western bloc, on the other hand, was centred on the most dynamic centres of the world economy; it possessed and developed legitimate state and inter-state institutions; and it maintained its cohesion, successfully containing both popular pressures and inter-state rivalries.

The radical change was therefore that during the Cold War, a more or less united West dominated global economy, culture and politics. For the first time the greater part of the world's space was incorporated within a single geopolitical sphere. Centred on the greatest single state, the United States, the post-1945 West also subsumed the historic European world empires. Most of the residue of bipolarity, the Third World, was clearly within Western-dominated world systems. Even in the Cold War epoch, it was generally thought appropriate to define Soviet-bloc states – and those Third World states which attempted autonomous development – in terms of the degree of their integration into these world systems.

Three points about this transformation are important to emphasise. First, it was the *state* integration of the West (chiefly the transatlantic alliance of North America and Western Europe together with Japan) which created the conditions for a single global space. Secondly, state integration played an essential role in *enabling* the rapid growth of economic, cultural and political globalisation in this space throughout the late twentieth century. Thirdly, the decisive turning-point in globalisation was therefore the mid-century military-political transition (1945–47). It was a *contingent* result of the Second World War and Cold War.

It is only in the light of this major transition that we can understand the significance for globalisation of the secondary transition of 1989–91. This change – the end of the 'short twentieth century' as Eric Hobsbawm[4] has called it – was momentous because it completed and made manifest the full meaning of the earlier change. Once again a state-level transformation unlocked wider changes. The collapse of the Soviet bloc, the Cold War and the Soviet state itself removed the remaining major political division of the world.

This transition enabled the former Communist world to be incorporated more clearly and fully within Western-dominated world markets, systems and institutions. Even more important, it enabled a world which had been sub-stantially unified since the mid-century transformation to recognise itself, at last, as one world. Hence, this perhaps explains – since the owl of Minerva flies at dusk – the upsurge of globalisation debates in the 1990s rather than in the previous decade when the ideology of market liberalisation was rampant.

In historical perspective, then, the (long) nineteenth century (1760–1914, according to Mann[5]) saw the creation of the economic infrastructure of globalisation within politically divided forms. The (short) twentieth century (1914–89) was an era of inter-state struggle, with key mid-century changes – completed in the late-century upheavals – leading to political unification. By this token too, the twenty-first century has already begun in the messy transformations of the 1990s, and those who are waiting for New Year's Eve 1999 have missed the bus.

It is appropriate that the new century also marks a new millennium, since at last – after half a millennium of world change – the global transformations of modern economics, politics and culture are manifest. The global revolution has been a long time in the making and its major transition occurred half a century ago, but it is clear why it is at the current juncture that it has become transparent. The end of the Cold War division into competing world orders marks a crucial substantive and symbolic transition to single-world economic, cultural and political orders.

Global Theory in the Social Sciences

The new transparency of global relations in the 1990s has brought with it a conceptual crisis in the social sciences. The modern tradition of social theory and analysis has encapsulated the essentially political tension at the heart of globalisation. On the one hand, the master-theories of social science, developed from the late eighteenth to the early twentieth centuries, centred on concepts of universal and implicitly global significance – civil society, capitalism, industrialism, modernity. On the other hand, the twentieth-century institutionalisation of the social sciences in academic disciplines, research and teaching practice nationalised these concepts. Theory and analysis came to refer, implicitly if not explicitly, to the national frameworks of state and society which dominated social relations in the mid-century heyday of the nation-state.

The core disciplines of the social sciences, whose intellectual traditions are reference points for each other and for other fields, have been *domesticated* – in the sense of being preoccupied not with Western and world civilisation as a whole but with the social forms of particular national societies. In sociology and political science, for example, the particular was often assumed to represent the general – for example British society, state and capitalism with all their idiosyncracies were held to typify society, state or capitalism as such. Jan Aart Scholte has called this tendency 'methodological nationalism'.[6]

Where the general pattern of social relations on a world scale came to be represented by more than a single case, it was not usually by the forms of global, transnational or even international relations but by the *comparative* method. Comparing the different particular social forms came to substitute for understanding the relations between them and the general structures within which these comparisons might be explained. National and comparative sociology and politics increasingly dominated these core disciplines in practice.

International Relations conformed to this pattern as the exception to the rule. In the early post-war decades when realism was codified, the global could only be conceived in terms of the international. In a world of nation-states, it represented the relations between the units under this single, simple rubric. The inter-national, of course, meant inter-state, since states were assumed, by definition, to represent 'their' nations in an unproblematic, indeed symbiotic relationship. International Relations, even more than the core social sciences, was a Cold War American product. It represented the bifurcation of superpowers and blocs rather than the burgeoning global relations which underlay them.

The division of labour between the domesticated disciplinary social sciences and International Relations reflected the curious reality of the Cold War West. Although nation-states were casting off the military rivalries of centuries to create common institutions, national forms remained dominant. Western integration was first of all the cooperation of the national states and, reflecting them, national societies which had emerged from the era of total war. Commonality presented itself first as the *alliance* and *similarity* of distinct units. Only later would the Western world and its European sub-unit begin to see themselves as integrated wholes.

No wonder, then, that the comparative method became so influential in Western social science and that instead of global knowledge, international research generated comparative studies. The genre has gained new life with the increasing dependence of much European research on European Union funding, with its inbuilt balancing of national interests, and the incorporation of Central and East European nation-states within the Western social science orbit.

The possibility of genuinely global, or at least trans- rather than inter-national, knowledge reflects the partial overcoming not just of the Cold War but of the way in which integrationary tendencies were understood during it. The removal of the border of violence between two distinct world orders has accelerated the tendency to see all national borders as partial and relative.

The dissolution of the ideological world orders has released the power of identity – most obviously but not exclusively in ethnic and national forms. But it has simultaneously loosened still further the sense of discrete nation-state units which were the building blocks of the Cold War. For all the posturing of nationalists, the nation-state is indeed constantly relativised, as so much literature has stressed. The links between people can no longer be squeezed into the national–international strait-jacket. This is as true of social relations 'within' states as it is of those 'across' their borders.

Instead, social relations increasingly are grasped in all their genuine complexity, as interpersonal, familial, professional, local, regional, transnational, world-regional, global – as well as international. Most social relations still have some national-international aspect: for example, even my e-mail address ends in 'uk'. But this signifier is of trivial importance since neither the content nor the mechanism of my communications depends on its national character. Although this is an extreme case, increasingly the international is a residual category of convenience in global relations.

Since social relations are now understood in a variety of spatial terms, some oppose regional or transnational to global change. Global categories have, however, emerged as the main forms of the new theoretical discourse of the social sciences. This is not accidental: the global is the largest and most inclusive framework of social relations. To talk of global transformations does not mean that all relations are of a spatially global kind. Rather, global includes regional and transnational in a way which neither of the others can include the global. In the emerging twenty-first century, therefore, social theory is becoming conscious of a global revolution.

This revolution represents a deep crisis for the social sciences. It is constituting the most important transformations of the structures of social knowledge in recent times. At the centre of these transformations is the question of whether the core disciplinary subjects can escape from their methodological nationalism and reconstitute themselves in global terms. So far, the evidence is that the theoretically constitutive subjects of economics, sociology and politics have indeed been disabled by this tendency. Despite a few new shoots, the mainstreams have hardly been globalised.

Sociology, for example, was organised around concepts of industrial society – or in the Marxist version, capitalist society – which clearly held a potential for global understanding. But these overwhelmingly were operationalised as national categories and the comparative sociology of national societies substituted for global knowledge.[7] The new Marxism failed partly because – with exceptions such as 'world-systems' theory which had their own characteristic weaknesses – it adapted itself to the national contexts of existing social science. Since the Marxist revival petered out, if anything there has been a further domestication of sociology, pragmatically integrating it in national and sub-national contexts while eschewing the understanding of politics, the international and the global. Although these bigger issues have been addressed by major thinkers, including Giddens and Mann, they have impinged only slowly on the institutionalised intellectual context of the discipline.

Political science is equally afflicted. In its case, the standard demarcation of national and international is especially disabling. Comparative politics suffers from much the same weaknesses as comparative sociology. If there is hope, it lies particularly in political theory and philosophy where, because of the normative agenda of globalisation, major issues arise. Nevertheless, as David Held stresses in his recent study of *Democracy and Global Order*, what is at stake is nothing less than a fundamental recasting of political theory as it has developed *within* the liberal democratic nation-state.[8] It remains to be seen if political science can respond to such challenges. As to the third constitutive discipline, economics, it is symptomatic that the issue of the economic relations of globalisation is picked up more substantively in the burgeoning field of International Political Economy, within International Relations rather than conventional economics.

This is an interesting case of a general trend, that global issues are often best addressed through interdisciplinary fields – such as environmental, development, communications and cultural studies – and in subjects which are less constitutive of the social sciences as a whole. Three subjects – anthropology, geography and International Relations – have shown the greatest openness. All are fields in which historically the national–international nexus was not just a methodological bias, but explicitly constitutive. Their openness to globalisation debates reflects theoretical and ideological transformations, which began earlier in the post-war period, in which nationalist constructions of their objects were challenged and abandoned. In geography and International Relations, at least – but not in anthropology – these changes also made disciplinary definitions become increasingly problematic.

The old colonial-inspired traditions of social anthropology distintegrated with the independence movements of the 1960s, which required new ways of conceiving global relations. The discipline's bias towards the study of less formal social relations facilitated an interest in relations across as well as within state borders. In geography, similarly, the old geopolitical foundations long ago collapsed, although in this case the result has been the decline of a distinctive disciplinary sense, with research increasingly informed by economic and sociological thought. Its major concept, space, has been peculiarly problematised by globalisation, and it has accommodated broad social theorising of global issues. In International Relations, the historic statist core eroded from the period of *détente* in the 1970s and imploded after 1989. This has opened up the subject (in some eyes at least) as an interdisciplinary field of global social science.

Contradictions of International Relations

International Relations has had the unique advantage for global purposes that, while it assumed the national, it was at least constituted above the national level. The transformation is, however, problematic, because of a core contradiction between the international and the global. International Relations is currently one of the most highly theoreticised of the social sciences, its intellectual ferment testifying to serious issues at stake.

The diversity of theories which results – a wide range of critical approaches jostling with the remnants of realism and neo-realism – can seem like a Tower of Babel to the uninitiated. The challenge is no less than whether International Relations can be a discipline and an interdisciplinary field at the same time. As the subject moves towards reconstituting itself as a field of global social science in general, in which economy, society and culture are as much its objects as the state-system, what happens to its claims to disciplinary status? It is not far-fetched to see this tension as a fundamental crisis. There seem to be two polar possibilities for its resolution:

1. The maintenance or restoration of traditional International Relations, based on a modified state-centric approach which gives due recognition to the roles of economic, social and cultural realities and non-state actors in the inter-state system.
2. The reconstitution of International Relations as, essentially, a multi- or interdisciplinary field of global social science, in which not only state-centric international politics but politics in general are relativised.

Neither is an adequate solution. A restoration would not do justice to the depth of the challenge from non-traditional International Relations. A simple pluralisation of International Relations as a field of *de facto* global social science would discard the inter-state problematic contributed by traditional International Relations and abdicate the task of specifically theorising global politics. In practice International Relations will undoubtedly include diverse discourses, some of them quasi-realist and others broadly political-economic and global-sociological. We need to ask, however, what should comprise the central, constitutive intellectual dynamic.

Instead of being constituted simply by either international politics or global society, International Relations should be reconstituted as global politics, centred on the *relationships* between global politics and global society. The field should certainly take on a leading role in the development of global social science, but it should focus on the *nature and role* of politics in global society. This involves a dual problematic: the ways in which global politics helps to *constitute* and are *transformed by* global society.

Although global politics is about more than state relations, critical to this whole enterprise is rethinking the concept of state. It is symptomatic of the failures of domesticated social science that there is little debate about the contemporary meaning of the state in either sociology or political science. While International Relations' realist theoretical traditions provide no answers, critical international theory ought in principle to be able to do so. In reality, however, it has often involved a partial critique of 'state-centrism' which has failed to challenge realist theorising on the state.[9]

The deficiency of realism is often seen as lying in an excessive concern with the state in general and its military-political aspect in particular. Critical theorists frequently see the state as by-passed by globalisation, and the task of a global approach as the unravelling of what Richard Falk calls a 'post-statist world order'.[10] This approach rests on two mistakes. The more obvious, which critics of extreme globalisation approaches have noted, is that the nation-state is far from irrelevant.[11] The more fundamental, however, which these critics share with the extreme globalisers, is that the contemporary state is not simply national in form. The relative weakening of the nation-state heralds not a post-statist world, but one in which state forms undergo critical transformations.

Much anti-state-centric international theory has echoed this debate by diminishing the role of the state – or at least its military aspect – in its analyses. Thus international and global political economy has tended to see the state mainly in its economic role, neglecting the traditional military core of state power. Social movement approaches have contributed to a radical agenda for 'global governance' in which international institutions and civil society are seen as more important than states.

Such theoretical tendencies fall down on three counts. First, by arguing that a *focus on* military state power rather than the *explanation of* it is the problem, they concede too much to realism – failing to challenge it on its own ground. Secondly, they understate the state core of global governance – the extent to which even nation-states are important directly, as components of international (i.e., inter-state) institutions and as foci of civil society activity. Finally, they too fail to tackle the fundamental question of theorising the new forms of state in an increasingly globalised era.

In the remaining sections of this chapter, I provide the outlines of a framework for answering both the general problems of a global social science and the specific dilemmas of International Relations. These are intimately linked: the general reconceptualisation of society and culture at a global level, which I begin to offer in the next section, is necessary in order to provide the foundations for a redefinition of the International Relations project. Conversely, the resolution of the crisis in International Relations, centred on the reconceptualisation of the state and inter-state system, is necessary to complete the reconstruction of social theory in global terms.

Understanding Global Society

The problem for the new, globalised elements of the social sciences in general is that while they have incorporated global *issues*, global *theory* is still in the early stages of development. The problem is not just how to understand globalisation, as debates in most fields have suggested. The defining issue is how to understand society, culture and politics under the impact of the global revolution. As Mann notes: 'In major transitions the fundamental interrelations, and very identities, of organizations such as "economies" or "states" become metamorphosed. Even the very definition of "society" may change.'[12] What is at stake is no less than a reconstitution of the central concepts of social science in global terms.

This fundamental reconceptualisation remains to be realised. In this section, I advance the task by examining how two of the master-concepts of social theory, society and culture, should be redefined. Part of my purpose is to develop the arguments which are needed generally in globalising social science, as a basis for my later reconsideration of the concept of state. I take the concepts of society and culture together, therefore, not to conflate them or deny the need for specific consideration of each, but because they pose the same central issues in the global context.

Both society and culture are problematic concepts, with a double meaning embodying the same fundamental contradiction. On the one hand, each can be understood as *process*: society as social relations, culture as symbolic interaction. Social relations in general and symbolic relations in particular (I see culture as an aspect of social relations) are in this meaning dynamic and open-ended, involving constant transformation and change.

On the other hand, we have ideas of *a* society and *a* culture, or societies and cultures, which particularise the concepts and introduce the idea of the *boundedness* of social and cultural interaction. In some versions, society and culture are relatively static, closed systems – as in Talcott Parsons's classic self-regulating 'social system' with its functionally interdependent sub-systems.[13] This concept was criticised on many grounds, but it is worth noting its implicit nationalism, equating social system with national context (America).

Conceptual discussion of societies and cultures in this sense has fallen out of favour. Few have attempted post-functionalist definitions. This probably reflects greater interest in the open-endedness and dynamism of social relations – how boundaries are broken down in an era of rapid socio-cultural change and globalisation. Mann, for example, writes that 'societies are constituted by multiple, overlapping networks of interaction', but he does not deal with the problem of what defines when such sets of networks become societies.[14]

If conceptual discussion has faltered, particularist concepts are still widely used. Domesticated sociology and politics routinely assume national societies and employ the comparative method. Anthropologists have not stopped talking about particular cultures. Cultural theorists even particularise cultures further as sub-cultures. International Relations theorists are only just in-corporating the idea that society and culture are important and they often fall for traditional conceptions. Thus when Ole Wæver recently defined 'societal security', he identified society with national, ethnic and religious communities rather than with more open, plural or transnational relations.[15]

We need to adjudicate the status of particularist concepts of society and culture. Neither society nor culture has ever been fully defined by boundaries. The implicit openness of social and cultural relations means that boundaries were always there to be crossed, relative and subject to transformation. Even the most isolated tribal societies were defined by relations with other societies, which should not be seen as relations between social wholes but as more or less institutionalised interactions between people. In the world of nation-states, national societies and cultures have *always* been highly permeable. There have always been manifold relations across boundaries. At the peak of the nation-state system, most came to be seen just as international, although many were transnational rather than international in a specific sense.

In what sense, if any, can particularist concepts of society and culture be upheld? Clearly we could reject them altogether – arguing that there are only social and cultural relations and that to conceptualise them within particular societies and cultures is illusory and ideological, reifying boundaries. But this goes too far: social and cultural life has always been and still is informed by particularistic concepts. Boundaries, while relative, are real. Thus it makes partial sense to talk of, say, British, Kurdish or Zulu society and culture, as well as many other networks and sub-cultures at sub-national and transnational levels. All such differentiations are abstractions from the flux and openness of society and culture understood as process and relationship.

Compared to other forms of differentiation, we can define societies and cultures as those contexts which are *inclusive* and *constitutive* of social and cultural relations in general. The degree of inclusiveness or constitutiveness of a particular society or culture is subject to variation and transformation. Not all contemporary national societies or cultures are inclusive and constitutive to the same degree. The same national societies and cultures are more or less inclusive and constitutive in different historical periods.

Similarly, since the boundaries of societies and cultures are relative to society and culture in general, a range of particularistic concepts may coexist and overlap. It makes good analytical sense to talk simultaneously of Welsh, British, European and Western, and of Kurdish, Iraqi, Arab and Islamic, and of Zulu and South African societies and cultures. Such concepts are not mutually exclusive.

Following this general conceptual unpacking, *global* society and culture can be said to exist to the extent that global relations are inclusive and constitutive of social and cultural relations in general. Empirically, we could say that global society exists to the extent that global relations of production, trade, politics, military power, culture and communication have become inclusive and constitutive sets of relationships. Global culture exists to the extent that global cultural relations include and constitute cultural relations in general. The concepts of global society and culture, as of other societies and cultures, do not represent static systems or end-states. They are abstractions from the flux of social relations: they vary over time and they coexist with more particularistic concepts.

While a society or culture is an inclusive set of relations, it does not consist merely of relations at its particular level. National societies and cultures partially include and constitute sub-national relations of many kinds. Global society and culture partially include and constitute relations at all other levels – world-regional, transnational, international, national, sub-national, etc. It makes most sense to emphasise that global society and culture are emergent realities. They are becoming *more* defining frameworks of social relations, while national frameworks – although still important – are becoming *less* defining.

The global is not only more inclusive of transnational relations in general – which in one sense is true by definition – but is also constitutive of them in a way which they are not of it. Increasingly transnational, regional – and international – relations are informed by a sense of the world as a social and cultural context, more than this global sense is informed by the international, regional or transnational.

The point of comparing global society and culture with other particular concepts is to demonstrate the distinctiveness and novelty of these forms. Although global society is still a bounded concept, it is not bounded in the same way, since it can be said to include society in the sense of social relations in general. It is a maximum concept, defined not like national or tribal societies in relation to other societies of the same kind, but in relation to more particular societies which it includes.

So far I have not distinguished society and culture. There are, however, ways of defining society which involve their relationships, making culture central. David Lockwood classically distinguished 'system integration', the factual integration of a society, and 'social integration', its normative integration.[16] This argument implies that a society cannot be defined *as* a system, as Parsons believed, but that its degree of 'systemness' is an empirical question. Indeed, as Giddens suggests, rather than seeing society as a system we should recognise a number of distinct 'abstract systems' with variable articulation which provide the infrastructure of social relations.[17]

Lockwood also says that the factual or systematic interconnectedness of a society is not the same as its degree of normative interconnectedness, the degree to which it is integrated by common values. We cannot assume common values but need to investigate how far they exist. Applying this distinction, we might argue that there is an increasing degree of system(s) integration in global society, as measured by globalisation studies, but that value integration is highly problematic.

However, such a way of posing matters neglects the implicit interconnection between the spread of common systems and the development of common values and norms. Minimally, even the development of global markets involves a global market culture; globally organised production systems involve common cultures of production; and the growth of global communications involves common cultures of communication as well as common cultural content through a greater sharing of symbols and myths.

However, these lowest-common-denominator dimensions of commonality need to be supplemented by a more distinctive normative consensus. Without looking for the 'central value system' beloved of Parsons, the development of global culture – and hence global society – are confirmed by the growth of common values. The extent to which Western values like human rights and democracy become globalised, and a genuine global politics develops around them, are of critical importance.

As I noted above, many have defined global politics in terms of plural forms of governance based at the international and civil society as well as state levels. International are, however, generally inter-state forms, and the politics of civil society cannot be defined without reference to state forms.

This is as true of global as of national civil societies. Global politics does not develop merely through state institutions, but the forms of state are essential to any reconceptualisation of global society and politics.

Forms of State in the Global Era

Both globalisation debates in general and critical International Relations in particular have failed to address the nature of the state in a global era.[18] State discourse is the extreme case of methodological nationalism: it has remained trapped within a nation-centred understanding. Even Mann writes, 'The state has become a *nation-state*',[19] but the concept of state is *not* identical with that of nation-state. We need to recognise multiple qualifications and transformations of the nation-state concept.

First, even the dominant form of state which was given from the long nineteenth century was actually the European world-empire, with a *more-or-less* nation-state core, rather than the nation-state as such. And it is even more accurate to describe this state-form as a plurality of imperial nation-states in the context of a wider state-system. These forms were the products, moreover, of the 'multi-power-actor' Western civilisation which developed over centuries and is the historic core of the emergent global society.

Secondly, within the state-system there has been a fundamental 'internationalisation' of state organisation. Western states (through NATO, the European Union (EU) and various economic organisations), and to a lesser extent nation-states in general (through the United Nations system), have engaged in a comprehensive pooling of state sovereignty since 1945. This has formed the basis for two very distinctive developments: first, the relatively unified *Western* state which developed during the Cold War, and secondly, the globalisation of state power and an emergent, if problematic *global* state.

Both these terms obviously need elaboration and justification. The global state in particular is an unfamiliar concept, although much of its difficulty is cultural: since political and international theory are centred on a concept of state as centralised nation-state, a global state can only be understood in terms of a 'world government' which obviously does not and is not likely to exist. I use the term in a rather different way.

In order to explain this, let us first define state. In particular, the continuing significance of military-political power as the primary criterion for the existence of a state needs to be explained. Most discussion of states has incorporated an implicit slippage from a military-centred definition towards a juridical or economic-management-based definition. Because of this slippage, many have concluded that the state is weakened by globalisation. I assume that the classic military-political definition is still relevant. Military relations still define the relations between distinct states and hence the parameters of the world-system of power.

To pursue the issue of what is a state – and when is a state not a state

– I turn to Max Weber: 'A compulsory political organization with continuous operations will be called a "state" insofar as its administrative staff successfully upholds the claim to the monopoly of the legitimate use of physical force in the enforcement of its order.'[20] This definition has been widely endorsed, but Mann proposes that it should be amended to four looser points:

1. The state is a differentiated set of institutions and personnel
2. embodying centrality, in the sense that political relations radiate to and from a centre, to cover a
3. territorially demarcated area over which it exercises
4. some degree of authoritative, binding rule making, backed up by some organized political force.[21]

This definition abandons the idea of a monopoly of legitimate force: there is merely 'some degree of authoritative rule making' and 'some organized political force'. Although designed to explain nineteenth-century states, it is particularly suited to the complex, overlapping forms of state power which exist in the late twentieth century in conditions of globalisation.

Before 1945, state leaders often acted as if Weber's definition was true and they did in fact hold a monopoly of legitimate violence. In a world of nation-states, the demarcation of one state from another was the potential for violence between them. What then happens to states, and to our understanding of state, when this potential is removed, as it has since 1945 between Western states – and more problematically since 1989 between Western states and Russia?

The control of violence ceases to be divided vertically between nation-states and empires but is divided horizontally between different levels of power, each of which claims some legitimacy and thus fragments the nature of 'state'. On the one hand, there is the internationalisation of legitimate force. On the other, there are the processes of privatisation (or reprivatisation) of force, in which individuals, social groups and non-state actors are more widely using force and claiming legitimacy for their usage.

The internationalising processes are my first concern. In what senses can we refer to them under the rubric of 'globalisation of state power', let alone 'global state'? First, while the transatlantic Western state of the Cold War period was a regional form of state power in Europe, it was also an incipiently global form of state power, aspiring to regulate violence on a world scale. Secondly, the internationalisation of Western state power was partly constitutive, I argued above, of the single global space in which many globalising processes developed. Thirdly, the Western bloc organised a series of economic institutions which became effectively forms of global regulation.

The Western state in the Cold War era was therefore a pre-global state. It could not recognise itself or be recognised as a global state because of the limit of Cold War competition with a major, even if weaker rival centre. Legitimate global institutions, centred on the United Nations, were largely neutralised by Cold War rivalry. The end of the Cold War, however, removed these constraints. The rival centre dissolved and its principal successor, the Russian Federation, became an ally, however reluctant at times.

In a series of major issues, the Western nuclear powers and Security Council members, the United States, the United Kingdom and France, together with the wider Western bloc of NATO, the European Union, Japan and their various regional allies, were able to dominate the global agenda and mobilise the UN to legitimate their actions. Interestingly, this happened despite the manifest reluctance of the main Western governments to pursue a global leadership role. At rare moments, such as the Gulf mobilisation, the Somalian and Haitian interventions and the Dayton settlement, they appear to have chosen leadership. The scarcity of these moments, compared to the occasions on which they have seemed to want to turn their backs, suggests, however, that they have had leadership thrust upon them.

It is the logic of the new global political-military situation, including the articulation of domestic politics with global issues, which has compelled the West and especially the United States to act as the centre of an emergent global state. The fact that this has happened despite the manifest reluctance and ideological unpreparedness of the leaders is testimony to the structural significance of these events in global society.

The global state is constituted, therefore, by the Western state together with the legitimation framework of the UN. It acts as a global state due to the pressures and contradictions of global governance: not merely the threats to Western interests (as with Kuwaiti oil or the danger of a wider Balkan war), but also the imperatives of globally legitimate principles (human rights, democracy), the claims of insurgent and victimised groups (such as Kurds and the Bosnians), the contradictions of global media coverage and the demands of an emergent global civil society.

These pressures function to hold together, more or less, a West-centred global state, just as the pressures of world war and Cold War were the context of earlier stages in the development of a coherent Western state. The fact that contemporary pressures are more diffuse does not necessarily mean that they are ineffectual, although it does raise a question-mark over the long-term coherence of the process. While global crises push forward and make visible the process of global state formation, they also bare its weak coherence and contradictions, including the internal conflicts of the Western core.

The 'global state' can be defined as a state in line with Mann's four criteria. First, states, according to Mann, involve 'differentiated sets of institutions and personnel' – differentiated, I take him to mean, both internally and in relation to society. The important word here is actually 'sets'. Mann makes it clear that states are not necesarily homogenised and closely integrated institutions, but consist of more or less discrete, often disjointed apparati. 'Under the microscope, states "Balkanize"', he argues, quoting Abrams's formulation that, 'The state is the unified symbol of an actual disunity'.[22] Mann introduces, indeed, the idea that states are institutional 'messes' rather than the homogeneous structures of ideal type.[23]

Just as global society is highly distinctive in 'including' a large number of national societies, the global state is unusual in 'including' a large number of nation-states. Nevertheless, this is not entirely unprecedented. Multinational states do not always take the relatively neat centralised forms of the United Kingdom or (in a different sense) the former Soviet Union. Mann himself analyses the highly complex (and from an ideal-typical point of view, idiosyncratic) forms of the Austro-Hungarian Empire.

The Western and global state is, however, an aggregation of institutions of an *unprecedented* kind and on an unprecedented scale. If one examines it in action, for example in Bosnia-Herzegovina, we see an amazing plethora of global, Western and national state institutions – political, military and welfare – complemented by an equally dazzling and complex array of civil society organisations. As this example underlines, the global state is truly the biggest 'institutional mess' of all.

The second big question is in what sense the global state meets Mann's criterion of 'embodying centrality, in the sense that political relations radiate to and from a centre'. To put the issue another way, we can ask when is an institutional mess so messy that it cannot be seen as a single set of institutions at all? In what sense do the UN, NATO, the United States and the various Western nation-states constitute a single set of institutions?

Clearly there is no straightforward constitutional order in the global state – but there is a constitutional order nevertheless. The main centre – Washington rather than New York – seems clear, and the fact that political relations radiate to and from it has now been confirmed in all serious global crises of the post-1989 period, from Kuwait to Dayton. The continuing centrality of the United States to war-management world-wide and to all major 'peace processes' from the Middle East and Yugoslavia to South Africa and even Northern Ireland underlines this point.

There are two apparent anomalies in this situation which lead probably to much of the theoretical confusion. First, the centre of the Western and emergent global state is constituted primarily by a nation-state, the United States. Secondly, political relations radiate to and from this centre through diverse sets of institutions. There is the UN itself, which confers global legitimacy on the US state (and in which it has a constitutional role as a permanent member of the Security Council, and a *de facto* role far beyond that). There is NATO, confirmed as the effective organisation of Western military power. There are numerous Western-led world economic organisations, from the exclusive G8 to the increasingly global World Trade Organisation (WTO). Last but not least, there are bilateral relations between the American state and virtually all other nation-states.

Of course, other nation-states, especially the United Kingdom and France but in different ways Germany and Japan, Russia and China, as well as regional organisations, notably the European Union (EU), have very important roles in the developing global state. These roles are all contested, problematic and changing, and in the Russian and Chinese cases especially unstable, but they are nonetheless real.

Mann's third criterion, that a state possesses a 'territorially demarcated area' over which it exercises some degree of authoritative, binding rule-making, backed up by some organised political force, is also problematic but does not negate the concept of a global state. The territorially demarcated area of global power is, in principle, the world. The fact that other state organisations claim lesser territorial jurisdications, regional in the case of the EU, national in the case of nation-states, does not contradict this. The idea of overlapping territorial jurisdictions is not new, and it has a particular salience in today's world. There is a systematic sharing of sovereignty which is relativising the previously unique sovereignty of the nation-state.

This leaves us with the existence of 'some degree of authoritative, binding rule making', backed up by 'some organised political force'. The authoritative rule-making takes several forms. Institutional arrangements bind states to-gether in the various inter-state organisations, regulating the internal structure of the global state and the roles of nation-states within it. The body of international law binds individuals and institutions in civil society as well as state institutions. Rule-making is undoubtedly patchy and in some areas incoherent, but it proceeds apace. Mann's 'some degree' seems apposite.

Rule-making in the global state clearly has the backing of 'organised political force': the armed forces of the United States, United Kingdom, France, in some circumstances Russia, and many other states are deployed in the names of NATO and the UN. International law is also acquiring a machinery of courts and police, even if it remains heavily dependent on nation-states, has selective application and limited real enforcement capacity.

The global state meets at least this definition of a state. However, although Mann's definition clearly permits a conceptualisation of overlapping levels of state power, it says nothing specifically about the ways in which different 'states' in this sense will articulate. We need therefore to add a new criterion: that a state (particular) must be, to a significant degree, *inclusive* and *constitutive* of other forms or levels of state power (i.e., of state power in general in a particular time and space).

This criterion is essential. Clearly, nation-states, in the present period, are still generally inclusive and constitutive of sub-national forms, although less so than in the recent past. To a considerable extent they also constitute world-regional and global forms of state – as well as (by definition) the international. In contrast, local and regional forms within nation-states are generally only weakly constitutive, while the inclusiveness and constitutiveness of the various transnational forms of state is not easy to determine.

Clearly, global state institutions such as the UN have been inclusive but, to date, only weakly constitutive. On the other hand, the Western state became highly constitutive of its component nation-states during the Cold War. The European state (European Union) has gradually strengthened both its inclusiveness and its constitutiveness of member nation-states – although this is very much a matter of contention – but its articulation with the transatlantic Western state is increasingly problematic.

Once we examine this criterion, the global state is evidently a problematic level of state power. In many ways its Western core remains stronger than the global form itself. It is evident, however, that the Western state is operating globally, in response to global imperatives and with global legitimation. It has begun to be constituted within broader global rather than narrowly Western parameters. The global level rather than the narrowly Western one is *becoming* constitutive, too, of the component nation-states. Still, the global state, even more than global society or culture, is an emergent, contingent and problematic reality.

The key issue is the articulation of the global state and the regional and national states which it partly includes and constitutes. These relationships are plural and variable. The European state is a key component of the Western state in general as well as constituting a unique state form. It too meets all of Mann's criteria, in some cases better than the global state, but with one key qualification. The forms of force available to it are very limited and its capacity for mobilising military power, or even political power to deal with military issues, is very weak.

To clarify the concept of global state, it is also essential to explicate its varied relations with nation-states. In the West, these vary from the United States and post-imperial Britain and France, which all retain a clear capacity for independent military action in some circumstances, to the Canadian, Benelux and Scandinavian states which have largely surrendered the capacity for independent initiative to NATO and the UN. Beyond the Western state lies a never-never land of minor nation-states, like the Eastern Europeans, smaller East Asian states and many Latin American and African states, most of which also have weak autonomous power and shelter under Western power but are only weakly integrated into it.

A general point in analysing the relations of nation-states to regional, Western and global state forms is that these are increasingly institutionalised. Mann labels the period after 1945 'the age of institutionalised nation-states', partly because states were based on institutionalised compromises between classes, but also – and for our purposes more relevantly – because relations between states were highly institutionalised.[24] The role of each nation-state corresponded to a complex set of understandings and systems of regulation within the West as a whole.

One reason for our difficulty in recognising global state developments is that they are manifested in complex, rapidly changing and often highly contrasting forms. Different theoretical approaches tend to latch on to different sides of these developments. For Marxists and 'third worldists', for example, the Gulf War represented a manifestation of imperialism, centred on strategic control of oil. In contrast, Western military action to protect Kurdish refugees, following the war, represented for many International Relations analysts a new form of humanitarian intervention.

These and other paradigms compete to offer simple characterisations of global state power. In reality, however, global state power crystallises as *both* imperialist and humanitarian, and indeed in other forms. Mann's argument that states involve 'polymorphous crystallisation', and that different crystallisations dominate different institutions, is relevant here.[25] He gives as an example the American state, crystallising 'as conservative-patriarchal one week when restricting abortion rights, as capitalist the next when regulating the savings and loans banking scandal, as a superpower the next when sending troops abroad for other than national economic interests. These varied crystallisations are rarely in harmony or in dialectical opposition to one another; usually they just differ. They mobilise differing, if overlapping and intersecting, power networks.'[26] We need to extend this analysis in understanding the emergent global state. Without understanding the diversity, we will lapse into one-sidedness or confusion and fail to grasp global political change.

Towards Global Ethics and Politics

Theorising the global state takes International Relations beyond the international, but leaves it still focused on the political. It is a decisive step because it finally transcends the 'state–global divide'[27] which threatens to bifurcate the subject. It is also of fundamental importance to the social sciences as a whole, since the nation-state is the central obstacle to re-conceptualising boundaries in social relations in general. The idea of national societies and cultures as more-or-less fixed units depends implicitly on the nation-state. Once we overcome the idea of the national as the inevitable form of the state, it can hardly be the necessary form of society or culture.

Global-level entities – society, culture and state – have been presented in this chapter as maximum forms. It has been pointed out that, as such, they have unique characteristics. They are inclusive of social, cultural and state relations in general, and blur the distinction between social relations and societies, or between society and *a* society. The development of global-level entities means that our perceptions of boundaries is transformed: they are now necessarily within society, and necessarily relativised.

This development has huge significance for ethical thought. Global theory recontextualises normative questions. In bounded forms of society, there is a contradiction between humanist universals, as theorised by liberal, democratic and socialist political theories for example, and the particularistic context of social relations. Global society and culture offer the possibility of resolving this contradiction, by grounding universals in social relations. Universals are not normative concepts imposed on particularistic realities, but concepts corresponding to global social realities. The sterile debate between cosmopolitan and communitarian ethics can be overcome.

The concept of global state is of huge significance for our understanding of global society and universal values. Global society is constituted by global social relations in general, and not simply at the state level. Nevertheless, the possibility of globally legitimate authority – which in our times can only be located in state institutions – is essential to its realisation in stable and secure forms. The consolidation of the global state in forms which transcend its narrower Western origins and which command genuine world legitimacy is a uniquely important task.

In the twenty-first century, therefore, we need a global politics which aims to construct a new relationship between the emergent global society and culture and state institutions. The new global politics will be based, as many have argued, partly in the developing global civil society. But it will also be based partly in, and have the aim of transforming, state power as well as social relations.

CHAPTER 14

The International Relations of Global Environmental Change

David Humphreys

This chapter analyses the perspectives on global environmental change offered by the International Relations theories of realism, neo-liberal institutionalism and neo-Marxism. It also considers critically two discourses on environmental sustainability, namely ecological modernisation and post-modernism, the latter of which, while not an environmental discourse *per se,* does offer insights on an environmentally sustainable future. While these theories and discourses help illuminate, in different measure, the causes and effects of, and potential solutions to, global environmental change, none offers a complete view. Reference is also made to Dobson's distinction between environmentalism and ecologism. Environmentalism concerns the cooption of green ideas into other ideologies, such as liberalism, whereas ecologism is an ideology in its own right that critiques prevailing political, economic and social practices and envisages a post-industrial future.[1]

Environmentalism and ecologism may be seen as two poles of a continuum of green thought, with environmentalists seeking to achieve system mainten-ance by greening the state and industry, whereas ecologism, which views the state and business as sources of the environmental crisis, essentially seeks system transformation. Features of ecological thought include the rejection of global solutions, the debunking of the concept of development, an emphasis on the empowerment of the local and a scepticism of science and economics.[2] Attention turns first to the realist paradigm.

Realism

Although the possession and control of natural and environmental resources is a key attribute of the realist concept of power, with more powerful states tending to cause more environmental degradation,[3] realism has very little to say on environmental problems. Global environmental degradation challenges realist claims that the state can provide for the security of its citizens, with the result that the environment has entered realist thought through attempts to redefine security. This has resulted in the 'hybridisation'[4] of the traditional realist concern with security with an extraneous concern, namely the environment, to yield the notion of environmental security.[5] However, proponents of environmental security fail to explore the important differences between the realist notion of security and environmental security. Realism deals with the security of states, privileges the military as an interest group, accepts that there are conditions when the use of force is justified, is exclusionist in principle with its emphasis on a culture of secrecy, and depends in large part on technological progress. Green security, on the other hand, seeks to deal with the security of ecosystems and individuals, challenges the protected position of the military, rejects the use of force, is inclusionist in principle with its emphasis on a culture of transparency, and is sceptical of the notion of technological progress.[6] Although future inter-state conflicts may originate from resource conflicts, for example over water, the environment has yet to become a central concern of realist thought. To Lafèrriere, 'the call to arms by realism turns nature into raw materials and legitimises warfare',[7] while Conca, Dalby and Finger consider that the militarisation of the environment is a likely consequence of viewing environmental degradation as a security issue.[8] The concept of environmental security is inadequate as an operational tool and, with respect to the environment, realism remains better suited to explaining why states will not cooperate (unless they stand to achieve relative gains by environmental conservation measures) and why international institutions and international regimes are unlikely to deal meaningfully with environmental deterioration.[9]

Neo-liberal Institutionalism

Neo-liberal institutionalism redefines state interests to yield the notion of 'common interests' which, it is claimed, has sustained international cooperation and the growth of international regimes in the post-war era. Regime theory, which emerged in the 1970s, originally sought to explain why states cooperate on problems of international economic management, but with increasing intergovernmental cooperation on the environment, regime theory has since colonised environmental issues. The environment was seen as offering new case studies to which the hypotheses of regime theory could be applied and tested. However, no consideration was given to the ways in which environmental problems differ from economic ones, and the global environment, like the global economy, was treated as a management issue.

Unlike realists and neo-realists, who assume that states seek to maximise their self-interest in a conflictual international system by achieving relative gains, to neo-liberal institutionalists states will cooperate where they can realise absolute gains, irrespective of the gains made by other states. Neo-liberal institutionalism's emphasis on cooperation and the importance of institutions in a condition of international anarchy successfully explains international cooperation on some environmental issues, such as climate change.[10] However, neo-realism remains better suited to explaining why states fail to cooperate, in particular when environmental conservation is linked to other issues in a bargaining game. For example, during the forest negotiations for the United Nations Conference on Environment and Development the G77 developing countries refused to meet the North's demand for a global forest convention which would require the G77 to conserve its forests unless the North paid for this in the form of increased aid and technology transfers. This stance was designed to realise relative gains for the G77 *vis-à-vis* the North.[11] Continued assertions of sovereignty and the fact that on some issues at least states continue to search for relative gains provide grounds for questioning the degree to which intergovernmental cooperation can conserve the global environment.

The remainder of this section considers five weaknesses that arise from an uncritical usage of regime theory. First, regime theory strives for a methodological parsimony across the entire universe of regimes, irrespective of differences in the nature of the issue, the political and economic interests affected, geographical area or time. Hence, in a collaborative research project Young and Osherenko tested various hypotheses for the formation of regimes on the conservation of the Svalbard archipelago (created in 1920), the preservation of Arctic fur seals (1911) and polar bears (1973), the regime to prevent ozone layer depletion (1985, amended 1987) and the convention to prevent long-range transboundary air pollution in Europe (1979). Not surprisingly, given the diversity of cases, of the nineteen hypotheses tested only one – the role of leadership in regime creation – was found to be confirmed for all five cases.[12] Anomalies and inclusive results have led to the academic's recourse to the need for further research, rather than to a re-examination of the methodology of the regime theorist or to an acceptance that different regimes created at different points of history with different geographical scopes may require different conditions for creation.

Secondly, regime theory is primarily state-centric. Regime theorists have paid only limited attention to the role of non-governmental organisations (NGOs) in lobbying states to join environmental regimes, in pressing for regime change and in policy verification and implementation. The role of non-governmental regimes, which represent a new type of transnational norm-governed cooperation among non-state actors, is also neglected. One such example is the Forest Stewardship Council which seeks to implement a global labelling scheme for timber harvested from well-managed forests.[13] Regime theory also ignores transnational corporations, many of which are central to the political economy of environmental degradation. Susan Strange's powerful and still valid critique of regime theory argues that the 'who-gets-what' of the international economy 'is more likely to be captured by looking not at the regime that emerges on the surface, but underneath, at the bargains on which it is based'.[14] Such bargains involve not just states, but also transnational corporations (TNCs). Nor should the role of actors at the sub-state level be neglected. Once a regime is adopted, national authorities must bargain with local authorities and private sector interests over the implementation of regime provisions; this bargaining process can delay implementation, and may result in a state failing to honour its international commitments.[15]

Thirdly, regime theory assumes a priori that there are universally valid norms, rules and environmental management techniques. While universal prescriptions and proscriptions may be applicable in some cases, this should not be a starting assumption for all environmental problems. For example, many ecologists deny that there is such a thing as a technocratic fix, and the idea of universal rules is dismissed by some as 'ecocratic'. To Wolfgang Sachs the ecocrat,

> likes universal ecological rules, just as the developmentalist view liked universal economic rules. Both pass over the rights of local communities to be in charge of their resources ... global resource planning protects nature as environment around the economy, while local conservation efforts protect nature as environment around the home.[16]

Elsewhere Sachs opposes, in language similar to the regime theorist's, the way in which 'the state assumes the task of gathering evidence on the state of nature and the effects of man, of enacting norms and laws to direct behaviour, and enforcing compliance with the new rules'.[17]

Fourthly, regime theory takes the current intergovernmental system and the neo-liberal economic system as the starting points of its analysis.[18] While early twentieth-century liberal internationalism may be seen as a radical discourse, in that it offered an alternative to the then dominant power politics of realism,[19] the price that liberalism has paid for its seeming triumph is the loss of this radicalism. While Young and Osherenko note that, 'some international institutions are broad and encompassing (for example, the international economic order)' and that regimes 'deal with a set of well-defined activities or a specific area of geographical interest',[20] they do not consider the relationship between 'the international economic order' and environmental regimes, nor whether environmental conservation is possible within this order. Other International Relations scholars are more sensitive to questions of world order. To Cox, assumptions of the fixity of world order are 'not merely a convenience of method, but also an ideological bias',[21] with the bias favouring actors whose interests are served by the neo-liberal norms of the global political economy. Cox distinguishes between two types of theory. Problem-solving theory 'takes the world as it finds it, with the prevailing social and power relationships and the institutions into which they are organised, as the given framework for action'.[22] According to this definition, regime theory is clearly a problem-solving theory. Critical theory 'stands apart from the prevailing order' and 'allows for a normative choice in favour of a [different] social and political order'.[23]

A fifth problem concerns disagreement as to what constitutes regime effectiveness. Effectiveness was given no consideration until 1986 when two members of the German Tübingen group, Wolf and Zürn, first considered the question. Following Wolf and Zürn, Rittberger elaborates that,

> ... a regime is said not to have come into existence if the pertinent norms and rules are disregarded by states at their discretion ... norms and rules which do not shape the behaviour of states cannot be considered reliable predictors of states' behaviour capable of producing convergent expectations.[24]

The question as to how regime effectiveness should be defined is an important one. Until recently, most American theorists had not considered this question, although they are now devoting some attention to it. In 1993 Haas, Keohane and Levy wrote that an international institution, including an international regime, may be considered effective if 'the quality of the environment or the resource [is] better because of the institution'.[25] In other words, an institution is deemed effective if environmental quality would be worse if the institution did not exist. Referring to themselves as 'pragmatists', Haas, Keohane and Levy state that institutions are effective if they 'retard the rate of environmental decline, even if they fail to confront the underlying causes of such decline'.[26] Such an uncritical view allows for continued, even accelerating, environmental decline, with institutions only mitigating the worst effects of environmental destruction. But, as Karen Litfin argues, the

> strongest indictment of existing institutions comes from the recognition that, despite the flurry of institution-building over the past two decades, the quality of the global environment has degenerated over the same period. If we are to be honest with ourselves, environmental quality must be the principal measure of effectiveness.[27]

Litfin's emphasis differs from that of Haas, Keohane and Levy, with the former stressing maintenance of environmental quality, while the latter stress the mitigation of environmental degradation. To Andrew Hurrell, regime effectiveness may be seen as deriving from 'the extent to which they tie states into a continuing and institutionalised process of negotiation'.[28] John Vogler distinguishes between three notions of regime effectiveness. A regime may be considered effective according to the extent to which its norms and principles are authoritative in terms of international law, to the extent to which states transfer authority to the regime, or to the extent to which states modify their behaviour to take account of the norms and principles of the regime.[29]

The failure of regime theorists to agree on what constitutes effectiveness stems from their failure to consider what should be the objectives and functions of regimes. As Matthew Paterson notes, the criterion 'that regimes are judged to be effective if they affect behaviour assumes that the contents of any particular regime ... are desirable', with the value-free analysis of regime theorists limiting the opportunity to introduce normative questions of justice and the rights of future generations.[30] There is a need for students of international regimes to be clear as to how they define effectiveness and how it is to be achieved; in the final analysis the Litfin view that effectiveness should mean environmental quality must be the principal criterion. One possibility for the future development of regime theory, if it is to move from being more than merely an academic pursuit to a tool that contributes to genuine environmental conservation, is for the next generation of regime theorists to move beyond a mechanical consideration of the factors that contribute to regime formation, and concern themselves with an investigation of those factors necessary to ensure the long-term maintenance of environmental quality. Such an enterprise allows regime theorists to exhibit a critical potentiality, if it can be demonstrated that genuine environmental quality cannot be achieved within the contemporary global political economy. While theories of neo-liberal institutionalism may help explain inter-state cooperation, they have little to say about the root causes of environmental decline. In the next section the lenses are reversed, and we enquire what causes environmental degradation, with particular reference to tropical deforestation.

Neo-Marxism and Ecologism

The question of whether conservation of the global environment is possible within the contemporary economic order is not addressed by regime theory; it is not even asked. In this section, it is argued that the causes of tropical deforestation are rooted in the global economic system. The view is forwarded that, while neo-Marxism has almost entirely neglected environmental degradation, its radicalism has nonetheless contributed strongly to the radicalism of ecologism. The similarities and differences between neo-Marxism and ecologism are considered and the causes of tropical deforestation are described using an analysis that owes an intellectual debt to neo-Marxism.

There is no single, coherent neo-Marxist view, hence it is first necessary to draw out the commonalties and similarities of dependency school and world-systems theorists in the neo-Marxist camp, in particular André Gunder Frank, Samir Amin and Immanuel Wallerstein. Neo-Marxism views the world as an intrinsically exploitative global capitalist system. A class relationship, a legacy of colonialism, has evolved between the developed metropolitan countries of the centre and the underdeveloped satellite countries of the periphery. The periphery is dependent on the centre for capital investment, while the centre exercises an exploitative relationship over the periphery.

Johan Galtung develops this analysis to argue that there are centres and peripheral areas within centre and periphery countries. A harmony of interests exists between the periphery–centre and the centre–centre, while there is a disharmony between the two peripheries.[31] The Galtung concept of the periphery–centre corresponds closely to what other writers refer to as the comprador class whose interests are tied to transnational capital. The periphery–centre (comprador class) occupies an intermediary position, exploiting the periphery–periphery, yet is itself exploited by the centre–centre. Bodenheimer sees the comprador as a clientele class, occupying a 'dual position as junior partners of metropolitan interests, yet dominant elites within their own societies'.[32] Central to neo-Marxism is the channelling of surplus (profit) from centre to periphery.[33] The periphery–centre acquires a share of this surplus, accrued from the investment of transnational capital which provides and sustains its leading role in the periphery, while the elites of the centre (the centre–centre) extract the greater share.

Wallerstein's world-system theory develops core–periphery analysis and introduces the notion of the semi-periphery. Semi-periphery countries consist of rising peripheral countries and declining centre countries; their existence is necessary for the global capitalist economy to function smoothly.[34] The concept of underdevelopment is at the heart of neo-Marxism; to Frank, underdevelopment is the inevitable consequence of a country's involvement on the periphery of the world economy. Development in the satellites cannot occur if the satellites maintain their links with the metropolis, hence the satellites experience greatest economic development when their ties to the metropolis are weakest.

Before the similarities between neo-Marxist and ecological theories are explored, it is necessary to note the differences between them. Each provides a critique of the global political economy, but for different reasons. Five fundamental differences should be noted. First, the concerns of neo-Marxism and ecologism differ. Neo-Marxists are concerned with development, or more precisely with underdevelopment, in the periphery. Ecologists, however, are concerned with environmental degradation, in both centre and periphery. While neo-Marxists continue to see a role for development, the assumption that 'development' and 'economic growth' is progressive is not shared by ecologists.[35] Its centrality to neo-Marxism stems, notes Michael Redclift, from assumptions under capitalism adopted by the Marxist socialist project.[36] Whereas neo-Marxists favour an economistic project, the ecologist is anti-economics, arguing that the environment has an infinite value which cannot be internalised into a monetary figure through pricing.

Secondly, the exploitation of labour is a central concern of neo-Marxists, whereas the exploitation of nature is not.[37] With few exceptions, such as Amin (see below), most neo-Marxists have ignored environmental degradation until very recently. However, to ecologism, developmentalism treat both labour and nature as resources to be exploited and managed. Developmentalist culture assigns instrumental value to nature, whereas to ecological culture nature has intrinsic value and its limits should be respected.

Thirdly, neo-Marxist theorists have a benign view of the state whereas ecologism views the modern industrial state as central to the problem of environmental degradation. To dependency theorists there will remain a role for the state in peripheral economic and development planning. Ecologists, however, are distinctly anti-statist and anti-elitist and seek the disempower-ment of centralised political and economic elites with a concomitant shift in power and property relations to the local level.

Fourthly, the objectives of neo-Marxism and ecologism differ markedly. Dependency theorists argue that peripheral countries can enable economic development by delinking from the centre.[38] To adopt the terminology of Galtung, the dependency school favours the delinking of the periphery from the centre, whereas the ecologists, with their inherent belief in the ability of the local community to care for its local environment, favour the delinking of all peripheries from all centres, with the empowerment of the former. Hence, while both favour delinking, the ecologist carries the logic of this process further than the neo-Marxist.

Fifthly, although both neo-Marxists and ecologists are structural in their assessment of the global economic relations, only the former are structural in their policy prescriptions for the future. The dependency school wishes to reform the present international economic structure to make it more equitable. Ecologists, however, incline towards the abolition of all institutions that fill a top-down economic or development planning role. In this respect, the neo-Marxists can rightly be called structuralist whereas the ecologists, in their policy prescriptions, are essentially 'anti-structuralist'.

Despite these not insignificant differences, many analysts of an ecological persuasion describe the economic and political forces behind environmental degradation using, in part, neo-Marxist language. The similarities are especially strong with respect to centre–periphery relationships. For example, Marcus Colchester of the World Rainforest Movement focuses on the progression from slavery through to colonialism and the modern state which, he argues, has led rural communities to the verge of collapse in Equatorial Africa. Continuity between the policies under colonialism and those after in-dependence has been 'assured by an elite of French-educated Africans'.[39] Colchester notes the importance of patron–client networks which 'enrich the indigenous elite and outside commercial interests'. With regard to logging operations in the Congo, 'foreign companies, or joint operations dominated by foreign capital, produce the vast bulk of the timber'.[40] The similarity between Colchester's view and neo-Marxism is clear. However, Colchester's central concern is the relationship between the ecological balance and the land rights of local rural communities. Whereas neo-Marxism would advocate delinking between centre and periphery to promote development, Colchester argues that, for the ecological balance of the region to be restored, it is necessary to rebuild community institutions.[41] Similarly, Nicholas Hildyard argues that it is 'incontestable' that the chief perpetrators of ecological destruction in the South 'are Northern interests, acting in conjunction with

Southern elites'.[42] But Hildyard would not envisage further empowerment of Southern elites; this would not answer the central questions of '*who* owns the land, *who* controls decision-making, *who* should manage the commons, and in *whose* interest'.[43]

The brief analysis of the causes of deforestation that follows illustrates the similarity between the analyses of ecologism and neo-Marxism. Concerns that neo-Marxism and ecologism share are the role of TNCs and international capital, external debt, Structural Adjustment Programmes, poverty and inequitable patterns of land ownership. The environmental impact of these processes, which are distinguished below for analytical purposes and which should not be seen as distinct in the real world, varies according to region, country and forest type.

To the neo-Marxist, TNCs play a central role in the extraction of surplus from centre to periphery, thus limiting the opportunities for development in the latter. For example, Dale Johnson sees peripheral countries progressively losing control of their industries to Northern-based TNCs which take advantage of low-cost factors of production in the periphery, an arrangement that benefits only those members of the local comprador class collaborating with TNCs. In the international tropical timber trade, valued at US$100 billion in 1996,[44] TNCs provide the economic linkages between the felling of timber and the international timber market. The environmentally destructive practices of timber TNCs, in particular those attached to Japan as a core state, have attracted attention, especially in Papua New Guinea. Japanese TNCs were accused in 1990 by a judicial enquiry (the Barnett Report) of widespread transfer pricing, a mechanism whereby TNCs transfer profits from a periphery country to a core country by, in the case of the timber industry, declaring a sale price for timber purchased that is below the current market value. The sum of money transferred in this way escapes tax in the tropical forest country. Japanese TNCs created subsidiary companies in Papua New Guinea to facilitate transfer pricing. To give one such example, during the period 1986–87 the Stettin Bay Lumber Company made a hidden profit in excess of US$3 million for its parent company, the Japanese TNC Nissho Iwai.[45] The Barnett Commission concluded that in the Papua New Guinean timber industry transfer pricing 'was a major preoccupation of the great majority of companies being studied'.[46]

Neo-Marxist theorists see the World Bank and the International Monetary Fund (IMF) as agencies of imperial power perpetuating the dependence of periphery on centre. Frank notes that the role of World Bank and IMF-imposed policies in Latin America have led to currency devaluation and balance of payments difficulties causing increased dependence on the IMF and metropolitan loan and investment institutions.[47] The relationship between external debt and underdevelopment is a further concern for neo-Marxists who argue that in order to repay past debts, the periphery has became increasingly dependent on the metropolis. External debt is also a concern for ecologists. Susan George notes two debt-environment connections: first, the act of borrowing, often to finance projects that are environmentally destructive; and secondly, paying for them by exporting natural resources.[48] To Patricia Adams, a large debt burden can help save the environment. External debt was accumulated from borrowing for large environmentally destructive development projects. With many creditors no longer willing to lend money, it is no longer possible to finance such projects.[49] Adams's argument is an indictment against the destructive effects of transnational capital, rather than an argument in favour of high debts in tropical forest countries.

The high external debts of many countries has resulted in intervention by Structural Adjustment Programmes (SAPs). Designed by the World Bank and the IMF in conjunction with national elites, SAPs, which usually by-pass local communities, are intended to curb inflation, promote economic growth and cut public spending, thus restoring a balance of payments equilibrium. However, the export-oriented growth strategy that SAPs promote has damaged environments. Research by Friends of the Earth concludes that there is a generalised link between SAPs and deforestation.[50] Berthoud sees SAPs as putting economic efficiency above social justice; they are 'the attempts of the IMF and the World Bank to impose liberalism on a worldwide scale'.[51] A special edition of *Third World Resurgence* outlined several objections to SAPs. Some of these objections fit with neo-Marxist theory; SAPs benefit no more than a small elite in the South. Other objections adhere more to an ecological view; the role of SAPs in environmental degradation.[52] Once again it can be seen that neo-Marxists and ecologists share similar concerns, though for very different reasons.

Poverty receives some consideration from neo-Marxists. To Cockcroft, Frank and Johnson, poverty is rooted in the global political economy and is perpetuated by metropolitan elites and the comprador class who pursue their interests at the expense of the poorer classes. Indeed, the poor become dysfunctional for the capitalist system when money is spent on their subsistence and welfare needs.[53] Poverty is also a concern for the ecologists, although they reject suggestions that the poor *cause* deforestation,[54] arguing instead that the poor are agents of deforestation, with the causes lying in deeper structural factors. Poverty in tropical forest countries contributes to deforestation due to, for example, increased demand for woodfuel and land for agricultural smallholdings. Clearly, certain causes of poverty lie at the country-level, such as national development policies that displace populations or give low priority to rural areas. Poverty in the South therefore has its origins in both national policy and global economic relationships and consumption patterns. However, poverty is not just a function of global economic forces and of government development policies. It is also related to a further factor, namely inequities in land ownership.

Neo-Marxists note that the globalisation of capitalism has resulted in the commercialisation and commodification of land as a factor of production.

Neo-Marxist theories see land reform as essential to the implementation of social equity. A focus on inequities in land tenure and the role of the landless poor is also central to ecologism. With respect to deforestation, one view is that inequities in land tenure cause rural poverty, driving the landless poor into tropical forests in search of land for agriculture. This theme emerges from a series of studies conducted by the World Rainforest Movement where elements of the neo-Marxist approach are visible in the argument that 'inequitable patterns of land use and ownership in the tropics have been exaggerated by the incorporation of the third world into the global market'.[55] To Friends of the Earth, inequitable land distribution restricts the poor to the least fertile agricultural lands, 'whilst traditional elites reap most of the benefits of their countries' natural resources'.[56] This emphasis on land concentration as a factor that strengthens local economic elites, marginalises the poor and consequently plays a role in forest degradation owes a clear debt to neo-Marxist thought.

It has been noted that, despite certain dissimilarities, there are strong commonalties between the analyses of neo-Marxism and ecologism. Both consider that a major barrier to the type of world they wish to inhabit lies in the global political economy. Both focus on the importance of alliances between the elites of North and South. Both offer a critique of TNCs and Structural Adjustment Programmes, and focus on external debt, poverty and inequitable patterns of land ownership. But whereas the central concern of the early neo-Marxists was underdevelopment, that of the ecologist is the degradation of nature.

How have neo-Marxists responded to the environmental crisis? The environment generally has not been a concern of dependency theorists, although Samir Amin is a notable exception. In 1977, Amin argued that problems of environmental degradation 'are rooted in the very structure of the capitalist economic and social system'.[57] While noting that environmental problems accrue to all humanity, he argued that the centre benefits in economic terms, while the periphery bears the costs, for example, in terms of soil erosion and deforestation. In 1992, Amin restated his environmental concerns, but proceeded further and argued that the ideology of development has been eroded 'to the point where it is now finished'.[58] He then re-states, but also redefines, the importance of delinking. Delinking should not mean the severance of all economic and trade ties or the complete separation of centre from periphery in order to achieve development. Amin talks of an alternative development based on 'the objective need for social justice and the development of peoples'.[59] In contrast to SAPs, which seek to adjust a country's economic relations to external factors, Amin sees delinking as the submission of external relations to the logic of internal development. The delinking principle is a relative one with 'no clear or universal recipe for implementation'.[60] Amin thus favours endogenous development that emerges from within societies according to their values and cultures, rather than exogenous development, driven by the values and priorities of external actors.

In recent years Wallerstein has paid some attention to the environment, although it has yet to become a central concern in his work. Like Amin, he notes the increasing ecological burden borne by the South, especially since the global expansion of production in the 1970s and 1980s which 'saw a shift in locus of the major ecological costs from core to peripheral and semi-peripheral areas'.[61] Wallerstein also argues that the problem of pollution is 'too dramatic to be affected by minor adjustments' and that paying for clean-up costs 'threatens to overwhelm the possibility for the continued accumulation of capital'.[62] Frank has also departed from some of his earlier assumptions and questions the role of modernising development when arguing that evidence of oppression and poverty 'has now raised serious doubts about the very concept of development as a progressive, integral, and integrating process'.[64] With such a view Frank moves himself towards ecological thought, and in particular towards those such as Sachs who contest the very concept of development. In different ways, therefore, Amin, Wallerstein and Frank voice reservations about contemporary patterns of modernising development, as well as concern for the destruction of nature.

While neo-Marxism helps explain why environmental degradation occurs, it offers a bleak and pessimistic prognosis for the future. The above view explains only why environmental degradation is likely to continue, not how it may be arrested. Yet if the problems of environmental degradation are rooted in the global political economy, some degree of structural change is clearly necessary. The next section speculates how such change may occur.

Two Views of the Future: Ecological Modernists and Post-modernists

In his theory of structuration, Anthony Giddens parts company with the inert structural determinism of neo-Marxism which assigns no real role to independent agents. To Giddens, agents are more than mere structural proxies and are never totally powerless. Agents can 'make a difference',[64] although Giddens avoids pure voluntarism by acknowledging the existence of structural properties which mediate behaviour.[65] Structuration theory, which deals with the production and reproduction of society, thus allows for the evolution of new and different social systems; the theory is therefore 'intrinsically incomplete if not linked to a conception of social science as critical theory'.[66] Jan Aart Scholte also notes the potential for social change: 'Personal and group choices erect, reaffirm, undermine and/or reconstruct patterns of social order at the same time that the social order delimits and constrains these choices.'[67] To Robert Cox, historical structures are 'persistent social practices, made by collective human activity and *transformed through collective human activity*'.[68]

In this section brief consideration is given to two views on how global patterns of social organisation may shift to an environmentally sustainable basis. Each view recognises that a systemic fault of modernity is institutionalised environmental destruction, although they differ on the capacity of modernity to respond effectively to this problem. The first view advocates the continued development of modernity to a new and environmentally sustainable stage by a process of *ecological modernisation*. In contrast to ecological modernising theories, *post-modernism* considers environmental degradation to be an intrinsic feature of modernity, and advocates the undermining of the institutions of modernity so that society is reorganised along post-industrial lines.

Ecological modernisation theory draws from Giddens's theory of structuration. To Giddens, the 'acceptability' of a social practice includes two elements: there must be agreement as to what constitutes an acceptable act; and there must be an evaluation of such acts according to moral rules and norms that evaluate conduct.[69] Hence, the dominant norms and morals of society can only change if the 'acceptability' of social practices is first questioned. Giddens refers to this process as reflexivity, namely 'the monitored character of the ongoing flow of social life'.[70] To Giddens, reflexivity is a central feature of modernity; new knowledge and moral questions cause action to be monitored in a new light. Ecological modernisation theories adopt Giddens's notion of reflexive modernity to argue that concerned agents reappraise and redefine social practices with the purpose of eliminating the environmental risks generated by modernity.[71] To Mol, reflexive modernity deals with the environmental crisis by 'the routine incorporation of new (ecological) information and knowledge in social conduct and institutional forms, transforming the institutional order'.[72]

Ecological modernisation theory is defined by Hajer as 'the discourse that recognises the structural character of the environmental problematique but none the less assumes that existing political, economic and social institutions can internalize the care for the environment'.[73] To Weale, 'Instead of seeing environmental protection as a burden upon the economy the ecological modernist sees it as a potential for future growth.'[74] Hence some governments now talk of 'no-regrets policies' that benefit the economy while arresting environmental risks.[75] While there is no generally accepted formulation of ecological modernisation theory, the following features are shared by ecological modernists.[76] First, the theory has a benign view of the modern state and assumes that an ecologically reformed state can play an enabling role in providing a regulatory framework for sustainable development. Secondly, ecological modernists advocate the ecological reform of the industrial production so that environmental sustainability is integrated into the production process from source, rather than dealt with by 'end of pipe' solutions. However, ecological modernisation theory forestalls accusations that it merely promotes technocratic fixes to deep structural problems by advocating the contraction of technological systems that fail to adhere to strict ecological standards.[77] Thirdly, the theory emphasises a central role for a reformed market. According to this view, capitalist markets have an inbuilt instinct for self-preservation and will respond to the environmental crisis by promoting the production and consumption of products manufactured on a sustainable basis. The internalisation of external environmental and social costs into market mechanisms is seen to be an important feature of the ecological modernisation of markets.

Clearly ecological modernisation theory places a heavy emphasis on self-regulation and the self-monitoring characteristics of social systems and assumes a priori that an environmentally sustainable modernity is possible. Proponents of ecological modernisation theory acknowledge these weaknesses. To Mol, social change is usually preceded by social struggle and disputes, factors that ecological modernisation theory rarely emphasises,[78] while to Hajer ecological modernisation theory fails to acknowledge that waste, instability and insecurity are 'inherent aspects of capitalist development'.[79] Nonetheless, the principle of ecological modernisation has gained widespread acceptance in many industrialised countries, in particular in the European Union.[80]

Ecological modernists would be seen by Chris Brown as critical theorists, among those 'unwilling to abandon the Enlightenment Project, even though they realize it can no longer be defended in the same way'.[81] In contrast to the critical theory approach, post-modernism, defined here as an approach that rejects the Enlightenment notions of universal laws and the rationality of science, challenges the industrial system and modern state. Hence to Saurin, 'global environmental degradation arises out of the *normal and mundane practices of modernity* and not from the accidental or abnormal',[82] while to Matthias Finger, 'post-modern politics can be considered the new expression of societal fragmentation and the erosion of the project of modernity' with key characteristics being 'the erosion of the nation-state as the most legitimate unit of action and the subsequent emergence of other equally legitimate levels of political action'.[83]

Here it is instructive to return to Dobson's distinction between environmentalism and ecologism. Dobson acknowledges that post-modernism's criticism of totalising discourses and celebration of diversity informs much ecological thought.[84] Ecological modernisation theory, however, is closest to the environmental end of the environmentalism–ecologism continuum, although with its advocacy of a limited degree of industrial restructuring it should not be equated with pure environmentalism.

Post-modern environmental politics – a sub-set of post-modernism – differs with ecological modernisation on a number of points: by arguing for the deconstruction of the state; by advocating the empowerment of the local; and by rejecting science, the market and economic development. A further difference is that while ecological modernisation emphasises institutional learning and the ecological reform of the institutions of modernity, post-modernism seeks the abolition of such institutions, rejecting the view that they can learn, at least to the degree necessary to ensure long-term sustainability. A characteristic of post-modernism is that the environment–development interface represents a zero-sum game, that is, there can be either development or environmental conservation but not both. However, a characteristic of ecological modernisation theories is that environmental protection is considered to be a positive sum game, that is by further modernisation, the environment can be protected. Finally, while both ecological modernists and post-modernists have a vision of the future, only the former is prepared to offer policy prescriptions and models intended to realise sustainability; to post-modernists, the generation of policy documents, models and blueprints belongs to the discredited modernist order.

Post-modern views are not without their critics. As Piers Blaikie notes, in advocating the empowerment of the local, post-modernism is silent on the role of non-local exogenous groups, such as 'progressive developmentalists' focusing on poverty alleviation, justice and sustainable crop yields. Secondly, the post-modern view that the environment can be saved with a shift in power relations to the local presumes *angélisme* on the part of local communities, and the possibility that local elites may emerge and exploit a resource to the detriment of the wider community is not addressed.[85] Many Northern-based NGOs working in the South often experience difficulty obtaining local partners accepted by all sections of a local community. Post-modernism fails to acknowledge that there is rarely an homogeneous view at the local level any more than there is at the global level.

Concluding Thoughts

Although none of the five perspectives considered in this chapter – realism, neo-liberal institutionalism and neo-Marxism and the discourses of ecological modernisation and post-modernism – offers a complete view of the causal processes of, and potential solutions to, environmental degradation, none of the views should be rejected entirely. While the perspectives are silent in many respects, they have explanatory utility in many others, although further theoretical development is necessary before the full picture of global environmental politics can be gleaned. Realism helps explain why environmental degradation is due in part to the quest for state power and why states may disagree over global environmental policies; however, realism has little to say about environmental conservation, and its notion of environmental security fails to convince. Neo-liberal institutionalism explains claims to explain increased levels of intergovernmental cooperation, although it tends to avoid the role of non-state actors, lacks a critical dimension and is divided on the question of effectiveness. Neo-Marxism has contributed significantly to ecological thought, and a modified neo-Marxism that includes within its framework the exploitation of nature indicates that environmental degradation has its locus in the global political economy; this view, however, says more about why degradation will continue, rather than how it can be arrested. In different ways, ecological modernists and post-modernists each acknowledge that the origins of environmental degradation lie in the contemporary model of global capitalism, but their views of the future differ: an environmentally sustainable modernity in the case of the former; a post-modern society in the case of the latter. Each view is open to criticism. While ecological modernists generate policy prescriptions for the short-to-medium term, they offer an essentially benign view of the state, science, the market and industry, and do not consider what should happen if ecological modernisation fails to achieve the desired results. Post-modernists draw attention to the diversity of local cultures and eco-systems and introduce a healthy scepticism of the role of science and 'global solutions' in dealing with environmental problems. However, they avoid policy prescriptions and consequently are unsure how to operationalise their desired world view, and while they readily offer critiques, they also offer an overly optimistic view of the local.

As William Sunderlin argues with respect to the classical paradigms of sociology, it is usual for students of global environmental change to argue from a position drawing from just one paradigm, a phenomenon he refers to as 'paradigm isolation'.[86] The same may be said for many students of International Relations. The study of global environmental change encompasses a consideration of the political, economic and social consequences of environmental change, the environmental and social consequences of political and economic policy, and informed speculation of the political, economic and social changes necessary to ensure environmental sustainability. No single view can fill any one of these functions, and while a complete synthesis of all 'paradigms' is clearly impossible,[87] it also makes little sense to analyse global environmental change while striving for paradigmatic consistency, especially when the global environment continues to deteriorate.

Finally, different normative positions underlie the paradigms of International Relations. In the case of realism it can be argued that the state, or at least the democratic state, is the best vehicle for promoting democracy and international security. Despite the claimed positivism of its proponents, the norms of cooperation, free trade, development and economic prosperity underlie neo-liberal institutionalism, while neo-Marxism has traditionally been informed by the norms of economic justice and equality of opportunity.[88] There is a need for those students who care for the environment to make explicit their own normative positions – such as eco-centrism, environmental quality and local community empowerment – irrespective of their home paradigm or discipline. While there will be some disagreement over what these norms should be, this is nonetheless preferable to the unaffordable luxury of supposedly 'value-free' analysis of political and economic processes that result in an increasingly ecologically frail planet.

CHAPTER 15

The Internet as an Object of International Relations Interest

Keith Webb

Civilisation progresses in proportion to the number of important things that can be done automatically. (Alfred North Whitehead)

Its not that she's got anything that any other woman hasn't got, but she's got it across the corridor. (Tony Hancock)

There is little doubt that the nature of human communication and changes in communication radically affect the character of society and relations between societies. Without communication there could be no society and definitely no international society. Communication, broadly and simply defined, may be considered as the transmission of goods, information or ideas between individuals or societies. These are not, of course, exclusive categories; the transmission of goods may carry with it information and ideas that affect behaviour, or be given meanings by the receiver that are very different from those intended by the sender. An example might be the Cargo Cults of the Melanesian Islands; manufactured goods from Europe were considered as magical since they appeared without work.[1] Neither must we constrain the idea of communication to intentional transmission. Body language or other unintended emissions will often convey 'messages' that are not intended by the emitter but are picked up by the receiver. A similar issue, which will be discussed later, is whether the extension of the Internet globally is an extension of what has been called the 'coca-cola' ideology; it may not be the explicit intention of America or individual Americans to proselytise culturally with respect to less developed countries, but in the acceptance or reaction to American cultural artifacts this may be the result.

While this chapter is about the Internet, it should be noted that this is only a small part of global communication. The Internet, is conceived here as 'computer-mediated communication' (CMC). Global communication, in line with the definition above, includes also trade and commerce, telephone, television, film, newspapers and books, travel, and a host of other inter-national and inter-cultural interactions and inter-penetrations. However, there are problems of delineation which, rather than becoming clearer through time, will become more difficult, due to the ubiquity of computer usage. For example, a computer is used to typeset a newspaper; this is transmitted *in toto* to another site and a regional adaptation is produced. Telephone exchanges are computerised and the travel booking process depends on computers. The international money markets, now open twenty-four hours a day, depend on the electronic transmission of information. And in the future, an increasing linkage of the entertainment and the computer industry will further blur the distinction, particularly with the continuing development of technology. Thus, in one sense, much of contemporary communication is 'computer mediated'.

There is a great deal of overstatement about the Internet. It is frequently conceived of as something new and revolutionary. What *is* new and revolu-tionary is the ease and quantity of communication; qualitatively, the Internet is merely an extension of changes in social and technological trends that have been occurring over the past one-and-a-half centuries. An example may demonstrate this. In 1820 there was an insurrection in Glasgow. It was put down by the locally based armed forces and the leaders hung almost before the government in London knew that there was an insurrection. Perhaps the major innovation was the telegraph. By 1836 Samuel Morse had developed a working model of the telegraph, and in 1844 an experimental line was constructed between Washington and Baltimore. The legendary Pony Express, charging $5 an ounce for mail, in fact lasted less than two years before being put out of business by the telegraph in 1861.[2] Along with this came the capacity of governments to centralise decision-making, reducing the *de facto* autonomy of distant provinces, actors and regions, leading in some cases to regional resistance to distant control. Alexander Bell, beating a competitor by a few hours, filed what has been termed 'the most valuable patent ever issued' in 1876, and within a short time telephone began its growth towards universality. And Bell himself pointed out, the telephone betters:

> all other telegraphic machines [that] produce signals which require to be trans-lated by experts, and such instruments are therefore extremely limited in their application, but the telephone actually speaks, and for this reason it can be utilized for nearly every purpose for which speech is employed (from an address Bell made in 1878).[3]

To quote Jarrod Wiener, what both the telegraph and the telephone did was to begin the 'collapse of time and space'.[4] But these were not the first. In an important sense the printing press contributed to the process, and in a different way so did canals, metalled roads, railways and clipper ships. To these may be added the later developments of radio, cinema, and television, without which today's world would not be recognisable.

The Development of the Net

The claims for the Internet are legion.

> We know only that we cannot say for certain what the future of the Net may
> be. But that it is of tremendous importance to the future history of humanity
> cannot be disputed. Changes in computer mediated communication have now
> gone beyond doing the same old thing the same old way only faster and better;
> the machines are now rewriting the software of Man.[5]

In spite of the communications revolution that preceded the Internet, it is
a uniquely modern phenomenon, an evolution possible and understandable
only in the context of rapidly developing technology. This is as true today
as it was in the past; what is true of the Net now will be out of date
tomorrow. Many claims and predictions made about the Net may be ex-
travagant in the short term and conservative with respect to the long term.
These range from those who see the Net as something that is going to
transform radically the nature of human societies, to those who see the Net
as merely an extension of already extant changes; the former we may refer
to as the 'Gutenburg Complex' (in that the changes are seen as being as
fundamental as the invention of the Gutenburg Press) and the latter as the
'developmentalists'. For example, Wilson argues that the Net is a means
whereby the Third World can by-pass the information deficit; children in
African schools will be able to access learning programmes in multimedia
form, and in addition:

> People in underdeveloped countries or developing countries, (or whatever the
> PC term is this month) are ALREADY looking to the InterNet as a way of
> bypassing all the obstacles to higher-learning that developed countries faced.
> They cannot wait the many years it will take to create modern universities with
> good facilities, including a good library and a good faculty. They want and need
> all the educational advantages that the InterNet can provide, and are already
> hoping it will be their salvation.[6]

Others would claim, as Hardy notes, that the Net 'represents the growth of
a new society within the old'; that it is 'the first intelligent artificial intelligence'; or that it is the 'greatest free marketplace of ideas that has ever
existed'. However, while, as we shall note later, a powerful developmental
potential undoubtedly exists, at present the infrastructure of many less
developed countries is such that they cannot support the hardware needs of
the Net.

Others have claimed that the Net has intimate links with the spread of
democracy; from this point of view, the democratisation of information
world-wide is the death knell of thought control. Here the examples of
personal electronic communications in the failed Russian coup or Tiananmen
Square are cited. Others look to the Net as the beginning of the end of the

nation-state; communications penetrate national boundaries by a multitude of routes that cannot be controlled, a recent confirmation of the 'cobweb' model of international society.[7] Some, of a more conservative bent, see the Net as a major threat both to the integrity of the state and to its security. Others see the Net, particularly in its commercial extensions, as being the agent of enormous change in the life-style of every individual in the developed world; in twenty years time not being 'on the Net' will be a sign of extreme disadvantage, akin to being bankless, telephoneless, carless or without a television today. Whatever one thinks of the Net, there is little doubt that it is important from a number of points of view, and that this significance will undoubtedly accelerate. A small measure of this is the rate of growth of the Net; effectively it is doubling in size every year.[8]

The initial development of the Net was stimulated by military and security concerns in the context of the Cold War.[9] The first articulation came in paper in 1964 by Paul Baran of the RAND corporation. The military problem was this. In the event of a nuclear attack, how could military communication structures in the United States remain intact? An analogy was made with the evolution of transport. The road system in the United States had been constructed in such a way that it could not be interrupted by nuclear attack. There were always multiple ways to anywhere. There was no centre to the transport system. The proposed solution to the communications conundrum was similar; the establishment of large numbers of interconnected computers that could route messages in multiple ways. Because there was no centre to the communications structure – each node was equal to all other nodes – a nuclear strike on one or many sites would not disable the communication system. Communication would just go through another route. In addition, information would go in 'packets', and by different routes, and would be reassembled when all arrived at the destination. The history of the Net thus really begins in the 1960s with the establishment of the packet-switched networks. Packet-switching is a method of fragmenting messages into sub-parts, routing them to their destinations, and reassembling them. Packetising information has several advantages. It facilitates allowing several users to share the same connection by breaking up the data into discrete units which can be routed separately. While this was in some respects an inefficient and slow means of communication, in other respects it was a rugged and almost indestructible means of communication. Thus, from the very inception of the Net, the concept of anarchy was built in, in the sense of there being no overarching authoritative centre, first as a military necessity, but later as a culture.

The National Physical Laboratory in Britain was the first to set up a network on these principles in 1968, and was soon followed by a much larger and more ambitious project sponsored by the Pentagon in 1969. The first node was established at UCLA, soon followed by three further nodes. The mini-network was named ARPANET (Advanced Research Project Agency

NET). The primary aim of ARPANET was to enable the transmission of data files and long-distance computing, including accessing data and research files at distant sites. The latter was particularly important given the scarcity and cost of the 'supercomputers' of the time. However, within a very short time the main usage of the Net was very different. In 1972 an electronic mail programme was constructed that allowed the distribution of messages across a network.[10] Other purposes such as personal messages using email (it was a matter of months before the first email romance was consummated[11]) became popular. Research collaboration at a distance became possible. And, with the introduction of the mailing list, like-minded individuals could form groups. One of the first was a science fiction mail list. In 1973 the first international connections to ARPANET were established with Britain and Norway.[12] Today there are literally thousands of mail lists, discussion groups covering virtually every aspect of human existence.

Within a relatively short time other networks were established and networked through ARPANET. For example, TELENET, a commercial version of ARPANET came on-line in 1973. There were three reasons for this rapid growth and development, particularly following the publication of a 'Transmission Control Programme' (TCP) by Cerf and Kahn, which was a major breakthrough in standardisation and flexibility.[13] First, the software was in the public domain and was free. Secondly, the TCP/IP software could handle many kinds of machines. Thirdly, just as a telephone is of little use unless a great many people have one, linking to the ARPANET allowed the identification of other users. In time ARPANET became an insignificant part of the Internet as more and more networks were established and more and more machines became linked. In 1983 the military component of ARPANET became a separate network MILNET, now just one network among hundreds. In 1989 ARPANET 'formally expired', but its demise was scarcely noticed since all of its functions continued to be performed anarchically at hundreds of sites. In the years since then the Net has continued to grow at an astonishing rate, as noted previously. One factor that has ensured its continued expansion is the introduction of the World Wide Web, through which the Internet became graphical as well as interactive.

There are perhaps five factors that account for both the past growth of the Net and the expectation of future growth. The first is purely economic. Just a few years ago the cost of the hardware and software needed to access and use the Net was prohibitive except for wealthy individuals and institutions. The price of access level technology has, however, dropped dramatically, bringing it within financial capability of many more people. Due to the cut-throat competition in the computer industry, which applies also to servers who proffer services in the expectation of high future profits, the fall in access costs can be expected to continue.

Secondly, young people are increasingly being educated in the use of the Net. In the comparatively recent past the Net was the province of academics, the military and research establishments. Business – particularly the financial information sector – realised the benefits, and started using the Net seriously. Today, especially in the university sector, the Net on both a local (LAN) basis and nationally and internationally is used on a daily basis by many students. Further, schools are beginning to use the Net more fully. As ever the United States is ahead in this respect, but in Britain and Europe there are increasing numbers of schools using the Net for a variety of purposes. An additional factor in this respect is the fact that many youngsters learn at least basic keyboard skills and familiarity with computers through computer games. Unlike James Thurber's grandmother, who was reputed to put all the plugs in the house into their sockets at night so the electricity would not leak out, children are normally far more conversant, familiar and at ease with modern technology than many of their seniors. The technology is not a threat or a problem but is increasingly a normal part of their environment.

Thirdly, there is much more awareness of the Net; even though many people do not use it, they will be aware that it exists. There are three reasons for this. Perhaps the most important factor in consciousness arousal is the activity of the media. By the very nature of their business it is to be expected that the media in its various forms would early on realise the benefits of computer communication. It is an every-day tool in at least some of its aspects for most journalists. Because of their enchantment with the new means of communication, it is difficult to pick up a newspaper these days without some mention of the Net. Major broadsheets such as *The Independent* and *The Guardian* have weekly sections devoted to the Net, while the *Sun* and *Daily Mirror* regularly have reports on the amount of pornography on the Net. The journalist in this respect typically projects his or her view of the world on a public which, in the main, is not conversant with that aspect of the world. Thus, even though accessing the Net is still very much a minority activity, many more people are aware of it than actually use it.

A fourth factor, which is as important as any other, is the increasing ease of usage. In this respect the Net follows computer usage as a whole. To hoary old computer users, brought up on green and brown punch-cards and computers running on vacuum valves which were always breaking-down, the modern computing environment with which most new users are acquainted, must seem very easy. Apple Macintosh recognised early the importance of ease of use, but because of their pricing policies failed to clean-up in the marketplace. But Microsoft were forced to introduce their Windows system to meet the challenge, followed by Windows 95 and NT. In general, whether we are talking about statistical packages, databases, wordprocessing, desktop publishing or operating systems, the move has been to greater ease of usage and hence a much shallower learning curve for the technological novice. And, in general, the easier it is for people to access those things perceived as desirable, the more probable it is that they will do so. The Net has kept pace with, or even surpassed this move to increased simplicity. The additional hardware power needed for Net access has been forthcoming at reduced cost. The facilities provided by the public utilities, particularly telephones for the private user, have been improved continually. These two factors have improved dramatically the speed of the system, reducing the frustration of long waiting times. But much more than this, the introduction of new software, allowing access to the World Wide Web which is easy to install, easy to use, and in many cases free, has led to a massive increase in Net usage. The initial writing of HTTP (HyperText Transfer Protocol) was done by Tim Berners-Lee in 1989. It came on-line only in 1993. It was accompanied by an extremely easy-to-use programming language, HTML (HyperText Mark-up Language), which allowed even comparative novices to write their own individual 'homepage' for external consumption. Further, in the last two or three years applications have become available that translate wordprocessed documents into HTML so that Web authors can know only very little about hypertext programming. But even if this is not done, programmes such as Netscape, Internet Explorer or Mosaic allow the user, at the click of a mouse button, to access the Internet on a global basis and reach the 700 million 'pages' that are currently available.[14] More than this, however, the technology of the Web with its hypertext linking allows the most un-sophisticated user to surf unhindered and at relatively low cost.

The final factor that explains the increased usage of the Net is its 'function-ality'. Just as only one person having a telephone is of little use, so a small number of people and institutions connected to the Net is of limited value. However, when nearly everybody has a telephone, it becomes a nearly indispensible tool of communication. So too with the Net. The exponential growth rate of the Net means that it makes much more sense to be connected now than in the past. The very growth itself means that more information is accessible and more connectivity is possible. This is true for research, commercial and private usage. It is, of course, possible to argue that there is too much information on the Net – what can we do with it all? – but with the development of faster search engines, such as Alta Vista, HotBot, Lycos, Webcrawler, Metacrawler and indexes such as Yahoo and the Yellow Pages, to mention just a few, the capacity to search the Net keeps pace with the amount of sources and sites on the Net. Such search engines and relatively sophisticated means of searching become necessary when one realises that between 1 AD and 1500 AD the amount of publically available information doubled, while today it is doubling at a rate of between eighteen months and five years.[15] Further, in so far as the Net becomes important for advertising and selling, the competitive pressures will tend to enforce connectivity.

Looking at the recent past of the Net, and the astonishing present, it is difficult to conceive of a future where computer-mediated communication does not exercise a considerable influence. But it is unlikely to be the future we envisage. Just as email was set up for research purposes and rapidly led to romance on the Net, or the Zapatistas used the Peace and Conflict Nets to inform the world of their plight, people in the future will use the Net in ways that, as yet, we do not envisage. There are precedents for this. At the inception of newspapers, Thomas Paine saw them as a means of reaching all humanity and spreading ideas inimical to monarchy and totalitarianism.[16] The technology was such that anyone could set up a news sheet and publicise their views. The future was not, however, as he envisaged it; within a comparatively few years, partly driven by commercial pressures, newspapers were controlled and run by press 'barons' such as Rothermere, Beaverbrook, Hearst, and Murdoch, while in totalitarian countries the media was used to persuade and control populations. Whether the Net will fulfil the aims of Paine and reinvent the world in the image of the common man − 'We have it in our power to begin the world over again' − as argued by Katz, or whether it will take a different path, is at present difficult to estimate.

The Consequences of Communication

At a very basic level it can be argued that one of the fundamental features of humanity in comparison to the rest of the animal world is the ability to communicate in a sophisticated and flexible manner employing linguistic design features not found elsewhere.[17] Chomsky, indeed, relates this to the structure of the brain, arguing that 'deep structure' displays an underlying similarity of all human languages.[18] This is not to argue that animals do not communicate, but that in the main they employ signals rather than signs and where they do begin to approach human communication, it is in a much more simple way.[19] It is difficult to imagine human society evolving without communication;[20] indeed, Deutsch *defines* a society in terms of the boundaries or disjunctures in communication.[21]

Not only is communication a basic feature of the human creature and human societies, but the mode and form of communication structures our construal of the world in many ways. At one level we may argue that language influences what we can say or think; Mannheim, for example, comes close to cultural determinism here,[22] as indeed does Whorf.[23] Foucault, in his many works, draws attention to the relationship between language and power, in so far as social relationships, hierarchies, and stereotyping with subsequent behaviour are a consequence of linguistic typifications.[24] Marshall McLuhan, on the other hand, draws attention to not just what is communicated but to how it is communicated, arguing that the very mode of communication affects the meaning of what is transmitted with significant social consequences.[25]

As communication is so fundamental to human beings and societies, it is unsurprising that changes in communications can have dramatic affects on the nature of both. Throughout most of human history, because of the limited mode of communication, cross-cultural communication was fairly limited, mainly constrained to marginal trade, war and migration usually enforced by natural disaster.[26] McNeill points out that as far as war was concerned, transport and provisioning were vital, but with the introduction of the horse and the chariot the constraints lessened and with them the ability to make war over a greater distance thus enhancing control and communication.[27] The ability to increase military reach and thus communication was a consequence of changes in technology.

Examples abound of where changes in the nature of communication have affected the lives of people and society. Perhaps the most well-known is the invention of the printing press. This, among other effects, had the consequence of freeing understanding of the Bible from priestly interpretation, aiding the development of the Protestant belief in a direct rather than mediated relationship to God. Congruent with this was the development of literary forms of indigeneous languages, facilitating the development of nationalism. Similarly, throughout Europe, improvement in canals and roads led not only to an enhancement of trade, but also to the ability of government to extend the degree of control to distant provinces. Further, the Industrial Revolution in Britain, which set a model for the world, would not have been possible were it not for the ability to transport goods and food, and the same capacity for transport, allied to technological supremacy, was an important element in the growth of colonialism and imperialism. A consequence of this has been a universalisation of nationalism as the major vocabulary of dissent and affirmation.

The invention of the printing press, the telegraph, the telephone, the radio and the television have wrought other significant changes. The world is a smaller place, or if not a smaller place, people's awareness of it is larger. Whereas a thousand years ago serfs were tied to villages and their major source of news were the rumours brought by travellers, or what was conveyed by the priest or the town-crier, today what is happening now is seen now, communicated by an all-pervasive media. For many of the world's population the inhibitions of parochialism have gone, but with this has come uncertainties with respect to identity. The more cosmopolitan and open the world becomes, and the greater the variety of competing perspectives that people are exposed to, the greater is the choice of values, goals and ideals. Pick-and-mix identities and ideologies become possible as the simplicities appropriate to a different age fade away.

Communication is a part of all social interaction. Social change is facilitated by communication, and changes in communication lead to social change. Through most of human history social change and the invention of new social forms has been comparatively rare, usually caused by exogenous factors such as famine, disease or conquest. Modern humankind, with perspectives derived from the Enlightenment, is not only socialised to change, but because of the belief in the essential manipulability of the world, expects and desires change. The new technology of communication, computer-mediated communication, will be taken up and, like past innovations in communications, will change society. The vision of McLuhan, of a deproximated electronically connected global village, with corresponding changes in work patterns, a view supported by Bill Gates,[28] may not come to pass, and yet there will be change. We may only be able to glimpse through the gap in the curtain, but the glimpse that we get shows a social landscape re-forming.

The Net as a Disciplinary Resource

As a disciplinary resource the Net has two basic functions, as a means of communication and as a source of material. These are undoubtedly revolutionising the discipline with respect to the speed with which work can be done, and the range of work which is possible. To some extent, while for purposes of discussion these functions are separated, in practice they often overlap. For example, frequently on the mailing lists there will be requests for information or sources on particular subjects; the request may come from Washington and the answer from Finland or Japan. It is important to recognise that we are as yet in the infancy of this development. What is unusual now will become commonplace in the future, and uses will emerge which as yet we have not imagined.

If electronic means of communication and research is going to become common in academic life in general, and International Relations in particular, this has implications both for teaching and for the training of the next generation's academics. Already one occasionally sees the rather sad spectacle of the middle-aged academic teaching graduate students who are, at least in terms of access to information, far ahead of him or her. While the teacher may read one or two newspapers and wait for the next book or journal article on the subject, the student is able to access dozens of today's news sources and by monitoring the maillists and bulletin boards find out what is going down on the ground now. One student recently, for example, was able to monitor the rebellion in Mexico as it happened through an American maillist and incorporate this into his coursework. Clearly, the teacher, with many years of experience behind him or her, may be much more sophisticated in theory, approaches, and methodology, and yet in other areas will be overtaken by the technologically sophisticated student. And, what is increasingly becoming common, versions of papers which *will* appear in journals are published on home pages for the astute student to read. Hence it is often possible to be ahead of the literature. Students, who are the next generation of academics, are leading the way in many respects. The problem will solve itself as one generation succeeds another, but for some of today's cohort of teachers, for whom the wordprocessor is seen as a novel innovation, some effort to master the Internet would pay great dividends.

Communication on the Net can be of several kinds. Perhaps the most common is the use of mailing lists. These are, in Britain, largely run through Mailbase which is sited at Newcastle University and is funded by the Joint

Information Systems Committee, though today many developed countries have their own similar services. Scholars both start and join lists and take part in the discussions of the list.[29] Lists can vary in the quality or usefulness of the discussion; in general, it would seem that the narrower the focus of the list the higher the probability that it will be of use. Many of the more general lists have a high proportion of noise to content, but even in this case useful contacts can be made and new insights gained. In all cases a decision has to be made as to the time taken scanning mail against what is to be gained from participation. Unlike ordinary mail (sometimes referred to as 'snail mail'), the conventions of emailing are such that most of the courtesies are omitted with the consequence that messages tend to be briefer and to the point. Scanning mail thus tends to be much quicker. Further, most maillist systems also have an archival facility that allows searching for particular topics or discussions, which, again, can save a lot of time.

Lists can be of two kinds, moderated or unmoderated, closed or open. The moderated list is where the 'owner' of the list, usually the person or persons who started the list, controls the input into the list. Usually this means merely screening out 'noise' (contentless messages, or communications that should be done on a bilateral rather than public basis) rather than the imposition of any censorship. The aim is to increase the utility factor of the list. The unmoderated list, on the other hand, is open to all input and no contol is exercised by the owner. A closed list is where the participants to the list are limited; joining the list is not open to everyone. While this may seem somewhat constraining, it does mean that academics working on a research project can communicate with each other only rather than the world at large. In such a case the relevance of the communications to the participants is increased. As far as usefulness is concerned, different kinds of lists are useful in different ways. For example, while a closed list might be of more use with respect to a group of scholars working on a particular project, advertising a conference, or a call for papers for a special issue of a journal, would be more successful on an open list.

One of the great advantages of mailing lists is their ease of use and the nature of participation. Joining is easy and participation simple. Further, the participation is usually international rather than merely national. Hence it becomes possible to identify a community of scholars around the world. As we will note later, this international participation is limited by levels of national development and by constraints placed on Net participation by states for either political or religious reasons. It does, however, point to an accelerating trend in both research and the nature of the academic community; it is increasingly an international community. Clearly, to some extent, the discipline of International Relations, partly because it is an academic discipline and partly because of the nature of its subject matter, has always been 'international' in its scope and communications structure. But what is happening is a strengthening of that tendency. Structurally, within Europe, this is marked by such factors as the growth of the ECPR,[30] the European Standing Group on International Relations,[31] and the increasing inter-linking of universities through various staff and student exchange programmes. Beyond Europe, academic boundaries continue to fade; sometimes, for example, it is difficult to know merely from the email address exactly where someone is communicating from. The reason for the dissolving of academic boundaries is clear to see; from my desk at the University of Kent it is as easy to communicate with someone in Berlin or Colorado as with someone in London.

The internationalisation of communication, together with the institutional regionalisation of International Relations, should have other consequences. In the past, partly due to sheer numbers and partly due to the resources devoted to the subject, there has been a tendency for the intellectual centre of the discipline to be dominated by scholars in the United States. As boundaries fade, however, the participation of scholars from around the world becomes possible in the discourse of the discipline, and scholars in the United States will become increasingly exposed on a daily basis to other perspectives. One function of the Net is to reduce ethnocentricism. In addition, resources which previously were not accessible to many scholars outside of North America will become available to all.

A further use of the Internet for research is in the exchange of papers or chapters. Where the research is of an international collaborative nature, it is possible to speed up the feedback, especially if this involves joint authorship, by a factor of many times. To some extent this can be done by the use of faxes, but here the problem is that the material is not in computer memory which slows down re-writing or re-editing, even with the capacity to scan. To do a file transfer, on the other hand, leaves the material in computer memory and available for re-working. In a recent eight-country study jointly edited by the author, where there were problems of language as well as substance, the file transfer mechanism saved a great deal of time.[32] A chapter was transferred, edited and commented upon, and returned to the sender in one day, a process which by ordinary mailing procedures would have taken at least three weeks.

The Internet and Development

One of the more exciting ideas about the Internet is that it might be used to fuel a new revolution in education. The usual degree of hyperbole has been noticeable in the writings about this on the Net and elsewhere, and yet the potential is there for tremendous change. There is, however, a utopian vision of the relationship between the Net and development education that is propagated on the Net itself. We suspect it is a vision generated by well-intentioned educators in developed countries with little or no first-hand experience of the conditions of grinding poverty, where the maintenance of life itself absorbs all the energy of what is often a long day, and where the labour of children is necessary to the well-being of the family. What is this vision? It is a picture of millions of people in the Third World sitting at computers taking degree courses and vocational qualifications, run from the developed countries by academics. The Net from this point of view, is a form of educational development aid, replacing some of the educational activities of the Peace Corps, the VSO, or religious charities. It would be far more efficient than past educational aid, in that the material and reading would be on-line, and would be written and structured according to the most up-to-date perspectives in any particular discipline. Neither would it be dependent on the meagre local teaching talent, for the enterprise would be truly global. Thus it would be possible for an inhabitant of Papua New Guinea or the Gambia to gain an MBA from Harvard without ever leaving his or her home country. In some ways it is a beautiful vision, but unfortunately the reality is and will be very different. Like all utopian visions, though, it should not be dismissed entirely. What it does is provide motivation and define goals, and if the dream cannot be realised in full, perhaps there is some residual fall-out that can be realised. Where, however, the Net may come into its own is with respect to the 'semi-periphery' countries, those that are developed but distanced, such as Australia, New Zealand or Argentina.

The idea simply put is that through this medium, the Third World can jump a generation in development through accessing the best education available. In many Third World countries, access to higher education is restricted by both finance and the availability of personnel. Libraries tend to be bare of many essential texts, and certainly of modern texts and journals. The finance in Third World countries is just not available or is needed for more urgent tasks, often related to food, water or the development of basic infrastructure. Education is recognised as being of immense importance, but in a Third World context, there are so many things that fall into the same category.

However, it is probably the case that the dream of universal education through the Net will have to wait a while, merely because it is itself dependent on other aspects of development. For example, only a few years ago there were just seven land telephone lines going out of Asmara, the capital of Eritrea. It is difficult to see the development of any but the most primitive international communications in the near future. In China, in some ways a relatively advanced developing country, only in 1995 was an email network being set up between the top one-hundred universities. This is of the most basic kind, and it is unlikely that it will be extended to an international communications facility widely available to the academic community. If one looks at the distribution of servers throughout the world, one sees large areas of the globe largely bereft of these resources.

Further, one of the main things needed by a computer is electricity.[33] In many countries this is found only in the major cities, and even there it can be somewhat intermittent. It is, of course, possible to run computers with battery power, but these would need to be purchased and charged. A further major problem is the maintenance of computers. In one such country visited recently, a large number of 486 PCs had been donated as part of an aid package. However, when a machine went down, there were no spare parts available and no money with which to purchase them. With some ingenuity, machines were cannibalised, with the consequence of a constantly decreasing number of machines.

In addition, before the full educational potential of the Net as an engine of development can be realised, it is probably necessary for there to be a prior development in primary education. This would involve at a minimum literacy and numeracy, and, of course, some minimal skills in computing. It might also be the case that some language capability would be necessary. It seems unlikely that a course in, say, geology, on the Internet, would be translated into Hausa, Bangladeshi, or Aharu.

If the Internet is going to be an agent of change in the Third World from the point of view of education, then almost certainly for the foreseeable future it is going to be an urban phenomenon. It is only the urban areas which will be able to provide the basic infrastructure needed for the Net. Access to the Net will also probably be restricted to the upper echelons of the society, for only those are likely to have minimal skills needed to use the Net, since access to education in many Third World countries is very stratified. The first users will probably also be young; it is difficult to see large numbers of older people using the Net. The age profile in this respect will probably not be too different from that in developed countries. If these assumptions are correct a profile of an expected clientele emerges. It will tend to be urban, upper-class, young, and male dominated. Any spread of the use of the Net in education is likely to be nodal in form, with the initial take-up confined largely to capital cities, with only gradual spread to other urban areas.

There is, however, another factor that is likely to be of some importance. At least initially, and probably for some time to come, access to the Net will be institutionally based, rather than on an individual basis. In much of the developed world any individual can get on to the Net merely by the purchase of a machine and modem, by having the relevant skills and a telephone line and by suscribing to one of the increasing number of servers. Gateways exist from these to the wider Net. Other individuals will have access either through business linkage or through the academic networks. Mostly this is available at the cost of a local telephone call.

As far as the institutional base for the Internet is concerned, two particular structures come to mind: universities and state aid/representative organisations of developed countries. Universities, in most cases grossly under-funded, would only be able to afford the equipment and infrastructure through aid. To put this point into context, at the People's University in

Beijing, one of the 'top' universities in China with some 7,000 students, there were only two fax machines in 1995, and it has to be remembered that in terms of developing countries, China is one of the more dynamic economies with an annual growth rate of around 11 per cent. Many countries are far less fortunate, often ravaged by famine or drought, internal warfare, or rampant disease. One estimate, for example, suggests that among young people in Uganda, 10 per cent are carriers of the AIDS virus, while in Eritrea 40 per cent of the food supply is externally donated due to the economy being devastated by a thirty-year war of independence. Cases such as these could easily be multiplied around the world.

Another institutional scenario, however, is possible. Some developed countries have organisations in less developed countries that perform both educational and representative functions. In Britain this is the British Council, which is both a conduit for grants and scholarships, exchange schemes, etc., and which often has large libraries in the developing country. The British Council is funded by government grant via the Foreign and Commonwealth Office. A similar function, though often on a larger scale, is performed by the American ISO, the Information Services Office. If courses *were* available on the Net, then instead of funding scholarships for individuals from less developed countries, which due to their expense are limited in number, they could be run from the British Council offices or the ISO or similar organisations. A bank of some twenty or thirty networked PCs would cost little more than the cost of a few scholarships, and give far more people access to the education that many of them desire avidly. As a form of aid it would be cheap, and if properly organised, effective. It would fall short of a best-case scenario since there would be little personal face-to-face interaction which is an important element in education, but would provide good opportunities for education which are currently unavailable to all but the very privileged few.

The assumption throughout this chapter thus far is that access to the Net is a 'good thing', and that the education it potentially offers is a valued commodity. Experience in the Third World suggests that among many young people, education is seen as the golden gate out of poverty. The idea of education is espoused with enormous enthusiasm, and along with this enthusiasm goes an admiration of the developed world and a desire to achieve, particularly, the material prosperity of the First World. Politically, however, this is far from universally true. Education is never an entirely neutral product. It always contains within it the values of the educator and in certain circumstances can produce political paranoia. In Britain, where liberal educational values are strong and in the main unquestioned, attacks (wholly unjustified) were made in the early 1980s by the then Minister of Education on Open University teaching material as being too 'marxist'.

In so far as education is a liberal education, it holds to certain values. It believes in open discourse and debate, and the consideration of alternative and often contradictory perspectives. Truth, particularly in the humanities and social sciences, is not a given, and its nature is itself a matter of debate. Indeed, a contemporary trend in the humanities and social sciences, post-modernism, denies in some of its manifestations that there can be any truth above personal interpretation. Part of the liberal doctrine, that was strongly influenced by the writings of John Stuart Mill, is an acceptance of deviance. All points of view are arguable, and if they are to be sustained as live beliefs rather than dead rote dogma, they must be defended in the marketplace of ideas. Edmund Burke earlier had the same notion: 'He that wrestles with me is my friend, for he strengthens my muscles.'

Yet it is only recently that Iran banned the use of satellite dishes that were used to watch foreign television stations. Saudi Arabia follows a similar policy. In China, except at a few select hotels and university libraries, access to foreign newspapers and books is very difficult. It is not so long ago, after all, that Iran described the United States as 'the Great Satan'; the religious authorities are hardly likely to look kindly on a communication media which is imbued with liberal values and which is driven by American technology. In all these cases, thought policing is at work, an activity that is wholly opposed to the idea of education as understood in most developed countries, and which is completely antithetical to the spirit of the Internet as understood by most of its users. This does mean that some countries will not allow access to the Net, for the Net is far more subversive of authority than newspapers or television. And it is probably true to say that it is not possible in the long run for political authority to allow access for some purposes (such as business) and not for others. It is reasonable to argue that you either take the whole package or you take none. Any technical proscriptions that an authority attempts to impose will soon be circumvented by bright and ingenious users. For example, many universities in the developed world have attempted technically to proscribe access to pornographic material on the Internet, yet one bright second-year student found three separate ways to circumvent the censorship. The history of computing, particularly with respect to hacking, demonstrates that the mere presence of barriers is an incentive to find a way around them.

In general, then, while the Net may in the long run bring many benefits to less developed nations, it is difficult to see this happening in the short term. What is far more likely to happen is that as access to the Net deepens in developed countries, the gap between the 'haves' and the 'have nots' will widen.

Democracy and the Globalisation of Opinion

There is a belief, widespread on the Net, usually emanating from America, that the Internet can make a significant impact on 'democracy'.[34] The general nature of the argument covers at least two different themes which are often not differentiated, leading to a degree of confusion. The first theme is that through CMC participation can be increased, leading to greater degrees of popular control. The second theme is that through CMC a 'world opinion' can be created that can by-pass the restrictions of boundaries and bureaucracies leading to international grassroots participation. The former argument was beautifully satirised in a Peter Cook film in 1970, where voting buttons were mounted on every television, and everyone was required to vote on everything.[35] The outcome was dictatorship.

'Democracy' is without doubt an 'essentially contested concept'.[36] However, for the present discussion we can take the relevant meaning of democracy to be liberal and representative democracy, and the potential usage via the Internet to be some version of direct democracy. The former version of democracy is marked by organised pluralism – political parties legitimately expressing a variety of views in the contest for power – and election of representatives by the mass-public. These representatives are removable through future elections. There are many other things that we could say about liberal representative democracy – particularly the role of pressure groups in the formation of opinion between elections – but these two features are the important ones for our purposes.

'Direct democracy', the idea of which comes down to us from Greek times, means that the people themselves are the decision-makers, excepting, of course, barbarians, slaves and women. Perhaps the most powerful advocate of direct democracy was Jean-Jacques Rousseau who denied that representative democracy was democracy, since the sovereignty of the individual could not be represented.[37] Some support for this view would come from the analysts of political elites, particularly Pareto, Mosca and Michels. In Michels' work, for example, socialist parties with a founding egalitarian myth and representative democratic organisation were studied to explain how, in spite of this, they evolved into unrepresentative oligarchies. 'He who says organisation says oligarchy' – this was seen as an 'iron law'. The people, in spite of elections and recall, lost power to the elites.[38]

We thus have these two ideas of democracy which imply very different roles for the citizen. In the former version there is a tendency – perhaps even an expectation – that the majority of the citizenry is essentially passive except for particular political moments when the role of elector is adopted. The elector then selects between competing parties and programmes and confers power for a given period of time. The influence of the individual is thus indirect and episodic. In this model of democracy there are other avenues of influence such as through pressure groups, through the media, and sometimes by direct action and protests. Through these channels, however, the citizen does not act in the interests of the state as a whole, but is concerned to pursue particular interests within the polity. But perhaps the most powerful influence the citizen has is the desire of power-holders to retain office, and the desire of power-seekers to gain office; in this contestation, parties will seek the goodwill of the electorate through their policies. The citizenry is thus a consumer of policies and an audience before whom the political drama is enacted. Essentially, though, the mass-public is for most of the time apolitical or non-political; politics is a specialised role within a pluralistic society.

In the direct version of democracy, however, the role of the citizen is very different. Here every citizen is seen as a political being. Politics is at the heart of social life and every man and woman is deeply involved in decision-making. Direct democracy, if it is to be real direct democracy, must involve the citizenry in both the framing of the political agenda and the debate about issues on that agenda.

Those who advocate direct democracy argue that liberal representative democracy is not democracy. Movement should be encouraged towards empowering the citizen, so that every man and woman can take a meaningful part in the governance of the state. The counter-argument to this might be that from four points of view the advocacy of direct democracy is unrealistic. First, from the point of view of efficiency, it would be impossible for all the citizens of a modern state to take part in political debate in a meaningful way; there is not time or space for this to happen. Participation can be increased in many ways, by regional assemblies and local decision-making units relevant to particular issue areas, but these will still be representative. Secondly, it is not the case that all citizens *want* to take part in politics in any intensive manner. Liberal democracy is essentially pluralist, and many citizens may have deep and time-consuming interests in other things, such as making money, art, or football. It would be an imposition on the citizenry to insist that they also become politically active. Thirdly, it could be argued that a great many citizens in modern mass democracies are not capable of meaningful participation due to their level of knowledge about politics. Opinion polls do indicate a great deal of ignorance about political matters. However, as a counter-argument to this, it might be suggested that people would not be ignorant if their participation were efficaceous and meaningful; the opportunity-costs of effective participation are so high that many are deterred from entering the political fray. They may care about education or public health, but since they perceive that decisions over which they have no influence are taken elsewhere, the incentive to gather information is lessened. Further, the charge that many citizens are incompetent to take part in public debate may rest on a particular definition of 'politics'; politics is what happens at Westminster, Brussels or Washington, rather than politics being about the everyday life and circumstances of the individual.[39] Fourthly, it could be argued that were there mass participation on a large scale, this would be an indicant of the intense politicisation of society, a measure of dissension, discontent and divisiveness.

If the Net is going to have any effect on the nature and practice of democracy – that is if the citizen is going to be more of a participant in the democratic process as opposed to being a passive audience – four functions have to be fulfilled. First, the capacity to identify and communicate with a significant group must be present. Secondly, there must be the capacity to mobilise; by this is meant the ability to aggregate opinion for the purposes of political action. Thirdly, there is the need to access relevant information about issues of interest. Finally, there must be means of inputting aggregated views into the political process which is legitimated and potentially politically efficaceous.

Before proceeding with the discussion of these dimensions a preliminary point needs to be made. While the Net in some of its manifestations is twenty years old, the most user-friendly and used part of the Net – the World Wide Web – is barely five years old! As noted previously, we are at the inception of the development. What we need to consider is not the Net as it is at the moment, but where it will be and what it will be used for in five or ten years, in an effort to assess its potential impact. Some indication of future possibility may be gleaned from the American experience, where in most areas the use of the Net is more extensive than elsewhere.

We also need to recognise, however, that while at present the Net may be democratic in the sense that it confers equality on all – on the Net a private individual has the same right of access as a corporation – some of the views expressed on the Net are profoundly *undemocratic*. While there are many groups which aim at empowering the individual for democratic or humanitarian ends, there are also many groups that use the Net for extreme racist and authoritarian purposes.[40] Further, as the encryption debate demonstrates, the state is not always willing to be excluded from the private communication of its citizens. While this is justified on the grounds that encryption and total privacy (or even Pretty Good Privacy) allows criminals, and particularly those involved in the drugs trade, inviolable means to communicate freely, the result is equivalent to an attack on the state in so far as the free movement of drugs is facilitated. The argument is not dissimilar to that with respect to phone-tapping or mail interception. The danger is, of course, the age-old Platonic question 'Who guards the guardians?'. Given the humanitarian record of governments both in historical and contemporary perspectives, allowing powers to government for particular purposes does not guarantee that those powers will be used only for those purposes.

Politics in contemporary society is always a group activity. If the Internet is going to move the practice of democratic politics more towards the direct democracy model through better access to elites, and improved capacity to exert pressure, then this means that relevant groups must be identified and communicated with. If it is the case that the Net merely enhances the capacity of already existent groups to communicate more effectively with themselves, without enlarging or reaching new constituencies, then the potential of the Net is reduced considerably. Perhaps it is possible to go further than this, and suggest that if the main function of the Net is to intensify within-group communication, the potential for a 'lock-in effect' is enhanced.[41] It is unlikely that Net communication has a great capacity to persuade apart from those who are already like-minded due to its essentially literary and cerebral form of communication, although it may bring information to those who are already sympathetic. A recent example might be the international indignation concerning the French nuclear tests. Looking at the communication on both the peace and environmental Nets, one is struck by both the volume of it and the inability of this internationalised protest to affect the course of events in any way whatsoever. The only form of real pressure that was suggested that would be likely to have any (and at that very minimal) effect, was to overload the French government's computers with email. However, so long as the source of legitimation resides within state boundaries, the cross-national expressions of popular indignation are unlikely to be effective.

A further important point to recognise is that, if we are talking about democracy and the Net, most states in the world are not democracies in either a direct or representative sense. Iran has attempted to ban satellites on the grounds of their moral content, while China is very wary of the Internet as a source of destabilising perspectives that would reach the heirs of Tiananmen Square. To square the circle of economic liberalisation while maintaining an authoritarian stability may well mean controlling access to information. In such cases there is no immediate relationship between democracy and the Net. However, in so far as the use of the Internet is associated with contemporary business and potential economic development, it may prove difficult for reluctant governments to exploit the benefits without also having to accept other kinds of access. Fukuyama may have grossly overstated his case about 'the end of history', yet contemporary movement in both Eastern Europe and Africa does tend to suggest movement towards normative acceptance of democracy internationally.

There is another aspect here that is important, but one which may just be a temporary phenomenon. To what extent is the Net merely an extension of the 'chattering classes'? Cross-nationally there is great variation; even though Net take-up is increasing, in the less developed world the gap will remain enormous for the foreseeable future. Within the developed world there is variation, with no country even beginning to rival the United States for density. But, and what may be just as important, even within the developed state, the take-up and use of the Net is very uneven and is partially predicted by age, income, and education. Younger people will tend to feel easier with new technology; to use that technology in a domestic rather than business context demands an income both for the hardware and the on-line costs; and computational skills and the sense of efficacy to employ them are usually associated with a reasonable level of education. The characteristics of this cadre would also define those who are in any case more potentially politically active with or without the Net.

Britain is one of the most technologically advanced countries in the world. In Britain, however, while academics, journalists, researchers and businesses use the Internet on a daily basis, to most of the population the Internet is still a completely foreign land. It is my habit to visit a local hostelry for a pint of beer on a Friday night. There I meet with a great many people selling cars, insurance, family trees, travel, dogs, etc. There is little cognisance of the Net or its capacities among those for whom it is not a professional necessity, and even those who use it professionally, such as travel agents, *will often not use it for other purposes,* and will not be aware of, or interested in, its other uses.

In reaching the general population, income is important. For the United States, with an average income above that of the United Kingdom and any other European country, the average income of the Net user is way above that of the average wage.[42] The same appears to be true of the United Kingdom. In the United States two further demographic characteristics are important, which again have reflections in the non-US context. First, the US usage is disproportionately white, and in the parts of the world where white is not the predominant characteristic, a disproportionality in this direction is still noticeable. Further, if we look at the gender distribution, in the United States over 80 per cent report themselves as being male, while for non-US sources, this rises to 90 per cent and for Europe (of which the United Kingdom represented 39 per cent of the sample) it was 92 per cent. In a further study, conducted by Yahoo Inc. and Jupiter Communications, and reported in the *New York Times,*[43] further interesting data comes to light. Around 10 million Americans subscribe to on-line services, an increase of 78 per cent from the previous year, with 14,000 new commercial on-line service accounts opening every day. This means that *at the moment,* over 20 per cent of the population are connected in some way. Compared with Africa, where only two in every thousand are connected (with most of these being in South Africa), America has by far the most dense electronic communications. We can expect, though at very different rates of development, the rest of the world to follow the United States out of commercial necessity.

This brief excursion into the demographics of the Internet is not without relevance to the democractic argument. We can draw a crude profile of the 'average' Net user as predominantly white, predominantly male, and in general wealthier than the society at large. With median age of the US Net user being thirty-five, and outside the United States being thirty-one, we have a picture of the Net user. The Net is primarily being used by those who have access to the system in any case. It is, as with many things, a case of 'to those who have shall be given'. It is true that governments and international organisations of many kinds are putting vast amounts of information on the web, but those who will access this information are those who would have had considerable access in any case. The Net at the moment is in the main not empowering those who are at present dis-empowered, but adding to the empowerment of those who are empowered already. It may be the case that in the future access to the Net may become as common as owning a telephone or television (at least in the developed world), but at the moment this is not the case.

From the perspective developed in this section, it would seem unlikely that the Internet will have any significant effect on the practice of politics in democratic societies, and neither will the capacity for opinion formation across national boundaries have any marked effect. Where the Internet and other forms of cross-national communication may have more effect in both the short and long term is on economically developing countries which are not democratic.

Security and the Net

'Security', as used in International Relations, is a term that has become more complex with the passage of time. Indeed, one of the criticisms of contemporary Critical Security Studies is that it has become almost coterminous with the study of International Relations. The term here will be used in a manner similar to that expressed by Buzan, writing from a neo-realist perspective.[44] A distinction is made between different levels of security such as individual, social, economic and state security, and it is in these terms that the problem of security and the Internet will be discussed. A problem of security exists where there is a sense of threat.

For the individual the Internet has the possibilities of both expanding capabilities and increasing vulnerabilities. For the disabled, the housebound or the isolated, the Internet can provide an interactive gateway to the world of unparalleled freedom. However, in the last analysis, the Internet is about *information*. The power of the Internet resides in the linking of millions of computers that hold information. Just imagine a situation such that it was possible to access information about individuals from their bank records, their credit card details, social security records, employment records, where and what they surf, what they buy and who they talk to by telephone, etc., there would be very little about that person that would not be known. Privacy would become a thing of the past. The essence of the individual would be encapsulated electronically. Commercial enterprises would be able to target their potential customers with great accuracy; to some degree this is already happening with the amount of unsolicited junk mail increasing daily. A very real potential for blackmail also arises. Perhaps more importantly, the possibility of governments obtaining such information for political use arises; the state as 'Big Brother' becomes a real possibility. The technology for such a development exists, but at the moment is constrained by law and the norms of society. But not all societies are liberal democracies, and not all liberal democracies are as liberal as others, and as technology develops, the potential for such developments expands.

It is in this context that the encryption debate has taken place. Governments, particularly the American government, have argued that a surveillance capability must be possible for the security of the state, while liberal-minded individuals have argued that such a capability is an infringement of personal liberty, the argument being fought out in terms of constitutional interpretation. Both sides are in some sense right. Were it possible that terrorist groups, drug smugglers or paedophiles, for example, were able to communicate in codes that were unbreakable, as was promised by the use of the clipper chip, there would be little that law enforcement agencies could do about it. The US government, which developed the technology, initially attempted to bring about a state of affairs such that it alone would have access to all the encryption-decryption codes. The computer manufacturers complained about government interference in industry and commerce, and liberal opinion pointed out that good governments come and go; had the technology been available during the Hoover era of FBI control, or during the McCarthy persecutions, there would have been instant access to people's political opinions. The US government retracted, but still argue that they should have access to the key codes as and when necessary. In fact, however, there are other technologies – such as PGP (Pretty Good Privacy) – that provide a high level of privacy in that while theoretically not unbreakable, the time it would take would probably render the utility of decoding unfeasible. The US government also showed its concern by attempting to prevent the more powerful versions of these programs being sold or sent abroad; this was a complete failure as the following day they were obtainable from a Finnish source.

The Internet is also seen as a threat to the *moral* values of the individual, particularly with respect to pornography. The perception of threat comes from four directions: women's rights groups, who see pornography as fundamentally degrading; from those who are concerned about children and adolescents gaining instant access; from those who wish to protect children from paedophilia; and from the moral right for whom all pornography is iniquitous. There is no doubt that the Net is awash with pornography that can be accessed with great ease. Feeding key words into the major search engines rapidly yields hundreds of sex-oriented sites. Images, videos, erotic literature, interactive on-line strippers, and all manner of unusual sexual preferences are readily available at the click of a mouse. In addition there is a plethora of special-interest newsgroups; if you are a foot-fetishist, the Internet is the place for you. There have been various attempts to control pornography on the Internet, with as yet not a great deal of success. Pleas for self-censorship of the commercial purveyors have not elicited an effective response; there is clearly so much money involved and the competition so fierce that commercial survival often depends on out-extreming the opposition. A second attempt was to place the responsibility for control on the server, such as America On-line, or CompuServe. The larger servers have in some cases responded marginally to these pressures, but often, such is the flow of overall traffic, their capacity to act as policeman or watchdog is limited. In addition, they complain that restrictions are being applied to them that are not applied to other media. A telephone company is not held responsible for the content of telephone calls, nor is a librarian expected to be conversant with the contents of all the books in the library. Other attempts operate at the level of the user. Programs such as CyberNanny or SurfWatch are installed on the home computer and forbid access to certain sites. However, any reasonably determined twelve-year-old can circumvent these programs, probably without his or her parents knowing. Similarly, commercial enterprises, colleges and universities that attempt to set up 'firewalls' are doomed to failure. Neither has straight legislation proved successful, for two reasons. The first is that it is seen as a form of censorship, and particularly in the United States is seen as contravening constitutional rights. The second reason is more interesting. The Internet is not controllable nationally; it is *international*. Germany, Britain and the United States can all pass domestic legislation, but have no control at present over the Dutch, Swedes, or, extrapolating to a possible future, the Mongolians or the Gambians. The Net consequence of this is that without harmonisation of legislation – an unlikely development given the commercial interests involved and national normative differences in attitudes to pornography – and given the anarchic nature of the Net, pornography is unlikely to be controlled in any serious sense in the near future. The same may be said about other areas of disquiet about the Net, such as incitement to racism, denial of the Holocaust, or instructions on bomb-making. Jarrod Wiener, in an innovative study of money laundering by electronic means, has pointed out the extreme difficulty of control because of the speed of transaction, the international nature of transactions, and the lack of harmonisation of law.[45]

In 1989 Clifford Stoll published a fascinating book called *The Cuckoo's Egg*.[46] In this, working as a sysop, he found a small accounting discrepancy of 75 cents, and in his quest to account for it discovered a computer spy operation accessing US military computers run from Germany. In September 1994 a young unemployed man was charged in London with entering with intent to tamper with computers in US military installations.[47] There are books written about the 'legendary' Kevin Mitnick.[48] Numerous other examples could be given.[49] Most hacking is fairly harmless – in the sub-culture of the hacker, the thrill of overcoming the challenge is the motivation rather than attempts to tamper with or damage information. There are numerous guides to hacking, constantly updated to cope with new systems and technologies, that teach the novice how to hack. However, harmlessness is not always the case; in 1994 British banks were reported as having paid millions of pounds to a computer terrorist gang to avoid having their databases wiped.[50] There are other kinds of behaviour that the speed and the ubiquity of the Net allows, and that is the threat of theft of intellectual materials. Wiener, in his article on copyright law and the Net, suggests that until there is harmonisation of law internationally, there is not too much that can be done about it.[51] Since 'intellectual property' constitutes the second-largest American export, it is understandable that the United States is most concerned about this issue. In general, however, in an age of electronically stored information, commerce, industry, the military, and governments are always at risk. There is little prospect of this changing for the better; as in other areas of crime, every advance in protective technology is met by a corresponding ingenuity. And, since the potential rewards are so high, the prospect is for an increase rather than a decrease in computer-based crime. Governments, industry and commerce cannot manage their affairs in a modern world without computers, but with them there is always an element of risk.

The ability to hack and tamper, however, is not restricted to the amateur hacker or the computer criminal. It is also a capacity sought and developed by governments. Advanced contemporary warfare is very dependent on CMC, and the ability to interfere with the enemy's communications, or even to feed false information, is seen as a vital capacity, as is the need to defend one's own communication structures. Information warfare, as the activity is known, may be defined as:

> Any action to deny, exploit, corrupt, or destroy the enemy's information and its functions; protecting ourselves against those actions; and exploiting our own military information functions.[52]

The seriousness with which this aspect of war is viewed can be seen by the appointment of a presidential commission in the United States,[53] and by the establishment of an apparently well-funded research institute,[54] and the rise of 'information warriors'.[55] Information has always been vital in warfare, but with the advent of CMC as an important factor in the contemporary military, an entire new technology of warfare has emerged.

There is little doubt that in recent years the dominant form of communal and international conflict has been about identity. With the removal of the overlay of the Cold War this has intensified. The fear is often expressed that with the diminution of space and time in communications, and the dominance of this market by the United States, indigenous cultures will come under threat. The argument has been made that 'communities' or 'cultures' can be created over the Internet,[56] but a more important question is whether the Internet can or will destroy, modify or pose a threat to existing cultures. The only honest answer to this question is to recognise that we don't know and it is difficult to see how we could ever know. The problem is that the Internet as a cultural phenomenon cannot be separated from the myriad of other cultural influences – radio, television, videos, films, music, etc. The suspicion must be that for less developed countries, the Internet will be a very minor factor in comparison to other influences, merely because of the demographic factors of usage. Those in such situations who do use the Internet already are exposed to other cultural influences. Perhaps of more importance in the long run, from the point of cultural imperialism, is the fact that the language of the Net is predominantly English.[57] It is no accident that the United States' government has invested so heavily in the Net and suffers free-riders gladly. In so doing it strengthens the use of English as the international tongue, with commercial benefits to follow.

If the term 'security' refers, however, to the perception of threat, it is possible that some of the uses of the Internet may act to reduce the degree of threat and thus increase security. One of the tenets of conflict resolution is that most conflicts are marked by misperception. This does not mean that conflicts are always caused by parties initially misperceiving the intentions or goals of others, but that as a conflict develops there is a lessening of communication congruent with heightened anxiety, hostility, and often distrust. In such cases where communication lessens there is an increased tendency to apply a worst-case analysis to the intentions and actions of other parties, which is often reciprocated. The consequence is increasing misperception. In the last few years there have been attempts to set up Internet connections across battle zones and between conflictual parties.[58] One such is the ZaMir network that was set up in Sarajevo in 1991,[59] and there are currently attempts to set up a cross-communal network in Cyprus. At present such schemes are unlikely to be too effective, merely because of the low levels of access, which are in any case likely to be lessened in a war situation. However, such developments do point towards a potential use of the Internet to increase security.

Conclusion

The Internet is a fascinating phenomenon that raises all kinds of questions and makes many things possible that were not so previously. But from this examination of the Internet from the point of view of International Relations, the following major points have emerged. First, the Internet is a continuation of other communications trends that began long ago. Secondly, many of the influences of the Internet cannot be separated from other developments; as the Net develops it will become more and more difficult to discern something called 'the Net' as technologies mesh and merge. Thirdly, many of the claims made for the Net regarding development are rash over-statements. Fourthly, both within and between societies, the technology of the Net will merely add to those already empowered. Fifthly, the Internet does pose security threats of various kinds and at different levels that are unlikely to lessen. Finally, considering International Relations from a teaching and research perspective, the Internet is rapidly becoming an indispensible tool.

CHAPTER 16

Feminism and the Concept of Community in International Relations

Beverley Neufeld

All new approaches to International Relations challenge the foundations of the mainstream discipline, and feminist theory has undertaken this task for so long that perhaps it ought no longer to be considered 'new'. But in spite of the powerful and compelling challenges feminism makes to the core assumptions of International Relations, this 'new' approach still operates at the edges of the discipline, and continues to centre on critique. At the same time, though, that much of its critique has focused on core concepts of International Relations, feminism has also brought into the discipline a range of other issues that International Relations tends to overlook. One of these neglected concepts is community, and this chapter examines the implications of the feminist critique of International Relations for the concept of community.

As a central but often hidden concept in International Relations, the absence of community in the international realm is the basis of Martin Wight's contention that there is no International Relations theory.[1] However, Wight's suggestion that the discipline cannot theorise the international in the absence of community seems to be contradicted by the evidence: the absence of a definition of community, and the limited nature of discussion of the concept in the discipline has not prevented the development of theory in International Relations. This does not, however, diminish Wight's point; on the contrary, it emphasises its continued importance. For while the discipline has concentrated mainly on developing strategies for survival and, at the same time, allowed for normative questions about the nature and content of community, the concept of community itself remains undefined and vague, and largely dismissed as unimportant.

Indeed, despite recent efforts to explore the concept of community, little of this work has examined the conflation of community and the state in

International Relations, and its implications for theorising in the discipline.[2] The intent of this chapter is therefore not to develop a feminist theory of community, but to argue that theorising community is an important and neglected aspect of International Relations.[3] It is the contention of this chapter that feminist theory illustrates the weaknesses of current conceptions of community in International Relations, and also provides the theoretical tools with which to rethink the concept.

Unlike mainstream International Relations, feminist theory problematises the concept of community. First, feminist theory challenges received wisdom concerning subjectivity and identity, in part contesting the notion of the state as the ideal form of community, and in turn the understanding of citizenship as the ideal identity. Secondly, questions of territory are also raised in feminist theory, contesting the bounded limits of the political in the discipline. Thirdly, feminist theory addresses Wight's concerns with politics and competing notions of what may constitute the good life, which in International Relations are often overtaken by questions of right (and often only statist) behaviour.

The chapter begins with a review of feminist theory in International Relations, exploring how and why feminist theory engages with the discipline. Secondly, a critique of the ideal of community is considered, in part to examine how feminist critiques are applied to specific issues in International Relations – in this case to the concept of community – and in addition, to set out the particular points of critique upon which an alternative conception of community in International Relations might be developed. This second section focuses on the work of two feminist theorists: Iris Marion Young and Shane Phelan. The third section examines how community is (inadequately) conceptualised in International Relations in light of feminist theory. It begins with a review of the traditional International Relations conception of community as the state, revisiting Young's critique in terms of Warren Magnusson's work on the state and community, and concludes with an analysis of the work of Andrew Linklater on community in light of feminist critiques. Finally, the chapter concludes with a discussion of Phelan's feminist theory of community, which incorporates the work of Jean-Luc Nancy in attempting to move beyond critique to theorise the concept of community in International Relations.

Feminist Theory and International Relations

Like all approaches to International Relations, feminism is neither unified nor harmonious. In *The Blackwell Encyclopaedia of Political Thought*, feminism is defined as '[a] generic term for a complex phenomenon ... defined in part by contests generated over its meaning'.[4] As a consequence of its diversity and debate, summarising feminism is problematic.[5] One typology often adopted is Sandra Harding's, who outlines three feminist theories of knowledge: feminist empiricism, feminist standpoint theory and feminist post-modernism.[6]

Feminist empiricism claims that there is a male bias in empiricism which directs the types of problem chosen for investigation, which in turn means that the scientific method may achieve objective truth only if this male bias is removed, or a (balancing) female 'bias' is added. Feminist standpoint theory, on the other hand, rejects the notion of objective truth as attainable, instead relying on obtaining truth from within a certain perspective, in this case from the standpoint of feminism. Feminist post-modernism, finally, rejects the notion of objective truth entirely, seeing knowledge and reality instead as socially constructed and in need of sceptical deconstruction.[7]

In terms of International Relations and less specifically epistemological concerns, Marysia Zalewski includes an additional three feminisms in her historical/political typology: liberal feminism, Marxist/socialist feminism, and radical feminism.[8] Liberal feminism is the classical equal rights feminism of individual freedom and autonomy, also known as 'the "add women and stir" variety of feminist thought',[9] while Marxist and socialist feminism see patterns of gendered oppression directly linked to repressive and exploitative economic and social systems. Finally, radical feminism triumphs the notion of the personal as political, interpreting all aspects of life – public or private – as permeated by male domination and in need of redescription and fundamental change.[10]

Thus at first glance it appears that the various lists of, and debates about feminisms, involve little more than wide-ranging disputes over highly contested terrain. However, while there is no question that there are important and complex distinctions between feminist schools of thought, it is still possible to identify shared characteristics throughout feminist theories. Feminist theory is, first and foremost, *critical* theory. Critical in this context has a double meaning, referring both to the general notion of challenging received wisdom concerning women and gender, but also referring to the Frankfurt School and post-structuralist variants of post-Marxist critical theory. This view of feminism, as seeking to problematise the existing social order, is perhaps the most useful characterisation of feminism as a whole, in terms of understanding the shared characteristics of feminisms, as well as the debates among them.

In *Critical Theory in Political Practice*, Stephen Leonard suggests that while feminist theory is deeply suspicious of universalising or grand theory, critical feminist theory 'can accommodate the plurality of life experiences and the particular forms of domination and struggle reflecting this plurality'. Specifically,

> what feminists have shown is that critique cannot be grounded in an ahistorical, transcendental or abstract understanding of knowledge and self that is separated from a particular, historically contingent context. Nor can it simply assume that

the contingency of knowledge and identity reduces critique to nothing more than a radical skepticism. [Thus, r]ather than asking how an emancipatory political practice can be theoretically defined and defended ... feminists ask instead what theory must look like if it is to speak to practical concerns. The issue for feminists is, in short, less one of realising theory in practice than it is of realising the practical demands theory must meet.[11]

Thus, feminist critical theory addresses three interrelated political problems: autonomy/solidarity, theory/practice, and subjectivity/identity, because its imperative is based in its origins as a social movement in which theory must meet the needs of political and social goals.

As a consequence, identity and subjectivity are pivotal questions in feminism. As Leonard points out, asking 'what does it mean?' prompts the feminist reply 'to whom?', '[a]nd in terms of these questions, many feminists have come to realise that much of modern discourse means "objectivity" from the standpoint of a "disinterested" observer who in reality is neither objective nor disinterested, but rather objectively male'.[12] Thus, there are again multiple meanings at work in the seemingly straightforward observation that the subject of feminism is women: subjectivity (and thus objectivity) is contested, and feminists debate as to whether women as opposed to gendered subjects ought to be their addressee. Indeed, a further step posits a difference between women and 'women'.[13] Christine Sylvester's reason for using the scare quotes is to reduce the apparent ontological clarity of 'women', for she wants to problematise the subject of feminism – the socially constructed identities of masculine and feminine, men and women.

Such dualisms represent for feminist theories what Sylvester calls 'the pattern of certainty and oppressive bifurcation that marks modern knowledge'.[14] Bifurcation 'implies a modernist/positivist separation of fact/value, known/knower, epistemology/ontology, which conjures up a strait-jacketed view of the world and how we think about it'.[15] Thus another concern central to most feminist theories is an argument that identity is not either/or, fixed or stable, but fluid and multiple. In this context, feminists explicitly seek ways to break down dualisms, arguing that they are socially constructed.

The difficulty with this deconstructive element of feminist theory is how to centralise the issues of concern to feminists – including the role of women – and at the same time decentre social constructions such as gender. For, as Kimberly Hutchings suggests, feminists seem to risk falling into the trap of debating between 'false knowledge and no knowledge at all', in which '[t]he logic of the feminist standpoint itself seems to push us into a plurality of viewpoints, yet the abandonment of the idea of a standpoint leaves us without anchor in a sea of contending narratives, with no possibility of distinguishing between those that are meaningful and those that are not'.[16] In International Relations, feminist theory has encountered similar problems, beginning with, a deep dissatisfaction with existing orthodox approaches to the understanding of the international, a dissatisfaction with both theoretical and practical dimensions. On the one hand, traditional approaches are seen as perpetuating actual discrimination against women in both economic and political spheres, and on the other hand those same approaches are seen as incapable of yielding a proper understanding of the international sphere itself.[17]

Thus one of the main concerns in feminist approaches to International Relations has been to problematise the discipline's dominant (realist) paradigm, including: 'the assumption of the state as a given; conceptions of power and "international security"; and the model of a rational human individual standing apart from the realm of lived experience, manipulating it to maximize his own self-interest'.[18]

The feminist critique of mainstream International Relations centres on two related arguments. First, the bounded nature of state-based politics is contested as inadequate. Feminists argue that women are ignored as actors in state-centric International Relations, because 'women and the feminine constitute historically underprivileged, under-represented, and under-recognized social groups and "standpoints"'.[19] Secondly, feminists contest the notion that the good life necessarily exists within states, not only because its bounded notion of politics and exclusion of women limits debate as to what may constitute politics and thus the good life, but also because of the realist focus on rational, self-maximising action which prioritises questions of right behaviour over questions of what is good.[20]

Feminism therefore offers a subversion of the ontological, epistemological and methodological bases of International Relations. In *Feminism as Critique*, Seyla Benhabib and Drucilla Cornell aptly summarise the problem facing feminists in International Relations, asking: 'where do we go beyond the politics of gender? To a radical transcendence of the logic of binary oppositions altogether or to a utopian realization of forms of otherness, immanent in present psychosexual arrangements, but currently frozen within the confines of rigid genderized thinking?'[21] The problem for feminist theory, then, does not end with its critique, which opens up the problems of the politics of gender, the logic of binary oppositions, and rigid genderised thinking. The problem, given that feminist critical theory is about developing an alternative vision of the social order, is to decide upon the step beyond critique that applies the subversive nature of feminism to problems in International Relations.

There are three central characteristics of feminist theories which suggest a way to move beyond critique. First, the challenge feminist theory makes to apparently unbiased notions of identity and subjectivity means that the apparent ontological soundness of social constructions – like masculine or feminine, women and 'women' – are called into question. Moreover, such dualisms are further challenged in epistemological terms through the feminist engagement with questions of knowledge and of identity, and particularly in the feminist assertion that identity is neither fixed nor singular. Secondly, the feminist critique of state-centrality in International Relations highlights the question of territory and thus problematises the limits of politics within states, and, thirdly, the feminist critique of the state also challenges the International Relations state-based notion of what is right, to instead open up debates about what constitutes the good life.

These central characteristics of feminism highlight the potential in feminist theory for developing a transformative approach to International Relations theory. However, as Zalewski warns, a feminist re-working of International Relations has dangerous implications because it does not set its own terms, relying instead on those already set by the discipline.[22] At the same time as she warns against simply developing a feminist version of International Relations though, Zalewski also emphasises the subversive nature of feminism, noting that 'when the notion of subversion is stripped of its derisory connotations, applied to it by defenders of the status quo, subversive strategies provide a foundation from which to emancipate and liberate'.[23]

Thus future directions for feminist theory in International Relations are based on developing an emancipatory theory beginning from its existing critique of the discipline and the unique perspective feminism brings to theorising the international. This perspective may be applied powerfully to theorising community, because feminist theory implicitly (and sometimes explicitly) addresses the core concerns surrounding that concept. Indeed, feminist critiques highlight just how inadequately community is now theorised in International Relations. But before turning to a discussion of the International Relations' understanding of that concept, the next section examines feminist critiques of the concept of community, focusing on the work of Iris Marion Young and Shane Phelan.

Feminist Theory and the Concept of Community

While much of feminist theory in general addresses issues which are central to the concept of community, relatively little of this literature specifically deals with that concept. Two feminist theorists who do explicitly address the concept of community are Iris Marion Young and Shane Phelan. In her discussion of 'The Ideal of Community and the Politics of Difference', Iris Marion Young considers the concept of community, mainly addressing her critique to the local or urban, rather than the international, context of this concept. Shane Phelan, in 'All the Comforts of Home: The Genealogy of Community', follows Young's critique but also proposes an alternative conception of community. This section examines the critiques of the concept of community by both Young and Phelan in turn, but postpones discussion of Phelan's alternative approach to conceptualising community to the final section of the chapter.

Young's work focuses on three features which are of concern to feminists:

the good life, identity and subjectivity, and territory. She argues that community is an ideal which 'privileges unity over difference, immediacy over mediation, [and] sympathy over recognition of the limits of one's understanding of others from their point of view'.[24] Young begins her discussion of community with a central feminist concern: abstract individualism. This philosophy 'considers individual human beings as social atoms, abstracted from their social contexts, and disregards the role of social relationships and human community in constituting the very identity and nature of individual human beings'.[25]

Young supports critiques of this liberal individualist social ontology. However, while recognising its importance, she objects to the routine and (for her) largely unquestioned substitution of community in its place. She is particularly critical in this regard because of the lack of content in these substituted communities; the ideals invoked, Young argues, fail to 'ask what [community] presupposes or implies, or what it means concretely to institute a society that embodies community'.[26] Moreover, Young rejects the dualistic notion of community versus individualism as either/or, arguing that this dualism '... is integral to political theory and is not an alternative to it'.[27]

Beyond problems with the fuzziness of invoked values of the ideal of community, Young has specific objections which stem from the three central problems raised by feminist theory. First, she considers questions of subjectivity and identity, arguing that the ideal of community produces a denial of difference between subjects, replacing difference with social wholeness and identification. Secondly, Young addresses questions of territory, arguing that denial of difference is reinforced by the utopian dream of 'decentralized face-to-face' communities, which are impractical at best. Finally, Young addresses questions of the good life, arguing that the ideal of community poses 'an opposition between authentic and inauthentic social relations' which 'provides no understanding of the move from here to there that would be rooted in an understanding of the contradictions and possibilities of existing society'.[28]

Sabina Lovibond's comments on what she calls the 'Kantian vision ... of a universal rational community' parallel Young's concerns with the ideal of community in terms of its denial of difference.[29] Capturing the essence of the problem of universal identity (for feminists and others), Lovibond notes that:

[t]he furthest point to which one might be carried by this movement of recoil from universalism would be the point of inability to accept *anything* public as capturing the content of one's thoughts or feelings. How (one might ask) could I allow my unique subjectivity to be made to submit to some *abstraction*, some *general idea*, which would mediate between me and other subjects by furnishing us with a common thought – and so with a point of intellectual identity? Isn't this process of mediation, as Nietzsche maintained, necessarily one of

vulgarization – a systematic infliction of violence on the inexpressible in order to make it fit the expressive forms available within some arbitrary language?[30]

Young recognises that this suppression of difference has been countered by some theorists: '[u]nlike reactionary appeals to community which consistently assert the subordination of individual aims and values to the collective, [there are] radical theorists [who] assert that community itself consists in the respect for and fulfilment of individual aims and capacities. The neat distinction between individualism and community thus generates a dialectic in which each is a condition for the other.'[31] However, Young goes on to argue that this dialectical relationship between individual and society still reflects a totalising desire because of a failure to address the feminist critique of identity and subjectivity:

> [a]ll these formulations seek to understand community as a unification of particular persons through the sharing of subjectivities: Persons will cease to be opaque, other, not understood, and instead become fused, mutually sympathetic, understanding one another as they understand themselves. Such an ideal of shared subjectivity ... denies difference in the sense of the basic asymmetry of subjects [because] ... persons necessarily transcend each other because subjectivity is negativity. The regard of the other upon me is always objectifying. Other persons never see the world from my perspective, and I am always faced with an experience of myself I do not have in witnessing the other's objective grasp of my body, actions, and words.[32]

Thus the feminist critique of identity and subjectivity is crucial here for, as Marysia Zalewski notes, who women are is not the only question that arises in feminist theory, because where and how and what women are must also be considered.[33] In other words, just as not all feminists agree on what constitutes feminist theory because no one theory can possibly represent the views, interests, identities, and concerns of all women, neither would all members of a community be able to accept one unified and singular vision of that community, or, indeed, of themselves.

Furthermore, this failure to address the significance of the feminist critique of subjectivity and identity in considering the concept of community leads to the related problem of knowledge and 'presupposes that a subject can know himself or herself and express that knowledge accurately and unambiguously to others'.[34] Feminist theory rejects such a conception of both knowledge and subjectivity; Young points out that '[n]ot only does this ideal of shared subjectivity express an impossibility, but it has undesirable political implications ... because it denies difference in the concrete sense of making it difficult for people to respect those with whom they do not identify'.[35] As a consequence, Young concludes that '[t]he desire for community relies on the same desire for social wholeness and identification that underlies racism and ethnic chauvinism on the one hand and political sectarianism on the other'.[36]

Young's critique of the ideal of community extends beyond this central discussion of identity and difference. She also problematises community as an ideal which 'implies a model of the good society as consisting of de-centralized small units, which is both unrealistic and politically undesirable'.[37] Her discussion in this context focuses on two related problems, addressing questions of both territory and the good life, which stem from the idea that community must consist of face-to-face relationships in which social relations are intimate and immediate. Young argues that the world in which we live simply does not lend itself to such an ideal of social relations. This ideal of community is unrealistic because it 'would require dismantling the urban character of modern society, a gargantuan physical overhaul of living space, work places, places of trade and commerce ... [and i]f we take seriously the way many people live their lives today, it appears that people enjoy cities, that is, places where strangers are thrown together'.[38]

Thus Young contests the notion that such intimate and immediate social relations are somehow more authentic than those mediated by the reality of time and space. In highlighting the political undesirability of such relations, she argues that '[t]heories of community are inclined to privilege face-to-face relations ... because they wrongly identify mediation and alienation'.[39] Young rejects this dualism of authentic and inauthentic social relations, particularly as a way of identifying what constitutes the good life, noting that while 'mediation is a necessary condition for alienation [this] does not entail the reverse implication: that only by eliminating structures of mediation do we eliminate alienation'.[40] Indeed, Young sees 'both face-to-face and non-face-to-face relations [as] mediated relations, and in both there is as much the possibility of separation and violence as there is communication and con-sensus'.[41]

Young's critique of the ideal of community thus focuses on three main areas. First, she addresses the problem of identity and subjectivity in terms of denial of difference. Secondly, Young problematises the notion that the good life can be found by opposing supposedly authentic versus inauthentic social relations, based, thirdly, on territory and the idea that intimate social relations occur only in decentralised small units.[42] This penetrating critique seems to suggest that there may be little of interest in the concept of community for feminists. However, Shane Phelan disagrees with Young's conclusions, and in applying the same concerns (with the good life, identity and subjectivity, and territory) seeks to apply this critique to develop an alternative conception of community.

In 'All the Comforts of Home: The Genealogy of Community', Phelan agrees with Young's critique, but rather than rejecting the ideal of community as Young does, Phelan offers an alternative conception of it. First, Phelan explores two conceptions of community: voluntarist and ascriptive. These are the ideals of community which Young critiques and which Phelan characterises as 'identitarian'. An ascriptive community is one in which 'we understand ourselves not simply as "like another" in certain discrete ways but as sharing a common identity, a common membership within a concrete community'.[43] Voluntarist community, on the other hand, is not based on such natural or organic relationships, but on members of community who share common goals, values, and behavioural norms.[44] Phelan points out, however, that this dualistic notion of identitarian communities is not as straightforward as it appears:

> [w]hat is involved here is a rearticulation that reascribes us, as it were, not necessarily by challenging notions of primordial or 'true' identity, but by re-locating our identities. We may thus refer to 'created communities', not in stark contrast to 'natural' (ascriptive) ones, but along a continuum of relations between space and time on the one hand and consciousness on the other.[45]

Based on a critique which reiterates Young's, Phelan concludes that '[n]either ascriptive nor voluntarist conceptions of community ... do the work that feminist theory and politics require'.[46]

Specifically, Phelan (like Young) problematises the notion of community as a substitute for the state, on the grounds that it does not necessarily embody more authentic social relationships than those in states, and because identitarian community denies difference by failing to problematise identity, thereby resulting in 'the closure of the political'.[47] Phelan therefore proposes an alternative understanding of community which addresses these concerns, and which stem from the notion that community need not deny politics and difference. But before turning to Phelan's alternative theory of community, the next section addresses the problems and concerns raised by feminist critiques of the ideal of community for International Relations.

The Concept of Community and International Relations

The concept of community is receiving increased attention in International Relations. Andrew Linklater, in fact, suggests that debates about theories of community are now so common that '[i]magining new forms of political community has emerged as a major enterprise in the contemporary theory of the state and international relations'.[48] However, the concept of com-munity remains undefined and vague in mainstream International Relations, and largely dismissed as unimportant. Indeed, even a definition of this concept remains the exception rather than the rule:

> 'community' has a high level of use but a low level of meaning ... [O]n the one hand it appears to identify particular forms of social interaction, though what these are has been a matter of dispute; on the other hand its use is usually meant to imply something positive and valuable about the social relationships thus defined, though across the political spectrum there is disagreement as to where its value resides.[49]

Consequently, debate about the concept of community – as Linklater's comment demonstrates – either is limited to a search for an imagined international community, by conceptualising it as some sort of mystical entity to be conjured up, or it is largely ignored in favour of theorising the state. Both are deficient, as feminist critiques of the ideal of community illustrate.

This section considers the feminist critiques of Young and Phelan with reference to International Relations approaches to the concept of community. It opens with a look at the substitution in the mainstream discipline of the state for community. Picking up Young's feminist critique (on over-emphasising the importance of territory, as well as the issues of identity and subjectivity, and of what constitutes the good life in states), the work of Warren Magnusson on 'The Reification of Political Community' is considered. Secondly, this section assesses approaches in the discipline which seek explicitly to theorise community, specifically focusing on the work of Andrew Linklater in light of the feminist critique of the concept of community.

Mainstream IR: Community as the State International relations is dominated by realist approaches which focus on the state. As a result, mainstream International Relations tends to identify community, if this question arises at all, with the state. In 1960, when Martin Wight found only paucity and intellectual and moral poverty in international theory, he suggested that international theory does not exist because political theory is about theorising the good life, possible because the state is a community, whereas international theory cannot theorise the good life because it lacks this stable, predictable setting. As a result, the absence of community in the international realm may explain the 'recalcitrance of international politics to being theorized about' which concerned Wight.[50] Even after thirty years most, if not all, debates about the concept of community in International Relations still begin and end with the state.

Feminist critiques of the state in International Relations highlight the consequences of failing to problematise the concept of community, and of the resultant substitution of the state for community.[51] In particular, feminist theory challenges the presumption that states are 'abstract unitary actors whose actions are explained through laws that can be universalised across time and place and whose internal characteristics are irrelevant to the operation of these laws'.[52] This (realist) perspective is challenged on a number of related grounds in feminist theory, which revolve around the three questions raised by Young and Phelan on the concept of community.

First, feminism addresses the question of what constitutes the political, in seeking to expose the state as a masculinist construction privileging male-oriented values. Secondly, feminist theory also problematises the separation of public and private realms of power and politics which privilege public/ male activities over private/female experiences and limits them to these roles. This takes the question of politics further and invokes problems of identity and subjectivity as well as concerns with what is understood to constitute the good life. Thirdly, feminist theory seeks to contest the notion of the closed state, to reveal that masculinist politics affect it at all levels. This criticism problematises territory-based politics, and what may constitute the political within such boundaries. Finally, feminism seeks to challenge state-based dualisms in both identity and knowledge/epistemology, with a particular concern with the notion of fixed identities tied to citizenship.

Picking up on this range of issues raised by feminist (and other) critiques of the state, Warren Magnusson addresses the concept of community and is critical of its identification as the state. His concern is that,

> [t]he key assumption is that political community requires enclosure – that politics proper is impossible without a protected space where ideals can be realized and interests ideally adjudicated. ... Serious thought about the relation between what is contained in and what is excluded from the political enclosures is extremely rare, and is usually distorted by the assumption that political community – and the values associated with it – depend on enclosure. That there might be forms of political community that resist enclosure or are stifled by it is barely considered. How these forms might sustain or extend common political ideals is not a serious subject.[53]

Thus Magnusson is also concerned with what Young sees as the problem of denial of difference in the ideal of community. Moreover, he sees the substitution of the state for community as resulting in (self-imposed) limitations. Specifically, as Young's critique of community suggests, one of the problems with unquestioningly substituting the state for community is that its politics and thus the locus of power within it are circumscribed. Just as Young sees politics eliminated along with difference in community, so Magnusson sees politics limited by this mainstream International Relations conception of community as the state. Magnusson therefore argues that the reification of the state stems from a failure to problematise the concept of community in the first place, which in turn limits the scope of politics, and of what may be theorised at all.[54]

As a consequence of substituting the state for community, then, International Relations theories mistake varieties of political organisation for varieties of politics. Magnusson, therefore, suggests that,

> [b]y freeing ourselves from standard conceptions of political community, we can begin to examine politics as people actually experience and practice it. ...
> In part, this is a matter of [people] confronting, challenging, or participating in practices of domination, some (but not all) of which are organized by the state. But it is also a matter of their creative social interaction: inventions, not just resistances.[55]

In other words, challenging the substitution of the state for community is crucial. This does not mean that states cannot be communities, but it does mean that theorising community must not end with the state. However, feminist theory also challenges the notion that it should begin with the state.

Indeed, identifying community as the state limits politics, as Wight predicted, to a question of survival, and thus to an ability to conceive only of a politics of resistance, rather than, as Magnusson proposes, allowing for a politics of invention. By defining community as the state, alternative approaches to politics – as to what may constitute the good life, for example – are ignored or overlooked.

Therefore, the core International Relations conception of community, which simply ignores it in favour of theorising the state, is problematic for feminists. However, the point of feminist critique in this regard is not to eliminate consideration of the state from International Relations. Rather, feminist critiques of the state as community suggest that this approach is insufficient, and that, consequently, the absence of questions about the concept of community is a shortcoming that must be addressed in the discipline.[56]

Among those in International Relations who recognise this shortcoming is Andrew Linklater. Throughout his work, Linklater has identified community as an important concept for International Relations, and has attempted to move beyond the bounds of state-centricity in theorising community. The remainder of this section will thus consider Linklater's approach to the concept of community in International Relations as one which has been concerned to theorise community explicitly, in contrast to the traditional International Relations substitution of the state for community.[57]

Critical IR: The Expansion of Community Whereas mainstream International Relations substitutes the state for community, other approaches in the discipline question this approach. One International Relations theorist who attempts to theorise community is Andrew Linklater, who suggests that '[t]he recurrent philosophical questions in modern international relations theory have been concerned with the grounds for conferring primacy upon any one of three competing visions of community – the nation-state, the society of states, or a community of humankind'.[58] He argues that the practical problems arising from these philosophical issues are also three-fold: whether 'the purpose of foreign policy [is] to advance the interests of the exclusive nation-state, to strengthen a more inclusive society of states, or to promote a logic of moral inclusion by establishing a community of humankind'.[59] Linklater suggests that the key to resolving these dilemmas lies with the state and its 'capacity to attract human loyalty and structure political identity', while '[t]he key question of whether industrialization would erode the power and authority of the state and generate consensual forms of world politics continues to set the terms of the debate'.[60]

There are a number of problems highlighted by feminist theory in Linklater's approach to the concept of community. Setting aside the question of whether a 'community of humankind' is simply paradoxical, there is an irony in Linklater's apparent contention that the development of community somehow rests upon the state. Whether, as he puts it, states seek to advance their interests, strengthen the society of states, or promote the moral inclusion of humankind, the force behind and aim of each is the state. For Linklater, then, it seems that the concept of community is a consideration only in terms of the erosion of the 'power and authority of the state'. It seems that he believes that community would produce consensus in world politics, and thus prevent the further erosion of the state. But whether such a consensus is possible, let alone desirable, goes unquestioned, and this call for consensus is also puzzling in terms of intent. Perhaps it is meant to lead to the good life, which in itself is a debatable point, but, more importantly, Young's concerns with identity and subjectivity in terms of sameness and the suppression of difference in the ideal of community also apply here.

Indeed, Linklater's desire to 'promote a logic of moral inclusion by establishing a community of humankind' based on the territorial state seems illogical, not to mention implausible, and also illustrates the relevance of Young's concerns about supposedly authentic versus inauthentic social relations. Not only does Linklater's view leave the concept of community as something to be conjured up in the imagination, but neither its content nor its plausibility seem to be a consideration either. Some of the difficulty with Linklater's conception of community may stem from his characterisation of what is at stake: '[w]e may characterise this problem in different ways: as the issue of the proper relationship between the obligations which men may be said to acquire *qua* men and the obligations to which they are subject as citizens of particular associations; or, as the question of reconciling the actual or potential universality of human nature with the diversity and division of political community'.[61]

This characterisation of the problem of community attempts to address and perhaps surpass the state-centricity of mainstream International Relations. But it fails in this regard, for instead of substituting the state for community, Linklater substitutes (state-based) citizenship for identity. Thus Linklater fails to consider feminist critiques on questions of identity and subjectivity which challenge the idea that identity is immutable and that it can be captured within a (statist) conception of community. Moreover, this substitution fails to address problems of the good life, presuming that one's identity as citizen may simply be transferred to some apparently more meaningful locus – the community. Finally, it also ignores feminist concerns with issues of territory, because Linklater wants to extend what he sees as authentic (because they are intimate) social relations outward to a community of humankind, while at the same time maintaining that states and citizenship provide the basis for this new theory of community.

Feminist critiques of the concept of community are thus crucial here. Young challenges the very idea that the social relations of the ideal of community are somehow more authentic than those which take place within states. Relatedly, Young questions the preceding assumption that the good life exists within states in the first place, let alone that it can simply be transferred to some sort of community invoked by imagination, which ignores problems of both time and space. Furthermore, Young's concern with the denial of difference and problems of subjectivity and identity (as sameness) in community problematise Linklater's assumption that citizenship equals, or is sufficient for, identity. Feminist theory not only challenges this notion of immutable identity, but it also problematises the role gender plays in citizenship.[62]

Therefore, Linklater's work is a good start but does not go far enough. He makes a valuable contribution to theorising community in International Relations, because Linklater's characterisation of the problem at least recognises that community is inadequately theorised in the discipline. At the same time, however, his search for a solution is conducted within the statist terms of International Relations, and ends with the same denial of difference Young questions, though even more narrowly focused on citizenship. Thus Linklater's argument that International Relations ought to examine 'the prospects for extending community to represent outsiders and for deepening community to represent insider groups which have long been marginal' seems to address the concerns of feminists.[63] However, debates about universal-particular relations are, in feminist theory, important because of concern with the suppression of difference which seems inevitable in the ideal of community, and Linklater's conception of community does not address adequately these (among many other) concerns. Linklater's approach, then, is a good start, but ultimately falls short of its own liberating and emancipatory goals, and those of feminist theory as well.

Thus efforts to theorise community in International Relations constitute little more than an opening for further critique. For while debating the merits of various conceptions of community is a positive start, it is at the same time unsatisfying because the concept of community, or proposed solutions to the problem of community, still remain bound up with the state in these debates. The inadequacy of such an approach is criticised by feminist theory on the grounds of both intent and feasibility: locating the good life in an imagined territorial community, and identity in citizenship, neither addresses feminist concerns nor seems plausible. As a consequence, this approach to the concept of community is as incomplete as that of the mainstream discipline which substitutes the state for community. The next section thus returns to Shane Phelan's work on the concept of community, which critiques conceptions of community in International Relations and also proposes an alternative understanding of the concept.

Feminism and the Concept of Community in International Relations

Given feminist critiques of International Relations approaches to the concept of community, this section examines the potential in feminist perspectives for theorising that concept. Shane Phelan proposes a theory of community which addresses the elements that both she and Young believe to be crucial: problems of identity and subjectivity, questions of the good life, and the question of territory.

First, while Phelan agrees with many of Young's critiques of the ideal of community, she disagrees with Young's conclusions. Phelan does not, like Young, see community as a denial of politics, but instead as a potential locus for politics:

> Community has been firmly entrenched within the logic of the same that man-dates self-identity and unity among members. In such definitions, community becomes an essence, a thing to be studied and acted upon and used. In [Jean-Luc] Nancy's terms, such essentialising amounts to 'the closure of the political' ... shutting us off from the insecurity and instability of actually being-in-common [i.e., community] and wrapping us in common being, in sameness. Politics, the art of being-in-common, is eliminated when we fix identities and locations in this way. This helps us to see that our 'common understandings' of community trap us into antipolitical postures even as we try to valorise 'dif-ferences'.[64]

Thus Phelan posits a theory of community which moves beyond identitarian conceptions that understand community as sameness and that denies differ-ence. Phelan's central concern is with questions of subjectivity, identity and difference, and with ensuring that questions of what constitutes the good life are not lost in a quest for authentic or intimate social relations. Moreover, Phelan is also concerned with the question of territory, recognising the problem of social relations which are of necessity mediated by time and space. She addresses these concerns in her argument that '[c]ommunities are not formed of or by individuals with pre-existing "characteristics" ... [r]ather, the characteristics are created over time as part of building a community ... [thus w]e are still constituted by community, but that does not give to community a prior, separate existence, for community is simultaneously constituted by us'.[65]

In following Jean-Luc Nancy's work on the concept of community, Phelan proposes an understanding of community as 'being-in-common' as opposed to (its opposite) 'being common' or being the same. In this conception of community, subjectivity and identity are not reduced to sameness or to a denial of difference. Moreover, it also addresses the problem of what may constitute the good life, because differences are recognised as real and not dissolved in community. Thus with no closure of the political in this con-ception of community, competing questions of what constitutes the good life may find expression.

Therefore, politics may be allowed to flourish through a conception of community as 'being-in-common' for two reasons. First, the notion of identity as both pre-existing and fluid is accepted: the self is not assigned a stability and autonomy that must consequently be suppressed by membership in community. Secondly, community itself is also (untypically) seen as neither unified nor fixed. In fact, answering Young's concern about shared subjectivity and thus supposedly more-authentic and intimate social relations, community is understood to be unstable and thus insufficient at providing its members with a singular and fixed identity. In allowing for difference, then, it also allows for the opportunity to explore (competing) questions of the good life.

The central point is that understanding community and individuals to be mutually constitutive does not lock either into a fixed identity, does not insist on intimate and direct social relations as the only authentic type, and thus allows for politics, for a consideration of what is good. Indeed, Phelan suggests that '[r]ather than being a source of support, Nancy's 'being-in-common' is the locus of anxiety and vertigo that the Western philosophical tradition has fled from'.[66] As Nancy argues:

> thinking of community as essence – is in effect the closure of the political. Such a thinking constitutes closure because it assigns to community a *common being* whereas community is a matter of something quite different, namely of existence inasmuch as it is *in* common, but without letting itself be absorbed into a common substance. Being *in* common has nothing to do with communion, with fusion into a body, into a unique and ultimate identity that would no longer be exposed. Being *in* common means, to the contrary, *no longer having, in any form, in any empirical or ideal place, such a substantial identity, and sharing this* (narcissistic) *'lack of identity'*.[67]

Thus Phelan's conception of community (*pace* Nancy) addresses the three-fold feminist critique of the ideal of community. Moreover, it also addresses the International Relations deficiency in theorising community. For while Linklater yearns for the transposition of community (as the state) to the international realm with the goal of consensus, Phelan argues that this idealistic notion of the inherent goodness of communities is problematic. The point of community for her (and for Nancy) is not safety, comfort, consensus and therefore lack of politics. Rather, it is the opposite – a recognition of the fact that differences and insecurities and, thus, politics exist.

Phelan's view of the concept of community, therefore, does not deny reality, nor does it simply wish it away. Instead, Phelan seeks for a way to cope with it – with insecurity and with politics – at the same time as she illustrates what is unsatisfying, and thus what might be changed, in those politics. This conception of community, therefore, in recognising difference and the mediated nature of social relations, allows for the expression of competing conceptions of what constitutes the good life.

Conclusion

Feminist critiques of the concept of community in International Relations demonstrate that theorising community is an important (missing) element in

International Relations. Feminism highlights the need to recognise that theorising community must consist of more than either (re)-analysing the state or dreaming up replacements for it. Both are now occurring in International Relations, in part due to feminist critique, but both are also insufficient.

Thus, feminist theory points to three essential axes of analysis for theorising community in International Relations: the (political) question of what constitutes the good life, the issue of the limitations of territory-based politics, and the problems of fixed and inflexible notions of identity and subjectivity. All three are well-developed points of critique in feminism, and developing the concept of community in International Relations requires that these factors be taken into account.

The feminist critique of International Relations and its conception of community, therefore, opens up opportunities for developing more complete theories of community than those that presently exist in the discipline. Given that the concept of community underlies much of International Relations theory, it is vital to address its current underdevelopment. Feminist theory does so by revealing the nature of the hidden concept of community in International Relations, in addition to the means by which the concept might be coaxed out of its disciplinary closet.

This work is crucial, especially since International Relations continues to grapple with the implications of not only the end of the Cold War, but also increasing globalisation. Both developments raise fundamental questions concerning the relevance and meaning of community, and as Jean-Luc Nancy suggests: '[t]he gravest and most painful testimony of the modern world, the one that possibly involves all other testimonies to which this epoch must answer ... is the testimony of the dissolution, the dislocation, or the conflagration of community'.[68] It is through feminist critique that this problem is most clearly articulated as one that International Relations has failed to recognise. If International Relations is to do more than, at best, marginalise the concept of community, then the compelling challenges that feminist theory poses for the discipline can no longer be ignored.

CHAPTER 17

The End of History and the First Man of the Twenty-first Century

Paul Bacon

In this book the reader is invited to contemplate the significance of the end of the millennium. Is 2000 a number which holds genuine significance for International Relations, or are we imbuing it with a spurious significance which relates principally to our habit of counting in tens? Is the end of the millennium accompanied by new realities which render traditional theory redundant, and if so, what kind of original theorising might be required to frame the most significant problems of International Relations in the coming century? These are big questions, and any collection of papers which purports to address them would be radically incomplete were it not to contain an evaluation of the Big Answer with which Francis Fukuyama explained the (still comparatively) recent unravelling of bipolar International Relations. Fukuyama has argued that the international history of the past ten to fifteen years signifies,

> not just the end of the Cold War, or the passing of a particular period of postwar history, but the end of history as such: that is, the end point of mankind's historical evolution and the universalisation of Western liberal democracy as the final form of human government.[1]

For those who hold to such a view, the idea that we require new theory with which to confront the conundra of the new millennium is redundant. We already have the answer; Fukuyama believes that what we have been witnessing is the,

> unabashed victory of economic and political liberalism. ... The triumph of the West, of the Western *idea*, is evident first of all in the total exhaustion of viable systematic alternatives to Western liberalism. ... there are powerful reasons for believing that it is the ideal that will govern the material world *in the long run*.[2]

These claims are clearly controversial and have provoked heated debate. Fukuyama's writings have provoked ire, condescension, and faint praise in roughly equal measure.[3] Most academics seem to have a strong opinion about the worth of Fukuyama's contribution, and it is imperative to stress that there are 'vulgar' versions of Fukuyama's argument in circulation which should not survive a close engagement with his text. Fukuyama's arguments have all too frequently been misrepresented or misunderstood, or have simply not been given the close attention that they deserve.[4]

There is a further important sense in which the significance of Fukuyama's contribution has not been appreciated, however. In *The End of History and the Last Man*, the arguments contained in the original journal article are developed to the extent that the concluding section casts considerable doubt on the original thesis that we have in fact witnessed the end of history. The principal objective of this chapter is to offer a fair representation of Fukuyama's arguments, and to clear up some of these basic misunderstandings.

The End of History and the Last Man

In restating and defending the arguments contained in his earlier article, Fukuyama asserted that what he believed had come to an end was 'not the occurrence of events, even large and grave events, but History: that is, history understood as a single, coherent, evolutionary process, when taking into account the experience of all peoples in all times'.[5] This process 'dictates a common evolutionary pattern for *all* human societies – in short, something like a Universal History of mankind in the direction of liberal democracy'.[6] This evolution in the direction of capitalism is 'in some sense inevitable for advanced countries', and for this reason, '[w]e who live in stable, long-standing liberal democracies ... have trouble imagining a world that is radically better than our own, or a future that is not essentially democratic and capitalist'.[7] In the first section of the text, Fukuyama believes that it is possible to speak of a directional History of mankind that culminates in liberal democracy for two reasons, the first to do with economics, the second with what he calls the 'struggle for recognition'.

Fukuyama accepts that the idea of a directional History as outlined by Hegel and Marx has been the subject of vigorous critique, and also that many of the most profound thinkers of the century have concluded that history is not a coherent or intelligible process. The evidence against such a proposition is provided by the political disasters of the first half of the twentieth century: the world wars, the rise of totalitarian ideologies, the development of nuclear weapons, and environmental damage. In a century which gave witness to the excesses of Hitler, Stalin and Pol Pot, it is said, it is not difficult to see how the idea of directional Historical progress would attract few adherents.

Despite the gloomy context, Fukuyama identifies what he believes to be remarkable developments in the international political landscape in the late twentieth century. The world's dictatorships, both of the military-authoritarian Right and the communist-totalitarian Left, have proved to be weak, despite all appearances to the contrary. From Latin America to Eastern Europe, from the Soviet Union to the Middle East and Asia, dictatorships have been falling over the last two decades. While Fukuyama accepts that not all of these states have evolved into stable liberal democracies, 'liberal democracy remains the only coherent political aspiration that spans different regions and cultures around the globe, ... [and] liberal principles in economics – the free market – have spread, and have succeeded in producing unprecedented levels of material prosperity, both in industrially developed countries and in countries that had been, at the close of World War II, part of the impoverished Third World'.[8]

Fukuyama believes that these positive developments deserve closer inspection. Is this successful liberal conjunction accidental, a matter of luck, or is it evidence of some deeper phenomenon at work, unfolding in history? Fukuyama believes that the question of the existence of a Universal History of mankind was begun in the early nineteenth century, but broken off in the light of the international political disasters of the first half of the twentieth century. Fukuyama argues that we need to look again at the possibility of Universal History, and proceeds to offer two sets of arguments in support of his end-of-history thesis.

First, Fukuyama argues that modern natural science is by common consensus both cumulative and directional, even if the impact of this accumulation of knowledge on human happiness is ambiguous. Fukuyama believes that the development of natural science has had a uniform effect on all societies that have experienced it. First, 'technology confers decisive military advantages on those states that possess it, and given the continuing possibility of war in the international system of states, no state that values its independence can ignore the need for defensive modernisation'.[9] Secondly,

> modern natural science establishes a uniform horizon of economic production possibilities. Technology makes possible the limitless accumulation of wealth, and thus the satisfaction of an ever-expanding set of human desires. This process guarantees an increasing homogenisation of all human societies, regardless of their historical origins or cultural inheritances. All countries undergoing economic modernisation must increasingly resemble one another: they must unify nationally on the basis of a centralised state, urbanise, replace traditional forms of social organisation like tribe, sect, and family with economically rational ones based on function and efficiency, and provide for the universal education of their citizens.[10]

Fukuyama advances a number of related propositions which develop this theme. These homogenised, modernising societies increasingly have become linked through global markets and the spread of a universal consumer culture.

For Fukuyama, 'the logic of modern natural science would seem to dictate a universal evolution in the direction of capitalism'.[11] While the highly centralised economies of the Soviet Union, China and other socialist countries suffice to reach the level of industrialisation achieved in Europe in the 1950s, these types of economy cannot create complex 'post-industrial' economies.

Fukuyama believes that modern natural science can explain a great deal about the way in which modern societies have changed and become more uniform. Modern natural science cannot, however, account for the phenomenon of democracy. For Fukuyama, 'There is no question but that the world's most developed countries are also its most developed democracies ... but there is no economically necessary reason why advanced industrialisation should produce political liberty.'[12] Fukuyama notes that a liberal revolution in economic thinking has sometimes preceded, sometimes followed, the move towards political freedom around the globe. He claims that stable democracy has emerged in pre-industrial societies, citing the United States as an example, and also that technologically advanced capitalism can coexist with political authoritarianism, citing Meiji Japan, Bismarckian Germany, and present-day Singapore and Thailand as examples. There is no necessary conjunction between liberal economics and liberal politics, and it is also often the case that authoritarian states can produce rates of growth which are unattainable in democratic societies.

Fukuyama concedes, therefore, that his first attempt to establish the basis for a directional history is only partly successful. What he calls the 'logic of modern natural science' offers an economic interpretation of change, but this account alone is incomplete because man is not merely an economic animal. Fukuyama moves to his second, parallel account of the historical process, and draws on Hegel's non-materialist account of History to illustrate what he refers to as 'the struggle for recognition'.

According to Hegel's account, humans share with animals natural needs and desires for objects outside themselves, such as food, drink, shelter, and bodily safety. But man also desires the desire of other men, in the sense that he wants to be recognised as a human being, a being with dignity and worth. Hegel believes that man initially derives his sense of worth from a willingness to risk his life in a struggle for prestige. This is seen as evidence that man and only man can overcome baser animal instincts, such as the need for self-preservation, in pursuit of more elevated and abstract goals. The Hegelian desire for recognition drives primordial combatants to risk their lives in battle. Fear of death eventually leads one to submit, and the relationship of master and slave is born. The stakes in this battle, which occurs at the beginning of history, are not baser animal needs, but pure prestige. According to Fukuyama, it is 'precisely because the goal of the battle is not determined by biology that Hegel sees in it the first glimmer of human freedom'.[13]

Fukuyama asserts that although this concept of the desire for recognition may appear unfamiliar, it has deep roots in Western political philosophy. He claims that the desire for recognition was addressed by Plato in the *Republic*, where he suggested that there were three parts to the soul: a desiring part, a reasoning part, and a part that he called *thymos*, or spiritedness. Although much of human behaviour can be explained in terms of the first two parts, desire and reason, 'human beings seek recognition of their own worth, or of the people, things, or principles that they invest with worth'.[14] Today, we call this self-esteem, and Fukuyama argues that the feeling of self-esteem derives from that part of the soul which he refers to, after Plato, as *thymos*. There is an equilibrium at work here: people have a concept of their own worth, and when they are not treated accordingly, they experience anger. When they fail to live up to their own conception of their worth they experience shame, and they experience pride when they are evaluated appropriately in proportion to their worth. It is important to understand that according to Hegel the desire for recognition and the related emotions of anger, shame and pride are critical to political life, and, in fact, drive the historical process.

This Hegelian desire for recognition manifested itself at the beginning of history in a battle to the death for prestige. As a result of this battle human society divided into a class of masters and a class of slaves, the former willing to risk their lives, the latter yielding to their fear of death. Although this relationship between master and slave has taken a variety of forms throughout history, it ultimately proves unsatisfactory in that it fails to satisfy the demands for recognition of either masters or slaves. Slaves are clearly not recognised as human, but the recognition which is afforded to the masters is also incomplete, because the only recognition which they receive is from slaves whose capacity to recognise is incomplete. Societies characterised by the master–slave relationship contained fundamental contradictions which necessitated, in Hegel's view, further stages of historical development.

The contradictions inherent in such societies were overcome, Hegel believed, by the French and American revolutions:

> These democratic revolutions abolished the distinction between master and slave by making the slaves their own masters and by establishing the principles of popular sovereignty and the rule of law. The inherently unequal recognition of masters and slaves is replaced by universal and reciprocal recognition, where every citizen recognises the dignity of every other citizen.[15]

Hegel asserted that with these revolutions history had come to end, because the struggle for recognition which had animated history was now resolved in democratic societies. Democratic institutions satisfy the struggle for recognition better than could any other social arrangements, and because of this no further progressive historical change is possible.

Fukuyama believes that the desire for recognition provides the missing link between liberal economics and liberal politics. Referring to Plato's tripartite division of the soul, Fukuyama asserts that desire and reason together explain the process of industrialisation, and a good part of economic life in general. Desire and reason cannot, however, explain the drive for liberal democracy, which derives from *thymos*, that part of the soul which demands recognition. Industrialisation, and in particular education, unleash a demand for recognition which does not appear as strong in poorer and less literate societies. Fukuyama claims that as living standards increase people demand more recognition of their status. This is why people are not, in his view, content to live in relatively prosperous market-oriented authoritarian states, which leads them to demand democracy. Importantly, '[c]ommunism is being superseded by liberal democracy in our time because of the realisation that the former provides a gravely defective form of recognition'.[16]

The struggle for recognition has clear implications for International Relations. There are clear links between the account of the original battle for prestige between two individual combatants which leads to a master and slave relationship, and imperialism and world empire. As Fukuyama puts it, 'The relationship of lordship and bondage on a domestic level is naturally replicated on the level of states, where nations as a whole seek recognition and enter into bloody battles for supremacy.'[17] Nationalism has been the vehicle for the struggle for recognition for the last hundred years, and although modern, it is not a fully rational form of recognition. The result of struggles for recognition pursued on this basis has been the power-politics familiar to all students of International Relations.

Fukuyama is optimistic that the end of history has positive consequences for International Relations. He believes that,

> if war is driven by the desire for recognition, it stands to reason that the liberal revolution which abolishes the relationship of lordship and bondage by making former slaves their own masters should have a similar effect on the relationship between states. Liberal democracy replaces the irrational desire to be recognised as greater than others with a rational desire to be recognised as equal. A world made up of liberal democracies, then, should have much less incentive for war, since all nations would reciprocally recognise one another's legitimacy. And indeed, there is substantial empirical evidence from the past couple of hundred years that liberal democracies do not behave imperialistically toward one another.[18]

This optimism is, however, tempered in the final part of Fukuyama's argument, in which he returns to the question of the end of history and asks what sort of human being is produced by liberal democracy, what the 'last man' actually looks like. Fukuyama notes that much of the response to his original *National Interest* article focused on the question of whether there were viable alternatives to liberal democracy, whether Communism was really dead, or whether Islam would continue to develop into a serious challenge to the West. Fukuyama believes that the most important question is 'the goodness of liberal democracy itself', whether liberal democracy retains internal contradictions that will eventually undermine it from the inside as a political system.

At this point Fukuyama turns to the writings of Alexandre Kojève, referred to here as Hegel's great interpreter.[19] Kojève agrees with the thrust of Hegel's argument, that the universal and homogeneous state definitely solves the question of recognition, and that liberal democracy renders the demand for recognition 'completely satisfied'. Fukuyama is less sure. He understands that resolving the struggle for recognition has been the central problem of politics, 'because it is the origin of tyranny, imperialism, and the desire to dominate'.[20] Although the struggle for recognition 'has a dark side', it cannot be avoided, and its positive and destructive effects must be harnessed, for the good of the political community:

> If contemporary constitutional government has indeed found a formula whereby all are recognised *in a way that nonetheless avoids the emergence of tyranny*, then it would indeed have a special claim to stability and longevity among the regimes that have emerged on earth.[21]

Importantly, Fukuyama now doubts that the recognition available to citizens of contemporary liberal democracies is completely satisfying, although he believes that the long-term future of liberal democracy and its alternatives ultimately hinges on this question. In addressing this issue, Fukuyama examines two arguments which claim that liberal democracy is unsatisfying, one from the Left, and one from the Right. According to the first argument, recognition in liberal democracy is clearly incomplete because capitalism requires economic inequality and a division of labour in order to function. According to the second argument, which Fukuyama finds more compelling and to which he devotes more time, 'modern democracy represented not the self-mastery of former slaves, but the unconditional victory of the slave and a kind of slavish morality'.[22] Here Fukuyama is invoking the arguments of Nietzsche; liberal democracy produces 'men without chests' who possess desire and reason but lack *thymos* – 'last men' who have succumbed to comfortable self-preservation.

What are the implications of Fukuyama's argument for International Relations? Fukuyama identifies two clear trends. The first is the cumulative homogenization of mankind, aided by modern economics and technology, and accompanied by the spread of the belief that liberal democracy is the only legitimate basis of government. The second is a resistance to that homogenisation manifested in a reassertion of cultural identity. The number of forms of acceptable economic and political organisation has diminished considerably this century, but there remain a varied number of possible interpretations of capitalism and liberal democracy. Fukuyama believes that although ideological differences will decrease, important differences between states will remain, but will exist on the plane of culture and economics. For Fukuyama these differences mean that 'the existing state system will not collapse anytime soon into a *literally* universal and homogeneous state'.[23] Nations will remain the focal point of identification for some considerable time, even though an increasing number of nations will organise their political and economic affairs in similar ways.

Fukuyama's Critique of Realism

This observation that the state system is not about to collapse necessitates a consideration of what relations between states will look like, and how relations between liberal democratic states differ from traditional accounts of International Relations. Fukuyama believes that the existence of a directional history would have important consequences for International Relations. If the relationship of lordship and bondage can be overcome at the individual level within societies, then the spread of the universal homogeneous state would seem to suggest that lordship and bondage between nations could also be overcome, entailing the end of imperialism and wars based on imperialism.

Fukuyama notes that pessimism about the possibility of progressive change within societies, although marked, is less pervasive than the pessimism with which relations between states are regarded, and acknowledges the significance of realist theory in shaping our conceptions of International Relations. It is, he claims, the dominant framework for understanding International Relations, 'and shapes the thinking of virtually every foreign policy professional today in the United States and much of the rest of the world'.[24] Fukuyama wants to argue that while realist theory may have been appropriate at certain times this century, this is no longer the case.

Realist theories start from the assumption that insecurity is a universal and ever-present feature of international order. Due to the anarchic nature of the system, in the sense that there is no international sovereign, states are potentially under threat, and arm themselves accordingly. The process of armament engenders misperception and can lead to arms races. States seek to maximise their power, and competition and war are the inevitable result. According to realist theory, the international pursuit of power is not affected by the internal characteristics of states. Because the drive for power is similar in all states, the issue is not whether certain types of state are more likely to be aggressive, but whether power is balanced appropriately within the international system or not; the distribution of power between states in the international system is the single most important determinant of war and peace. Nation-states are viewed as billiard balls whose internal attributes are irrelevant to a consideration of their behaviour in international politics. Waltz, for example, 'seeks to explain international politics purely on the basis of the system's structure without any consideration whatsoever of the domestic character of its component nations. In an astonishing reversal of customary linguistic usage, he calls theories that take account of domestic politics "reductionist", in contrast to his theory, which reduces the entire complexity of the "system", of which one can know essentially one fact: whether it is bipolar or multipolar.'[25]

Realism is both descriptive and prescriptive. Fukuyama distils the following prescriptions from realist thought. The ultimate solution to the problem of international insecurity is to be found through maintenance of a balance of power against one's potential enemies. Friends and enemies should be chosen primarily on the basis of their power. Statesmen should look more closely at military capabilities rather than intentions, and moralism should be excluded from foreign policy. Fukuyama identifies a paradox here; realists are continually seeking to maintain a balance of power based on military force, but for precisely this reason they are the most likely to seek accommodation with powerful enemies. The realist position holds that conflict between states is permanent and universal, and so changes in the ideology or leadership of hostile states will not alleviate the central problem of international insecurity. Realists such as Metternich and Kissinger, therefore, advocate the dispassionate balancing of power, free of consideration of ideology. It is for this reason that Kissinger was happy to broker *détente* between a liberal democratic United States and an unreconstructedly Communist Soviet Union.

Fukuyama believes that realism 'played a large and beneficial role in shaping the way Americans thought about foreign policy after World War II', and that realism was 'an appropriate framework for understanding international politics in this period because the world operated according to realist premises'.[26] It is not that realist theory confers timeless truth, but rather that the world was sharply divided, and international politics was characterised by the aggressive clash of fascism, communism and liberal democracy. Liberal internationalism was inadequate, and derived from precisely the liberal ideology that fascist and communist states were attempting to overthrow.

However, realism has 'serious weaknesses [as] a framework for viewing international relations, both as a description of reality and a prescription for policy'.[27] To support this claim, Fukuyama identifies what he believes to be two seriously flawed arguments. The first is offered by Gaddis, who suggested that the West should have tried to keep the Warsaw Pact alive on the grounds that it was the bipolar division of Europe that was responsible for the European peace since 1945.[28] The second is offered by Mearsheimer, who claimed that the end of the division of Europe would lead to greater instability in Europe than was the case during the Cold War, which could be remedied through the managed proliferation of nuclear weapons to Germany.[29] For Fukuyama these arguments are akin to continuing to give chemotherapy to a cured cancer patient on the grounds that it has worked in the past. 'Treating a disease that no longer exists, realists now find themselves proposing costly and dangerous cures to healthy patients.'[30]

Fukuyama believes that realism rests on two questionable foundations: first, that it is reductive with regard to the motives and behaviour of human societies; and secondly, that it does not address the question of History. Realist thought is premised on a certain view of the person. Insecurity, aggression and war are permanent possibilities in International Relations, because they are rooted in an unchanging view of human nature. This condition does not change as specific forms and types of human society change. According to Mearsheimer, 'Conflict is common among states because the international system creates powerful incentives for aggression. ... States seek to survive under anarchy by maximising their power relative to other states.'[31] For Fukuyama, this is highly reductionist, and covertly attributes agency to the system rather than to the units that comprise this system. There is no prima-facie reason why states should feel threatened by each other, unless one had good reason to believe that human societies were inherently aggressive.

Fukuyama notes the connection between the realist account of international politics and the Hobbesian state of nature, where man is in a state of war of all against all. Self-preservation alone is not sufficient to explain this war of all against all, however; the state of war arises because self-preservation coexists with the desire for recognition. Hobbes himself would argue that the primordial state of war would only arise if some men sought to impose their views on others. Rousseau also argues for a peaceful state of nature, since he believes that man is naturally fearful and solitary, and can be essentially peaceful because his few selfish needs are easily met. Original anarchy can also produce peace. To return to Hegelian terms, a world of slaves would be free of conflict, because it is only masters who are driven to mortal combat. Similarly, it is possible that anarchic state systems could be peaceful, if the states in such a system were inhabited by Rousseauian man or Hegel's slave who are only interested in self-preservation. From these arguments Fukuyama draws the conclusion that realist thought is not so much systemic as premised on a 'hidden assumption that human societies in their international behaviour tend to resemble Hegel's master seeking recognition, or the vainglorious first man of Hobbes, rather than the timid solitary of Rousseau'.[32]

It is important to note that Fukuyama is here offering us an international political theory that aims to subvert Waltz's structural realism, and to locate cause at the unit-level rather than at the system-level:

> The fact that peace in historical state systems has been so difficult to obtain reflects the fact that certain states seek *more* than self-preservation. Like giant thymotic individuals, they seek acknowledgement of their value or dignity on dynastic, religious, nationalist, or ideological grounds, and in the process force other states either to fight or submit. The ultimate ground of war among states is therefore *thymos* rather than self-preservation. Just as human history began with the bloody battle for pure prestige, so international conflict begins with a struggle for recognition among states, which is the original source of imperialism.[33]

If this is true, the bare fact of power distribution within the international system is meaningless, and becomes meaningful only in the context of the attributes of the societies that constitute the system, and whether their principal motivation is mere self-preservation or the struggle for recognition. For Fukuyama, the realism of Morgenthau, Kennan, Niebuhr and Kissinger is preferable to Waltz's structural realism, because the former writers recognised that to be intelligible, conflict had to be understood as derived from human desires for domination, rather than from structural imperatives. Even these more sophisticated variants of realist thought, however, remain reductionist in Fukuyama's eyes.

States do seek power in the sense that they strive to achieve national objectives, and this seeking of power is indeed universal, but the statement is so general as to be trivial. Although states do attempt to become wealthy, this is invariably for the purposes of domestic consumption; it is not the case that states are always seeking to maximise military power. For Fukuyama, states do not simply engage in a pursuit of power, 'they pursue a variety of ends that are dictated by concepts of *legitimacy*'.[34] The concept of legitimacy serves to constrain the pursuit of power for its own sake, and states can invariably ill afford to disregard conceptions of legitimacy. It is in terms of these observations that Fukuyama explains the end of the Cold War in Europe. The events of 1989 and 1990, the disintegration of the Warsaw Pact and the reunification of Germany constituted a massive shift in the balance of power, despite the fact that 'not a single tank in Europe was destroyed in combat'.[35] There was no shift in the material balance of power. Crucially, 'the shift occurred entirely as a result of a change in standards of legitimacy'.[36] Communist power was discredited in Eastern Europe, and the Soviets themselves did not retain sufficient faith in the regime to restore its military pre-eminence. This concept of legitimacy constitutes what Vaclav Havel referred to as 'the power of the powerless',[37] and confounds realist attempts to define power in terms of capabilities and not intentions.

The fact that conceptions of legitimacy can both evolve and dissipate so dramatically leads to Fukuyama's second critique of realism, that it does not take account of history.

> In sharp distinction to every other aspect of human political and social life, realism portrays international relations as isolated in a timeless vacuum, immune from the evolutionary processes taking place around it. But those apparent continuities in world politics from Thucydides to the Cold War in fact mask significant differences in the manner in which societies seek, control, and relate to power.[38]

At this juncture Fukuyama introduces a new concept – that of *megalothymia*, which he defines as the master's desire to be recognised as superior. This, according to Fukuyama, is the wellspring of imperialism, the forcible domination of one society by another. The thymotic drive that leads to the conditions of lordship and bondage within societies are replicated at the level of international relations, and continues until the master achieves world empire or dies. As a result of this, and in direct contradiction of Waltz, '[t]he desire of masters for recognition, and not the structure of the state system, is the original cause of war'.[39] Imperialism and war are related to the existence of a certain class, the masters, or aristocracy. In aristocratic societies, 'the striving of princes for universal but *unequal* recognition was widely regarded as legitimate. ... Wars of territorial conquest for the sake of an ever-expanding dominion were seen as normal human aspiration.'[40]

The struggle for recognition need not manifest itself solely in imperialism, but could take other forms, such as the desire for religious mastery. Fukuyama believes that manifestations of *thymos* in dynastic and religious expansionism,

> were to a large extent displaced in the early modern period by increasingly rational forms of recognition whose ultimate expression was the modern liberal state. The bourgeois revolution of which Hobbes and Locke were the prophets sought to morally elevate the slave's fear of death over the aristocratic virtue of the master, and thereby to sublimate irrational manifestations of *thymos* like princely ambition and religious fanaticism into the unlimited accumulation of property.[41]

Political liberalism in England ended the religious wars between Protestants and Catholics, and new zones of civil peace were constituted by the modern liberal European nation-state. Once again, Fukuyama is keen to suggest that the civil peace engendered in political liberalism has its analogue in International Relations. Imperialism and war are caused by the masters in aristocratic societies. Liberal democracy abolishes this distinction between masters and slaves by making the slaves their own masters. Liberal states will therefore not be imperialistic. In reaching this conclusion Fukuyama has clearly been influenced heavily by the arguments of Joseph Schumpeter. Schumpeter argues that democratic capitalist societies are not warlike or imperialistic because they provide alternative outlets for energy, or for the struggle for recognition.

> The competitive system absorbs the full energies of most of the people at all economic levels. Constant application, attention, and concentration of energy are the conditions of survival within it, primarily in the specifically economic professions, but also in other activities organized on their model. There is much less excess energy to be vented in war and conquest than in any precapitalist society. ... A purely capitalist world can therefore offer no fertile soil to im-perialist impulses. ... The point is that its people are likely to be of an unwarlike disposition.[42]

For Schumpeter, therefore, imperialism is not a universal characteristic which all societies possess, but can be located in relation to the emergence of aristocratic orders whose moral basis is oriented towards war. Once again, realist theory is too simplistic and mistaken in its ascription of similar motives to quite different types of state.

Pacific Union?

For Fukuyama it is clear that modern liberal societies are driven by the consciousness of the slave rather than the master, or more specifically by Christianity, which is 'the last great slave ideology ... manifest in the spread of compassion, and a steadily decreasing tolerance of violence, death, and suffering'.[43] In developed countries capital punishment is gradually disappearing, and there is low tolerance of casualties sustained in warfare. Fukuyama also argues that the economics of war have changed fundamentally. Before the Industrial Revolution, princes could increase their wealth only by seizing someone else's land and peasants. After the Industrial Revolution, however, land, population and natural resources declined in significance in comparison to technology, education, and the rational organisation of labour. Economic gains through labour productivity became far more certain and significant than the economic spoils potentially on offer through territorial conquest. Given that access to resources 'can be obtained peacefully through a global system of free trade, war makes much less economic sense than it did two or three hundred years ago'.[44] The economic costs of war have also increased greatly with advances in the sophistication of military technology. By the end of the First World War, technology was such that states were undermined by participation in war, even if they were on the winning side.

Liberal democratic states, according to Fukuyama, are unlikely to be warlike or imperialistic. That liberal societies are not warlike is evidenced by the 'extraordinarily peaceful relations they maintain among one another. There is by now a substantial body of literature noting the fact that there have been few, if any, instances of one liberal democracy going to war with another.'[45] Here, Fukuyama refers in particular to the well-known research of the political scientist Michael Doyle, who suggests that in the two hundred years or so in which modern liberal societies have existed, there have been no instances in which two liberal democracies have fought each other. Fukuyama acknowledges that this conclusion depends to a significant extent on exactly what one is prepared to define as a liberal democracy, but on the whole concludes that 'Doyle's conclusions are both correct and striking'.[46]

Some realist thinkers have tried to confound Doyle's Perpetual Peace thesis by arguing that liberal democracies have not historically been neighbours (and have therefore been unable to fight each other), or have cooperated only in the light of a strong military threat from non-liberal societies. The most significant variable with which to explain peace in Europe since 1945 is not the common commitment to liberal democracy, but rather the common fear of the Soviet Union which animated the construction of NATO and the European Community.

Fukuyama does not agree with this argument, and claims that such conclusions could be reached only if one conceived of states as billiard balls and disregarded what was going on within them. He argues that it is the peaceful influence of liberal ideas on foreign policy which best illustrate the changes which have taken place in the former Soviet Union and Eastern Europe since the mid-1980s. Realist theory dictates that the strategic objectives of the Soviet Union would remain the same regardless of its internal constitution. This is patently not what happened. Soviet foreign policy changed as a result of 'new thinking' which entailed a thoroughgoing re-appraisal of the security threats which confronted the Soviet Union. The Soviets themselves came to realise that military aggression against socialism by Western powers was most unlikely, and that 'bourgeois democracy serves as a definite barrier in the path of unleashing such a war'.[47]

While certain countries such as Syria and Iraq do ally periodically against Israel, relations between the two are generally hostile, as evidenced by the Gulf War. There is no such hostility between the democratic countries that lined up against the Soviet Union; it is unthinkable that France and Germany, Holland and Denmark, and Canada and the United States could go to war.

Fukuyama's reasons for thinking this, however, are not as comforting as one might imagine.

> The anarchic state system of liberal Europe does not foster distrust and insecurity because most European states understand each other too well. They know that their neighbours are too self-indulgent and consumerist to risk death, full of entrepreneurs and managers but lacking in princes or demagogues whose ambitions alone are sufficient to start wars.[48]

It is hopefully becoming clear that Fukuyama is by no means an unreconstructed triumphalist, and that he is all too aware of the role that nationalism has played in the major conflicts of this century, and the threat that it may pose in the future to the peace of post-communist Eastern Europe. Fukuyama believes that he can account for the significance of nationalism by identifying it as an outlet for *thymos* which lies between domestic and religious ambition, and the fully modern resolution that it ultimately finds in the universal and homogeneous state.

The Domestication of Nationalism?

Nationalism lies at an intermediate stage between these states and contains elements of both. Nationalism is specifically modern because it replaces the relationship of lordship and bondage with mutual and equal recognition, but extends this recognition only on grounds of ethnic or national solidarity, and is not therefore fully rational. Nationalism is a more democratic and egalitarian conception of legitimacy than many forms of aristocratic rule, but the dignity that nationalists seek to have recognised is not universal human dignity, but group dignity. This raises the potential for conflict between different groups seeking recognition for their particular version of dignity. Nationalism is therefore capable of replacing dynastic and religious ambition as a basis for imperialism. The persistence of imperialism and war after the bourgeois revolutions of the eighteenth and nineteenth centuries is due, according to Fukuyama, to the fact that 'the masters *megalothymia* was incompletely sublimated into economic activity'.[49]

Non-liberal states constantly displayed irrational forms of *thymos*, and all states were affected by nationalism to some degree. European nationalisms were closely interrelated, and the disentanglement of Eastern and South-eastern European nationalisms into separate nation-states was a great source of conflict. Fukuyama acknowledges that liberal societies would wage wars against non-liberal states, and that ostensibly liberal states attacked and ruled over non-European societies, and failed to universalise their concepts of right by basing citizenship on race or ethnic origin. While Fukuyama accepts that 'mass populations motivated for war by nationalism ... could rise to heights of thymotic anger seldom seen in dynastic conflicts',[50] it is necessary to put the phenomenon of nationalism in perspective. The importance of nationalism is exaggerated by scholars who view the 'nations' on which nationalism was based as timeless social entities. Nationalism is not an elemental force in history which will eventually overcome liberalism. It is not permanent and all-conquering, but rather a recent and contingent phenomenon that accompanied the Industrial Revolution, 'which forced all societies undergoing it to become radically more egalitarian, homogeneous, and educated. ... Nationalism was therefore very much the product of industrialisation and the democratic, egalitarian ideologies that accompanied it.'[51]

Importantly, in relation to his overall argument, Fukuyama believes that,

> nationalisms have a certain life history. At certain stages of historical development, such as in agrarian societies, [nationalisms] do not exist at all. They grow most intense just at or past the point of transition to industrial society, and become particularly exacerbated when a people, having gone through the first phases of economic modernisation, is denied both nationality and political freedom. ... But for national groups whose identity is more secure and of longer standing, *the nation as a source of thymotic identification appears to decline*. The passing of the initial, intense period of nationalism is most advanced in the region most damaged by nationalist passions, Europe. ... Having experienced the horrendous irrationality latent in the nationalist form of recognition, Europe's populations have gradually come to accept universal and equal recognition as an alternative.[52]

This acceptance of universal and equal recognition is most manifest in the momentum behind the creation of the European Union. Although the EU obviously has not abolished national differences, arguments that take place between Member states are a highly domesticated version of the nationalisms that provoked two World Wars.

Fukuyama believes that those who say that nationalism is too potent to be thwarted by liberalism and economic self-interest should consider the fact that '*liberalism vanquished religion in Europe*'.[53] Although religion was once all-pervading in European politics, it has now been relegated to the sphere of private life. Fukuyama predicts that a similar phenomenon will happen to nationalism, and that 'where individualistic nationalisms accept a separate but equal status with their fellows, the nationalistic basis for imperialism and war will weaken'.[54] Although many people believe that the drive for European integration is a short-term response to the Second World War and the Cold War which is doomed to failure, Fukuyama believes that the two World Wars of this century may transpire to possess a significance for nationalist senti-ment comparable to that of the wars of religion in the sixteenth and seventeenth centuries for the fate of religion. 'Like religion, nationalism is in no danger of disappearing, but like religion, it appears to have lost much of its ability to stimulate Europeans to risk their comfortable lives in great acts of imperialism.'[55]

Fukuyama is not suggesting that Europe will be free from nationalist conflict in the future. He regards nationalism as a 'necessary concomitant' to the spread of democratisation, and acknowledges that many nationalisms are likely to be quite primitive – intolerant, chauvinistic, and externally aggressive. However, Fukuyama believes that because the most intense nationalist surges would take place in the least modernised parts of Europe, there was little danger of them affecting the evolution of Europe's older nationalisms in the direction of liberal toleration. The broader impact of new nationalist conflicts on broader European security would be negligible, especially compared to 1914. There are now no great powers in Europe remotely interested in exploiting nationalist conflict for their own advantage. Indeed, the most pressing concern facing most great powers is that of avoiding entanglement. Fukuyama believed that many of the new nation-states would emerge as liberal democracies, and that their nationalisms would eventually mature in much the same way that the nationalisms of Western European states have. In short, people have over-estimated the world historical significance of nationalism.

> It is curious why people believe that a phenomenon of such recent historical provenance as nationalism will be so permanent a feature of the human social landscape. Economic forces encouraged nationalism by replacing class with national barriers and created centralised, linguistically homogeneous entities in the process. Those same economic forces are now encouraging the breakdown of national barriers through the creation of a single, integrated world market. The fact that the final political neutralisation of nationalism may not occur in this generation or the next does not affect the prospect of its ultimately taking place.[56]

Fukuyama's typology of evolutionary nationalism, then, informs us that nationalism has been domesticated by certain states, yet remains significant in certain regions of the world, even if it is ultimately to pass into history.

Post-historical International Relations

Until such a time, however, power politics will prevail in the relations between non-democratic states. There will be a sharp distinction between the behaviour of Third World states and the industrial democracies. Fukuyama believes that, '[f]or the foreseeable future, the world will be divided between a post-historical part, and a part that is still stuck in history'.[57] In the post-historical world the key issues between states are economic, and power politics has decreasing relevance. There will be high levels of economic competition, little military competition, and market and production-driven economic rationality will undermine traditional conceptions of sovereignty. The post-historical world will still consist of nation-states, but post-historical nationalism will have made its peace with liberalism. The historical world will, however, remain mired in religious, national and ideological conflict according to the stage of development of particular countries, and relations here will continue to be governed by relations of power. The nation-state will remain the primary vehicle for political identification in the historical world.

Fukuyama concedes that the dividing line between the historical and post-historical world can sometimes be difficult to draw, but believes that these two worlds 'will maintain parallel but separate existences, with relatively little interaction between them'.[58] There are three exceptions to this generalisation: oil, immigration, and world-order questions. Oil production is centred in the historical world, but is also crucial to the post-historical world's well-being. There is at present a constant flow of immigration from the historical world to the post-historical world which could be accelerated still more by events in the historical world. This flow, or potential flow, of immigrants from the historical world will raise the post-historical world's awareness of, and interest in, events in the historical world. Fukuyama believes that there are two reasons why it is difficult for post-historical countries to bar immigration. First, the post-historical world has had 'difficulty formulating any just principle of excluding foreigners that does not seem racist or nationalist, thereby violating those universal principles of right to which they as liberal democracies are committed'.[59] The second is the fact that there remain shortages of unskilled or semi-skilled labour in nearly every developed country.

In the interests of world order, post-historical countries will oppose and seek to prevent the spread of technology to the historical world. This means preventing the spread of nuclear weapons, ballistic missiles, and chemical and biological weapons. There is also a threat to environmental interests posed by the prospect of unregulated technological proliferation. Fukuyama claims that post-historical countries will have a related common interest both in protecting themselves from external threats, and in promoting the cause of democracy in the historical world.

Realist principles will continue to govern the interactions of the historical world, and the post-historical world must also avail itself of realist policies when dealing with the historical world. Despite growing economic inter-dependence between the two worlds, 'force will continue to be the *ultima ratio* in their mutual relations'.[60] Fukuyama believes that realist theory is relevant to certain relationships between certain types of state at certain points in their world-historical evolution. As we have seen, Fukuyama agrees that realism was an appropriate framework within which to understand International Relations during the Cold War, and the relationship between the historical and post-historical world at present. Realism does not possess a *timeless* relevance for International Relations, however.

> The human historical process has engendered a series of concepts of legitimacy – dynastic, religious, nationalistic, and ideological, leading to as many possible bases for imperialism and war. Each of these forms of legitimacy prior to modern liberalism was based on some form of lordship and bondage, so that imperialism was in a sense dictated by the social system. Just as concepts of legitimacy have changed over history, so has international relations; while war and imperialism may have seemed constant throughout history, wars have been fought for very different objectives in each age.[61]

Concepts of legitimacy have changed over history; all forms of legitimacy prior to liberal democracy rested, to varying degrees, on the relationship of lordship and bondage. Liberalism abolishes this distinction between masters and slaves, and it therefore follows logically for Fukuyama that such an abolition would lead to the pursuit of altogether different foreign policy objectives. This is not merely because states would share a common concep-tion of legitimacy, but rather that '[p]eace will arise instead out of the specific nature of democratic legitimacy, and its ability to satisfy the human longing for recognition'.[62]

Although Fukuyama argues that realist principles were appropriate to the governing of Soviet–American relations during the Cold War, he does acknowledge an unresolved tension between hard-nosed policies of mutual accommodation with non-democratic states, and a concern with foreign policy issues consonant with the moral concerns of liberal democracies. A good example of such tension was the criticism directed at Reagan for suggesting in 1987 that the Soviets should tear down the Berlin Wall. Much of this criticism came from the Germans, to whom the Wall was of course un-welcome, but who had also long since absorbed the political reality of Soviet power. Because the Wall did come down, the injunctions turned out to be both morally satisfying and practically prudent, but there is of course no guarantee of this always being the case. 'Revolutions of the sort that occurred in Eastern Europe in 1989 are rare events, even unprecedented ones, and a democracy can not predicate its foreign policy on the imminent collapse of each dictatorship that it confronts.'[63] This notwithstanding, liberal democracies should remember Havel's injunction that legitimacy is the power of the powerless, and that superficially strong states are actually quite weak without this power. Democratic societies that ally consistently with other democratic societies are likely to have stronger and more durable alliances. Because democracies are peaceful, they have a long-term interest in preserving and expanding the scope of democracy where possible. The post-historical world holds out the promise of peace and prosperity.

Liberal International Relations

The suggestion that democracies should work together to promote peace is not new. It was most famously discussed in Kant's *Perpetual Peace: A Philosophical Sketch*, and *Idea for a Universal History*.[64] Kant argues that although there are gains in man's move from the state of nature to civil society, these gains are nullified by the state of war held to characterise the nature of relations between states. As Fukuyama notes, Kant's writings on international relations became an intellectual buttress for the ideas of liberal internationalism advanced by the Americans in their attempts to establish the League of Nations and the United Nations. The failure of these organisations to provide security against challenges to international order by Japan, Germany, and Italy led to the discrediting of Kantian internationalism, international law, and idealist international relations in general.

Fukuyama argues that attempts to discredit Kant as a result of the shortcomings of these two international organisations is wide of the mark. Kant's own precepts had not been followed in the inauguration of either organisation. Kant's First Definitive Article for perpetual peace stipulated that the constitution of states in the state system should be republican, or liberal democratic, and his Second Definitive Article affirms that the law of nations should be founded by free nations, or states that share republican constitutions.[65] Democracies, he argued, are less likely to accept the costs of war than despotisms, and an international federation can only work if the states which are party to it share common liberal principles of right.

Many of the members of the United Nations patently do not meet these criteria. Membership of the United Nations was 'open to any state possessing certain minimal formal criteria of sovereignty, regardless of whether they were based on popular sovereignty or not'.[66] Stalin's Soviet Union was a founding member of the organisation, with a seat on the Security Council and the right to veto resolutions. Many of the post-colonial states who later became members of the organisation did not share liberal principles, and found the United Nations to be a useful instrument for the pushing of illiberal political agendas. The UN is not characterised by any consensus on order or rights, and as such it is not surprising that the organisation has little of any substance in the critical area of collective security. The League of Nations was more homogeneous, but was fatally undone by the fact that Japan and Germany were important players, but were undemocratic, and unwilling to play by the League's rules.

The prospects for the United Nations seemed brighter with the un-precedented consensus for the use of force against Iraq to liberate Kuwait, but Fukuyama maintains that the integrity of the Security Council remains vulnerable to possible regression on the part of incompletely reformed countries such as Russia and China, and that the General Assembly remains populated by nations that are not free. He is sceptical about the possibility that the United Nations might successfully underpin a new world order in the immediate future. Instead, he believes that if we wanted to build a league of nations that was faithful to Kant's precepts, such an organisation would look much more like NATO than the United Nations. This would be a league of free states, genuinely united by common belief in liberal principles, and clearly capable of defending itself from threats which arise in the historical world in the future. This Kantian international order evolved organically during the Cold War. The use of force to settle disputes between these countries is unthinkable. This means that the post-historical liberal democracies will have to come to terms with the fact that their interrelations are not to be governed by geopolitics, and that the major issues will be economic, to do with unemployment, budget deficits, and the like. Universal and rational recognition has replaced the struggle for domination.

The First Man of the Twenty-first Century

Thus far I have outlined in uncritical fashion the liberal conclusions which Fukuyama draws from the earlier part of his analysis. Fukuyama believes that it is intelligible to talk of an evolutionary and cumulative history, and of the end of history. There is an historically significant conjunction between liberal politics and liberal economics which produces both economic success and democracy, which features fully constituted rights-bearing individuals. Realist theory is no longer relevant to International Relations between liberal states, which have domesticated nationalism and resolved the struggle for recognition, and a Pacific Union, or zone of peace, has emerged between these states, which can confidently be expected to expand concomitantly with the spread of liberal democracy and the gradual homogenisation of culture. These are exactly the type of arguments which one would expect Fukuyama to employ to buttress an extended defence of his thesis, in that they remain faithful to the tone and conclusions of his original journal article. As I indicated in the introduction, however, Fukuyama is far more sanguine about the prospects for his original thesis throughout his book, and particularly the concluding section, than he is given credit for. In the next stage of the exposition I want to look in more detail at a possibility which Fukuyama believes could eventually undermine his thesis; the possibility that disillusioned last men might be tempted to restart history in the post-historical world.

Fukuyama claims that people will argue about whether they have reached the post-historical world, or whether International Relations will produce further empires, dictatorships, civilisational surges or unfulfilled nationalisms, or whether alternatives as yet unimagined will emerge. This preoccupation, he warns, may be misplaced; it is clear at this moment in time that liberal democracy is superior to alternative forms of political organisation, and has served as 'needed shelter from the desperate storms of the twentieth century'.[67] At some point, however, Fukuyama claims that it must be asked whether liberal democracy is worthy of choice in itself, whether it leaves us completely satisfied.

For Kojève, the struggle for recognition drove history from the very beginning, but now history has ended because liberal democracies which embody reciprocal recognition fully satisfy this longing. The major historical phenomena which we have witnessed over the last few centuries, such as religion, nationalism and democracy, can all be understood as attempts to resolve the struggle for recognition. For Fukuyama,

> [t]he question of the end of history then amounts to a question of *thymos*: whether liberal democracy adequately satisfies the desire for recognition, as Kojeve says, or whether it will remain radically unfulfilled and therefore capable of manifesting itself in an entirely different form.[68]

Fukuyama outlined two paths to a Universal History, one guided by modern natural science and the logic of desire, the other by the struggle for recognition. As I suggested earlier in the text, both culminated in the same point, capitalist liberal democracy. Now, Fukuyama is not so sure. '[C]an desire and *thymos* be so neatly satisfied by the same sorts of social and political institutions? Is it not possible that what satisfies desire is not satisfying to *thymos*, and vice versa, so that no human society will be satisfying to "man as *man*"?.'[69] Fukuyama is at this juncture acknowledging the possibility that liberal democracy may not simultaneously be able to satisfy both desire and *thymos*, but in his concluding remarks he goes further still. 'No regime – no "socio-economic system" – is able to satisfy all men in all places. This includes liberal democracy. ... Thus those who remain dissatisfied will always have the potential to restart history.'[70] Fukuyama has come to the conclusion that rational recognition in the universal state is not self-sustaining, and must rely upon pre-modern, non-universal forms of recognition to function properly.

> Group rather than universal recognition can be a better support for both economic activity and community life ... not only is universal recognition [as merely equal] not universally satisfying, but the ability of liberal democracies to establish and sustain themselves on a rational basis over the long term is open to some doubt.[71]

Fukuyama, it would appear, now tends towards Aristotle's view of history. Aristotle believed that history was cyclical, because all regimes possess imperfections which will serve as a stimulus for change, and Fukuyama suggests that we could say the same of modern democracy. 'Following Aristotle, we might postulate that a society of last men composed entirely of desire and reason would give way to one of bestial first men seeking recognition alone, and vice versa, in an unending oscillation.'[72] It is difficult to imagine a conclusion less in keeping with the original thesis of the journal article, and the earlier sections of the book.

Liberal Economics, Authoritarian Politics?

What has stimulated this development in Fukuyama's thought? It is at this juncture that we need to look in more detail at the work of Kojève. In his *Introduction to the Reading of Hegel*, Kojève's lectures on Hegel's *Phenomenology of Spirit*, Kojève states that:

> I was able to conclude that the 'American way of life' was the type of life specific to the post-historical period, the actual presence of the United States in the World prefiguring the 'eternal present' future of all humanity. … It was following a recent visit to Japan [1959] that I had a radical change of opinion on this point. There I was able to observe a Society that is one of a kind, because it alone has for almost three centuries experienced life at the 'end of History'. … This seems to allow one to believe that the recently begun interaction between Japan and the Western world will finally lead not to a rebarbarization of the Japanese, but to a 'Japanization' of the Westerners.[73]

This tension between East and West is also present in Fukuyama's writings. Fukuyama believes that modern economics is having a homogenising effect, and destroying a number of traditional cultures. But also he warns that modern economics might not win every battle, and that certain cultures and certain manifestations of *thymos* are hard to absorb. If there are obstacles to economic homogenisation, following Fukuyama's argument, then the process of democratisation is also thrown into doubt. Although many peoples desire capitalist prosperity and liberal democracy, not everyone will be able to achieve it. There are therefore two ways in which as yet unseen authoritarian alternatives to liberal politics and liberal economics may arise. Some may experience economic failure for cultural reasons, but others may successfully combine authoritarian politics with liberal economics. Indeed, Fukuyama believes that:

> The most significant challenge being posed to the liberal universalism of the American and French revolutions today is coming … from those societies in Asia which combine liberal economics with a kind of paternalistic authoritarianism.[74]

As a result of this, Asia in general, and Japan in particular, are at a 'critical turning point with regard to world history'.[75] It is possible to envisage Asia moving in one of two directions as it continues to develop economically in the next few years. The first possibility is that Asia's increasingly cosmopolitan and educated elites could absorb and inculcate Western ideas of universal and reciprocal recognition, further the spread of democracy, and deepen the purchase of the principles of freedom and equality in their own societies, leading to a concomitant decline in the significance of group identification. The second is that Asians come to believe that their economic success is actually rooted in their successful integration of traditional Asian values with modern business practice rather than the importing of Western values whole-sale. Fukuyama acknowledges that although the logic of modern natural science entails the development of capitalist free markets, there is no guarantee that this will be accompanied by liberal democracy, and claims that '[t]he beginnings of a systematic Asian rejection of liberal democracy can be heard'.[76]

At this juncture Fukuyama returns to a persistent theme of his book, the breakdown of community life in America. Although Fukuyama claims that Japanese democracy is somewhat authoritarian by American or European standards, he is prepared to concede that Asian societies possess a sense of community which Western liberal democracies lack. Asians derive status from membership of· a series of interlocking groups rather than from individual ability or worth, but also, and crucially, 'the individual self-interest at the heart of Western liberal economic theory may be an inferior form of motivation to certain forms of group interest. ... The highly atomistic economic liberalism of the United States or Britain, based exclusively on rational desire, becomes economically counter-productive at a certain point.'[77] We can conclude from these observations, scattered throughout the text, that Fukuyama believes that atomist Western societies possess less of a sense of community, and in the long run will therefore prove to be less economically competitive than the group-oriented societies of the East, and possibly even less normatively desirable.

> The breakdown of community life in the United States begins with the family, which has been steadily fractured and atomized over the past couple of genera-tions. ... Yet it is precisely a sense of community that is offered by Asian societies, and for many of those growing up in that culture, social conformity and constraints on individualism seem to be a small price to pay.[78]

Fukuyama's view of the desirability of Asian-style democracy is therefore ambiguous. He catalogues the social shortcomings of Asian authoritarianism, but also extols its economic and social virtues in relation to Western liberal democracy.

Fukuyama's thesis began its life as a Hegelian/Kojèvian assertion of the triumph of Western liberal democracy. Yet now Fukuyama's thesis appears to be that Western democracy is in danger of being usurped by Confucian neo-authoritarianism precisely because it is in fact *insufficiently* Hegelian, in a manner that Kojève's writings are not equipped to address. What Fukuyama laments is the lack of intermediate associations between the level of state and individual in the West; what Hegelians refer to as civil society. Significantly, '[b]oth Tocqueville and Hegel emphasised the importance of associational life as a focus for public-spiritedness in the modern state'.[79] Associational life consists in membership of institutions such as political parties, private corporations, labour unions, churches, literary societies, sports clubs and the like. Such institutions, however small, constitute communities of recognition and solidarity, and Fukuyama reads Tocqueville as implying that strong community life is democracy's best guarantee that its citizens do not turn into last men. Hegel also thought that 'associations organized spontaneously by civil society ... served as a focus for community and virtue'.[80]

Earlier in his argument, Fukuyama had advised us to assume the existence of 'a new synthetic philosopher named Hegel–Kojève',[81] but it is clear from Fukuyama's own remarks that the two philosophers' views are at odds with regard to the issue of civil society, a concept which plays a clear role in Fukuyama's change of opinion.[82] The existence of civil society is our best hope of obtaining the recognition which prevents us from becoming last men, and constitutes a superior form of recognition to that conferred by the Asian 'empires of deference ... which may produce unprecedented prosperity, but also ... a prolonged childhood for most citizens, and therefore an incompletely satisfied *thymos*'.[83] The recognition conferred by such liberal yet constitutive societies would also make it less likely that alienated first men would be tempted to restart history, but ultimately,

> [t]he decline of community life suggests that in the future, we risk becoming secure and self-absorbed last men, devoid of thymotic striving for higher goals in our pursuit of private comforts. But the opposite danger exists as well, namely, that we will return to being first men engaged in bloody and pointless prestige battles, only this time with modern weapons. ... The two problems are related to one another, for the absence of regular and constructive outlets for *mega-lothymia* may simply lead to its later resurgence in an extreme and pathological form.[84]

Notes

Foreword

1. See, for instance, Damian Thompson, *The End of Time: Faith and Fear in the Shadow of the Millennium*, Sinclair-Stevenson, London, 1996.
2. Steve Smith, 'Power and Truth: A Reply to William Wallace', *Review of International Studies*, Vol. 23, No. 4, 1997.
3. On the 'inarticulacy of the good' in International Relations, see Mark Neufeld, 'Identity and the Good in International Relations Theory', *Global Society: Journal of Interdisciplinary International Relations*, Vol. 10, No. 1, 1996, pp. 43–56; and the reply by Roger Epp, 'On Making a Place for the "Good" in International Ethics: A Response to Mark Neufeld', *Global Society: Journal of Interdisciplinary International Relations*, Vol. 10, No. 2, 1996, pp. 191–3.

2. The Construction of Ideologies in the Twentieth Century

1. These four perspectives are derived from the useful categorisation made by Ngaire Woods in 'The Uses of Theory in the Study of International Relations', in Ngaire Woods (ed.), *Explaining International Relations since 1945*, Oxford University Press, Oxford, 1996, pp. 13–20.
2. For recent reassessment of the impact of the idealist tradition in IR see David Long and Peter Wilson (eds), *Thinkers of the Twenty Years Crisis*, Clarendon Press, Oxford, 1995. In the United States realist scepticism towards the pretensions of idealism really took off in the middle 1930s following the establishment of the Yale Institute of International Studies in 1935. It was also aided by the work of Howard M. Earle at the Institute for Advanced Study at Princeton. See Grayson Kirk, *The Study of International Relations in American Colleges and Universities*, Council on Foreign Relations, New York, 1947.
3. Hans Morgenthau, *Politics Among Nations: The Struggle for Power and Peace*, Alfred A. Knopf, New York, 1967, pp. 83–4.
4. Alan Cassels, *Ideology and International Relations in the Modern World*, Routledge, London, 1996, p. 240.
5. E. H. Carr, *The Twenty Years Crisis*, Macmillan, London, 1939.
6. Long and Wilson (eds), *Thinkers of the Twenty Years Crisis*.
7. Ronen P. Palen and Brook M. Blair, 'The Idealist Origins of the Realist Theory of International Relations', *Review of International Studies*, Vol. 19, 1993, pp. 385–99. See also Martin Thom, *Republics, Nations and Tribes*, Verso, London, 1995, for a more detailed historical treatment of this theme.
8. This was also a time when close links were forged between IR departments in the US and the foreign policy establishment in Washington.
9. For an analysis of this debate, see Nathan Liebowitz, *Daniel Bell and the Agony of Modern Liberalism*, Greenwood Press, Westport, CT, 1985.

10. Noam Chomsky, *American Power and the New Mandarins*, Penguin Books, Harmondsworth, 1969.

11. Franz Schurmann, *The Logic of World Power*, Pantheon Books, New York, 1974, p. 561.

12. Ibid., p. 403.

13. Immanuel Wallerstein, *The Capitalist World Economy*, Cambridge University Press, Cambridge, 1977, p. 22.

14. See in particular Robert Keohane and Joseph Nye, *Power and Interdependence*, Little Brown, Boston, 1977.

15. Long and Wilson, (eds), *Thinkers of the Twenty Years Crisis*.

16. John A. Hall, 'Ideas and the Social Sciences', in Judith Goldstein and Robert O. Keohane (eds.), *Ideas and Foreign Policy*, Cornell University Press, Ithaca, NY and London, 1993, pp. 31–54.

17. Andrew Linklater, 'The Problem of Community in International Relations', *Alternatives*, Vol. 15, 1990, pp. 135–53.

18. I am currently involved in a project to explore the impact of this fourth dimension entitled *Weapons States and Warlords: The Militarisation of Ethnic and Sub-state Conflict* (Macmillan, London, forthcoming).

19. John Vincent, *Realpolitik*, in James Mayall (ed.), *The Community of States*, Allen and Unwin, London, 1982, p. 76. See also Cassels, *Ideology and International Relations*, p. 70.

20. Cited in Barry Rubin, *Paved with Good Intentions: The American Experience and Iran*, Penguin Books, Harmondsworth, 1981, p. 100.

21. Shah to President Eisenhower, 20 November 1956, *Eisenhower Library*, cited in ibid., p. 97.

22. Larry Cable, *Conflict of Myths: The Development of American Counter Insurgency Doctrine and the Vietnam War*, New York University Press, New York and London, 1986, p. 5.

23. Fred Halliday, 'The Sixth Great Power: On the Study of Revolution and International Relations', *Review of International Studies*, Vol. 16, 1990, p. 215.

24. This process is examined in more detail in Paul B. Rich and Richard Stubbs (eds), *The Counter Insurgent State: Guerrilla Warfare and State Building in the Twentieth Century*, Macmillan, Basingstoke, 1997.

25. Ahmad Ashraf, 'From the White Revolution to the Islamic Revolution', in Saeed Rahnema and Sohrab Behdad (eds), *Iran After the Revolution: Crisis of an Islamic State*, I.B.Tauris, London, 1995, p. 22.

26. Rubin, *Paved with Good Intentions*, pp. 104–15. Raymond Seidelman, *Disenchanted Realists: Political Science and the American Crisis*, New York State University Press, Albany, NY, 1985.

27. Ashraf, 'White Revolution', p. 35.

28. Rubin, *Paved with Good Intentions*, p. 130.

29. For an assessment of Al-e Ahmad's thought, see Roy Mottahedeh, *The Mantle of the Prophet*, Penguin Books, Harmondsworth, 1985, esp. pp. 287–323. See also Nikki R. Keddie, *Roots of Revolution: An Interpretative History of Modern Iran*, Yale University Press, New Haven, CT and London, 1981, esp. pp. 183–205.

30. Mehrzad Boroujerdi, 'Gharbzadegi: The Dominant Intellectual Discourse of Pre- and Post-Revolutionary Iran', in Samih K. Farsoun and Mehrdad Mashayekhi (eds), *Iran: Political Culture in the Islamic Republic*, Routledge, London and New York, 1992, pp. 36–41.

31. Mottahedeh, *Mantle of the Prophet*, pp. 330–31.

32. Theda Skocpol, 'Rentier State and Shi'a Islam in the Iranian Revolution', *Theory and Society*, Vol. 11, 1982, pp. 265–83. Repr. in *Social Revolutions in the Modern World*, Cambridge University Press, Cambridge, 1994, pp. 240–54.

33. See Said Amir Arjomand, 'Iran's Islamic Revolution in Comparative Perspective',

World Politics, Vol. XXXVIII, No. 3, April 1986, p. 387. A reassessment of the role of cultural and ideological factors has begun to take place among theorists of revolution. See for example, Jack A. Goldstone, 'Ideology, Cultural Frameworks, and the Process of Revolution', *Theory and Society*, Vol. 20, 1991, pp. 405–53; John Foran, 'Theories of Revolution Revisited: Toward a Fourth Generation', *Sociological Theory*, Vol. 11, No. 1, March 1993, pp. 1–17; Arthur N. Gilbert and James F. Cole, 'Cambodia, Iran and Modern Revolutionary Theory', paper presented to the International Studies Association Convention, Acapulco, 23–27 March 1993.

    34. Fred Halliday, *Islam and the Myth of Confrontation*, I.B.Tauris, London, 1996, pp. 46–7.

    35. Said Amir Arjomand, 'Traditionalism in Twentieth-Century Iran', in Said Amir Arjomand (ed.), *From Nationalism to Revolutionary Islam*, Macmillan, Basingstoke, 1984, pp. 195–231.

    36. Olivier Roy, *The Failure of Political Islam*, I.B.Tauris, London, 1994, pp. 174–5. See also Nikki R. Keddie, 'Why has Iran been so revolutionary', in H. Amirahmadi and N. Entessan (eds), *Reconstruction and Regional Diplomacy in the Persian Gulf*, Routledge, London and New York, 1992, pp. 19–32.

    37. Ibid., p. 172.

    38. H. E. Chehabi, 'Religion and Politics in Iran: How Theocratic is the Islamic Republic?', *Daedalus*, Vol. 120, No. 3, Summer 1991, p. 73; Roy, *Failure of Political Islam*, p. 174.

    39. Cited in Chehabi, 'Religion and Politics in Iran', p. 82.

    40. Ibid., p. 85.

    41. Philip G. Phillip, 'The Islamic Revolution in Iran: Its Impact on Foreign Policy', in Stephen Chan and Andrew J. Williams (eds), *Renegade States: The Evolution of Revolutionary Foreign Policy*, Manchester University Press, Manchester and New York, 1994, p. 122.

    42. See for example Daniel Pipes and Patrick Clawson, 'Ambitious Iran, Troubled Neighbours', *Foreign Affairs*, Vol. 72, No. 1, Spring 1993, pp. 1245–6.

    43. Adeed Dawisha, 'Islam in Foreign Policy: Some Methodological Issues', in Adeed Dawisha (ed.), *Islam in Foreign Policy*, Cambridge University Press, Cambridge, 1983, p. 4. Fred Halliday, 'Iranian Foreign Policy since 1979', in Juan R. I. Cole and Nikki R. Keddie (eds), *Shi'ism and Social Protest*, Yale University Press, New Haven, CT and London, 1986, pp. 88–107.

    44. R. K. Ramazani, *Revolutionary Iran: Challenge and Response in the Middle East*, Johns Hopkins University Press, Baltimore, MD and London, 1988, p. 82.

    45. David Hirst, 'Terror, Trade and the Lure of Oil', *The Guardian*, 4 February 1997.

    46. Crawford Young, *Ideology and Development in Africa*, Yale University Press, New Haven, CT and London, 1982.

    47. Evan Luard, *International Society*, Macmillan, Basingstoke, 1990, p. 103.

    48. Anthony Smith, 'National Identity and the Idea of European Unity', *International Affairs*, Vol. 68, No. 1, 1992, pp. 55–76.

    49. Yasemin Nuhoglu Soysal, 'Changing Citizenship in Europe: Remarks on Postnational Membership and the National State', in David Cesarani and Mary Fulbrook (eds), *Citizenship, Nationality and Migration in Europe*, Routledge, London and New York, 1996, pp. 17–28.

    50. Benyamin Neuberger, 'National Self-Determination: Dilemmas of a Concept', *Nations and Nationalism*, Vol. 1, No. 3, 1995, pp. 297–325.

3. International Relations after the Cold War

I am grateful to Dr Jarrod Wiener for his substantive comments and editorial advice in the preparation of this chapter.

1. See, for instance, Fred Halliday, *The Making of the Second Cold War*, Verso, London, 1983.

2. Donella H. Meadows, et al., *The Limits to Growth: A Report for the Club of Rome's Project on the Predicament of Mankind*, Pan, London, 1974.

3. Fernand Braudel, *The Mediterranean*, Harper & Row, New York, 1972.

4. Michael Mann, *The Sources of Social Power*, Cambridge University Press, Cambridge, 1986.

5. Hedley Bull, *The Anarchical Society*, Macmillan, London, 1977.

6. David Mitrany, *A Working Peace System*, Quadrangle Books, Chicago, 1966; John Burton, *Systems, States, Diplomacy and Rules*, Cambridge University Press, Cambridge, 1968; Karl Deutsch, *The Nerves of Government*, The Free Press, New York, 1963; and James N. Rosenau, *Linkage Politics*, The Free Press, New York, 1969.

7. See Michael Banks, 'The Evolution of International Relations Theory', in Michael Banks (ed.), *Conflict in World Society*, Harvester, Brighton, 1984, pp. 3–22.

8. For instance, Kenneth Waltz, *Theory of International Politics*, Addison-Wesley, London, 1979. See also Robert Keohane (ed.), *Neorealism and its Critics*, Columbia University Press, New York, 1986.

9. For instance, Robert Keohane and Joseph Nye, *Power and Interdependence: World Politics in Transition*, Little Brown, Boston, 1977.

10. Oran Young, *International Cooperation*, Cornell University Press, Ithaca, NY and London, 1989.

11. John W. Burton, *World Society*, Cambridge University Press, Cambridge, 1972.

12. Mitrany, *A Working Peace System*.

13. See the contribution of Martin Shaw in this volume.

14. Halford Makinder, *Democratic Ideals and Reality*, Henry Holt, New York, 1919; Alfred Thayer Mahan, *The Influence of Sea Power Upon History, 1660–1783*, Methuen, London, 1965; and Harold and Margaret Sprout, *The Ecological Perspective in Human Affairs*, Greenwood Press, London, 1979.

15. George Modelski, *Long Cycles in World Politics*, Macmillan, London, 1987; and Modelski (ed.), *Exploring Long Cycles*, Pinter, London, 1987.

16. Immanuel Wallerstein, *The Modern World System: Capitalist Agriculture and the Origins of the World Economy in the Sixteenth Century*, Academic Press, New York, 1974; and Wallerstein, *The Modern World System II: Mercantilism and the Consolidation of the European World Economy*, Academic Press, New York, 1980.

17. See Bull, *Anarchical Society*; and Martin Wight, *Power Politics*, Holmes and Meier, New York, 1979.

18. Michael Banks, 'Where We Are Now', *Review of International Studies*, Vol. 11, 1985, pp. 215–33, at p. 217.

19. John W. Burton and Tarja Värynen, 'The End of International Relations?', in A. J. R. Groom and Margot Light (eds), *Contemporary International Relations: A Guide to Theory*, Pinter, London, 1994, pp. 69–80, at p. 76.

20. See A. J. R. Groom and Dominic Powell, 'From World Politics to Global Governance: A Theme in Need of a Focus', in Groom and Light (eds), *Contemporary International Relations*.

4. Ideas and the Creation of Successive World Orders

1. Nicholas J. Cull, 'Selling Peace: The Origins, Promotion and Fate of the Anglo-American New Order during the Second World War', *Diplomacy and Statecraft*, Vol. 7, No. 1,

March 1996, p. 1; Eric Hobsbawm, *Age of Extremes: The Short Twentieth Century, 1914–1991*, Michael Joseph, London, 1994, p. 563.

2. John Lewis Gaddis, *We Know Now: Rethinking Cold War History*, Clarendon Press, Oxford, 1997, p. 283.

3. Francis Fukuyama, *The End of History and the Last Man*, The Free Press, New York, 1992. For a summary of Fukuyama's thesis, see Paul Bacon's contribution to this volume. For an excellent short analysis of Fukuyama, see Chris Brown, 'The End of History', in Alex Danchev (ed.), *Fin de Siècle: The Meaning of the Twentieth Century*, I.B.Tauris, London, pp. 1–19.

4. One example of the conspiracy approach is that of Noam Chomsky, whose *World Orders, Old and New*, Pluto Press, London, 1994, is a farrago of invective and unsubstantiated polemic against the United States and, on occasion, its 'loyal subsidiary' Britain. An otherwise excellent study that looks at the problem of global order but is a bit dated by taking the 'paradigms' of International Relations too seriously is R. D. McKinlay and R. Little, *Global Problems and World Order*, Pinter, London, 1986. Other writers use a more interesting historical framework and include John A. Hall's *International Orders*, Polity Press, Oxford, 1996, and Andreas Osiander, *The States System of Europe, 1640–1990: Peacemaking and the Conditions of International Stability*, Oxford University Press, Oxford, 1994, without forgetting, of course, Henry Kissinger, *Diplomacy*, Simon and Schuster, New York, 1994. It is in this latter tradition that this chapter would modestly like to be placed.

5. A good entry into de Tocqueville's way of thinking can be gained from François Furet, *Penser la Révolution française*, Editions Gallimard, Paris, 1978, p. 33.

6. Alfred Cobban, *National Self-Determination*, Oxford University Press/Royal Institute of International Affairs, London, 1945, p. 13.

7. Christopher Coker, *War and the Twentieth Century: A Study of War and Modern Consciousness*, Brassey's, London, 1994, p. 4.

8. Robert W. Cox with Timothy J. Sinclair, *Approaches to World Order*, Cambridge University Press, Cambridge, 1996.

9. The book is to be called: *Failed Imagination?: New World Orders of the Twentieth Century in Historical Perspective* (Manchester University Press, forthcoming).

10. Kissinger, *Diplomacy*, pp. 47 and 50.

11. I am thinking here in particular of the work of writers like Gabriel Kolko, William Appleman Williams and Gar Alperovitz. For an interesting discussion of their writing and that of their 'traditionalist' opponents see Gaddis, *We Know Now*, Chapter 10, 'The New Cold War History: First Impressions'.

12. The literature on Woodrow Wilson's foreign policy is of course vast. In particular we must mention the massive 42-volume edition of Wilson's speeches and writings by Arthur J. Link; Arno J. Mayer's *Political Origins of the New Diplomacy, 1917–18*, Vintage, New York, 1970, and his *Politics and Diplomacy of Peacemaking: Containment and Counterrevolution at Versailles*, Alfred A. Knopf, New York, 1967; Thomas J. Knock, *To End All Wars: Woodrow Wilson and the Quest for a New World Order*, Oxford University Press, Oxford, 1992, *passim*.

13. Knock, *To End All Wars*, pp. 76–8 and 112–15.

14. Wilson, quoted by Osiander, *The States System of Europe*, p. 254.

15. Quoted by Walter Kendall, *The Revolutionary Movement in Britain*, Weidenfeld and Nicholson, London, 1969, p. 96. For a detailed analysis of Bolshevik and Socialist moves for peace, see Mayer, *Political Origins*.

16. Point XIII, an observation that I owe to Heater. Heater has an interesting detailed discussion of the parallels and contrasts of Lloyd George's statements and those of Lenin, Trotsky and the Inquiry about Czarist Russian as well as Ottoman and Austro-Hungarian territories: Derek Heater, *National Self-Determination: Woodrow Wilson and his Legacy*, Macmillan, London, 1994, pp. 42–6.

17. Mayer, *Political Origins*, pp. 339–44.

18. A process described by James Der Derian as 'anti' or 'neo-diplomacy', Der Derian, *Diplomacy*, Blackwell, Oxford, 1986.

19. Arguably 'Human Rights' are also part of the NWO agenda in so far as they were mentioned within the Charter of the United Nations and then developed within the UN structure. However, a proper consideration of them would require far more thought than we have space for here and they arguably did not form a central part of the Wilsonian or Rooseveltian agendas but were rather a later development of them. For a discussion of the links to the NWO agenda, see Mortimer Sellers (ed.), *The New World Order: Sovereignty, Human Rights and the Self-Determination of Peoples*, Berg, Oxford, 1996. For a wider discussion of human rights, see R. J. Vincent, *Human Rights and International Relations*, Cambridge University Press, Cambridge, 1986, and Jack Donnelly, *International Human Rights*, Westview Press, Boulder, CO, 1993.

20. An excellent consideration of this point can be found in Seamus Dunn and T. G. Fraser (eds), *Europe and Ethnicity: World War I and Contemporary Ethnic Conflict*, Routledge, London, 1996. See also Daniel Moynihan, *Pandaemonium: Ethnicity in International Politics*, Oxford University Press, Oxford, 1993; and Walker Connor (ed.), *Ethnonationalism: The Quest for Understanding*, Princeton University Press, Princeton, NJ, 1994.

21. George Kennan, 'Russia and the Post-war Settlement', Summer 1942, Kennan Papers, Princeton University Library, Box 25/4, Princeton, NJ. The emphasis is Kennan's.

22. C. K. Webster, *British Diplomacy 1813–1815: Selected Documents Dealing with the Reconstruction of Europe*, G. Bell and Sons, London, 1921.

23. Osiander, *The States System of Europe*, p. 198.

24. Cobban, *National Self-Determination*, p. 124.

25. Heater, *National Self-Determination*, pp. 18, 43 and 95 (quoting Wilson's speech of 4 September 1919 (from Link et al., 1990, p. 10)). Point V of the Fourteen Points says that there should be 'A free, open-minded, and absolutely impartial adjustment of all colonial claims, based upon the principle that in determining all such questions of sovereignty the interest of the populations concerned must be given equal weight with the equitable claims of the government whose title is to be determined.'

26. Curzon wrote that Geddes (Lloyd George's main confidante in Cabinet) and Walter Long 'revel in the thought of the British flag flying over Constantinople, [and] ... think the Turk is not such a bad fellow after all ... and are firmly convinced that the only people who can solve this or any other problem are the British'. Curzon to Balfour, 20 August 1919, Balfour Papers, British Library, Mss 49734.

27. If the population of pre-war and post-war Hungary is calculated, it went from 18.2 million to 7.6 million, with 3.425 million of these being Magyar: see Miklos Molnár, *Histoire de la Hongrie*, Hatier, Paris, 1996, esp. Chapter VI.

28. The best contemporary study was produced by The Royal Institute of International Relations (RIIA), set up as a result of Versailles: see Cobban, *National Self-Determination*.

29. Hardinge quoted by Heater, *National Self-Determination*, p. 79, in turn quoting Jane Sharp, *The Versailles Settlement*, Macmillan, London, 1991, p. 156. Balfour to Curzon, 2 March 1919, and Curzon to Balfour, 2 March 1919, Balfour Papers, British Library, Mss 49734.

30. Heater, *National Self-Determination*, p. 78; Cobban, *National Self-Determination*, p. 28.

31. See James Mayall, *Nationalism and International Society*, Cambridge University Press, Cambridge, 1990; and Robert Jackson, *Quasi States: Sovereignty, International Relations and the Third World*, Cambridge University Press, Cambridge, 1990.

32. E. H. Carr, *The Twenty Years Crisis*, Macmillan, London, 1939.

33. Cobban, *National Self-Determination*, pp. 2–3.

34. Norman Angell, *The Great Illusion: A Study of the Relation of Military Power to National*

Advantage, William Heinemann, London, 1910. *The Great Illusion* stated the classic liberal belief that war had become impossible between the powers due to their economic interdependence. For a discussion of Angell's thinking see J. D. B. Miller, *Norman Angell and the Futility of War: Peace and the Public Mind*, Macmillan, London, 1986.

35. For a discussion of Keynes and Versailles, see Robert Skidelsky, *John Maynard Keynes: The Economist as Saviour, 1920–1937*, Macmillan, London, 1992; Karl Polanyi, *The Great Transformation: The Political and Economic Origins of Our Time*, Beacon Press, New York, 1957, originally published by Reinhart and Company, 1944.

36. John Maynard Keynes, *The Economic Consequences of the Peace*, Brace and Howe, New York, 1920, pp. 3–4 and 29.

37. Michael J. Hogan, *Informal Entente: The Private Structure of Cooperation in Anglo-American Economic Diplomacy*, Columbia University Press, New York, 1977, p. 1.

38. Ibid., p. 6.

39. Roosevelt to Eichelberger, 12 May 1941. The statement was probably drafted by Secretary of State Cordell Hull, whose central belief was in the possibility of spreading 'civilisation' through free trade. Roosevelt Official files, 4351.

40. John Foster Dulles, 'A North American Contribution to World Order', speech delivered on 20 June 1939 to a Canadian and American audience in New York State. It is significant that this was the first document considered by the Chatham House 'World Order (Group XIX)' in 1939, the main think-tank in Britain on the post-war order, which became the 'Committee on Reconstruction' in February 1941: Chatham House Archives, 9/18.

41. See, for example, Paul Hirst and Grahame Thompson, *Globalization in Question*, Polity Press, Oxford, 1996.

42. Peter Wilson, 'Introduction', in David Long and Peter Wilson (eds), *Thinkers of the Twenty Years' Crisis: Inter-War Idealism Reassessed*, Clarendon Press, Oxford, 1995, pp. 9–11.

43. David Long and Peter Wilson (eds), *Thinkers of the Twenty Years' Crisis: Inter-War Idealism Reassessed*, Clarendon Press, Oxford, 1995.

44. Zaki Laïdi, 'Power and Purpose in the International System', in Laïdi, *Power and Purpose after the Cold War*, Berg, Oxford, 1995, p. 9 and *passim*.

45. See my *Reorganising Eastern Europe* and *New Forms of Security: Views from Central, Eastern and Western Europe* (edited with Pal Dunay and Gabor Kardos), both Dartmouth Publishing, Aldershot, 1994 and 1995.

46. East European theorists of IR are now making some very interesting contributions to this debate: see, for example, Rein Müllerson (an Estonian), *International Law, Rights and Politics*, Routledge/LSE, London, 1994.

47. Hall, *International Orders*, p. 168.

48. The most vocal advocate of this latter belief is Chomsky, in his *World Orders, Old and New*. In an excellent review of this book Anthony Giddens manages to combine sympathy for Chomsky's polemic with the sad admission that 'Communism ... fell, not only, or even primarily, because of the hostile attitudes adopted by the Western powers: it collapsed because socialist thought ... turned out to have elemental shortcomings', Giddens, 'Oh, What a Profitable Peace!', *Times Higher Educational Supplement*, 18 November 1994.

49. Laïdi, *Power and Purpose*, pp. 11 and 12.

50. The thought comes of course from Francis Fukuyama, *The End of History and the Last Man*, p. xi.

51. Samuel P. Huntington, 'The Clash of Civilisations?', *Foreign Affairs*, Vol. 72, No. 3, Summer 1993, pp. 22–49; expanded in his *The Clash of Civilisations and the Remaking of World Order*, Simon and Schuster, New York, 1996. But see Donald Puchala, 'International Encounters of Another Kind', *Global Society: Journal of Interdisciplinary International Relations*, Vol. 11, No. 1, 1997, pp. 5–30.

52. In his excellent little book *Human Rights and International Relations*, John Vincent makes

the case that the notion of human rights is an essentially Western construct. Whether one takes the view that this therefore diminishes their validity depends on whether one thinks there are alternative viable or morally justifiable constructs that are 'better'. I think not, a personal prejudice based on a belief in the benefits of bourgeois individualism, the relative success of which we are all benefiting from here in Oxford.

53. Francis Fukuyama, *Trust*, The Free Press, New York, 1995, and his *The End of Order*, The Social Market Foundation, London, 1997; Zaki Laïdi, *Un monde privé de sens*, Fayard, Paris, 1994.

6. Europe and the International System

An earlier version of this chapter was published in Paul Bairoch and Eric Hobsbawm (eds), *Sotria d'Europa*, Vol. 5, Enandi, Turin, 1996.

1. The following discussion, encompassing both areas of previous research on my part, and issues on which my anterior competence was exiguous, owes a great deal to many people with whom I have discussed these issues over more than two decades. Colleagues in various discussion groups in which these themes have been discussed – the Transnational Institute, the *New Left Review*, and the 1990s Group – will recognise many issues debated there. I would also like to thank Maxine Molyneux, Geoffrey Best, Michael Mann, and the late John Vincent for their insights and suggestions.

2. Eric Hobsbawm, *The Age of Revolution, 1789–1848*, Weidenfeld and Nicolson, London, 1962, Chapters 2 and 3.

3. For a perceptive survey of the issues, see Volker Berghahn, *Militarism: The History of an International Debate, 1861–1979*, Berg, Leamington Spa, 1981.

4. William H. McNeill, *The Pursuit of Power: Technology, Armed Force and Society since AD 1000*, University Chicago Press, Chicago, 1982; Michael Mann, *States, War and Capitalism*, Basil Blackwell, Oxford, 1988; E. J. Hobsbawm, *Age of Extremes: The Short Twentieth Century, 1914–1991*, Michael Joseph, London, 1994, Chapter 1, 'The Age of Total War'.

5. Brian Bond, *Victorian Military Campaigns*, Hutchinson, London, 1967; Donald Featherstone, *Colonial Small Wars*, David and Charles, Newton Abbott, 1973.

6. Guy Wint and Peter Calvocoressi, *Total War*, Penguin, Harmondsworth, 1972.

7. Ibid.

8. Andrew Wilson, *The Disarmer's Handbook of Military Technology and Hardware*, Penguin, Harmondsworth, 1983, pp. 36–7.

9. Euphemistically characterised by some as 'the expansion of the West', this process must also be seen as the forcible, military, economic and cultural subjugation of the non-European world by a small group of coastal European states.

10. These included not only the Romanov, Habsburg and Ottoman Empires, but also the superficially homogeneous sections of the British Empire, i.e. 'west Britain' or Ireland.

11. The others were the three Baltic states, Finland, Hungary and Czechoslovakia, and Ireland.

12. Justin Rosenberg, *The Empire of Civil Society: A Critique of the Realist Theory of International Relations*, Verso, London, 1994, Chapter 5, esp. pp. 139–42, 'Historicizing the Balance of Power'; Herbert Butterfield, 'The Balance of Power', in Herbert Butterfield and Martin Wright (eds), *Diplomatic Investigations: Essays in the Theory of International Politics*, Allen and Unwin, London, 1966.

13. The term 'Europe' was originally applied to central Greece, then to the whole of Greece, and by 500 BC to the entire land-mass behind it. Subsequent shifts, a result of invasion and migration, and of shifting boundaries of Christian domains, have altered its

application. For one perceptive cultural history, see Gerrard Delanty, *Inventing Europe: Idea, Identity, Reality*, Macmillan, London, 1995.

14. As Perry Anderson has pointed out, the very conceptualisation of the 'European' political and social order in such writers as Montesquieu and Hegel was based on an explicit contrast with its Ottoman and, subsequently extended, 'Asian' counterpart, *Lineages of the Absolutist State*, NLB, London, 1975, pp. 395–401, 462–72. By contrast, Europe has never been assertively defined as against its alterity to the West, America, only residually, as the 'old world'.

15. George Mosse, *Towards the Final Solution. A History of European Racism*, University of Wisconsin Press, Madison, 1987.

16. Bernard Semmel, *Imperialism and Social Reform: English Social and Imperial Thought, 1895–1914*, George Allen and Unwin, London, 1960; Michael Howard, 'Empire, Race and War in pre-1914 Britian', in *The Lessons of History*, Clarendon Press, Oxford, 1991.

17. The psychoanalytic argument, that the origins of the First World War lay in such practices as tying young German boys to a punitive chair, the '*Schreberstuhl*', may not explain the causes of the First World War but tells us much about one of its preconditions. See Morton Schatzmann, *Soul Murder: Persecution in the Family*, Allen Lane, London, 1973.

18. See Berghahn, *Militarism*.

19. The search for a binding link between capitalism and war, or modernity and war, runs through much of European social theory (Berhahn, *Militarism, passim*). One powerful line is that running from Max Weber through to theorists of the nuclear age, such as C. Wright Mills.

20. Michael Mann, 'Capitalism and Militarism', in *States, War and Capitalism.*

21. Jacques Godechot, *La Grande Nation*, Aubier Montaigne, Paris, 1983; Geoffrey Best, *War and Society in Revolutionary Europe, 1771–1870*, Fontana, London, 1982; George Rude, *Revolutionary Europe, 1783–1815*, Fontana, London, 1964.

22. Carl von Clausewitz, *On War*, Penguin Classics, Harmondsworth, 1982; Raymond Aron, *Clausewitz, Philosopher of War*, trans. Christine Booker and Norman Stone, Routledge and Kegan Paul, London, 1983.

23. Immanuel Kant, *Schriften zur Anthropologie, Geschichtsphilosophie, politik und Pedagogik*, Vol. 1, Suhrkamp, Frankfurt, 1977, pp. 195–251.

24. Michael Doyle, 'Kant, Liberal Legacies and Foreign Affairs', *Philosophy and Public Affairs*, Vol. 12, No. 3, 1983, and Vol. 12, No. 4, 1983; Andrew Hurrell, 'Kant and the Kantian Paradigm in International Relations', *Review of International Studies*, Vol. 16, No. 3, July 1990.

25. This argument is present in the work of, *inter alia*, Otto Hintze and Charles Tilly. Felix Gilbert (ed.), *The Historical Essays of Otto Hintze*, Oxford University Press, New York, 1975; Charles Tilly, 'War Making and State Making as Organised Crime', in Peter Evans et al. (eds), *Bringing the State Back In*, Cambridge University Press, Cambridge, 1985.

26. McNeil, *The Pursuit of Power*, p. 196.

27. Ibid., Chapter 8, 'Intensified Military–Industrial Interaction, 1884–1914'; Eric Hobsbawm, *The Age of Empire, 1875–1914*, Weidenfeld and Nicolson, London, 1987, Chapter 13. For a broader analysis, laying stress on inter-state conflict, see Michael Mann, *The Source of Social Power, Vol. 2, The Rise of Classes and Nation States*, Cambridge University Press, Cambridge, 1993.

28. Clive Trevilock, 'British Armaments and European Industrialisation, 1890–1914', *Economic History Review*, Vol. 26, 1973.

29. The term 'conscription' originates from the French law of 5 September 1798 and was in English use from 1800. Slight inflections of origin and value can still be detected in the terms found in other European languages – '*Wehrpflicht*' (i.e. military duty, German),

'*leva*' (i.e. levy, Italian), '*servicio miltar*' (Spanish). The American 'draft' approximates most to the Italian.

30. Joseph Schumpeter, 'The Sociology of Imperialisms', in *Imperialism, Social Classes*, Meridian, New York, 1974.

31. D. K. Fieldhouse, *The Theory of Capitalist Imperialism*, Longman, London, 1967; Tom Kemp, *Theories of Imperialism*, Dennis Dobson, London, 1967.

32. Theda Skocpol, *States and Social Revolutions*, Cambridge University Press, Cambridge, 1979; McNeil, *The Pursuit of Power*, p. 184.

33. Eric Hobsbawm, *The Age of Revolution*; Jacques Godechot, *La Grande Nation*.

34. Edmund Burke, 'Letters on a Regicide Peace', in *The Works and Correspondence of Edmund Burke*, Vol. 5, Francis and John Rivington, London, 1852. I have gone into greater detail on these issues in *Rethinking International Relations*, Macmillan, London, 1994, Chapter 4.

35. Joseph Klaits and Michael Haltzel (eds), *The Global Ramifications of the French Revolution*, Cambridge University Press, Cambridge, 1994.

36. Goran Therborn, 'The Rule of Capital and the Rise of Democracy', *New Left Review*, No. 103, May–June 1977, traces the close relationship of world war and of concessions by established elites to pressure for electoral reform. What the First World War left unachieved (e.g. female suffrage in France, Italy and Belgium), the Second World War completed.

37. Gabriel Kolko, *Century of War*, New Press, New York, 1994, Chapters 5–7; Arno Mayer, 'Internal Crisis and War since 1870', in Charles Bertrand (ed.), *Revolutionary Situations in Europe, 1917–1922*, Montreal, 1977.

38. Bernard Semmel (ed.), *Marxism and War*, Oxford University Press, Oxford, 1981.

39. Christopher Coker, *War and the 20th Century: The Impact of War on the Modern Consciousness*, Brassey's, London, 1994; Martin Shaw, *Post-Military Society*, Polity Press, Cambridge, 1991.

40. Kenneth Waltz, *Man, the State and War. A Theoretical Analysis*, Columbia University Press, New York, 1959; Mann, *States, War and Capitalism*. For a lucid and, in the end, troubled survey of the argument, see Raymond Aron, 'War and Industrial Society: A Reappraisal', *Millennium*, Vol. 7, No. 3, 1978–79.

41. I am particularly grateful to colleagues in the 1990s Discussion Group for clarification on this question.

7. Virtual Security

1. See Richard Ashley, 'The Eye of Power: The Politics of World Modelling', *International Organization*, Summer 1983, pp. 495–535.

2. See James Der Derian, *Antidiplomacy: Spies, Terror, Speed, and War*, Blackwell, Oxford, 1992, pp. 19–39; and 'Antidiplomacy, Intelligence Theory, and Surveillance Practice', *Intelligence and National Security Journal*, July 1993.

3. *Independence Day* also made the 8 July covers of *Time* ('Aliens have landed!') and *Newsweek* ('"Out there" – from "Independence Day" to "The X-Files", America is Hooked on the Paranormal'). And as the corner ribbon: 'Terror in the Gulf: How Shaky are the Saudis?').

4. This is a *Daily News* headline from 15 August. When asked whether there is a real 'X-Files' division at the FBI, former supervisory special agent Gregg McCrary replied: 'As close as we come is the unit I was in, the "Profiling Unit." It deals with the behavioral sciences, and bizarre and unusual crimes – sex crimes, serial killers, etc. There isn't any real need for an X-Files because there aren't any aliens running around – but there's enough bizarre human behavior to keep us busy.' *Entertainment Weekly*, 'The War of the Worlds: In an Alien Nation, Whom Do You Trust?', 29 November 1996, p. 35.

5. See Ole Waever, 'Figures of International Thought: Introducing Persons Instead of Paradigms', in *The Future of International Relations: Masters in the Making?*, Routledge, London and New York, 1997, pp. 1–37.

6. And to put in a plug for the new on-line journal, *Theory & Event*: 'http://muse. jhu.edu./journals/theory_&_event'.

7. See Der Derian, *Antidiplomacy*; and 'The (S)pace of International Relations: Simulation, Surveillance, and Speed', *International Studies Quarterly*, September, 1990, pp. 295–310.

8. *Newseek*, 11 March 1991, p. 17.

9. In a footnote – the only footnote – in his most popular book, *Strategy*, Hart's contribution to the Salisbury Plain exercises is acknowledged. The strategy and tactics of the Mongols are dealt with more fully in the author's earlier book *Great Captains Unveiled*, which was chosen for the first experimental Mechanized Force in 1927. See B. H. Liddell Hart, *Strategy*, 2nd rev. edn, Signet, New York, 1974, p. 62.

10. See B. H. Liddell Hart, *Paris, or the Future of War*, New York, 1925; and B. H. Liddell Hart and Charles De Gaulle: 'The Doctrines of Limited Liability and Mobile Defense', in Gordon Craig and Felix Gilbert (eds), *Brian Bond and Martin Alexander, Makers of Modern Strategy from Machiavelli to the Nuclear Age*, Clarendon Press, Oxford, 1986, pp. 598–623.

11. Eric Barnouw, *A Tower in Babel: A History of Broadcasting in the United States*, Vol. 1 (to 1933), Oxford University Press, New York, 1966, p. 231.

12. Paul Virilio, *War and Cinema: The Logistics of Perception*, trans. Patrick Camiller, Verso, New York, 1989, p. 4.

13. Interview, Andrew Marshall, 21 June 1996.

8. Ideas and Economy in the Twentieth Century

1. See F. A. Hayek, *The Counter-Revolution of Science: Studies on the Abuse of Reason*, Liberty Fund, Indianapolis, 1979.

2. Mihaly Simai, 'The Changing State System and the Future of Global Governance', *Global Society: Journal of Interdisciplinary International Relations*, Vol. 11, No. 2, 1997, p. 145.

3. E. H. Carr, *The Twenty Years' Crisis*, Macmillan, London, 1939, pp. 80–1.

4. Francis Fukuyama, *The End of History and the Last Man*, Hamish Hamilton, London, 1992, p. 327.

9. Reconciling Regionalism and Multilateralism

1. E. H. Carr, *The Twenty Years' Crisis, 1919–1939*, 2nd edn, Macmillan, Basingstoke, 1991, p. 28.

2. See George Orwell, *Nineteen Eighty-Four*, Secker and Warburg, London, 1949.

3. Samuel P. Huntington, 'The Clash of Civilizations?', *Foreign Affairs*, Vol. 72, No. 3, Summer 1993, pp. 22–49.

4. Lester C. Thurow, *Head to Head: The Coming Battle among Japan, Europe, and America*, William Morrow and Company, New York, 1992, pp. 27–66.

5. Richard Stubbs and Geoffrey R. D. Underhill, 'Global Trends, Regional Patterns', in R. Stubbs and G. R. D. Underhill (eds), *Political Economy and the Changing Global Order*, Macmillan, Basingstoke, 1994, p. 331.

6. Louise Fawcett, 'Regionalism in Historical Perspective', in Louise Fawcett and Andrew Hurrell (eds), *Regionalism in World Politics: Regional Organisation and International Order*, Oxford University Press, Oxford, 1995, pp. 9–36.

7. John Gerard Ruggie, 'Multilateralism: The Anatomy of an Institution', in John Gerard Ruggie (ed.), *Multilateralism Matters: The Theory and Praxis of an Institutional Form*, Columbia

University Press, New York, 1993, pp. 8–14. Other key works examining the role of multilateralism in world order are: Robert W. Cox, 'Multilateralism and World Order', *Review of International Studies*, Vol. 18, No. 2, April 1992, pp. 161–80; and Philip G. Cerny, 'Plurilateralism: Structural Differentiation and Functional Conflict in the Post-Cold War World Order', *Millennium: Journal of International Studies*, Vol. 22, No. 1, 1993, pp. 27–51.

8. This contention is not made in ignorance of more limited forms of multilateralism. Rather, the term multilateralism is used here as a means of referring to a wider globalist agenda. Strictly speaking, multilateralism is taken to mean the organisation of inter-state activities in groups of three or more in accordance with certain generalised principles of conduct. Limited multilateralism such as NATO and EU are probably better described, as Karsten Voigt implies, as 'regional' multilateralism. See Karsten Voigt, 'German Interest in Multilateralism', *AussenPolitik*, Vol. 47, No. 2, 1996, pp. 107–16.

9. *General Agreement on Tariffs and Trade*, Article I.

10. *General Agreement on Tariffs and Trade*, Article I, paragraph 1.

11. On 30 September 1997 the Member states of the WTO agreed to terminate the plurilateral Bovine Meat and International Dairy Agreements effective from 1 January 1998. This action was taken in response to the establishment of WTO committees on Agriculture and on Sanitary and Phytosanitary Measures which deal, to a large degree, with trade policy-related matters affecting agricultural products.

12. James H. Mittelman, 'Rethinking the "New Regionalism" in the Context of Globalization', *Global Governance*, Vol. 2, No. 2, May–August 1996, p. 190. Also see Thomas O. Hueglin, 'Better Small and Beautiful than Big and Ugly? Regionalism, Capitalism, and the Postindustrial State', *International Political Science Review*, Vol. 10, No. 3, July 1989, p. 210.

13. Cerny, 'Plurilateralism', p. 36.

14. Paul Taylor, *International Organization in the Modern World: The Regional and Global Process*, Pinter, London, 1993, p. 7.

15. *General Agreement on Tariffs and Trade*, Article XXIV, paragraphs 2, 3, 4, 5, and 7.

16. Other instances exist where MFN can be suspended. These occur with regard to: adverse balance of payment situations (Article XII and XVII:*b* for less developed countries, GATT 1994, and Article XII of the GATS), newly-acceded Members (Article XIII of the WTO Establishing Agreement, and Article XXXV of the GATT), dumping (Article VI, GATT 1994), general and security exceptions (Articles XX and XXI, GATT 1994, and Articles XIV and XIV*bis* of the GATS), to sanction non-applying Members (Article XXII, Annex 2, WTO Establishing Agreement), and for the establishment of infant industries (Article XVIII:*a*, GATT 1994).

17. William R. Cline, 'Long-term Change in Foreign Trade Policy', in US Congress Joint Economic Committee Special Study on Economic Change, Volume 9, *The International Economy: US Role in a World Market*, US Government Printing Office, Washington, 1980, p. 188.

18. Bernard Hoekman and Michel Kostecki, *The Political Economy of the World Trading System: From GATT to WTO*, Oxford University Press, Oxford, 1995, p. 18.

19. Development became an issue in the GATT as early as 1954. See *Trends in International Trade: A Report by a Panel of Experts*, GATT Press, Geneva, 1958. On agriculture, see Jarrod Wiener, *Making Rules in the Uruguay Round of the GATT: A Study of International Leadership*, Dartmouth, Aldershot, 1995, pp. 62–95; and T. K. Warley, 'Agricultural Protectionism and Trade Policies', in Andrew Schonfield (ed.), *International Economic Relations of the Western World 1959–1971*, Vol. 1, Oxford University Press, London, 1976, pp. 292–336.

20. Mancur Olson, *The Logic of Collective Goods and the Theory of Groups*, Harvard University Press, Cambridge, MA,1965, p. 2.

21. See Keohane's interpretation of Axelrod and Richardson. Robert O. Keohane, 'Bar-

gaining Perversities, Institutions, and International Economic Relations', in P. Guerrieri and P. C. Padoan (eds), *The Political Economy of International Cooperation*, Croom-Helm, London, 1988, pp. 28–39. Also Robert Axelrod, *The Evolution of Cooperation*, Basic Books, New York, 1984; and Stephen D. Krasner, *Asymmetries in Japanese–American Trade: The Case for Specific Reciprocity*, Institute for International Studies, University of California, Berkeley, 1987.

22. *Regionalism and the World Trading System*, WTO Press, Geneva, 1995, p. 1.

23. WTO Press release, 18 April 1995.

24. *International Trade: Trends and Statistics*, WTO Press, Geneva, 1995, p. 11.

25. *Regionalism and the World Trading System*, p. 39.

26. *International Trade: Trends and Statistics*, p. 39.

27. Siegfried Schultz, 'Regionalisation of World Trade: Dead End or Way Out?', in Meine Pieter van Dijk and Sandro Sideri (eds), *Multilateralism versus Regionalism: Trade Issues after the Uruguay Round*, Frank Cass in association with the EADI, London, 1996, p. 31.

28. See, for example, Fred Halliday, *Islam and the Myth of Confrontation: Religion and Politics in the Middle East*, I.B.Tauris, London, 1996, p. 131.

29. However, as Bhagwati notes, this reasoning was developed after the inclusion of Article XXIV. See Jagdish Bhagwati, *The World Trading System at Risk*, Princeton University Press, Princeton, NJ, 1991, pp. 59–63.

30. Michael Hart, 'The GATT Uruguay Round, 1986–1993: The Setting and the Players', in Fen Olson Hampson (ed.), *Multilateral Negotiations: Lessons from Arms Control, Trade, and the Environment*, Johns Hopkins University Press, Baltimore, MD, 1995, p. 178.

31. Bruce Bueno de Mesquita, 'Multilateral Negotiations: A Spatial Analysis of the Arab–Israeli Dispute', *International Organisation*, Vol. 44, No. 3, Summer 1990, p. 317.

32. During the Uruguay Round, negotiations were also conducted in this manner as means of satisfying the need for domestic political elites to secure reciprocal satisfaction, as well as by employment of the principle–supplier rule, and other such methods. On political necessity, see Edmund Dell, 'Of Free Trade and Reciprocity', *The World Economy*, Vol. 9, No. 2, June 1986, p. 128; and Jagdish Bhagwati and Douglas Irwin, 'The Return of the Reciprocitarians – US Trade Policy Today', *The World Economy*, Vol. 10, No. 2, June 1987, pp. 111–12 and 117–19.

33. See S. H. Langhammer and J. P. Rolf, 'The Transatlantic Free Trade Area: Fuelling Trade Discrimination or Global Liberalization', *Journal of World Trade*, Vol. 30, No. 3, June 1996.

34. Stephen George, 'The European Union, 1992 and the Fear of "Fortress Europe"', in Andrew Gamble and Anthony Payne (eds), *Regionalism and World Order*, Macmillan, Basingstoke, 1996, pp. 26–8.

35. Paul Bowles and Brian Maclean, 'Regional Blocs: Can Japan be the Leader?', in Robert Boyer and Daniel Drache (eds), *States Against Markets: The Limits of Globalization*, Routledge, London, 1996, p. 156. Also see Andrew Gamble and Anthony Payne, 'Conclusion: The New Regionalism', in Gamble and Payne (eds), *Regionalism and World Order*, pp. 253–8.

36. Stephen Woolcock, 'Trade and Market Access Issues in US–EC Relations', *Paradigms: The Kent Journal of International Relations*, Vol. 7, No. 2, Winter 1993, p. 132. See also the updated version which appears as Woolcock, 'EU–US Commercial Relations and the Debate on a Transatlantic Free Trade Area', in J. Wiener (ed.), *The Transatlantic Relationship*, Macmillan, London, 1996, pp. 164–86.

37. Bowles and Maclean, 'Regional Blocs: Can Japan be the Leader?', p. 157.

38. Ibid., pp. 157–61.

39. UNCTAD, *World Investment Report 1995*, (TAD/INF/2620).

40. Malcolm Waters, *Globalization*, Routledge, London, 1995, p. 3.

41. Schultz, 'Regionalisation of World Trade', p. 33.
42. *Regionalism and the World Trading System*, p. 62.
43. The failure to implement strictly the specification of Article XXIV has been the concern of economists for years. See Bhagwati, *The World Trading System at Risk*, pp. 65–9.
44. *Regionalism and the World Trading System*, pp. 13–14.
45. Source: UNCTAD/WTO.
46. *International Trade: Trends and Statistics.*, pp. 27, 39.
47. See *WTO Focus*, January 1997, pp. 11, 15.

10. Foreign Direct Investment

1. UNCTAD, *UNCTAD Bulletin*, No. 26, May–June 1994, p. 3.
2. See Michael S. Minor, 'The Demise of Expropriation as an Instrument of LDC Policy', *Journal of International Business Studies*, Vol. 25, No. 1, 1994, esp. table on p. 180.
3. Stephen Hymer, 'The Multinational Corporation and the Law of Uneven Development', in J. N. Bhagwati (ed.), *Economics and World Order*, Macmillan, London, 1972, pp. 113–40. For a less radical thesis, see Raymond Vernon, *Sovereignty at Bay*, Basic Books, New York, 1971.
4. United Nations, General Assembly Resolution 1710 (XVI), 1961.
5. See Lawrence S. Finkelstein, 'The Politics of Value Allocation in the UN System', in Finkelstein (ed.), *Politics in the United Nations System*, Duke University Press, Durham, NC and London, 1988, pp. 1–41.
6. United Nations General Assembly Resolution 1803 (XVII) 1962. This hardened the language of previous Resolutions, such as that of United Nations General Assembly Resolution 626 (VII) of 21 December 1952 that provided that 'the right of peoples to use and exploit their natural wealth and resources is inherent in their sovereignty'.
7. Jiménez de Aréchaga, 'Stabilisation Clauses and International Law', *Receuil des Cours*, *Académie de Droit International*, 1978 (I), p. 159.
8. United Nations General Assembly Resolution 3281 (XXIX) of 12 December 1974, Chapter II, Article 2, 2(a).
9. United Nations Centre on Transnational Corporations (UNCTC), *Transnational Corporations in World Development: Trends and Prospects*, New York, 1988. It should be noted that there is a danger in extrapolating from this that the stock of private capital to developing countries has declined, since such figures mask the increase in mixed-ownership enterprises (MOEs) such as joint ventures between a host state and an MNC, particularly in former nationalised industries in the natural resource sector. Such new forms of investment (NFI) present a deviation from the relatively straightforward accountancy used to determine the stock of FDI in the developed world. See Peter Enderwick, 'Multinational Enterprises and Partial Privatisation of State-owned Enterprises', *International Business Review*, Vol. 3, No. 2, 1994, pp. 135–47; and A. M. F. Maniruzzaman, 'The New Generation of Energy and Natural Resource Development Agreements: Some Reflections', *Journal of Energy and Natural Resources Law*, No. 4, 1993, pp. 207–47.
10. See OECD, *Promoting Private Enterprise in Developing Countries*, OECD, Paris, 1990, p. 36.
11. This is, of course, a 'way forward' quite different from that envisioned by many Dependistas, such as that in the Conclusion of Leften S. Stavrianos's, *Global Rift: The Third World Comes of Age*, William Morrow, London, 1991.
12. See Minor, 'The Demise of Expropriation'.
13. For the latest articulation of his 'political ironies' thesis, see André Gunder Frank, 'Economic Ironies in World Politics: A Sequel to Political Ironies in the World Economy', *Economic and Political Weekly*, Vol. 26, No. 30, 1991.

14. See Mihály Simai, 'The Changing State System and the Future of Global Governance', *Global Society: Journal of Interdisciplinary International Relations*, Vol. 11, No. 2, 1996.

15. Minor, 'The Demise of Expropriation', p. 186.

16. The literature is voluminous. See, for example, André Gunder Frank, *Capitalism and Underdevelopment in Latin America*, Penguin, Harmondsworth, 1971; A. Emmanuel, *Unequal Exchange: A Study in the Imperialism of Trade*, New Left Books, London, 1972; Immanuel Wallerstein, *The Modern World System II: Mercantilism and the Consolidation of the European World Economy, 1600–1750*, Academic Press, New York, 1980.

17. Susan Strange and John Stopford, *Rival States, Rival Firms: Competition for World Market Shares*, Cambridge University Press, Cambridge, 1991, p. 228.

18. See 'Back in Fashion: Survey of Multinationals', *The Economist*, 27 March 1993.

19. 'See: 'Russians Invite Foreign Investment', *Financial Times*, 31 December 1991, p. 14; 'Moscow Aims for Foreign Investment', *Financial Times*, 14 April 1992, p. 2; 'Russia in Call for Oil Investment', *Financial Times*, 2 July 1992, p. 26; 'Russian Tax Holiday', *The Guardian*, 28 June 1994, p. 15.

20. See 'Ukraine Moves on Investment', *Financial Times*, 11 September 1991, p. 2.

21. See, for instance, Poland's 'Law on Companies with Foreign Participation', 4 July 1991, 30 *International Legal Materials*, 1991, p. 871, and the anticipation of it in 'Private US Funds for Poland', *The Times*, 22 March 1990, p. 8. See also: 'Great Eastern Gamble Starts to Look Safer', *The Times*, 29 October 1991, p. 33; 'The Worst May Well Be Over for Former Communist State in Transition', *The Guardian*, 9 January 1993, p. 13; 'Pace Hots Up in Dash for Cash', *The Guardian*, 22 May 1993, p. 39. Poland attracted US$2.7 billion of FDI in 1996, the most of all Eastern European states. See 'Emerging Market Indicators', *The Economist*, 1 November 1997, p. 146.

22. Vietnam's foreign investment law was amended in 1993. See (no author), 'Protection of Foreign Direct Investment in A New World Order: Vietnam – a Case Study', *Harvard Law Review*, Vol. 107, 1994. And in anticipation of this, see 'Vietnam May Lift Investment Curbs', *Financial Times*, 11 September 1992, p. 5.

23. 'North Korea Unveils Law on Foreign Investment', *Financial Times*, 21 October 1992, p. 6.

24. 'Cuba Opens Doors Wide to Foreign Investment', *Financial Times*, 11 June 1992, p. 6; 'Cuba to Facilitate Foreign Investment', *Financial Times*, 13 July 1992, p. 4.

25. 'Iran Removes Limit on Foreign Investment', *Financial Times*, 8 May 1992, p. 4.

26. F. J. Contractor, 'Do Government Policies Toward Foreign Investment Matter?', Rutgers University, *GSM Working Paper*, No. 90–15, July 1990.

27. 'Emerging Market Indicators', *The Economist*.

28. See S. Schneider and B. S. Frey, 'Economic and Political Determinants of Foreign Direct Investment', *World Development*, Vol. 13, No. 2, 1985, pp. 161–75; and UNCTAD, *World Investment Report 1993: Transnational Corporations and Integrated International Production*, (WIR93) United Nations Publications, Geneva, 1993.

29. Strange and Stopford, 'Rival States, Rival Firms', p. 30.

30. Minor, 'The Demise of Expropriation', p. 177.

31. See S. Friedman, *Expropriation in International Law*, Greenwood Press, Westport, CT, 1953 (1981), esp. pp. 1–5 and 140–2; Georg Schwarzenberger, *Foreign Investments and International Law*, Stevens and Sons, London, 1969, esp. p. 4; M. Sonorajah, *The Pursuit of Nationalised Property*, Martinus Nijhoff, Dordrecht, 1986, pp. 1–15.

32. Government of Eritrea, 'Investment Proclamation', Chapter 4, para. 13:1(a,b)2.

33. Maurice Mendelson, 'The Legal Character of General Assembly Resolutions: Some Considerations of Principle', in Kamal Hossain (ed.), *Legal Aspects of the New International Economic Order*, Pinter, London, 1980, esp. pp. 96–7.

34. Schwarzenberger, *Foreign Investments and International Law*, p. 188.

35. *Eastern Greenland Case* (1933), as cited in Ian Brownlie, *Principles of Public International Law*, 4th edn, Clarendon Press, Oxford, 1990, p. 18.

36. Cited by de Aréchaga, 'Stabilisation Clauses an International Law', p. 309. Emphases added.

37. United Nations General Assembly Resolution 1803 (XVII) of 14 December 1962.

38. 'Protection of Foreign Direct Investments in a New World Order', p. 1999.

39. See Friedman, *Expropriation in International Law*, pp. 204–11.

40. 'Russian Soviet Federated Republic: Law on Foreign Investments in the RSFSR' of 4 July 1991, *International Legal Materials*, Vol. 31, 1992, p. 397. After the dissolution of the RSFSR in 1991, this law came to refer to the Russian Federation.

41. 'Protection of Foreign Direct Investment in a New World Order', p. 2005.

42. In the case of Vietnam, there is also the issue that Article 23 of the Constitution, which has not been amended in light of the investment law, reserves the right of expropriation upon the payment of compensation, and it remains unclear as to whether the Law on Foreign Investment legally can supersede the Constitution. See Robert L. Wunker, 'The Laws of Vietnam Affecting Foreign Investment', *International Lawyer*, Vol. 28, No. 2, 1994, pp. 363–83, esp. p. 372.

43. 'Law on Foreign Investments in the RSFSR'.

44. See Martin Dixon, *Textbook on International Law*, Blackstone Press, Abingdon, 1990, pp. 149–54.

45. Minor, 'The Demise of Expropriation', p. 183.

46. Ingrid D. De Lupis, *Finance and Protection of Investments in Developing Countries*, Gower, Aldershot, 1987, p. 27.

47. A term used by O. Schachter, 'Stabilisation Clauses', Hague *Recueil des Cours, Académie de Droit International*, 1982 (V), p. 313.

48. It has been suggested that a choice-of-law clause stipulating international law can also be a stabilisation clause. However, as the only real legal effect of a stabilisation clause, as will be shown, is for the payment of compensation, and since an expropriation without compensation is an international delict, de Aréchaga contends that they are unnecessary (de Aréchaga, 'Stabilisation Clauses and International Law', p. 308).

49. *Texaco Overseas Petroleum and California Asiatic Oil Company v. The Government of the Libyan Arab Republic*, 53 *ILR* 1979, p. 395.

50. Ibid., p. 394.

51. *Libyan American Oil Company (Liamco) v. Government of the Libyan Arab Republic*, 62 *ILR*, (1982), pp. 169, 216.

52. Ibid., p. 170.

53. *Texaco v. Libyan Arab Republic, op. cit.*, p. 466.

54. *AGIP Spa v. The Government of the Popular Republic of The Congo*, 67 *ILR* 1984, p. 338.

55. *Liamco, op. cit.*, p. 192. For a discussion, see Alan Redfern, 'The Arbitration Between the Government of Kuwait and Aminoil', *British Yearbook of International Law*, Vol. 55, 1984, pp. 63–110, esp. pp. 101–2.

56. Samuel K. B. Asante, 'The Concept of Stability of Contractual Relations in the Transnational Investment Process', in Hossain (ed.), *Legal Aspects of the New International Economic Order*, esp. pp. 241–3.

57. A. M. F. Maniruzzaman, 'State Contracts with Aliens – The Questision of Unilateral Change by the State in Contemporary International Law', *Journal of International Arbitration*, Vol. 9, No. 4, 1992, p. 156.

58. Maniruzzaman, 'The New Generation of Energy and Natural Resource Development Agreements', p. 241.

59. See Sornarajah, *Pursuit of Nationalised Property, op. cit.*; Maniruzzaman, 'The New Generation of Energy and Natural Resource Development Agreements', and 'State Con-

tracts with Aliens', pp. 141–71; Pierre Barraz, 'The Legal Status of Oil Concessions', *Journal of World Trade Law*, Vol. 5, 1971, pp. 609–63.

60. *Aminoil, International Legal Materials*, Vol. 21, 1982, pp. 1021–22; Redfern, *Arbitration*, p. 102.

61. *Texaco v. Libyan Arab Republic*, p. 389.

62. *Liamco, op. cit.*

63. That is James N. Hyde, 'Permanent Sovereignty over Natural Wealth and Resources', *American Journal of International Law*, Vol. 50, 1956, pp. 854–67.

64. *Texaco v. Libyan Arab Republic*, para. 83.

65. *Liamco, op. cit.*, p. 189.

66. Maurice Mendelson, 'The Legal Character of General Assembly Resolutions: Some Considerations of Principle', in Hossain (ed.), *Legal Aspects of the New International Economic Order*, pp. 95–107.

67. Quoted in Sornarajah, *Pursuit of Nationalised Property*, pp. 122–3.

68. According to Article 53 of the Vienna Convention on the Law of Treaties.

69. Friedman, *Expropriation in International Law*, p. 128.

70. Brigitte Bollecker-Stern, 'The Legal Character of Emerging Norms Relating to the NIEO: Some Comments', in Hossain (ed.), *Legal Aspects of the New International Order*, p. 78.

71. See Sornarajah, *Pursuit of Nationalised Property*, pp. 91–5.

72. Cited in Philip Wood, *Law and Practice of International Finance*, Sweet & Maxwell, London, 1980, p. 5.

73. *Aminoil, op. cit.*

74. Schachter, 'Stabilisation Clauses', p. 314; de Aréchaga, 'Stabilisation Clauses and International Law', p. 307.

75. *Aminoil, op. cit.*, Article 17.

76. *Aminoil, op. cit.*, para. 88.

77. *Aminoil, op. cit.*, para. 94.

78. See Redfern, *Arbitration*, p. 102.

79. Rosalyn Higgins, 'Recent Trends in the International Law of Petroleum Concessions and Licences', *Recueil des Cours, Académie de Droit International*, 1982 (III), p. 303.

80. See Kamal Hossain, 'Introduction', in Hossain (ed.), *Legal Aspects of the New International Order*, p. 38.

81. 'Protection of Foreign Investments in a New World Order', p. 2000.

82. 'Russian Federation–United States Treaty Concerning the Encouragement and Reciprocal Protection of Investment', 17 June 1992.

83. 'Protection of Foreign Investments in a New World Order', p. 2000.

84. 'Argentina–United States: Treaty Concerning the Reciprocal Encouragement and Protection of Investment', 14 November 1991, *International Legal Materials*, Vol. 31, 1992, p. 124.

85. Friedman, *Expropriation in International Law*, p. 101.

86. Sornarajah, *Pursuit of Nationalised Property*, p. 40. See also p. 208.

87. Gillian White, 'The New International Economic Order: Principles and Trends', in Hazel Fox (ed.), *International Economic Law and Developing States: An Introduction*, The British Institute of International and Comparative Law, London, 1992, pp. 27–57, esp. pp. 44–7.

88. United Nations Centre on Transnational Corporations (UNCTC), *Bilateral Investment Treaties*, UN (1988), iii.

89. UNCTC, *Publications Review 1975–1989*, January 1989.

90. See DeAnne Julius, *Global Companies and Public Policy: The Growing Challenge of Foreign Direct Investment*, The Royal Institute of International Affairs and Pinter, London, 1990, esp. Appendix on pp. 109–22; Stopford and Strange, *Rival Strates, Rival Firms*, p. 37.

91. UNCTAD, *UNCTAD Bulletin*, No. 26, May–June 1994, p. 3.

92. 'Emerging Market Indicators', *The Economist*, 1 November 1997, p. 146.

93. International Monetary Fund, *World Economic Outlook, October 1992*, IMF, Washington, 1992, p. 5.

94. See Paul Hirst and Grahame Thompson, *Globalisation in Question*, Polity Press, Cambridge, 1995.

95. North American Free Trade Agreement, US Government Printing Office Publication 1992–330–817/70635, Art. 401 (b) and (d).

96. NAFTA, Annex 300–B, Section 2; Art. 404.

97. NAFTA, Arts. 402, 403.

98. See James Rochlin, *Discovering the Americas: The Evolution of Canadian Foreign Policy Towards Latin America*, UBC Press, Vancouver, 1994.

99. Canada had joined formally the OAS in 1972 as a Permanent Observer, but it took full membership, with voting rights, in 1989. See Rochlin, ibid, pp. 83, 193.

100. In 1941, Canada and Chile, along with other Latin American countries signed a number of Trade Agreements, and Canada opened a Trade Delegation in Chile the following year. See Rochlin, ibid., pp. 15–16.

101. Edward Boorstein, *Allende's Chile: An Inside View*, International Publishers, USA, 1977, pp. 109–26, 187–204.

102. For the Chilean Decree authorising this 'intervention' in ITT, see *International Legal Materials*, Vol. 10, 1971, p. 1234.

103. 'We [were] not labelled with the unfortunate association of attributed imperialist tendencies'. Department of Foreign Affairs and International Trade (DFAIT) document quoted in Rochlin, *Discovering the Americas*, p. 83.

104. *The Economist*, 13 October 1973, pp. 43–50, at p. 48.

105. See the Decree Law on the Nationalization of ITT Telephone Company of Chile, Decree Law No. 801, 10 December 1974, *International Legal Materials*, Vol. 13, 1974, pp. 781–3.

106. Rochlin, *Discovering the Americas*, pp. 88–9.

107. Canadian Imperial Bank of Commerce, 'Canada and Latin America', Toronto, Issue 1, 1976.

108. Most of these persons were supporters of the left-wing government of Allende. See Rochlin, *Discovering the Americas*, pp. 103–5; J. L. Granatstein and R. Bothwell, *Pirouette: Pierre Trudeau and Canadian Foreign Policy*, University of Toronto Press, Toronto, 1990, p. 271.

109. Rochlin, *Discovering the Americas*, pp. 243–6..

110. *The Economist*, 27 October 1973, p. 64.

111. Foreign Investment Statute Decree Law No. 1748, *International Legal Materials*, Vol. 17, 1978, pp. 134–8; Foreign Investment Statute Decree Law No. 600, 30 November 1985, *International Legal Materials*, Vol. 25, 1986, pp. 727–33.

112. Since 1990 there has been approximately $1 billion annually invested into Chile. Allan Rugman and Richard Hodgetts, *International Business: A Strategic Management Approach*, International edn, McGraw-Hill, London, 1995, p. 547.

113. Between 1975 and 1985 there was zero portfolio investment into Chile.

114. *The Economist*, 22 August 1992, p. 55.

115. *The Economist*, 13 June 1992, pp. 16–17, 83–4; See also, Ravi Ramamurti, 'Why Are Developing Countries Privatizing?', *Journal of International Business Studies*, Second Quarter, 1992, pp. 225–49.

116. *The Economist*, 24 May 1997, p. 73.

117. The education of a society is a strong indicator of its levels of development, as education issues are a middle-class concern. After the 11 December election, which Frei won with 58% of the votes, he set about educational reforms for the first time since 1973. *The Economist*, 27 November 1993, p. 76; *The Economist*, 18 December 1993, p. 6.

118. This was the motivation behind the Allende Government, which, though drawn closer to the Soviet Union through political ties, chose Marxist policies because of high levels of poverty. *The Economist,* 27 October 1973, p. 67.

119. Gary Macoein, *Chile: The Struggle for Dignity,* Coventure, London, 1975, pp. 8–9, 25.

120. *The Economist,* 26 December 1992, pp. 70–1.

121. *Latin American Journal,* 1989.

122. *The Economist,* 26 December 1992, pp. 70–1.

123. Rugman and Hodgetts, *International Business,* p. 547.

124. An International Labour Organisation report criticised Chile's privately managed pension programmes (Administradoras de Fondos de Pensions, AFPs) because of a fear that it could again collapse. The problem indicated in the ILO report was the lack of domestic outlets for investments. *The Economist,* 3 October 1992, p. 112.

125. *The Economist,* 13 September 1997, p. 67.

126. See *Cominco Business Outlook*: http://status.shh.fi/anet/education/cominco/business_outlook.html; and *Cominco-Quebrada Blanca*: http://www.rutgers.edu/Accounting/anet/education/cominco/chile_mine.html.

127. *The Economist,* 28 June 1997, p. 126.

128. This was ratified by the Chilean Parliament on 1 July 1997.

129. See, Department of Foreign Affairs and International Trade (DFAIT), *Canada–Chile Free Trade Agreement,* 24 March 1997, Chapter C.

130. Ibid., Chapter E.

131. Ibid., Chapter M.

132. Ibid.

11. Technology, Business and Crime

1. For an interesting discussion, see Herman M. Schwartz, *States versus Markets: History, Geography, and the Development of the International Political Economy,* St Martin's Press, New York, 1994, pp. 12–14.

2. Immanuel Wallerstein, *The Modern World-System: Capitalist Agriculture and the Origins of the European World-Economy in the Sixteenth Century,* Academic Press, New York and London, 1974, p. 349.

3. Anu Arora, *Electronic Banking and the Law,* 2nd edn, Banking Technology Ltd, London, 1993, p. 52.

4. Sarah Jane Hughes, 'Policing Money Laundering through Funds Transfers: A Critique of the Regulation under the Bank Secrecy Act', *Indiana Law Journal,* Vol. 67, Winter 1992, p. 283.

5. Testimony of Edward Kelly, Governor of Federal Reserve Board, Hearing of the House Banking and Financial Services Committee: Organised Crime and Banking, Chaired by Representative Jim Leach, *Federal News Wire,* 28 February 1996.

6. 'International Banking: Coping with the Ups and Downs', *The Economist,* Survey, 27 April 1996, p. 15.

7. Ian Robert Douglas, 'The Fatality of Globalisation'. Paper presented to the 21st Annual Conference of the British International Studies Association, University of Durham, 16–18 December 1996.

8. *The Economist* 'International Banking', p. 15; Gregory Millman, *Around the World on a Trillion a Day: How Rebel Currency Traders Destroy Banks and Defy Governments,* Bantam Press, London, 1995.

9. On which the reader is referred to two masterpieces: John R. Commons, *The Legal Foundations of Capitalism,* University of Wisconsin Press, Madison, WI, 1957; and J. B. Condliffe, *The Commerce of Nations,* George Allen & Unwin, London, 1951.

10. On the regulation of international finance, see Eric Helleiner, 'Explaining the Globalisation of Financial Markets: Bringing States Back In', *Review of International Political Economy*, Vol. 2, No. 2, Spring 1995; and Geoffrey Underhill, 'Markets Beyond Politics? The State and the Internationalisation of Financial Markets', *European Journal of Political Research*, Vol. 19, No. 2–3, 1991.

11. See Karl Erich Born, *International Banking in the 19th and 20th Centuries*, Berg Publishers, Leamington Spa, 1977.

12. Radio National Transcripts Background Briefing, Australian Broadcasting Corporation, 9 June 1996. Available at URL: http://www.abc.net.au/rn/talks/bbing/bb960609.htm; and 'Taking the Bite Out of Fraud', *The Virginian Pilot*, 2 October 1995, p. 10. See also, Hearing of the House Banking and Financial Services Committee, *op. cit.*

13. Bruce Zagaris and Scott B. MacDonald, 'Money Laundering, Financial Fraud, and Technology: The Perils of an Instantaneous Economy', *George Washington Journal of International Law and Economics*, Vol. 26, 1992, p. 63. See also Thomas F. McInerney III, 'Towards the Next Phase in International Banking Regulation', *DePaul Business Law Journal*, Vol. 7, Fall 1994, pp. 143–71.

14. Arora, *Electronic Banking and the Law*, pp. 45–52.

15. Hearing of the House Banking and Financial Services Committee, *op. cit.*

16. For an elaboration, see J. Wiener, 'Money Laundering: Transnational Criminals, Globalisation and the Forces of "Redomestication"', *Journal of Money Laundering Control*, Vol. 1, No. 1, 1997, pp. 51–63.

17. For an elaborate exposition of the ways in which this is already occurring between the United States and the European Union, see J. Wiener, *Symphony of Leviathans: Globalisation and the Harmonisation of Law* (forthcoming).

18. Barry Rider, 'The Financial World at Risk: The Dangers of Organized Crime, Money Laundering and Corruption', *Managerial Auditing Journal*, Vol. 8, No. 7, 1993, p. 11.

19. Barry Rider, 'Global Regulatory Trends – The Changing Legal Climate', *mimeo*, unpublished.

20. Susan Strange and John Stopford, *Rival States, Rival Firms: Competition for World Market Shares*, Cambridge University Press, Cambridge, 1991, p. 5.

21. Bill Gates, *The Road Ahead*, Basic Books, London, 1996.

22. See PL 102–94: 'The High Performance Computing Act of 1991', and the proposed amendment in US Congress HR 1757, 'High Performance Computing and High Speed Networking Applications Act of 1993' of 21 April 1993. For the Clinton administration's plans, see Executive Office of the President, 'The National Information Infrastructure: Agenda for Action', available through gopher.wiretap.spies.com. For a synopsis of recent developments of the National Information Infrastructure and the Global Information Infrastructure, see Ralph J. Andreotta, 'The National Information Infrastructure: Its Implications, Opportunities, and Challenges', *Wake Forest Law Review*, Vol. 30, Spring 1995, pp. 221–40.

23. This has also been called an 'Information Services Market'. For the EU programmes relevant to its information technology programme, see in particular, Commission of the European Communities, 'Proposal for a Council Decision Setting Up a Programme for an Information Services Market', COM(570) final, 23 January 1991. Available on World Wide Web Uniform Resource Locator (URL): http://www/echo.lu/programmes/en/DELTA_2.html. Martin Bangermann's report can also be accessed at: http://www.earn.net/EC.

24. 'Age of the Road Warrior', *Time International*, Special Issue, Spring 1995, pp. 34–6.

25. 'Ready for Prime Time?', *Time International*, 26 December 1994–2 January 1995, pp. 86–87.

26. Rosalind Resenick and Dave Taylor, *The Internet Business Guide: Riding the Information Superhighway to Profit*, Sams Publishing, Indianapolis, IN, 1994.

27. 'Secure Electronic Visa Purchases Begin', available URL: http://www.visa.com/cgi-bin/vee/vw/news/PRelc0042997.htm.

28. 'VISA, MasterCard Offer Secure Electronic Commerce', *Newsbytes*, 23 June 1995.

29. HR 1757, *op. cit.* Section 310 (b)(1) and (2): Applications for Libraries.

30. 'Networks Tap into Low Wages', *The Guardian*, 15 October 1994, p. 40.

31. Aileen A. Pisciotta and James H. Barker, 'Current Issues in Electronic Data Interchange: Telecommunications Regulatory Implications for International EDI Transactions', *Journal of International Law and Business*, Vol. 13, Spring/Summer 1992, p. 71.

32. George H. Windecker, 'The Eurodollar Deposit Market: Strategies for Regulation', *The American University Journal of International Law and Policy*, Vol. 9, Fall 1993, p. 366.

33. See Millman, *Around the World on a Trillion a Day*.

34. There is not space here to develop this point. For an elaborate discussion of the ways in which governments have been asserting their control over international finance, and the other aspects of the Internet discussed in this chapter, see Wiener, *Symphony of Leviathans* (forthcoming).

35. Malcolm Waters, *Globalisation*, Routledge, London, 1995, p. 88.

36. Phil Cerny, 'The Political Economy of International Finance', in Cerny (ed.), *Finance and World Politics*, Edward Elgar, Aldershot, 1993, p. 13.

37. Helleiner, 'States and the Future of Global Finance', p. 49.

38. Millman, *Around the World on a Trillion a Day*, p. xvii.

39. 'Accompanying Report of the National Performance Review to the Federal Coordinating Council for Science, Engineering, and Technology, High Performance Computing and Communications: Toward a National Information Infrastructure', Office of Science and Technology Policy, Washington DC, 1993.

40. 'Revealed: How Hacker Penetrated the Heart of British Intelligence', *The Independent*, 24 November 1994, various stories, pp. 1–3.

41. 'Brother Robot', Survey of Artificial Intelligence, *The Economist*, 14 March 1992, p. 24.

42. See J. Wiener, 'Transatlantic Trade: Economic Security, Agriculture, and the Politics of Technology', in J. Wiener (ed.), *The Transatlantic Relationship*, Macmillan, London, 1996, pp. 128–63, esp. pp. 146–57.

43. 'Transforming the Telescreen: Why Orwell was Wrong', *The Economist*, 12 February 1994, p. 14.

44. See the electronic summary of the case by Suzanna Sherry at lawprof@chicagokent.kentlaw.edu, distributed web-law-info by A.J.Charleswoeth@law.hull.ac.uk.

45. William J. Drake and Kalypso Nicolaidis, 'Ideas, Interests, and Institutionalization: "Trade in Services" and the Uruguay Round', *International Organization*, Vol. 46, No. 1, 1992, pp. 37–100, at p. 47.

46. See J. Wiener, 'Editor's Note', *Global Society: Journal of Interdisciplinary International Relations*, Vol. 1, No. 1, 1996, pp. 7–10.

47. Paul Virilio, *Pure War*, Semiotext(e), New York, 1983, p. 88.

48. This issue, along with breaches of copyright, have been 'settled' – unsatisfactorily, and for the time being – by placing the responsibility on the system operators, as established in *Playboy v. Frena*, *Sega Enterprises Ltd. v. MAPHIA*, *Frank Music Corp v. Compuserve*, and *Religious Technology Center v. NETCOM*. See Dan Burk, 'Patents in Cyberspace: Territoriality and Infringement on Global Computer Networks', *Tulane Law Review*, Vol. 68, No. 1, 1993; and William Galkin, 'Jumping the Gun on Sysop Liability', *The Computer Law Report*, No. 13, 6 November 1995, distributed by Galkin@aol.com.

49. See Martin Shapiro, 'The Globalisation of Law'; and Benjamin R. Barber, 'Global Democracy or Global Law: Which Comes First?', both in *Indiana Journal of Global Legal Studies*, Vol. 1, No. 1, 1993. Available at URL: http://www.law.indiana.edu/glsj/vol11/.

50. *First National Bank in Plant City v. Dickinson*. Reported in Carl Felsenfeld, 'Electronic Banking and its Effects on Interstate Branching Restrictions – An Analytic Approach', *Fordham Law Review*, Vol. 54, May 1986, pp. 1019–61.

51. See, for instance, 'CyberCash Launches PayNow Secure Electronic Check Service and Announces Agreement with International Billing Services to Develop Pilot Programs for Electronic Bill Presentment', *News Release of CyberCash*, 27 January 1997. Available at URL: http://www.cybercash.com.cybercash/news/releases/1997/.

52. Chris Reed, *Electronic Finance Law*, Woodhead-Faulkner, London, 1991, p. 34.

53. Felsenfeld, 'Electronic Banking', p. 1045.

54. For a list with hot-links to the various sites, see a Web page entitled 'Payment Mechanisms Designed for the Internet', available at URL: http://ganges.cs.tcd.ie/mpeirc.

55. David Van L. Taylor,'Doing Business on the Internet – a Question of Balance', *Business Communications Review*, Vol. 25, No. 8, August 1995, p. 35.

56. 'Electronic Money in the United States: Current Status, Prospects and Major Issues'. Fact-finding mission for the Financial Issues Working Group of the European Commission, 25 August–5 September 1996. Mission Report by Charles Goldfinger, Chairman FIWG. Available at URL: http://www.ispo.cec.be/infosoc/eleccom/elecmoney.html.

57. The Report by the Bank for International Settlements Committee on Payments and Settlements and the Group of Computer Experts of the G–10 can be accessed at http://www.bis.org/.

58. 'Market Study Sponsored by MasterCard, VeriFone and Visa Confirms Significant Opportunity for Internet Commerce', *PR Newswire*, 13 September 1995.

59. 'The National Consumers League Holds a News Conference on Combatting Fraud on the Internet', *FDCH Political Transcripts*, 27 February 1996.

60. Zagaris and MacDonald, 'Money Laundering, Financial Fraud, and Technology', p. 100. See also the testimony of Chuck Owens, Section Chief in the criminal investigative division of the financial crimes section of the FBI before the House Banking and Financial Services Committee, *op. cit.*

61. Ibid., p. 63.

62. Reported by Edward Kelly, Governor of the Federal Reserve Board, Testimony before the Hearing of the House Banking and Financial Services Committee, *op. cit.*

63. See Hearing of the House Banking and Financial Services Committee, *op. cit.* See also Sara Jankiewicz, 'Glasnost and the Growth of Global Organized Crime', *Houston Journal of International Law*, Vol. 18, Fall 1995, pp. 215–59.

64. 'VISA Delays "SET" Rollout while MasterCard Completes First Transaction', *Report on Electronic Commerce*, 14 January 1997. Available at: http://brp. com/netline/netline.html.

65. For the lower figure, see 'Credit-Card Companies OK Internet Security Deal', *San Francisco Examiner*, 1 February 1996, p. A–1. For the higher estimate, see ibid.

66. Robert M. Lewis, 'Allocation of Loss due to Fraudulent Wholesale Wire Transfers: Is There a Negligence Action against a Beneficiary's Ban after Article 4A of the Uniform Commercial Code?', *Michigan Law Review*, Vol. 90, August 1992, p. 2580.

67. Webster J, in *Royal Products Ltd. v. Midland Bank Ltd.*, cited in Peter Ellinger, 'Electronic Fund Transfer as a Deferred Settlement System', in R. M. Goode (ed.), *Electronic Banking: The Legal Implications*, The Institute of Bankers, Centre for Commercial Law Studies, London, 1985, p. 35.

68. Reed, *Electronic Financial Law*, p. 26.

69. Ibid., p. 18.

70. Ibid., p. 23.

71. Roy Goode, 'Electronic Funds Transfer as an Immediate Payment System', in R. M. Goode (ed.), *Electronic Banking*, p. 25.

72. Robert Pennington, 'Fraud, Error and System Malfunction: A Lawyer's Viewpoint', in Goode (ed.), *Electronic Banking*, p. 33.

73. Ibid., pp. 70–1.

74. Maria Chiara Malaguti, 'Legal Issues in Connection with Electronic Transfers of Funds', *Law, Computers & Artificial Intelligence*, Vol. 1, No. 3, 1992, pp. 275–90.

75. Lewis, 'Allocation of Loss due to Fraudulent Wholesale Wire Transfers', p. 2565.

76. See Pisciotta and Barker, 'Current Issues in Electronic Data Interchange', pp. 71–116.

77. Ibid., p. 2592.

78. Reed, *Electronic Finance Law*, p. 56.

79. Eric Woods, 'The Quantum and Limits of Liability', in Goode (ed.), *Electronic Banking*, p. 94.

80. See Jonathan Lass, 'Fraud, Error and System Malfunction: A Banker's Viewpoint', in Goode (ed.), *Electronic Banking.*, p. 61.

81. Reported in ibid.

82. *Foley v. Hill* ([1848] 2 HL Case 28), and *Joachimson v. Swiss Bank Corporation* ([1921] 3 KB 110). See Lord Chorley and P. E. Smart, *Leading Cases in the Law of Banking*, 4th. edn, Sweet & Maxwell, London, 1977, esp. pp. 1–6.

83. See Reed, *Electronic Finance Law*, p. 64.

84. Martin Karmel, 'Procedure and Evidence: The Maintenance of Transaction Records, Proving the State of Account in EFT Transactions', in Goode (ed.), *Electronic Banking*, p. 51.

85. Reed, *Electronic Finance Law*, p. 75.

86. Hearing of the House Banking and Financial Services Committee, *op. cit.*

87. Note that in practice, however, the financial institution may accept such losses from fraud for good commercial reasons.

88. Specifically, VISA and MasterCard have been in a joint venture with GTE, IBM, Microsoft, Netscape, SAIC, Terisa Systems, and VeriSign to develop the system. See 'VISA, MasterCard Offer Secure Electronic Commerce', *Newsbytes*, 23 June 1995; and 'MasterCard and VISA Announce Successful Completion of SET Compatibility Testing'. News Release, 30 April 1997. VISA Home Page. Available at URL: http://www.visa.com/cgibin/vee/news/PRmisc043097.html.

89. See 'Secure Electronic Visa Purchases Begin'. News Release, 29 April 1997. VISA Home Page. Available at URL: http://www.visa.com/cgibin/vee/vw/news/PRelco042997.hmtl.

90. By definition, of course, no one can be certain of the amount of something that cannot be seen. For the US estimates, see B. A. K. Rider, 'The Financial World at Risk: The Dangers of Organized Crime, Money Laundering and Corruption', *Managerial Auditing Journal*, Vol. 8, No. 7, 1993, pp. 3–14. For the global figure, see Matthew B. Comstock, 'GATT and GATS: A Public Morals Attack on Money Laundering', *Journal of International Law and Business*, Vol. 15, Fall 1994, pp. 139–77.

91. Daniel M. Laiffer, 'Putting the Super Back in the Supervision of International Banking, Post-BCCI', *Fordham Law Review*, Vol. 60, May 1992, pp. 467–500. See also Duncan E. Alford, 'Basle Committee Minimum Standards: International Regulatory Response to the Failure of BCCI', *George Washington Journal of International Law and Economics*, Vol. 26, 1992, pp. 241–91.

92. Sarah Jane Hughes, 'Policing Money Laundering'. See also the testimony of Edward Kelly, before the House Banking and Financial Services Committee, *op. cit.*, who stated that 'very candidly, it is indeed a problem in the electronic age to be able to effectively monitor the enormous numbers of very, very rapid transactions that take place'.

93. Barry Rider, 'Taking Money Launderers to the Cleaners'. Unpublished. 1 April 1995, p. 13.

94. On the US legislation, see G. Philip Rutledge, 'Bank Secrecy Laws: An America Perspective', *ms*; Jonathan J. Rusch, 'Hue and Cry in the Counting-House: Some Observations on the Bank Secrecy Act', *Catholic University Law Review*, Vol. 37, Winter 1988, pp. 465–88; and Frank C. Razzano, 'American Money Laundering Statutes: The Case for a Worldwide System of Banking Compliance Programs', *Detroit College of Law Journal of International Law and Practice*, Vol. 3, 1994, pp. 277–307.

95. The technique for evading this requirement is known as 'structuring' which refers to breaking up large transactions into more numerous, smaller-value ones in an attempt to fall under the $10,000 mandatory reporting threshold. It is an offence not only for anyone to structure, but to assist (i.e., by the bank) in structuring transactions.

96. For a thorough and concise exposition of these Acts, see Leonard Jason-Lloyd, 'Money Laundering – The Complete Guide', *ms*. See also Ross Cranston, 'Bankers Duty of Confidentiality: English Law'. Paper presented to the Cambridge International Symposium on Economic Crime, 11 September 1995. The sections cited relate to banks, financial advisors, or others who assist the criminals for the purposes of this exposition. The sections pertaining to the criminals themselves have been omitted.

97. On the Criminal Justice Act 1993, see Robert Finney, 'UK Money Laundering Law after the Reports of 1993', *Butterworths Journal of International Banking and Finance Law*, December 1993, pp. 530–7; Monica Bond, 'Money Laundering', *Accountants Digest*, No. 324, September 1994; Michael Clarke, 'How will the Money Laundering Regulations Work?', *Journal of Financial Regulation and Compliance*, Vol. 31, No. 1, 1995, pp. 36–42; and Gerard McCormack, 'Money Laundering and Banking Secrecy', *The Company Lawyer*, Vol. 16, No. 1, 1995, pp. 6–10.

98. Reported in 'Nations Worry about a Rise in On-line Money Laundering', *Wall Street Journal*, 17 March 1997.

99. 'Electronic Money in the United States: Current Status, Prospects and Major Issues', *op. cit.*

100. 'France Adopts E-Commerce Security Protocol'. Document available at URL: http://ganges.cs.tcd.ie/mepeirce/Projects/Press/cset.html.

101. At least, this is my agenda. See Wiener, *Symphony of Leviathans* (forthcoming).

13. The Global Revolution and the Twenty-first Century

1. Anthony Giddens, *The Consequences of Modernity*, Polity Press, Cambridge, 1990.

2. Michael Mann, *The Sources of Social Power*, Vol. I, Cambridge University Press, Cambridge, 1986.

3. Immanuel Wallerstein, *The Modern World-System: Capitalist Agriculture and the Origins of the European World-Economy in the Sixteenth Century*, Academic Press, London and New York, 1974.

4. Eric Hobsbawm, *The Age of Extremes: The Short Twentieth Century 1914–89*, Joseph, London, 1994.

5. Michael Mann, *The Sources of Social Power*, Vol. II, Cambridge University Press, Cambridge, 1993.

6. Jan Aart Scholte, 'Beyond the Buzzword: Towards a Critical Theory of Globalization', in Eleonore Kofman and Gillian Youngs (eds), *Globalization: Theory and Practice*, Cassell, London, 1996, pp. 43–57.

7. As we saw above, Mann argues that in periods of transition, the very definition of 'society' may change. Writing of the nineteenth century, Mann notes that, 'Throughout

this period the nation-state and a broader transnational Western civilization competed as basic membership units. Sociology's master-concept, "society", kept metamorphosing between the two.' *Sources of Social Power*, Vol II, p. 9.

8. David Held, *Democracy and Global Order*, Polity Press, Cambridge, 1995.

9. For a further development of the argument in this section, see my 'The State of International Relations', in Sarah Owen (ed.), *Globalisation and the State*, Macmillan, London (forthcoming).

10. Richard Falk, 'State of Siege: Will Globalisation Win Out?', *International Affairs*, Vol. 73, No. 1, 1997, p. 125.

11. Paul Hirst and Grahame Thompson, *Globalisation in Question*, Polity Press, Cambridge, 1995.

12. Mann, *Sources of Social Power*, Vol. II, p. 9.

13. Talcott Parsons, *The Social System*, Tavistock, London, 1952.

14. Mann, *Sources of Social Power*, p. 728.

15. Ole Wæver with Dave Carlton, *Identity, Migration and the New Security Agenda in Europe*, Pinter, London, 1993, Part 1, 'Societal Security', pp. 17–58; I have criticised this in Shaw, *Global Society and International Relations*, Polity Press, Cambridge, 1994, pp. 100–3.

16. David Lockwood, 'Social Integration and System Integration', in *Solidarity and Schism*, Clarendon Press, Oxford, 1992, pp. 399–412, and Shaw, *Global Society and International Relations*, pp. 10–11.

17. Anthony Giddens, *Modernity and Self-Identity*, Polity Press, Cambridge, 1992.

18. For a further development of the argument in this section, see my 'The State of Globalisation', *Review of International Political Economy*, 1997.

19. Mann, *Sources of Social Power*, p. 57.

20. Quoted by Mann, ibid., p. 55.

21. Ibid., p. 55.

22. Ibid., p. 53.

23. 'Like cock-up–foul-up theorists I believe that states are messier and less systematic and unitary than each single theory suggests.' Mann, *Sources of Social Power*, Vol. II, p. 88.

24. Michael Mann, 'As the Twentieth Century Ages', *New Left Review*, No. 214, November–December 1995, p. 116.

25. See Mann, *Sources of Social Power*, pp. 75–88. Mann identifies six 'higher-level' crystallisations in his analysis of nineteenth-century Western states, as capitalist, ideological-moral, militarist, patriarchal and at points on continua of representativeness and nationality. This categorisation needs expansion to deal with the greater complexities of late twentieth-century state crystallisations.

26. Mann, *Sources of Social Power*, p. 736.

27. Barry Gills and Ronen Palan (eds), *Transcending the State–Global Divide: A Neo-Structuralist Agenda in International Relations*, Rienner, London, 1994.

14. The International Relations of Global Environmental Change

Thanks are due to the Global Environmental Change Open University (GECOU) research group funded by the Economic and Science Research Council. The author is grateful to Tony McGrew for his helpful and constructive comments on an earlier version of this chapter. The usual author's disclaimers apply.

1. Andrew Dobson, *Green Political Thought*, HarperCollins, London, 1990, p. 205. Dobson's distinction between environmentalism and ecologism can be criticised for failing

properly to represent the rich diversity of green thought. See, for example, John Barry, 'The Limits of the Shallow and the Deep: Green Politics, Philosophy and Praxis', *Environmental Politics*, Vol. 3, No. 3, 1994, pp. 369–94.

2. 2. See Wolfgang Sachs (ed.), *The Development Dictionary: A Guide to Knowledge as Power*, Zed Books, London, 1992; and David Humphreys, 'Hegemonic Ideology and the International Tropical Timber Organisation', in John Vogler and Mark Imber (eds), *The Environment and International Relations*, Routledge, London, 1996.

3. Matthias Finger, 'The Military, the Nation State and the Environment', *The Ecologist*, Vol. 21, No. 5, 1991, pp. 220–5.

4. The term is borrowed from Robert Boardman, 'Ecological Discourse and International Relations Theory', *Global Society: Journal of Interdisciplinary International Relations*, Vol. 12, No. 1, January 1997, pp. 31–44.

5. See, for example, Barry Buzan, *People States and Fear: An Agenda for International Security Studies in the Post-Cold War Era*, 2nd edn, Harvester Wheatsheaf, Hemel Hempstead, 1991, pp. 19–20.

6. See the collection of essays in Jyrki Käkönen (ed.), *Green Security or Militarized Environment*, Dartmouth, Aldershot, 1994.

7. Eric Laferrière, 'Emancipating International Relations Theory: An Ecological Perspective', *Millennium: Journal of International Studies*, Vol. 25, No. 1, 1996, p. 66.

8. Ken Conca, 'In the Name of Sustainability: Peace Studies and Environmental Discourse'; Simon Dalby, 'The Politics of Environmental Security', in Käkönen (ed.), *Green Security or Militarized Environment*; and Finger, 'The Military, the Nation State and the Environment'.

9. Andrew Hurrell, 'A Crisis of Ecological Viability?: Global Environmental Change and the Nation State', *Political Studies*, Vol. XLII, 1990, p. 152.

10. See Matthew Paterson, 'IR Theory: Neorealism, Neoinstitutionalism and the Climate Change Convention', in Vogler and Imber (eds), *Environment and International Relations*, pp. 59–76.

11. David Humphreys, *Forest Politics: The Evolution of International Cooperation*, Earthscan, London, 1996, pp. 83–103.

12. The results are summarised in Oran R. Young and Gail Osherenko (eds), *Polar Politics: Creating International Environmental Regimes*, Cornell University Press, Ithaca, NY, 1993, pp. 223–61. See also Oran R. Young and Gail Osherenko, 'Testing Theories of Regime Formation: Findings from a Large Collaborative Research Project', in Volker Rittberger (ed.), *Regime Theory and International Relations*, Clarendon Press, Oxford, 1993, pp. 223–51.

13. David Humphreys, 'Regime Theory and Non-Governmental Organisations: The Case of Forest Conservation', *The Journal of Commonwealth and Comparative Politics*, Vol. XXXIV, No. 1, March 1996, pp. 90–115.

14. Susan Strange, '*Cave! hic dragones*: A Critique of Regime Analysis', in Stephen D. Krasner (ed.), *International Regimes*, Cornell University Press, Ithaca, NY, 1983, p. 354.

15. Kenneth Hanf, 'Implementing International Environmental Policies', in Andrew Blowers and Pieter Glasbergen (eds), *Environmental Policy in an International Context: Prospects for Environmental Change*, Arnold, London, 1996, pp. 203–4.

16. Wolfgang Sachs, 'Introduction', in Wolfgang Sachs (ed.), *Global Ecology: A New Arena of Political Conflict*, Zed Books, London, 1993, p. xvii.

17. Wolfgang Sachs, 'Environment', in Sachs (ed.), *Development Dictionary*, p. 33.

18. Matthew Paterson, 'Radicalising Regimes? Ecology and the Critique of IR Theory', in John MacMillan and Andrew Linklater (eds), *Boundaries in Question: New Directions in International Relations*, Pinter, London, 1995.

19. See, for example, David Long, 'The Harvard School of International Relations: A

Case for Closure', *Millennium: Journal of International Relations*, Vol. 24, No. 3, 1995, pp. 489–505.

20. Oran R. Young and Gail Osherenko, 'The Formation of International Regimes: Hypotheses and Cases', in Young and Osherenko (eds), *Polar Politics*, p. 1.

21. Robert W. Cox, 'Social Forces, States and World Orders: Beyond International Relations Theory', *Millennium: Journal of International Studies*, Vol. 10, No. 2, Summer 1981, p. 129.

22. Ibid., p. 128.

23. Ibid., pp. 129–30.

24. Klaus Dieter Wolf and Michael Zürn, '"International Regimes" und Theorien der Internationalen Politik', *Politische Vierteljahresschrift*, Vol. 27, 1986, pp. 201–21, cited by Volker Rittberger, 'Research on International Regimes in Germany: The Adaptive Internalization of an American Social Science Concept', in Rittberger (ed.), *Regime Theory and International Relations*, p. 9.

25. Robert O. Keohane, Peter M. Haas and Marc A. Levy, 'The Effectiveness of International Environmental Institutions', in Peter M. Haas, Robert O. Keohane and Marc A. Levy (eds), *Institutions for the Earth: Sources of Effective International Environmental Protection*, MIT Press, Cambridge, MA, 1993, p. 7.

26. Ibid.

27. Karen Litfin, 'Ecoregimes: Playing Tug of War with the Nation-State', in Ronnie D. Lipschutz and Ken Conca (eds), *The State and Social Power in Global Environmental Politics*, Columbia University Press, New York, 1993, p. 110.

28. Andrew Hurrell, 'International Political Theory and the Global Environment', in Ken Booth and Steve Smith (eds), *International Relations Theory Today*, Polity Press, Cambridge, 1995, p. 134.

29. John Vogler, *The Global Commons: A Regime Analysis*, John Wiley and Sons, Chichester, 1995, pp. 152–82.

30. Paterson, 'Radicalising Regimes?', pp. 213 and 218.

31. Johan Galtung, 'A Structural Theory of Imperialism', in Michael Smith, Richard Little and Michael Shackleton (eds), *Perspectives on World Politics*, Croom Helm/Open University, London, 1981, pp. 301–12. This piece is abbreviated from an earlier publication in *Journal of Peace Research*, Vol. 13, No. 2, 1971, pp. 81–94.

32. Susanne Bodenheimer, 'Dependency and Imperialism: The Roots of Latin American Underdevelopment', in Smith et al. (eds), *Perspectives on World Politics*, p. 318. This piece is abbreviated from an earlier publication in *Politics and Society*, Vol. 1, No. 3, 1971, pp. 327–57.

33. See, for example, André Gunder Frank, 'The Development of Underdevelopment', in Robert I. Rhodes (ed.), *Imperialism and Underdevelopment: A Reader*, Monthly Review Press, New York, 1970, p. 7. This piece first appeared in *Monthly Review*, September 1966, pp. 17–30. It is also published in abbreviated forms in James D. Cockcroft, et al., *Dependence and Underdevelopment: Latin America's Political Economy*, Anchor Books, Garden City, NY, 1972, pp. 3–17.

34. Immanuel Wallerstein, *The Capitalist World-Economy*, Cambridge University Press, Cambridge, 1979, p. 21.

35. See, for example, the collections of essays in Sachs (ed.), *Development Dictionary*, and Sachs (ed.), *Global Ecology*.

36. Michael Redclift, *Development and the Environmental Crisis: Red or Green Alternatives?*, Routledge, London, 1984, p. 122. Redclift is writing here on the approach of 'political economy … an approach to development which is derived principally from Marx' (p. 5).

37. Ibid., p. 122.

38. Frank, 'Development of Underdevelopment', p. 5.

39. Marcus Colchester, 'Slave and Enclave: Towards a Political Ecology of Equatorial Africa', *The Ecologist*, Vol. 23, No. 5, 1993, p. 168.

40. Ibid., p. 169.

41. Ibid., p. 172.

42. Nicholas Hildyard, 'Green Dollars, Green Menace', *The Ecologist*, Vol. 22, No. 3, 1992, p. 82.

43. Ibid., p. 83.

44. Environmental Investigation Agency, *Corporate Power, Corruption and the Destruction of the World's Forests*, Environmental Investigation Agency, London, 1996, p. 1.

45. Barnett Commission of Inquiry Final Report, Vol. 1, p. 7, cited in Asia Pacific Action Group, *The Barnett Report: A Summary of the Report of the Commission of Inquiry into Aspects of the Timber Industry in Papua New Guinea*, Asia Pacific Action Group, Hobart Tasmania, November 1990, p. 16.

46. Ibid., p. 15.

47. André Gunder Frank, *Capitalism and Underdevelopment in Latin America: Historical Studies of Chile and Brazil*, Monthly Review Press, New York, 1967, p. 311.

48. Susan George, *A Fate Worse than Debt*, Penguin, London, 1988, p. 156.

49. Patricia Adams, *Odious Debts: Loose Lending, Corruption and the Third World's Environmental Legacy*, Earthscan, London, 1991, esp. Ch. 5, 'The Debt Crisis' Silver Lining', pp. 49–57.

50. Dominic Hogg, *The SAP in the Forest: The Environmental and Social Impacts of Structural Adjustment Programmes in the Philippines, Ghana and Guyana*, Friends of the Earth, London, September 1993.

51. Gérald Berthoud, 'Market', in Sachs (ed.), *Development Dictionary*, p. 73.

52. *Third World Resurgence*, No. 28, 1992: Susan George, 'Debt as Warfare: An Overview of the Debt Crisis', pp. 14–19; IFDA Dossier, 'An indictment of the IMF and the World Bank', pp. 21–3; Michel Chossudovsky, 'Feeding on Poverty: India under IMF rule', pp. 24–7; Obinna Anyadike, 'Structural Adjustment: No Light at the End of the Tunnel', p. 28; Toye Olori, 'Nigeria: No Gain From the Pain', p. 29; Anon., 'Ghana: An Illusion of Success', pp. 30–1; and Anon., 'Chile: A "success story" – but for whom', pp. 32–3.

53. James D. Cockcroft, André Gunder Frank and Dale L. Johnson, 'Introduction', in Cockcroft et al., *Dependence and Underdevelopment*, p. xix.

54. See, for example, Vandana Shiva, *Forestry Crisis and Forestry Myths: A Critical Review of 'Tropical Forests: A Call for Action'*, World Rainforest Movement, Penang, 1987.

55. Marcus Colchester, 'Colonizing the Rainforests: The Agents and Causes of Deforestation', in Marcus Colchester and Larry Lohmann (eds), *The Struggle for Land and the Fate of the Forests*, Zed Books, London, 1993, pp. 11–12.

56. Friends of the Earth, *Poverty, Population and the Planet*, Friends of the Earth, London, 1992, p. 9.

57. Samir Amin, *Imperialism and Unequal Development*, Harvester Press, Brighton, 1977, pp. 137–43.

58. Samir Amin, 'Moving Beyond Structural Adjustment', *Third World Resurgence*, No. 28, 1992, p. 34.

59. Ibid., p. 35.

60. Ibid. On the subject of delinking, see also Samir Amin, *Re-Reading the Postwar Period: An Intellectual Itinerary*, Monthly Review Press, New York, 1994, pp. 166–7. It is noteworthy that in this volume Amin does not deal with environmental degradation.

61. Immanuel Wallerstein, 'The Global Picture, 1945–90', in Terence K Hopkins, Immanuel Wallerstein et al., *The Age of Transition: Trajectory of the World-System 1945–2025*, Pluto Press, London, 1996, p. 215.

62. Ibid., p. 225.

63. André Gunder Frank, 'World System in Crisis', in William R. Thompson (ed.), *Contending Approaches to World System Analysis*, Sage, London, 1983, p. 30.

64. Anthony Giddens, *The Constitution of Society*, Polity Press, Cambridge, 1984, p. 177.

65. Bas Arts, 'NGOs in Regime Formation: A Model Based on Structuration Theory'. Paper presented to the Second Pan-European Conference on International Studies, Paris, September 1995.

66. Giddens, *Constitution of Society*, p. 287.

67. Jan Aart Scholte, *International Relations of Social Change*, Open University Press, Buckingham, 1993, p. 128.

68. Robert Cox, *Production, Power and World Order: Social Forces in the Making of History*, Columbia University Press, New York, 1987, p. 4. Emphasis added.

69. Anthony Giddens, *Studies in Social and Political Theory*, Hutchinson, London, 1977, pp. 129–33.

70. Giddens, *Constitution of Society*, p. 3.

71. On environmental risks, see Ulrich Beck, *Risk Society: Towards a New Modernity*, Sage, London, 1992.

72. Arthur P. J. Mol, 'Ecological Modernisation and Institutional Reflexivity: Environmental Reform in the Late Modern Age', *Environmental Politics*, Vol. 5, No. 2, 1996, p. 304.

73. Maarten A. Hajer, *The Politics of Environmental Discourse: Ecological Modernisation and the Policy Process*, Clarendon Press, Oxford, 1995, p. 25.

74. Albert Weale, *The New Politics of Pollution*, Manchester University Press, Manchester, 1992, p. 76.

75. Angela Liberatore, 'The Social Construction of Environmental Problems', in Pieter Glasbergen and Andrew Blowers (eds), *Environmental Policy in an International Context: Perspectives on Environmental Problems*, Arnold, London, 1995, p. 64.

76. As noted in Mol, 'Ecological Modernisation', and Andrew Blowers, 'Environmental Policy: Ecological Modernisation or the Risk Society?', *Urban Studies*, Vol. 34, Nos 5–6, 1997, pp. 845–71.

77. Mol, 'Ecological Modernisation', p. 313.

78. Ibid., p. 318.

79. Maarten A. Hajer, 'Ecological Modernisation as Cultural Politics', in Scott Lash, Bronislaw Szerszynski and Brian Wynne (eds), *Risk, Environment and Modernity: Towards a New Ecology*, Sage, London, 1996, p. 255.

80. Weale, *New Politics of Pollution*, p. 76.

81. Chris Brown, 'Critical Theory and Postmodernism in International Relations', in A. J. R. Groom and Margot Light (eds), *Contemporary International Relations: A Guide to Theory*, Pinter, London, 1994, p. 58.

82. Julian Saurin, 'Global Environmental Degradation, Modernity and Environmental Knowledge', *Environmental Politics*, Vol. 2, No. 4, 1993, p. 62. Emphasis in original.

83. Matthias Finger, 'NGOs and Transformation: Beyond Social Movement Theory', in Thomas Princen and Matthias Finger (eds), *Environmental NGOs in World Politics: Linking the Local and the Global*, Routledge, London, 1994, p. 61.

84. Dobson, *Green Political Thought*, p. 158.

85. Piers M. Blaikie, 'Post-Modernism and Global Environmental Change', *Global Environmental Change*, Vol. 6, No. 2, 1996, p. 84.

86. William D. Sunderlin, 'Global Environmental Change, Sociology and Paradigm Isolation', *Global Environmental Change*, Vol. 5, No. 3, 1995, p. 211.

87. Keith Webb, *An Introduction to Problems in the Philosophy of Social Sciences*, Pinter, London, 1995.

88. On the norms invoked in the inter-paradigm debate, see Barry Buzan, 'The Timeless Wisdom of Realism?', in Steve Smith, Ken Booth and Marysia Zalewski (eds), *International Theory: Positivism and Beyond*, Cambridge University Press, Cambridge, 1996, esp. pp. 55–7.

15. The Internet as an Object of International Relations Interest

1. P. Worsley, 'Progress and Cults in Melanesia', *New Society*, Vol. 1, No. 3, 18 October 1962.

2. H. H. Frederick, *Global Communication and International Relations*, Wadsworth, Belmont, CA, 1993, pp. 29–30.

3. Dawne M. Flammger, *A History of the Telephone* (1995) on URL: http://www.geog. buffalo.edu/Geo666/flammger/tele2.html.

4. Jarrod Wiener, personal communication, 1997.

5. H. E. Hardy, 'A History of the Net', Master's thesis, Grand Valley State University, Allendale, 1993. Anonymous FTP from: umcc.umich.edu/pub/seraphim/doc/ nethist8.txt.

6. From dwilson@chaserv.almanac.bc.ca. In this context it is worth noting the development of the Global Network Academy (GNA), a nascent 'university of the internet'. The Open University, as well as other educational institutions, is also planning developments in this manner. It should be noted also that Iceland is netting most of its schools, a great advantage when it is remembered that many of these are in small and isolated communities. Netting gives all schools access to central teaching materials. See URL: http://rvik. ismennt.is/~fva/English/English.html.

7. See C. R. Mitchell, 'World Society as a Cobweb: States, Actors, and Systemic Processes', in Michael Banks (ed.), *Conflict in World Society*, Wheatsheaf, Brighton, 1984, pp. 59–77.

8. The number of Internet users is an open question, and will probably remain so. In merely estimating the Net there are serious difficulties. 'The most commonly quoted figure is from 30 to 75 million users. Some estimates focus on the United States; others are worldwide. Some estimates are of the core Internet, which includes only hosts using the Internet's TCP/IP protocol to connect to the backbone network operated by the National Science Foundation. Others include anyone who can exchange e-mail through Internet gateways like America Online, CompuServe or local bulletin board systems.' Downloaded from *HiTech Media* on 18/10/97 from URL: http://www.hitechmedia.com/ html/how_ big_is_the_net_.html.

A further commentator notes that: 'The appropriately-named "Irresponsible Internet Statistics Generator" (at www.anamorph.com/) says that in February 1995 there were 27,000 web sites and that number was doubling every 53 days.' See URL: http://www.xtra.co.nz/ soapbox/loggedon/. Downloaded on 18/10/97. In reality, it seems that no one is very sure about the size of the Net; all that various commentators seem to agree on is that it is very big and has a geometric growth rate.

9. Bruce Sterling, 'A Short History of the Internet', *The Magazine of Fantasy and Science Fiction*, Cornwall, CT, February 1993.

10. Robert Hobbes Zakon, Internet Timeline v1.4 (1994), Zakonhobbes@hobbes.mitre. org.

11. Interestingly, the same thing happened when the telegraph was introduced.

12. Vint Cerf (1994) [as told to B. Aboba] 'A Brief History of the Internet and Related Networks': gopher://is.internic.net/00/in guide/about internet/history/timeline.

13. Peter Salus, 'Pioneers of the Internet', *Internet World*, September 1994, pp. 70–2.

14. A page, in this context, may be single word, or a book.

15. Frederick, *Global Communication*, p. 8.

16. See Jon Katz, 'The Age of Paine', *Wired*, April 1995, pp. 64–9.

17. See C. F. Hockett, 'The Origin of Speech', *Scientific American*, No. 203, September 1960, pp. 89–96; and C. F. Hockett and S. A. Altman, 'A Note on Design Features', in *Animal Communication*, Indiana University Press, Bloomington, IN, 1968.

18. See N. Chomsky, *Language and Mind*, Harcourt, Brace & World, New York, 1968, *passim*.

19. See R. Byrne and A. Whiten, 'A Thinking Primate's Guide to Deception', *New Scientist*, No. 1589, December 1987, pp. 54–9.

20. See E. Sapir, *Language: An Introduction to the Study of Speech*, Harcourt, Brace & Co, New York, 1949, p. 1, where language is seen as a 'prerequisite for the development of culture as a whole'.

21. Deutsch writes: 'Membership in a people essentially consists in wide complementarity of social communication' (p. 97) while the end of community is marked by 'communicative barriers' (p. 100). See K. W. Deutsch, *Nationalism and Social Communication: An Inquiry into the Foundations of Nationality*, 2nd edn, MIT Press, Cambridge, MA, 1966.

22. K. Mannheim, *Ideology and Utopia*, Routledge & Kegan Paul, London, 1936, p. 19.

23. Whorf writes: 'We see and hear and otherwise experience very largely as we do because the language habits of our community predispose us to certain choices of communication.' See B. L. Whorf, *Language, Thought and Reality*, MIT Press, Cambridge, MA, 1956, p. 134.

24. M. Foucault, 'The Subject and Power', in H. L. Dreyfus and P. Michel Rabinow (eds), *Foucault: Beyond Stucturalism and Hermeneutics*, with an afterword by Foucault, Hassocks, Brighton, 1982.

25. See, for example, M. McLuhan on 'typographical man' in *The Gutenberg Galaxy*, Routledge & Kegan Paul, London, 1962.

26. C. J. Hamelink, *The Politics of World Communication*, Sage Publications, London, 1994, p. 5.

27. W. H. McNeill, *The Pursuit of Power: Technology, Armed Force and Society since AD 1000*, Basil Blackwell, Oxford, 1983, pp. 8–9.

28. W. Gates, *The Road Ahead*, Viking, London, 1996.

29. For a complete listing of academic lists in Britain, who are members and how to join a list, go to URL: http://www.mailbase.ac.uk/.

30. See European Consortium for Political Research at URL: http://www.essex.ac.uk/ECPR/index.htm.

31. See URL: http://www.ukc.ac.uk/international/sgir.html.

32. M. Girard, W.-D. Eberwein and K. Webb (eds), *Theory and Practice in Foreign Policy-making: National Perspectives on Academics and Professionals in International Relations*, Pinter, London, 1994.

33. It may be the case that technology itself may provide an answer. Recently, a British inventor, Trevor Baylis, invented a clockwork radio which is not dependent on external supplies of electricity. He has recently used the same principles to build a clockwork computer. See URL: http://www.emta.org.uk/enginuity/behind/clock.htm.

34. See, for example, Hazel Henderson, 'Computers: Hardware of Democracy', who writes: 'Democratizing computer and communication technology could provide maximum feasible participation in politics for virtually everybody.' Downloaded on 25/10/97 from URL: http://www.auburn.edu/tann/hazel/forum.html; and Hazel Henderson, 'Global Networks.' Downloaded on 25/10/97 from URL: http://www.context.org/ICLIB/IC36/Hendersn.htm.

35. *The Rise and Rise of Michael Rimmer* (1970). Directed by Kevin Billington, and starring Peter Cook and Denholm Elliott.

36. For a discussion of 'essential contestability', see K. Webb, *An Introduction to Problems in the Philosophy of Social Science*, Pinter, London, 1995, Ch. 3.

37. Jean-Jacques Rousseau, *The Social Contract and Other Later Political Writings*, Cambridge Texts in the History of Political Thought, Cambridge University Press, Cambridge, 1997.

38. Robert Michels, *Political Parties*, Dover Publications, New York, 1959.

39. See, for this argument, Carole Pateman, *Participation and Democratic Theory*, Cambridge University Press, Cambridge, 1970.

40. See, for example, Stormfront White Nationalist Resource Page on URL: http://www.stormfront.org/.

41. The 'lock-in' effect refers to the phenomenon whereby a group has intense within-group communications and few external communications. The consequence may be a continual reinforcement of within-group beliefs and an absence of external correctives to that point of view.

42. Figures come from GVU Center 3rd WWW User Survey. It should be noted that the methodology was such that the respondents were self-selected. See URLs: http://www.cc.gatech.edu/gvu/user_surveys/User_Survey_Home.html for the US results and http://www.clark.net/pub/granered/egworld.html for the non-US (including UK) results.

43. *New York Times*, 23 October 1995.

44. Barry Buzan, *People, States and Fear: An Agenda for International Security Studies in the Post-Cold War Era*, 2nd edn, Lynne Rienner, Boulder, CO, 1991.

45. Jarrod Wiener, 'Money Laundering: Transnational Criminals, Globalisation, and the Forces of Redomestication', *Journal of Money Laundering Control*, Vol. 1, No. 1, 1997, pp. 51–63.

46. Clifford Stoll, *The Cuckoo's Egg: Tracking a Spy through the Maze of Computer Espionage*, Bantam Doubleday Bell, New York, 1989.

47. See URL: http://news.uk.msn.com/news/3874.asp.

48. See, for example, Tsutomu Shimomura and John Markoff, *Takedown: The Pursuit and Capture of Kevin Mitnick, America's Most Wanted Computer Outlaw*, Hyperion/Littman, Jonathan, New York, 1996; *The Fugitive Game: Online with Kevin Mitnick*, Little, Brown and Company, New York, 1996.

49. For a listing of recent computer crimes of various kinds, see URL: http://www.georgetown.edu/users/samplem/iw/html/database.html.

50. 'Secret DTI Inquiry into Cyber Terror', *Sunday Times*, 9 June 1996.

51. Jarrod Wiener, *Symphony of Leviathans: Globalisation and the Harmonisation of Law* (forthcoming), Ch. 4, 'Harmonising Copyrights on the Internet'.

52. Attributed to Emmet Paige, the Assistant Secretary of Defense for Command, Control, Communications, and Computers, in Blake Harris, 'Advent of Information War'. Downloaded on 31/10/97 from: http://www.iwar.com/advent.htm.

53. See the President's Commission on Critical Infrastructure Protection. Downloaded on 31/10/97 from URL: http://www.pccip. gov/.

54. The Information Warfare Research Center can be found on URL: http://www.terrorism.com/infowar/wwwlinks.html.

55. 'Strategic War in Cyberspace', Rand Research Brief. Downloaded on 31/10/97 from URL: URL: http://www.rand.org/publications/RB/RB7106/RB7106.html.

56. See Harold Rheingold, *The Virtual Community*, Harper Perennial, New York, 1994; Rob Sheilds (ed.), *Cultures of Internet*, Sage, London, 1996; and S. G. Jones (ed.), *Cybersociety: Computer-mediated Communication and Community*, Sage, London, 1995.

57. There are pages in other languages – Japanese, Dutch, French, Spanish, etc. – but

these are a tiny minority compared to the pages in English. What is perhaps a telling point is that very often where there is, say, a page in Japanese, there is also an English version.

58. I am grateful to Dr Clem McCartney of the University of Ulster for drawing my attention to this.

59. See http://mediafilter.org/MFF/ZTN_InFo.html.

16. Feminism and the Concept of Community in International Relations

This chapter was originally presented at the International Studies Association Conference in Toronto, March 1997. I am grateful to Mairi Johnson, Bruce D. Jones and Bice Maiguashca for their critical insights and helpful comments on an earlier version of the chapter.

1. Martin Wight, 'Why is there no International Theory?', in Herbert Butterfield and Martin Wight (eds), *Diplomatic Investigations: Essays in the Theory of International Politics*, George Allen & Unwin, London, 1966.

2. The work of Andrew Linklater, explored later in this chapter, is the most obvious example of recent explorations of the concept of community in International Relations, and the communitarian–cosmopolitan debate in International Relations also engages this question, as do theorists such as R. B. J. Walker.

3. Developing a theory of community is beyond the scope of this chapter, but is part of my ongoing work.

4. 'Feminism', in *The Blackwell Encyclopaedia of Political Thought*, David Miller et al. (eds), Basil Blackwell, Oxford, 1987, p. 151.

5. Jacqui True offers one list of feminisms: 'conservative feminisms, liberal feminisms, Marxist feminisms and socialist feminisms ... radical feminisms, eco-feminisms, cultural feminisms ... lesbian feminisms, women of colour/Third World feminisms, and a complex group of postmodern critical feminist theories which draw variously on poststructuralist, French continental theory, psychoanalysis, postpositivist epistemologies and non-Western, multicultural feminisms'. Jacqui True, 'Feminism', in Scott Burchill and Andrew Linklater, et al., *Theories of International Relations*, Macmillan, Basingstoke, 1996, p. 212. For a recent (contentious) discussion and critique of feminist perspectives in International Relations, see Adam Jones, 'Does "Gender" make the World go Round? Feminist Critiques of International Relations', *Review of International Studies*, Vol. 22, No. 4, October 1996.

6. Sandra Harding, *Whose Science? Whose Knowledge? Thinking from Women's Lives*, Open University Press, Milton Keynes, 1991, pp. 105–37 and 164–87. See also Kimberly Hutchings, *Kant Critique and Politics*, Routledge, London and New York, 1996, p. 168.

7. Marysia Zalewski, 'Feminist Theory and International Relations', in M. Bowker and R. Brown (eds), *From Cold War to Collapse: Theory and World Politics in the 1980s*, Cambridge University Press, Cambridge, 1991, p. 120.

8. Ibid.

9. Ibid., p. 116.

10. Ibid. pp. 118–19.

11. Stephen Leonard, *Critical Theory in Political Practice*, Princeton University Press, Princeton, NJ, 1990, pp. 212–13.

12. Ibid., p. 217.

13. Christine Sylvester, *Feminist Theory and International Relations in a Postmodern Era*, Cambridge University Press, Cambridge, 1994. See also M. Zalewski, 'The Women/ "Women" Question in International Relations', *Millennium: Journal of International Studies*, Vol. 23, No. 2, 1994.

14. Sylvester, *Feminist Theory and International Relations*, p. 53.

15. Zalewski, 'Women/"Women"', p. 416.

16. Kimberly Hutchings, 'The Personal is International: Feminist Epistemology and the Case of International Relations', in Kathleen Lennon and Margaret Whitford (eds.), *Knowing the Difference: Feminist Perspectives in Epistemology*, Routledge, London, 1994, pp. 158–9.

17. Ibid., p. 155.

18. Jones, 'Does Gender make the World go Round?' p. 405.

19. Ibid., p. 406.

20. See, for example, Seyla Benhabib, 'The Generalized and the Concrete Other: The Kohlberg–Gilligan Controversy and Feminist Theory', in Seyla Benhabib and Drucilla Cornell (eds), *Feminism as Critique*, Polity Press, Cambridge, 1987. On the right and the good in International Relations, see Mark Neufeld, 'Identity and the Good in International Relations Theory', *Global Society: Journal of Interdisciplinary International Relations*, Vol. 10, No. 1, 1996, and Robert Jackson, 'Martin Wight, International Theory and the Good Life', *Millennium: Journal of International Studies*, Vol. 19, No. 2, 1990. For a (contrasting) feminist view on the potential for the good life in states, see Jean Bethke Elshtain, 'Sovereignty, Identity, Sacrifice', *Millennium: Journal of International Studies*, Vol. 20, No. 3, 1991.

21. Benhabib and Cornell, *Feminism as Critique*, p. 15.

22. Zalewski, 'Feminist Theory', p. 139.

23. Ibid., p. 142.

24. Iris Marion Young, 'The Ideal of Community and the Politics of Difference', in Linda J. Nicholson (ed.), *Feminism/Postmodernism*, Routledge, New York and London, 1990, p. 300.

25. Marilyn Friedman, 'Feminism and Modern Friendship: Dislocating the Community', in Cass R. Sunstein (ed.), *Feminism and Political Theory*, University of Chicago Press, Chicago, 1990, p. 143.

26. Young, 'Ideal of Community', p. 302.

27. Ibid., p. 306.

28. Ibid.

29. Sabina Lovibond, 'The End of Morality?', in Lennon and Whitford, (eds), *Knowing the Difference*, p. 68.

30. Ibid., p. 69. Emphasis in original.

31. Young, 'Ideal of Community', p. 307.

32. Ibid., p. 309.

33. Zalewski, 'Women/"Women"', p. 408.

34. Young, 'Ideal of Community', p. 310.

35. Ibid., p. 311.

36. Ibid., p. 302.

37. Ibid., p. 313.

38. Ibid., p. 316.

39. Ibid., p. 314.

40. Ibid., p. 315.

41. Ibid., p. 314.

42. Young proposes an alternative to the ideal of community: a politics of difference in 'the unoppressive city' which she describes in some detail, and which rejects community and its 'urge to unity'. See, ibid., pp. 317–20.

43. Shane Phelan, 'All the Comforts of Home: The Genealogy of Community', in Nancy J. Hirschmann and Christine Di Stefano (eds), *Revisioning the Political: Feminist Reconstructions of Traditional Concepts in Western Political Theory*, Westview Press, Boulder, CO, 1996, pp. 236–7.

44. Ibid., p. 238.

45. Ibid., p. 237.

46. Ibid., p. 238.

47. Ibid.

48. Andrew Linklater, 'The Transformation of Political Community: E. H. Carr, Critical Theory and International Relations', *Review of International Studies*, Vol. 21, No. 3, July 1997, p. 321.

49. 'Community', in *The Blackwell Encyclopaedia of Political Thought*, David Miller, et al. (eds), Blackwell Publishers, Oxford, 1987, p. 88.

50. Wight, 'Why is there no International Theory?' p. 33.

51. Three (of many) examples of feminist critiques of the state include: Catharine MacKinnon, *Toward a Feminist Theory of the State*, Harvard University Press, Cambridge, MA, 1989; V. Spike Peterson (ed.), *Gendered States: Feminist (Re)Visions of International Relations Theory*, Lynne Rienner, Boulder, CO, 1992; and Wendy Brown, *States of Injury*, Princeton University Press, Princeton, NJ, 1995.

52. J. Ann Tickner, *Gender in International Relations: Feminist Perspectives on Achieving Global Security*, Columbia University Press, New York, 1992, p. 42.

53. Warren Magnusson, 'The Reification of Political Community', in R. B. J. Walker and Saul Mendlovitz (eds), *Contending Sovereignties: Redefining Political Community*, Lynne Rienner, Boulder, CO, 1990, pp. 49–50. See also the development of his argument in W. Magnusson, *The Search for Political Space: Globalization, Social Movements and the Urban Political Experience*, University of Toronto Press, Toronto, 1996.

54. Magnusson is not alone in this contention: for an account of debates about the state in the communitarian–cosmopolitan debate, see, for instance, Molly Cochran, 'Postmodernism, Ethics, and International Political Theory', *Review of International Studies*, Vol. 21, 1995.

55. Magnusson, 'Reification of Political Community', p. 55.

56. Of course, there is also the question of how and why the appeal of the state as community has proved so compelling. See, for example, R. B. J. Walker, *Inside/Outside: International Relations as Political Theory*, Cambridge University Press, Cambridge, 1993; and Walker, 'Gender and Critique in the Theory of International Relations', in Peterson (ed.), *Gendered States*.

57. The development of Linklater's approach to the concept of community can be traced through most of his work, beginning with *Men and Citizens in the Theory of International Relations*, Macmillan, Basingstoke, 1990, to his more recent (1997) essay on 'The Transformation of Political Community', *op. cit.* Unfortunately, it is beyond the scope of this chapter to provide more than a brief (and therefore incomplete) summary of my analysis of Linklater's work on the concept of community.

58. Andrew Linklater, 'The Problem of Community in International Relations', *Alternatives*, Vol. 15, No. 2, Spring 1990, p. 136.

59. Ibid., p. 137.

60. Ibid.

61. Linklater, *Men and Citizens*, p. ix.

62. There is extensive literature on citizenship in feminist theory. See, for example: Elshtain, 'Sovereignty Identity, Sacrifice'; Kathleen Jones, 'Citizenship in a Women-Friendly Polity', *Signs*, No. 15, 1990; Christine Sylvester, 'Feminists and Realists View Autonomy and Obligation in International Relations', in Peterson (ed.), *Gendered States*. See also Andrew Linklater, 'Citizenship and Sovereignty in the Post-Westphalian State', *European Journal of International Relations*, Vol. 2, No. 1, 1996.

63. Andrew Linklater, 'Marxism' in Burchill and Linklater, *Theories of International Relations*,

p. 141. For his (sceptical) views on feminist theory, see Linklater, 'Dialogue, Dialectic and Emancipation in International Relations at the End of the Post-war Age', *Millennium: Journal of International Studies*, Vol. 23, No. 1, 1994, pp. 123 (n. 7) and 126.

64. Phelan, 'All the Comforts of Home', p. 239. Citation in quote from Jean-Luc Nancy, *The Inoperative Community* (Peter Connor, ed. and trans.), Minnesota University Press, Minneapolis, 1991, p. xxxviii.

65. Ibid., p. 239.

66. Ibid., p. 240.

67. Nancy, *The Inoperative Community*, p. xxxviii. Emphasis in original.

68. Ibid., p. 1.

17. The End of History and the First Man of the Twenty-first Century

1. Francis Fukuyama, 'The End of History?', *The National Interest*, No. 16, Summer 1989, p. 4. Fukuyama subsequently developed this article into a book, *The End of History and the Last Man*, Penguin, London, 1992. For reasons of scope, this chapter focuses on these two publications.

2. Ibid., pp. 3–4.

3. Derrida, for example, disparagingly describes *The End of History and the Last Man* as 'the disconcerting and tardy by-product of a "footnote"; *nota bene* for a certain Kojève who deserved better. ... [I]t remains essentially ... the schoolish exercise of a young, industrious, but come-lately reader of Kojève'. See Jacques Derrida, 'Spectres of Marx', *New Left Review*, No. 205, May/June 1994, p. 42.

4. As Fukuyama himself has observed, it can sometimes seem that a good many of his critics simply have failed to read his work with sufficient care. See his 'Reply to My Critics', *The National Interest*, No. 18, Winter 1989–90, p. 21.

5. Fukuyama, *End of History*, p. xii.

6. Ibid., p. 48.

7. Ibid., pp. 98 and 46.

8. Ibid, p. xiii.

9. Ibid., p. xiv.

10. Ibid, pp. xiv–xv.

11. Ibid., p. xv.

12. Ibid.

13. Ibid., p. xvi.

14. Ibid., p. xvii.

15. Ibid., pp. xvii–xviii.

16. Ibid., p. xix.

17. Ibid., p. xx.

18. Ibid.

19. Fukuyama notes that there is 'a legitimate question as to whether Kojève's interpretation of Hegel is really Hegel as he understood himself', but concludes that 'we are interested not in Hegel *per se* but in Hegel-as-interpreted-by-Kojève, or perhaps a new, synthetic philosopher named Hegel–Kojève'. Ibid., p. 144.

20. Ibid., p. xxi.

21. Ibid., p. xxii.

22. Ibid.

23. Ibid., p. 244.

24. Ibid., p. 246.

25. Ibid., p. 380.

26. Ibid., p. 251.

27. Ibid., p. 252.

28. See John Gaddis, 'One Germany – In Both Alliances', *New York Times*, 21 March 1990, p. A27.

29. See John Mearsheimer, 'Back to the Future: Instability in Europe after the Cold War', *International Security*, Vol. 15, No. 1, Summer 1990.

30. Fukuyama, *End of History*, p. 293.

31. Mearsheimer, 'Back to the Future', p. 12.

32. Fukuyama, *End of History*, p. 255.

33. Ibid., pp. 255–6.

34. Ibid., p. 257.

35. Ibid., p. 258.

36. Ibid.

37. Václav Havel et al., *The Power of the Powerless*, Hutchinson, London, 1985.

38. Fukuyama, *End of History*, pp. 258–9.

39. Ibid., p. 259.

40. Ibid.

41. Ibid.

42. See Joseph Schumpeter, *Imperialism and Social Classes*, Meridian Books, New York, 1955, p. 262.

43. Ibid., p. 261.

44. Ibid., p. 262.

45. Ibid.

46. Ibid., p. 383. See Michael Doyle, 'Kant, Liberal Legacies and Foreign Affairs I', and 'Kant, Liberal Legacies, and Foreign Affairs II', *Philosophy and Public Affairs*, Vol. 12. The articles appear in the Summer and Fall issues, respectively.

47. This fact was acknowledged in the Soviet Communist Party's theoretical journal *Kommunist*. See V. Khurkin, S. Karaganov and A. Kortunov, 'The Challenge of Security: Old and New', *Kommunist*, 1 January 1988, p. 45, cited in Fukuyama, *End of History*, p. 263.

48. Fukuyama, *End of History*, p. 265.

49. Ibid., p. 266.

50. Ibid., p. 267.

51. Ibid., p. 269.

52. Ibid., p. 270.

53. Ibid., p. 271.

54. Ibid.

55. Ibid., p. 272.

56. Ibid., p. 275.

57. Ibid., p. 276. Fukuyama intends this distinction to correspond to the old distinction between North and South, or between developed and underdeveloped countries.

58. Ibid., p. 277.

59. Ibid., p. 278.

60. Ibid., p. 279.

61. Ibid.

62. Ibid.

63. Ibid., p. 280.

64. Both contained in Immanuel Kant, *On History*, Bobbs-Merrill, Indianapolis, 1963.

65. See Kant, *Perpetual Peace*, in ibid., pp. 94, 98.

66. Fukuyama, *End of History*, p. 282.

67. Ibid., p. 284.
68. Ibid., p. 289.
69. Ibid.
70. Ibid., p. 334.
71. Ibid., p. 335.
72. Ibid.
73. Alexandre Kojève, *Introduction to the Reading of Hegel*, Cornell University Press, Ithaca, NY and London, 1980, pp. 161–2, in Williams, *Japan: Beyond the End of History*, Routledge, London, p. 160.
74. Fukuyama, *End of History*, p. 238.
75. Ibid., p. 242.
76. Ibid., p. 243.
77. Ibid., p. 233.
78. Ibid., p. 242.
79. Ibid., p. 322.
80. Ibid., p. 388.
81. Ibid., p. 144.
82. 'In this respect Hegel is quite different from Kojève's interpretation of him. Kojève's universal and homogeneous state makes no room for 'mediating' bodies like corporations or *Stande*; the very adjectives Kojève uses to describe his end state suggest ... a vision of a society where there is nothing between free, equal, and atomized individuals and the state.' Ibid., p. 338.
83. Ibid., pp. 243–4.
84. Ibid., p. 328.

Index